THE BOSPHORUS
Pages 136–149

EXCURSIONS
Pages 150–171

BEYOĞLU
Pages 100–107

Beyoğlu

BOSPHORUS

SERAGLIO POINT
Pages 50–67

Seraglio Point

SULTANAHMET
Pages 68–83

| 0 metres | 500 |
| 0 yards | 500 |

EYEWITNESS *TRAVEL GUIDES*

ISTANBUL

EYEWITNESS *TRAVEL GUIDES*

ISTANBUL

DORLING KINDERSLEY
LONDON • NEW YORK • SYDNEY • MOSCOW

A DORLING KINDERSLEY BOOK

PROJECT EDITOR Nick Inman
ART EDITOR Kate Poole
EDITORS Claire Folkard, Jane Oliver, Christine Stroyan
DESIGNERS Jo Doran, Paul Jackson
VISUALIZER Joy FitzSimmons
MAP CO-ORDINATORS Emily Green, David Pugh
RESEARCHERS Didem Mersin Alıcı, Hasan Kelepir

MANAGING EDITOR Georgina Matthews
MANAGING ART EDITOR Annette Jacobs
SENIOR MANAGING EDITOR Vivien Crump
DEPUTY ART DIRECTOR Gillian Allan

PRODUCTION Anna Pauletti, David Proffit
PICTURE RESEARCH Ellen Root
DTP DESIGNER Lee Redmond

MAIN CONTRIBUTORS
Rosie Ayliffe, Rose Baring, Barnaby Rogerson, Canan Sılay

MAPS
Paul Bates, Anne Rayski, Glyn Rozier (ESR Cartography Ltd)
Neil Cook, Maria Donnelly, Ewan Watson
(Colourmap Scanning Ltd)

PHOTOGRAPHERS
Anthony Souter, Linda Whitwam, Francesca Yorke

ILLUSTRATORS
Richard Bonson, Stephen Conlin, Gary Cross, Richard Draper,
Paul Guest, Maltings Partnership, Chris Orr & Associates,
Paul Weston, John Woodcock

•

Text film output by Graphical Innovations (London)
Reproduced by Colourscan (Singapore)
Printed and bound in China by L.Rex Printing Co., Ltd.

First published in Great Britain in 1998
by Dorling Kindersley Limited
9 Henrietta Street, London WC2E 8PS

Copyright 1998 © Dorling Kindersley Limited, London

Visit us on the World Wide Web at http://www.dk.com

A CIP CATALOGUE RECORD IS AVAILABLE FROM THE BRITISH LIBRARY.

ISBN 0 7513 9201 4

•

Every effort has been made to ensure that the information in
this book is as up-to-date as possible at the time of going to press.
However, details such as telephone numbers, opening hours,
prices, gallery hanging arrangements and travel information are
liable to change. The publishers cannot accept responsibility
for any consequences arising from the use of this book.

We would be delighted to receive any corrections and
suggestions for incorporation in the next edition. Please write to:
Senior Managing Editor, Eyewitness Travel Guides,
Dorling Kindersley, 9 Henrietta Street, London WC2E 8PS.

CONTENTS

**Madonna mosaic in the Church of
St Saviour in Chora**

INTRODUCING
ISTANBUL

**Tile panel in the Paired Pavilions
of Topkapı Palace's Harem**

◁ **The Blue Mosque and the church of Haghia Sophia, dominating Sultanahmet Square**

The great 6th-century Byzantine church of Haghia Sophia

TRAVELLERS' NEEDS

Men smoking bubble pipes in Çorlulu Ali Paşa Courtyard

BEYOND ISTANBUL

Simit seller

Ferry passing the waterfront of Karaköy below the Galata Tower

SURVIVAL GUIDE

Dolmabahçe Mosque with the skyline of Sultanahmet in the distance

HOW TO USE THIS GUIDE

THIS GUIDE helps you to get the most from your stay in Istanbul. It provides both expert recommendations and detailed practical advice. Introducing Istanbul locates the city geographically, sets Istanbul in its historical and cultural context and gives an overview of the main attractions. Istanbul Area by Area is the main sightseeing section, giving detailed information on all the major sights, with photographs, maps and illustrations. Greater Istanbul looks at sights outside the city centre, The Bosphorus guides you through a trip up the straits, and Excursions from Istanbul explores other places within easy reach of the city. Carefully researched suggestions for restaurants, hotels, entertainment and shopping are found in Travellers' Needs, while the Survival Guide contains useful advice on everything from changing money to travelling by tram.

FINDING YOUR WAY AROUND ISTANBUL

The centre of Istanbul has been divided into four sightseeing areas, each with its own chapter, colour-coded for easy reference. All sights are numbered and plotted on an area map for each chapter. The major sights are covered in more detail.

The area shaded pink is shown in greater detail on the Street-by-Street map on the following pages.

2 Street-by-Street map
This gives a bird's-eye view of the heart of each sightseeing area. Interesting features are labelled. There is also a list of "star sights" that no visitor should miss.

1 Area Introduction
This describes the history and character of the area and has a map on which the sights have been plotted. Other key information is also given.

Each area has colour-coded thumb tabs.

Locator Map

A suggested route takes in the most interesting and attractive streets in the area.

3 Detailed information
All the important sights are described individually. They are listed in order, following the numbering on the area map, with practical information about each.

ISTANBUL AREA MAP

THE COLOURED areas shown on this map (inside the front cover) are the four main sightseeing areas used in this guide. Each is covered in a full chapter in *Istanbul Area by Area (pp48–107)*. They are highlighted on other maps throughout the book. In *Istanbul at a Glance (see pp32–43)*, they help you to locate the top sights. The introduction to the Street Finder *(see pp238–255)* shows on which detailed street map you will find each area.

Introductory text gives an overview of the main sights in the Greater Istanbul area.

A map of the city shows Greater Istanbul and the areas covered in the chapter's sub-divisions.

4 Introduction to Greater Istanbul
Greater Istanbul has its own introduction, outlining what the city suburbs have to offer the sightseer. It is divided into five districts, shown on a map.

Practical information is provided in an information block. The key to the symbols used is on the back flap.

5 Introduction to Greater Istanbul areas
An introduction places the area in its historical context and provides a map showing the numbered sights.

The Visitors Checklist provides detailed practical information

6 The major sights
These are given two or more full pages. Historic buildings are dissected to reveal their interiors. Where necessary, sights are colour-coded to help you locate the most interesting areas.

INTRODUCING
ISTANBUL

Putting Istanbul on the Map

Istanbul stands astride the straits of the Bosphorus, straddling the European and Asian parts of Turkey and bordered to the south by the Sea of Marmara. The city is divided not only by the Bosphorus but also by the Golden Horn, an inlet forming a natural harbour. Although no longer the capital of Turkey (*see p29*), Istanbul is still the country's largest and most monumental city.

Satellite view of Greater Istanbul

KEY

☐	Greater Istanbul
✈	Airport
⛴	Ferry port
—	Motorway
—	Major road
—	Other main road
—	Railway
—	International frontier

0 kilometres   40

0 miles   40

◁ **Miniature depicting the lavish festivities staged for the circumcision of Ahmet III's sons in 1720**

GREATER ISTANBUL AND ENVIRONS

Haraççi

Kemerburgaz

Beykoz

Nalkalı

Istanbul and its Environs
*The sights in central Istanbul
are covered in detail on
pages 48–107 and a Street
Finder is provided on pages
238–55. Sights outside the
centre are covered on pages
108–49. Places of interest on
the Bosphorus and further
afield, still within easy reach
of the city, are explored on
pages 134–71.*

0 kilometres   7

0 miles   4

See next page

Black   Sea

Zonguldak

Ereğli

Devrek

Karabük   Yenice Irmağı

Şile

Kandıra

Karasu

Akçakoca

Kocaeli
(İzmit)

Sakarya
(Adapazarı)

Düzce

Bolu

Sapanca
Gölü

İznik
Gölü   İznik

Bilecik

Nallıhan   Beypazarı

Kırmir Çayı

ANKARA

Sakarya Nehri

Sarıyar
Barajı

K   E   Y

Milhallıççık

Eskişehir

Tuz
Gölü

EUROPE AND THE MEDITERRANEAN REGION

ESTONIA

SWEDEN   LATVIA

DENMARK   LITHUANIA

RUSSIAN
FEDERATION

UNITED
REP OF KINGDOM
IRELAND   NETHERLANDS   BELORUSSIA

POLAND

BELGIUM LUXEMBOURG GERMANY

CZECH REP.   UKRAINE

FRANCE   SLOVAKIA

SWITZERLAND AUSTRIA HUNGARY   MOLDAVIA

SLOVENIA CROATIA   ROMANIA

BOSNIA
HERZ.   YUGOSLAVIA BULGARIA

ITALY   Istanbul   GEORGIA

PORTUGAL   MACEDONIA

SPAIN   ALBANIA

GREECE   TURKEY

TUNISIA   SYRIA

LEBANON

MOROCCO   ALGERIA   ISRAEL   IRAQ

JORDAN SAUDI
ARABIA

LIBYA   EGYPT

Greater Istanbul

THE EXPANDING METROPOLIS of Istanbul
spreads along the Bosphorus to
the north, beyond the airport to the
west and inland from the Asian shore
in the east. Its official population is
put at a little over 9 million but the
actual population is probably much
higher. A new, integrated transport
system is being built to make getting
around this vast urban area easier.
Most visitors, however, stay in the
historical central parts where the
major sights are located.

Alibeyköy Barajı

Kırklareli

Edirne

GAZİOSMANPAŞA

BAYRAMPAŞA

EYÜP

ESENLER

BAĞCILAR

GÜNGÖREN

FATİH

BAHÇELİEVLER

ZEYTİNBURNU

BAKIRKÖY

YEŞİLKÖY

Sea of Marmara

0 kilometres   2

0 miles   2

KEY

Central Istanbul
Greater Istanbul
✈ Airport
⛴ Ferry boarding point
〰 Sea bus boarding point
🚇 Railway station
🚌 Bus station
= Motorway
▬ Main road
= Other road
— Railway

Central Istanbul

Shoe shine man outside the New Mosque

THIS GUIDE divides central Istanbul into four distinct areas, each with its own chapter. Three areas lie on the southern side of the Golden Horn. Seraglio Point is a raised promontory on which stands the sumptuous Topkapı Palace. Two architectural masterpieces, Haghia Sophia and the Blue Mosque, dominate the area of Sultanahmet. The pace of life is quite different in the Bazaar Quarter, a maze of narrow streets filled with frenetic commerce. North of the Golden Horn is Beyoğlu, which for centuries was the preferred place of residence of Istanbul's foreign communities, and is still markedly cosmopolitan in atmosphere.

İstiklal Caddesi, Beyoğlu
Old fashioned trams shuttle up and down the pedestrianized street that forms the backbone of this area (see pp100–7).

The Grand Bazaar, in the Bazaar Quarter
This quaint former coffee house stands at a junction in the labyrinthine old shopping complex at the heart of the city's Bazaar Quarter (see pp84–99).

KEY

▢	Major sight
⚓	Ferry boarding point
🚉	Railway station
Ⓜ	Metro or Tünel station
🚏	Tram stop
ℹ	Tourist information
🏛	Police station
🛁	Turkish bath
Ⓒ	Mosque
✝	Church
⊠	Post office

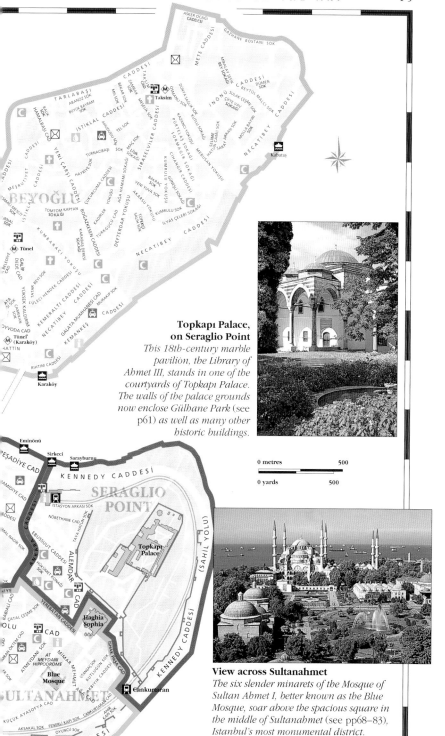

Topkapı Palace, on Seraglio Point
This 18th-century marble pavilion, the Library of Ahmet III, stands in one of the courtyards of Topkapı Palace. The walls of the palace grounds now enclose Gülhane Park (see p61) as well as many other historic buildings.

| 0 metres | 500 |
| 0 yards | 500 |

View across Sultanahmet
The six slender minarets of the Mosque of Sultan Ahmet I, better known as the Blue Mosque, soar above the spacious square in the middle of Sultanahmet (see pp68–83), Istanbul's most monumental district.

CONSTANTINE THE GREAT

In AD 324, after defeating his co-emperor Licinius, Constantine the Great (324–37) became sole ruler of the Roman Empire. One of his greatest achievements was to move the capital of the empire from Rome to Byzantium. Initially, Constantine preferred the site of Troy *(see p171)* for his capital, but was persuaded by advisers that Byzantium held a superior position for both defence and trade. Constantine's city was officially styled the "New Rome" but became widely known as Constantinople. The emperor quickly started on an ambitious programme of construction work, which included the Great Palace *(see pp82–3)* and various public buildings.

Gold aureus of Constantine

Constantine was also instrumental in the spread of Christianity. According to legend, he saw a vision of the cross before a battle in 312. Although not actually baptized until just before his death, he worked hard to create a coherent system of Christian belief out of the variant practices of the day. All of the early church councils took place in the city or near-by, the first being held in Nicaea, (modern-day İznik, *see p160*), and the second in Constantinople itself.

A successor of Constantine, Theodosius I (379–95), divided the Empire between his two sons, Honorius and Arcadius. When the Latin-speaking Western Empire fell to barbarian armies during the 5th century, the Greek-speaking Eastern Empire, thereafter known as the Byzantine Empire, survived.

THE AGE OF JUSTINIAN

The 6th century was dominated by the extraordinary genius of Justinian (527–65), who developed Constantinople into a thriving city and almost succeeded in reconquering the lost provinces of the Western Empire from the barbarians. At the time of his death the empire had expanded to its greatest size, and covered Syria, Palestine, Asia Minor, Greece, the Balkans, Italy, southern Spain and many territories in northern Africa, including Egypt.

Empress Theodora, wife of Justinian

Justinian's formidable wife, the ex-courtesan Theodora, had a great deal of influence over him. In 532 she persuaded the emperor to use mercenaries to put down an angry mob in the most notorious event of his reign, the Nika Revolt. In the carnage that followed 30,000 were killed inside the Hippodrome *(see p80)*.

Justinian was also responsible for much of the city's great architecture, including Haghia Sophia *(see pp72–5)*, Haghia Eirene *(see p60)* and parts of the Great Palace.

Relief from the Egyptian Obelisk *(see p80)*, showing Theodosius I and his courtiers

TIMELINE

324 Constantine becomes ruler of the Roman Empire	**330** Inauguration of Constantinople	**395** On the death of Theodosius I, the empire is divided into two	**476** The Western Roman Empire falls to barbarians	**532** Nika Revolt is put down by mercenaries; 30,000 are killed		**674** Five-year-long siege of Constantinople initiated by the Saracens
300		**400**	**500**	**600**		**700**
325 First church council meets at Nicaea	**337** Constantine is baptized a Christian on his deathbed	**412** Construction work begins on the Walls of Theodosius II *(see p20)*		**537** Emperor Justinian dedicates the new Haghia Sophia	**726** Leo III issues a decree denouncing idolatry, and many icons are destroyed	

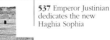

Walls of Theodosius II

THE HISTORY OF ISTANBUL

ISTANBUL WAS FOUNDED *in the 7th century BC on a naturally defensive site from which trade along the Bosphorus could be controlled. For 16 centuries it was a great imperial capital, first of the Byzantine Empire and then of the Ottoman sultans. Some knowledge of the histories of these two civilizations helps the visitor to appreciate the magnificent monuments found throughout the city.*

The topography of Istanbul was formed at the end of the last Ice Age, when meltwaters created the Bosphorus. The Stone Age cultures in the area were replaced by Copper Age villages and walled Bronze Age towns (notably Troy, *see p171*). The Bosphorus was an important trade route in the ancient world along which ships carried wine and olive oil north from the Mediterranean, and grain, skins, wool, timber, wax, honey, salted meat and salted fish south from regions around the Black Sea.

The area around the Bosphorus was subjugated by a series of peoples, starting with the Mycenaeans (1400–1200 BC). Between 800 and 680 BC the region was controlled by the kingdom of Phrygia. Later, in 676 BC, Greek expeditionaries founded the city of Chalcedon (on the site where modern Kadıköy now stands).

Septimius Severus, who devastated the city in the 2nd century AD

THE FOUNDATION OF BYZANTION

The foundation of Istanbul is usually dated to 667 BC when, according to legend, a Greek colonist, Byzas, led an expedition from the overcrowded cities of Athens and Megara to establish a colony on the European side of the Bosphorus. This colony, known as Byzantion, grew to be a successful independent city-state, or *polis*, one of the 40 most important such states throughout the Ancient Greek world. During the next few centuries, Byzantion worked in partnership with Chalcedon, using the same coinage and sharing the tolls exacted from passing sea trade.

But Byzantion had to struggle to maintain its independence in the mercurial politics of the ancient world. It endured Lydian (560–546 BC), Persian (546–478 BC), Athenian (478–411 BC) and Macedonian (334–281 BC) rule before briefly regaining its autonomy. In 64 BC it was subsumed into the Roman Empire as Byzantium. The city was almost destroyed in AD 195 by Septimius Severus because of its support for his rival for the imperial throne, Pescennius Niger. It survived the Goths' devastation of Chalcedon in 258 AD but trade in the region dramatically declined in the following years.

TIMELINE

Alexander the Great

c.676 BC Chalcedon, a Greek settlement, founded on Asian shore	**340 BC** Philip II of Macedonia unsuccessfully besieges city		**AD 195** Roman emperor Septimius Severus destroys Byzantium but later rebuilds it, laying out the Hippodrome	
600 BC	**400 BC**	**200 BC**	**AD 1**	**AD 200**
c.667 BC Byzantion reputedly founded by Greek colonists from Athens and Megara, led by Byzas	**334 BC** Alexander the Great crosses the Hellespont (Dardanelles) and conquers Anatolia	**64 BC** Pompey brings Byzantion into the Roman Empire, renaming it Byzantium	**AD 258** Goths destroy Chalcedon	

◁ **The Byzantine emperor Justinian the Great shown with one of his prefects in a mosaic**

THE BYZANTINES AT WAR

The Byzantine Empire never again attained the splendour of the reign of Justinian, but throughout the first millennium it remained rich and powerful. During the early Middle Ages, Constantinople was an oasis of learning, law, art and culture at a time when Europe was plunged into a

"Greek fire", used by the Byzantines against the Arabs

dark age of ignorance and illiteracy. Considering themselves to be the leaders of Christianity, the Byzantine rulers dispatched missionaries to spread their religion and culture among the Slavic nations, especially Russia.

During this period, Constantinople produced some capable emperors, in particular Heraclius (610–41), Basil the Macedonian (867–86), Leo the Wise (886–912) and Basil the Bulgar-Slayer (976–1025). Between them these rulers contributed a number of buildings to the city and recaptured lost provinces.

Never without enemies greedy for a share of the prodigious riches that had been amassed in the city, Constantinople was besieged by Slavs, Arabs, Avars, Bulgars, Persians and Russians, all without success because of the protection of the land walls. The surrounding seas, meanwhile, were under the control of Constantinople's powerful navy. Its main ship was the *dromon*, an oared vessel which could ram another ship but above all deliver the dreaded "Greek fire", an early form of napalm.

A 6th-century ivory carving of a Byzantine emperor, possibly Anastasius I (491–518)

In 1059 Constantine X, the first of the Dukas dynasty of emperors, ascended to the throne. The state over which the dynasty presided was a weakened one, divided between the over-privileged bureaucracy in the capital and the feudal landlords of the provinces. At the same time increasing dependency on foreign mercenaries placed the empire's defence in the hands of its most aggressive neighbours. These included the Normans from southern Italy, the Venetians and Turkic nomads from the east.

The Byzantine imperial army was totally destroyed at the Battle of Manzikert (1071) and again, a century later, at the Battle of Myriocephalon (1176) by the Seljuk Turks from the east. These losses effectively ended Byzantine rule of Anatolia, which had for so long been the backbone of the empire. The remarkable Comnenus dynasty (1081–1185) ruled for a century after the Dukas emperors, between these two defeats. Their main achievement was to succeed in holding the rest of the empire together.

Haghia Sophia mosaic

843 Icons are permitted again by seventh church council at Haghia Sophia		**1071** The Byzantine army is destroyed by the Seljuk Turks at the Battle of Manzikert. Emperor Romanus Diogenes is disgraced and deposed	**1138** John II Comnenus recovers Serbia	**1176** The Seljuk Turks defeat the Byzantine forces at the Battle of Myriocephalon
800	**900**	**1000**	**1100**	**1200**
		1054 The Orthodox and Catholic churches break away from each other because of differences over dogma	**1096** The armies of the First Crusade pass through Constantinople and assist Alexius I Comnenus to retake the Anatolian seaboard from the Seljuk Turks	

The City of Constantinople

Mosaic of the Virgin, St Saviour in Chora

For almost a thousand years Constantinople was the richest city in Christendom. It radiated out from three great buildings: the church of Haghia Sophia *(see pp72–5)*, the Hippodrome *(see p80)* and the Great Palace *(see pp82–3)*. The city also had a great many other fine churches and palaces, filled with exquisite works of art.

Daily life for the populace centred on the four market squares, or *fora*. Meanwhile, their need for fresh water was met by an advanced network of aqueducts and underground water cisterns.

Walls of Theodosius
Theodosius II's great chain of land walls (see p114) withstood countless sieges until the Ottoman conquest of the city in 1453 (see p24).

THE CITY IN 1200

At its height the magnificent city of Constantinople probably had about 400,000 inhabitants. The population density was relatively low, though, and there was space within the city walls for fields and orchards.

Mocius Cistern

The Golden Gate
was a ceremonial gate through the city's ramparts.

Church of St John of Studius
(see p116)

Walls of Constantine
(now totally destroyed)

Forum of Arcadius

Harbour of Theodosius

BYZANTINE CHURCH ARCHITECTURE

Early Byzantine churches were either basilical (like St John of Studius) or built to a centralized plan (as in SS Sergius and Bacchus). From the 9th century, churches, like the typical example shown here, were built around four corner piers, or columns. Exteriors were mostly unadorned brickwork, but interiors were lavishly decorated with golden mosaics. Although the Ottomans converted Constantinople's churches into mosques after their conquest of the city, many original features are clearly discernible today.

TYPICAL LATE BYZANTINE CHURCH

A central apse is flanked by two smaller side apses.

Four columns support the dome.

Brickwork may alternate with layers of stone.

The narthex, a covered porch, forms the entrance to the church.

Golden mosaics cover the ceilings and upper walls.

of the Italian city of Genoa, which was naturally disposed to fight against her rival Venice. Yet she still exacted a crippling price for her assistance. The Genoese established the colony of Pera across the Golden Horn from Constantinople, and effectively took control of the city's trade.

Constantinople's recapture and reconstruction caused a flowering of scholarship and artistic activity, known as the Palaeologue Renaissance after the family of emperors. An example of the many beautiful buildings dating from this period is the Church of St Saviour in Chora (see pp118–19).

During this period the double-headed eagle was adopted as the imperial crest, with the two heads symbolizing the western and eastern halves of the empire. Yet, within a few decades there was further discord in Constantinople, when a quarrel arose

Two-headed Byzantine eagle

between Andronicus II (1282–1328) and his grandson Andronicus III (1328–41) over the succession. This led to the disastrous civil war of 1321–54.

THE RISE OF THE OTTOMANS

The Ottoman state was born in 1301 when Osman I, a leader of warriors who were fighting for the Muslim faith on the eastern frontier of the Byzantine Empire, declared his independence. The new state quickly expanded and in 1326 captured Prusa (modern-day Bursa, see pp162–8), which became its capital. The judicious piety of the Ottomans soon won them the support of the general population of their territories, and even of some Christian brotherhoods. Meanwhile, a professional core of Janissaries (see p127) was created to add stability to an army which was otherwise too dependent on Turkic and renegade volunteer cavalry.

By 1362, with the Ottoman capture of Adrianople (Edirne, see pp154–7), Byzantium had been reduced to the city-state of Constantinople and a few minor outposts, isolated within Ottoman domains. Only a Mongol incursion in 1402 delayed the Ottoman invasion of Constantinople itself. In 1422 the Ottoman army made its first attack on the city's colossal land walls. As the threat increased, the Byzantine emperor made a last ditch effort to win the support of the Latin West in 1439. The Hungarians alone answered his call for help, forming a 25,000-strong crusade. However, in 1444 they were defeated en route by the Ottomans at the Battle of Varna on the Black Sea.

Mosaic of the Virgin and Child in St Saviour in Chora

Galata Tower

THE CONQUEST OF CONSTANTINOPLE
On 29 May 1453 Sultan Mehmet II (1451–81), known as "the Conqueror", entered Constantinople after a 54-day siege during which his cannon had torn a huge hole in the Walls of Theodosius II *(see p114)*. Mehmet's first task was to rebuild the wrecked city,

Sultan Mehmet II, "the Conqueror"

which would later become known as Istanbul. The Grand Bazaar *(see pp98–9)* and Topkapı Palace *(see pp54–7)* were erected in the years following the Muslim conquest. Religious foundations were endowed to fund the building of mosques such as the Fatih *(see p113)* and their associated schools and baths *(see pp36–7)*. The city had to be repopulated by a mixture of force and encouragement. People from all over the empire moved to Istanbul, and Jews, Christians and Muslims lived together in a cosmopolitan society.

Mehmet and his successors pushed the frontiers of the empire across the Middle East and into Europe. In the early 16th century, Selim I (1512–20) conquered Egypt and assumed the title of caliph *(see p27)*, as well as establishing the Ottomans as a sea power. He is also notorious for killing all his male relatives bar one son, to ensure that there were no rivals for the succession.

SÜLEYMAN THE MAGNIFICENT
Selim's one surviving son was Süleyman I, "the Magnificent" (1520–66), under whose rule the Ottoman Empire reached its maximum extent. At the time of his death the empire stretched

from Algiers to the Caspian Sea and from Hungary to the Persian Gulf. Much of western Europe only just escaped conquest when an Ottoman army was driven back from the gates of Vienna in 1529. Süleyman's

OTTOMAN EMPIRE
◼ *Maximum extent (1566)*

reign was a time of great artistic and architectural achievements. The architect Sinan *(see p91)* designed many mosques and other great buildings in the city, while the Ottoman arts of ceramics *(see p161)* and calligraphy *(see p95)* also flourished.

Depiction of the unsuccessful siege of Vienna

TIMELINE

1453 Mehmet the Conqueror enters Constantinople on 29 May	1456 The Ottomans occupy Athens		1536 Grand Vizier İbrahim Paşa is killed on the orders of Süleyman's wife, Roxelana *(see p76)*	1561 Süleyman executes his son Beyazıt on suspicion of treason	1571 Defeat of the Ottoman navy at the Battle of Lepanto
	1461 Trebizond on the Black Sea, the last part of the Byzantine Empire, is conquered				

1450	**1475**	**1500**	**1525**	**1550**	

1455 Yedikule Castle *(see p115)* is built and work begins on the Grand Bazaar	1478 Topkapı Palace completed		1533 Hayrettin Paşa, better known as Barbarossa, is appointed grand admiral	1556 Inauguration of Sinan's Süleymaniye Mosque *(see pp90–91)*	
	1470 Fatih Mosque is built over the Church of the Holy Apostles				

Süleyman I

THE SULTANATE
OF WOMEN

Süleyman's son Selim II
(1566–74), "the Sot", was
not such a capable ruler, although he added Cyprus to
the empire. The defeat of
his navy by the Venetians
at the Battle of Lepanto was
a heavy blow to Ottoman
ambitions to be a seafaring
power. This era was also

The Battle of Lepanto, a defeat for the Ottoman navy

the start of the so-called "Sultanate
of Women", when Selim's mother
(the valide sultan, *see p26*) and Nur
Banu, his principal wife (the first
kadın), effectively took over power
and exercised it for their own ends.
Corruption and intrigue became en-
demic, and after Selim's death Nur
Banu kept her son, Murat III (1574–
95), distracted by the women of the
harem so that she could maintain
her control over imperial affairs.

Osman II (1618–22) was the first
sultan to try to reverse the decline
of the empire. But
when the Janissaries
(see p127) learnt of
his plans to abolish
their corps, they
started a revolt
which eventually
led to his assassi-
nation. Murat IV
(1623–40) enjoyed
more success in his
attempts at reform
and significantly
reduced corruption

Osman II, who failed to halt Ottoman decline

during his stable period of rule.

The late 17th century saw many
years of capable government by a
succession of grand viziers from the
Albanian Köprülü family. Yet their
efforts were not sufficient to stem

the decline in imperial fortunes,
symbolized by a failed attempt to
capture Vienna in 1683. The Treaty of
Karlowitz in 1699 marked the start of
the Ottoman withdrawal from Europe.

THE TULIP PERIOD

Ahmet III (1703–30), on his succession
to the throne, left power in the hands
of his capable grand vizier, İbra-
him Paşa. The sultan preferred
pleasure to politics. During his
reign, beautiful Baroque palaces, such as Aynalı Kavak
Palace *(see p127)*, fountains,
mosques and yalis *(see p139)*
were built. Formal gardens
were laid out and filled
with tulips, Ahmet's fav-
ourite flower, which
lent their name to the
period of his rule. The
sultan even ordered
tulips to be scattered
over the floor at the
lavish festivals and
entertainments that
he staged for the
Ottoman elite. He also sent an ambassador, Mehmet Çelebi, to France to
investigate Western civilization and
culture. On his return, Western clothes
and costumes became not only acceptable for the first time, but fashionable.

1616 The Blue Mosque *(see pp78–9)* is finished after eight years of construction work by the architect Mehmet Ağa

1699 The loss of Hungary under the Treaty of Karlowitz marks the Ottomans' retreat from Europe

1600　　1625　　1650　　1700　　1725

1622 Revolt of the Janissaries. They murder Osman II in Yedikule Castle, the Prison of the Seven Towers

Domes of the Blue Mosque

1729 The first Ottoman printing press is set up in Istanbul and begins to print texts in Turkish

Ottoman Society

BENEATH THE SULTAN, Ottoman society was divided into a privileged ruling class (the *askeri*, which included the religious hierarchy, or *ulema*) and a tax-paying subject population *(reaya)*. Rank and honour, however, were not hereditary but could be gained through education or service in the army or administration. This social structure was modified during the reforms of the 19th century *(see p28)*, but Ottoman titles were only finally abolished in 1924 after the Turkish Republic was created *(see p29)*.

The grand vizier, the prime minister, was the sultan's right-hand man.

The sultan was at the apex of the social order and everyone owed allegiance to him. He lived a life of ease and luxury, as seen in this portrait of Mahmut I (1730–54). The Ottoman (Osmanlı in Turkish) sultans were always succeeded by one of their sons, but not automatically by the eldest.

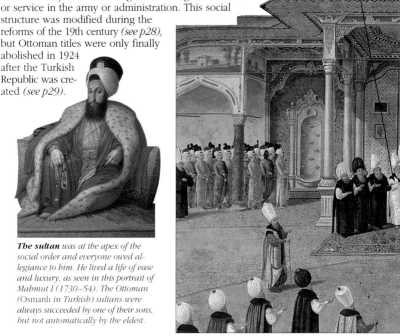

BAYRAM RECEPTION *(c.1800)*
In this painting by Konstantin Kapidagi, Selim III (1789–1807, *see p28)* presides over a parade of high-ranking officials during the celebration of a religious festival *(see p47)* at Topkapı Palace.

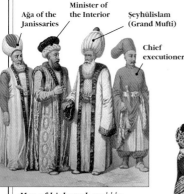

Ağa of the Janissaries

Minister of the Interior

Şeyhülislam (Grand Mufti)

Chief executioner

Men of high rank could be recognized by their different uniforms, above all their large and distinctive headgear, as seen in this portrait of four Ottoman officials. The turban was abolished by Mahmut II (see p28) in 1829 in favour of the more egalitarian fez.

THE WOMEN OF THE HAREM

Like all other Ottoman institutions the harem was hierarchical. It was presided over by the sultan's mother, the valide sultan. Next in order of importance came the sultan's daughters. Immediately below them were the four *kadıns*, the official wives or favourites. Then came the *gözdes* (girls who had recently caught the sultan's eye), and the *ikbals* (women with whom he had already slept). Apart from the sultan's family members, all these women had entered the harem as slaves. They were kept under a watchful eye by a powerful stewardess, the *kahya kadın*.

One of the sultan's favourites as depicted in a 19th-century engraving

Black eunuchs

Sword bearer to the sultan

The Gate of Felicity (see p54), in the second courtyard of Topkapı Palace, was used for such ceremonial occasions.

The sultan is surrounded by his courtiers. He is the only seated figure.

Şeyhülislam (Grand Mufti)

Chief lackey (footman)

Chief of the sultan's bodyguard

OTTOMAN TITLES

Ağa: leader of an organization. The most influential *ağas* were the commander of the Janissary corps, the sultan's elite troops (see p127), and the Ağa of the Abode of Felicity, or chief black eunuch, who was in charge of the harem (see pp58–9).

Chief black eunuch

Bey: governor of a district or province. The word is now used simply to mean "Mr".

Caliph: spiritual ruler of the Islamic world. The title was assumed by the Ottoman sultans, beginning with Selim the Grim in 1517.

Gazi: honorary title given to a victorious Islamic warrior.

Kadi: judge charged with interpreting Islamic law and Ottoman administrative codes.

Khedive: viceroy of Egypt under Ottoman rule (1867–1914). The autonomous khedives acknowledged the religious leadership of the Ottoman Empire.

Paşa: title bestowed on a senior civil servant or high-ranking army officer. According to his rank, a *paşa* was entitled to display one, two or three horsetails on his standard (see p56).

Sultan: political and religious ruler of the empire.

Şeyhülislam (Grand Mufti): head of the *ulema*, a religious institution which was made up of "learned men" responsible for interpreting and enforcing Islamic law (*sharia*).

Valide sultan: mother of the ruling sultan.

Vizier: minister of state. The four most senior ministers were called "viziers of the dome" because they attended cabinet meetings in the domed hall of the divan in Topkapı Palace (see pp54–9). From the 16th century, the divan was presided over by the immensely powerful grand vizier (the prime minister).

Grand vizier

Black eunuch   **Dancing women**   **Valide sultan**   **Dwarf**

*The **valide sultan**, the most powerful woman in the harem, is the centre of attention in this festive scene. The picture was commissioned c.1689 by Madame Giradin, wife of the French ambassador.*

A Janissary leaps to his death in a German painting of the Auspicious Event of 1826

THE REFORMING SULTANS

Abdül Hamit I (1774–89) resumed the work of reform and was succeeded by Selim III, who instituted a wide range of changes to the military and Ottoman society. He was deposed by a Janissary mutiny in 1807. Mahmut II (1808–39) realized that the Janissary corps *(see p127)* could not be reformed, so he replaced them with a modern army, but the Janissaries rebelled and were massacred on 15 June 1826 in the "Auspicious Event". Soon after, in 1829, the sultan introduced further modernizing measures including changes in the dress code.

Later in his reign Mahmut reorganized central government so that a regulated bureaucracy

replaced the old system of rule by military and religious powers. By doing this he paved the way for his sons Abdül Mecit (1839–61) and Abdül Aziz (1861–76) to oversee the Tanzimat (Reordering), a series of legislative reforms. Functionaries were given salaries to deter them from taking bribes and the grand vizier's post was replaced by that of prime minister.

A constitution was declared in 1876, creating parliamentary government. However, the Russian-Turkish War of 1877–88 led to Abdül Hamit II suspending it and ruling alone for the next 30 years. In 1908 a bloodless revolution by a collection of educated men – the so-called Young Turks – finally forced the sultan to recall parliament.

ATATÜRK AND WESTERNIZATION

Throughout the 19th- and early 20th-centuries, the Ottoman Empire steadily lost territory through wars with Russia and Austria, and to emerging Balkan nation-states such as Serbia, Greece and Bulgaria. Then, in World War I, despite famously winning the battle for Gallipoli in a valiant defence of the Dardanelles *(see p170)*, the Ottoman Empire found itself on the losing side. Istanbul was occupied by victorious French and British troops and much of Anatolia by Greek forces. The peace

Turkish artillery in action at Gallipoli

TIMELINE

Dolmabahçe clocktower

1807 Much of the city is destroyed during a Janissary revolt against Mahmut II

1845 First (wooden) Galata Bridge is built over the Golden Horn

1870 Schliemann begins excavation of Troy *(see p171)*

1888 Rail link with Paris leads to first run of the Orient Express *(see p66)*

1800	1825	1850	1875	1900

1826 Mahmut II finally destroys the Janissaries in their own barracks in the "Auspicious Event"

1856 Abdül Mecit I abandons Topkapı Palace for the new Dolmabahçe Palace *(see pp128–9)*

1875 The Tünel underground railway system, the third built in the world, opens in Galata

Orient Express poster

treaties that followed rewarded the victors with Ottoman territory and as a result stimulated Turkish nationalists to take over power from the sultan.

A portrait of Atatürk

The history of modern Turkey is dominated by the figure of Mustafa Kemal Paşa (1881–1938), a military hero turned politician, universally known as Atäturk, or "Father of the Turks". It was at his instigation that the Turkish War of Independence was fought to regain territory lost to the Allies and, in particular, Greece. At the conclusion of this war, the present territorial limits of Turkey were established. Atatürk then set in motion an ambitious programme of political and social change. The sultanate was abolished in 1922, and religion and state were formally separated when the country was declared a secular republic in the following year. His reforms included replacing the Arabic alphabet with a Roman one, allowing women greater social and political rights, encouraging Western dress (the fez was banned) and obliging all Turks to choose a surname.

MODERN ISTANBUL

Another part of this process was to move the institutions of state from the old Ottoman city of Istanbul to the more centrally located Ankara, which became the capital of Turkey in 1923. Since then, Istanbul has gone through a dramatic transformation into a modern city. As migrants from Anatolia have poured in, the population has increased, and although small communities of Jews, Arabs, Armenians and Christians remain within the city, they are now vastly outnumbered by Turks.

Modern tram *(see p232)*

A booming economy has led to the building of new motorways and bridges, and the public transport network has been revolutionized by the introduction of modern trams, light railways and fast catamaran sea buses *(see p235)*. Meanwhile Istanbul has geared itself up for tourism: its ancient monuments have been restored and many new hotels and restaurants have opened in recent years to accommodate increasing numbers of visitors.

But, like Turkey as a whole, Istanbul is forever wrestling with a divided half-Asian, half-European identity. The influences of these contrasting cultures remain widely evident today and create the city's unique atmosphere.

Suspension bridge spanning the Bosphorus

1915 Allied forces land at Gallipoli but are repulsed by Turkish troops	1919–22 British and French occupy Istanbul	1922 Sultanate finally ends	1928 Istanbul becomes the city's official name	1936 Haghia Sophia becomes a museum. Restoration starts	1938 Atatürk dies in Dolmabahçe Palace at 9:05am on 10 November *(see p129)*	1966 The city's old trams are taken out of service. A few are later reintroduced *(see p233)*	1973 A suspension bridge is built across the Bosphorus *(see p138)*, linking east and west Turkey	1993 The Islamicist Welfare Party takes control of the Greater Istanbul Municipality	1996 The United Nations Conference on Human Settlement (Habitat II) is held in Istanbul
1925		**1950**				**1975**			**2000**

Turkish flag

The Ottoman Sultans

THE FIRST OTTOMANS were the leaders of warlike tribes living on the borders of the Byzantine Empire. From the 13th century, however, the dynasty established itself at the head of a large empire. In their heyday, having captured Istanbul in 1453 *(see p24)*, the Ottoman sultans were admired and feared for their military strength and ruthlessness towards opponents and rival pretenders to the throne. Later sultans often led a decadent life-style while power was exercised by their viziers *(see p27)*.

Murat III (1574–95), whose *tuğra (see p95)* is shown above, fathers over 100 children

Selim II, "the Sot" (1566–74), prefers drinking and harem life to the affairs of state

Selim I, "the Grim" (1512–20), seen here at his coronation, assumes the title of caliph after his conquest of Egypt

Osman Gazi (1280–1324), a tribal chieftain, establishes the Ottoman dynasty

Murat I (1360–89)

Mehmet I (1413–21)

Beyazıt II (1481–1512)

1250	1300	1350	1400	1450	1500	1550

1250	1300	1350	1400	1450	1500	1550

Orhan Gazi (1324–59) is the first Ottoman to bear the title of sultan

Süleyman I, "the Magnificent" (1520–66), expands the empire and fosters a golden age of artistic achievement

Beyazıt I (1389–1402) is nicknamed "the Thunderbolt" because of the speed at which he takes strategic decisions and moves his troops from one place to another

Period of Interregnum (1402–13) while Beyazıt's sons fight each other over the succession

Murat II (1421–51), the greatest of the warrior sultans, gains notable victories against the Crusaders

Mehmet II, "the Conqueror" (1451–81), captures Constantinople in 1453. He then rebuilds the city, transforming it into the new capital of the empire

Mehmet III (1595–1603) succeeds to the throne after his mother has all but one of his 19 brothers strangled

Mustafa I (1617–18 and 1622–3), a weak and incompetent ruler, reigns for two short periods and is deposed twice

Abdül Mecit I (1839–61) presides over the reforms of the Tanzimat *(see p28)*

Mehmet VI (1918–22), the last Ottoman sultan, is forced into exile by the declaration of the Turkish Republic *(see p29)*

İbrahim, "the Mad" (1640–48), much despised, goes insane at the end of his short but disastrous reign

Mahmut II, "the Reformer" (1808–39), finally defeats the Janissaries *(see p127)*

Mehmet V (1909–18)

Mahmut I (1730–54)

Murat V (1876)

Mustafa II (1695–1703)

Mustafa III (1757–74)

Süleyman II (1687–91)

1650	1700	1750	1800	1850	1900

1650	1700	1750	1800	1850	1900

Osman III (1754–7)

Abdül Mecit II (1922–3) is caliph only, the sultanate having been abolished in 1922 *(see p29)*

Abdül Aziz (1861–76)

Mehmet IV (1648–87)

Abdül Hamit I (1774–89)

Murat IV (1623–40)

Mustafa IV 1807–08

Ahmet III (1703–30) presides over a cultural flowering known as the Tulip Period *(see p25)*

Osman II (1618–22)

Abdül Hamit II (1876–1909) suspends parliament for 30 years and rules an autocratic police state until toppled from power by the Young Turk movement

Ahmet I (1603–17) has the Blue Mosque *(see pp78–9)* constructed in the centre of Istanbul

Selim III (1789–1807) attempts Western-style reforms but is overthrown by a revolt of the Janissaries

ISTANBUL AT A GLANCE

MORE THAN 100 places worth visiting in Istanbul are described in the *Area by Area* section of this book, which covers the sights of central Istanbul as well as those a short way out of the city centre. They range from mosques, churches, palaces and museums to bazaars, Turkish baths and parks. For a breathtaking view across Istanbul, you can climb the Galata Tower *(see p105)*, or take a ride on a ferry *(see pp234–5)* to the city's Asian shore. A selection of the sights you should not miss is given below. If you are short of time you will probably want to concentrate on the most famous monuments, namely Topkapı Palace, Haghia Sophia and the Blue Mosque which are all located conveniently close to each other.

ISTANBUL'S TOP TEN SIGHTS

Topkapı Palace
See pp54–7

Archaeological Museum
See pp62–5

Blue Mosque
See pp78–9

Dolmabahçe Palace
See pp128–9

Haghia Sophia
See pp72–5

Basilica Cistern
See p76

Süleymaniye Mosque
See pp90–91

The Bosphorus Trip
See pp144–9

Grand Bazaar
See pp98–9

Church of St Saviour in Chora
See pp118–19

◁ **View of Haghia Sophia in central Sultanahmet, a great Byzantine church later converted into a mosque**

Istanbul's Best: Mosques and Churches

MOST VISITORS TO ISTANBUL will immediately be struck by the quantity of mosques, from the imposing domed buildings dominating the skyline to the small neighbourhood mosques which would pass unnoticed were it not for their minarets. Several mosques were built as churches, but converted for Islamic worship after the Ottoman conquest *(see p24)*. Some of the most outstanding of them have since become national monuments, but no longer serve a religious function.

St Saviour in Chora
The Dormition of the Virgin is one of many beautiful mosaics that fill this Byzantine church (see pp118–19).

Eyüp Mosque
The holiest mosque in Istanbul stands beside the tomb of Eyüp Ensari, a companion of the Prophet Mohammed (see p120).

Church of the Pammakaristos
An image of Christ Pantocrator gazes down from the main dome of what was one of the most important churches in the city (see p113).

GOLDEN HORN

Fatih Mosque
Rebuilt after an earthquake, this mosque was founded by Mehmet the Conqueror after his conquest of the city (see p24). The inner courtyard is especially fine (see p113).

Süleymaniye Mosque
Sinan, the greatest Ottoman imperial architect, built this mosque in honour of his patron, Süleyman the Magnificent (see p24). He placed ablution taps in the side arches of the mosque to serve a large number of worshippers (see pp90–91).

Atik Valide Mosque
The last major work of Sinan (see p91), this mosque was built in 1583 for the wife of Selim II. Its mihrab (niche indicating the direction of Mecca) is surrounded by İznik tiles (see p131).

Rüstem Paşa Mosque
The fine tiles decorating this mosque date from the mid-16th century, the greatest period of İznik tile (see p161) production (see p88).

Haghia Sophia
One of the world's greatest feats of architecture, Haghia Sophia dates from AD 537. The calligraphic roundels were added in the 19th century (see pp72–5).

BEYOĞLU

BOSPHORUS

SERAGLIO
POINT

HE BAZAAR
QUARTER

SULTANAHMET

ASIAN SIDE

Blue Mosque
Istanbul's most famous landmark was built by some of the same stonemasons who later helped construct the Taj Mahal in India (see pp78–9).

| 0 metres | 500 |
| 0 yards | 500 |

Church of SS Sergius and Bacchus
An intricate frieze with a Greek inscription honouring the two dedicatees of this former church has survived for 1,400 years (see p82).

Exploring Mosques

FIVE TIMES A DAY throughout Istanbul a chant is broadcast over loudspeakers set high in the city's minarets to call the faithful to prayer. Over 99 per cent of the population is Muslim, though the Turkish state is officially secular. Most belong to the Sunni branch of Islam, but there are also a few Shiites. Both follow the teachings of the Koran, the sacred book of Islam, and the Prophet Mohammed (c.570–632), but Shiites accept, in addition, the authority of a line of 12 imams directly descended from Mohammed. Islamic mystics are known as Sufis (*see p104*).

Overview of the Süleymaniye Mosque complex

The ablutions fountain (*şadırvan*) was used by worshippers for ritual washing.

The caravanserai or han (*see p96*) provided accommodation for travellers.

The kitchen (*imaret*) catered for mosque officials, students, the sick and the poor.

Hospital (*darüşşifa*)

Colleges (*medreses*) for general and theological education were built adjacent to the mosque. Most now serve other uses.

Turkish baths (*hamam*)

Courtyard (*avlu*)

Prayer hall (*cami*)

A mausoleum (*türbe*) was built for the founder of the mosque.

PLAN OF A TYPICAL MOSQUE COMPLEX (KÜLLİYE)

A large complex such as the Süleymaniye Mosque (*see pp90–91*), shown here, was built as a charitable foundation as well as a place of worship. It would typically include a hospital, school, Islamic study halls, caravanserai (lodgings for travellers), public kitchen for the poor, and bath house. Today most such buildings no longer fulfil their original functions.

INSIDE A MOSQUE

Visitors will experience a soaring sense of space on entering the prayer hall of one of Istanbul's great mosques. Islam forbids images of living things (human or animal) inside a mosque, so there are never any statues or figurative paintings; but the geometric and abstract architectural details of the interior can be exquisite. Men and women pray separately. Women often use a screened off area or a balcony.

***The* müezzin mahfili** *is a raised platform found in large mosques. The muezzin (mosque official) stands on this when chanting responses to the prayers of the imam (head of the mosque).*

***The* mihrab**, *an ornate niche in the wall, marks the direction of Mecca. The prayer hall is laid out so that most people can see it.*

***The* minbar** *is a lofty pulpit to the right of the mihrab. This is used by the imam when he delivers the Friday sermon (khutba).*

MUSLIM BELIEFS AND PRACTICES

Muslims believe in God (Allah), and the Koran shares many prophets and stories with the Bible. However, whereas for Christians Jesus is the son of God, Muslims hold that he was just one in a line of prophets – the last being Mohammed, who brought the final revelation of God's truth to mankind. Muslims believe that Allah communicated the sacred texts of the Koran to Mohammed, via the archangel Gabriel.

There are five basic duties for Muslims. The first of these is the profession of faith: "There is no God but God, and Mohammed is his Prophet". Muslims are also enjoined to pray five times a day, give alms to the poor, and fast during the month of Ramazan *(see p47)*. Once in their lifetime, if they can afford it, they should make the pilgrimage (hajj) to Mecca (in Saudi Arabia), the site of the Kaaba, a sacred shrine built by Abraham, and also the birthplace of the Prophet.

The call to prayer *used to be given by the muezzin from the balcony of the minaret. Nowadays loudspeakers broadcast the call across the city. Only imperial mosques have more than one minaret.*

PRAYER TIMES

The five daily prayer times are calculated according to the times of sunrise and sunset, and so change throughout the year. Exact times will be posted up on boards outside large mosques. Those given here are a guide.

Prayer	Summer	Winter
Sabah	5am	7am
Öğle	1pm	1pm
İkindi	6pm	4pm
Akşam	8pm	6pm
Yatsı	9:30pm	8pm

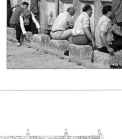

Ritual ablutions *must be undertaken before prayer. Worshippers wash their head, hands and feet either at the fountain in the courtyard or, more usually, at taps set in a discreet wall of the mosque.*

When praying, *Muslims always face the Kaaba in the holy city of Mecca, even if they are not in a mosque, where the mihrab indicates the right direction. Kneeling and lowering the head to the ground are gestures of humility and respect for Allah.*

VISITING A MOSQUE

Visitors are welcome at any mosque in Istanbul, but non-Muslims should avoid visiting at prayer times, especially the main weekly congregation and sermon on Fridays at 1pm. Take off your shoes before entering the prayer hall. Shoulders and knees should be covered. Men must remove their hats. Women need to cover their hair, so take a light scarf when sightseeing. Do not eat, take photographs with a flash or stand very close to worshippers. A contribution to a donation box or mosque official is courteous.

The loge (hünkar mahfili) *provided the sultan with a screened-off balcony where he could pray, safe from would-be assassins.*

The kürsü, *seen in some mosques, is a chair or throne used by the imam while he reads extracts from the Koran.*

Board outside a mosque giving times of prayer

Istanbul's Best: Palaces and Museums

AS THE FORMER CAPITAL of an empire that spanned from Algeria to Iraq and from Arabia to Hungary, Istanbul is home to a huge and diverse collection of treasures. Some, from musical instruments to priceless jewels, are housed in the beautiful former imperial palaces of the Ottoman sultans, which are worth visiting in any case for their architecture and opulent interiors. Topkapı and Dolmabahçe are the most famous palaces in Istanbul. The Archaeological Museum should also be on any itinerary of the city. This map points out these and other palaces and museums which are worth visiting for their splendid buildings or the exceptional collections they contain.

Aynalı Kavak Palace
This reclusive palace, with its airy feel and intimate proportions, shows subtler aspects of Ottoman taste. It houses a collection of Turkish musical instruments.

Archaeological Museum
Purpose-built in 1896, this superb museum has exhibits ranging from prehistory to the Byzantine era. They include this classical sculpture of the 2nd-century Roman Emperor Hadrian.

Museum of Calligraphy
Some of the texts in Istanbul's collection of Ottoman calligraphy (see p95) are by sultans, such as this panel by Ahmet III (1703–30).

GOLDEN HORN

BEYOĞLU

THE BAZAAR QUARTER

SERAGLIO POINT

SULTANAHMET

Museum of Turkish and Islamic Arts
This Seljuk example is one of the many carpets (see pp210–11) included in this museum's display of Turkish heritage. Other collections include glassware and ceramics.

Mosaics Museum
Gladiators fighting a lion are shown in one of the floors from the Great Palace (see pp82–3) displayed in this small museum.

Military Museum

A highlight of this museum is the famous Mehter Band, which gives regular outdoor concerts of Ottoman military music.

Şale Pavilion

One of a group of pavilions built in leafy Yıldız Park by 19th-century sultans, the Şale Pavilion has around 50 splendid rooms, including the Mother-of-Pearl Hall.

BOSPHORUS

THE ASIAN SIDE

Dolmabahçe Palace

This opulent 19th-century palace is home to such marvels as 2-m (7-ft) high vases, a crystal staircase and an alabaster bathroom.

Beylerbeyi Palace

Adorning one of the principal atriums of this 19th-century imperial summer palace is this elegant marble fountain. The palace was built to entertain visiting foreign dignitaries.

Topkapı Palace

This huge palace was used as the official royal residence for 400 years. The treasury contains a myriad of precious objects such as jewel-encrusted thrones and this ornate ceremonial canteen.

0 metres	750
0 yards	750

Exploring Istanbul's Collections

EACH MUSEUM in Istanbul contributes a piece to the vast cultural jigsaw of this cosmopolitan city. From Ancient Greek remains and early Chinese ceramics, which arrived in the city along the Silk Route, to 16th-century tiles commissioned for the great mosques and modern industrial machinery, each has its place in the history of Istanbul. Many of the larger museums have a wide range of exhibits and therefore feature under several of the headings below.

The *saz*, a type of lute

The Sarcophagus of the Mourning Women, Archaeological Museum

ARCHAEOLOGY

THE ARCHAEOLOGICAL fruits of the expansive Ottoman Empire are displayed in the **Archaeological Museum**, where the exhibits range from monumental 6th-century BC Babylonian friezes to exquisite classical sarcophagi and statues. Classical sculpture fills the ground floor. Upstairs there is a gallery for the archaeology of Syria and Cyprus. Ancient oriental finds are housed in an annexe. The **Museum of Turkish and Islamic Arts** features specifically Muslim artifacts, including early Iraqi and Iranian ceramics as well as beautiful displays of glassware, metalwork and woodwork.

Byzantine mosaic floor in the Mosaics Museum

BYZANTINE ANTIQUITIES

ALTHOUGH Constantinople was the capital of the Byzantine Empire *(see pp18–23)* for over 1,000 years, it can be hard to get a full picture of the city in that period. The best place to start is the **Archaeological Museum**, which has displays illustrating the city's Byzantine history. Its courtyard contains the purple sarcophagi of the Byzantine emperors.

For Byzantine church mosaics, visit the **Church of St Saviour in Chora** near the city walls which has some particularly fine examples vividly depicting the lives of Christ and the Virgin Mary. The impressive **Haghia Sophia** has a few brilliant gold mosaics remaining, some dating back to the reign of Justinian *(see p18)*. The galleries and upper walls of the **Church of the Pammakaristos** are covered with mosaics, although public access is restricted.

The **Mosaics Museum** houses mosaic floors and murals from the now-vanished Byzantine Great Palace *(see pp82–3)*, which were discovered by archaeologists in 1935. The **Sadberk Hanım Museum** also houses several Byzantine antiquities, including icons, ceramics and jewellery.

Mosque lamp from the Archaeological Museum

THE ARTS OF THE BOOK

IN THE DAYS BEFORE the printed word, Ottoman calligraphy *(see p95)* developed into a highly skilled artform, widely used both to ornament religious texts and to lend gravity to legal documents and decrees. The **Museum of Calligraphy** mounts a continuous series of temporary exhibitions, while beautiful early Koranic calligraphy can be viewed both in **Topkapı Palace** and in the **Museum of Turkish and Islamic Arts**.

CERAMICS

EXPERTS AND AMATEURS come from all over the world to view the collection of Chinese ceramics and porcelain on display in the kitchens of **Topkapı Palace**. The earliest examples provided the inspiration for Turkey's indigenous ceramic production at İznik *(see p161)*. Examples of İznik tiles can be seen on the walls of Topkapı Palace and in the city's mosques. İznik tiles and also pottery are on display in the **Çinili Pavilion**, an annexe of the **Archaeological Museum**, and at the **Sadberk Hanım Museum**. A wider selection of ceramics from all over the Islamic world can be found in the **Museum of Turkish and Islamic Arts**.

OTTOMAN INTERIORS

THE INTERIORS that can be visited in Istanbul run the gamut from the classical Ottoman styling of the older parts of **Topkapı Palace** to extravagant European-inspired 19th-century decor. In the latter category, the huge **Dolmabahçe Palace** set the style. It was decorated with Bohemian glass and Hereke carpets and has an

The opulent Süfera Salon in Dolmabahçe Palace

ornate central stairway fashioned of crystal and brass. The **Pavilion of the Linden Tree** and the Rococo **Küçüksu Palace**, although more intimate in scale, are equally lavish in their interior style.

TEXTILES

THE OTTOMANS were justifiably proud of their textile tradition, which can be admired in the huge imperial costume collection at **Topkapı Palace**, begun in 1850. The palace collection houses older materials, including kaftans dating back to the 15th century. The **Sadberk Hanım Museum** houses magnificent, mostly 19th-century pieces on the top floor and some fine examples of embroidery.

On a larger scale, there are huge imperial campaign tents in the **Military Museum**, which also has a collection of miniature Janissary *(see p127)* costumes. Uniforms, nomadic tents and fine carpets are on display in the **Museum of Turkish and Islamic Arts**. Antique carpets can also be seen in the **Vakıflar Carpet Museum**, housed in an annexe of the Blue Mosque. It contains some valuable old carpets that come originally from mosques all over Turkey.

Costume from Topkapı Palace

MUSICAL INSTRUMENTS

EXAMPLES OF typical Turkish instruments, such as the *saz* (lute), can be found in a museum devoted to them at **Aynalı Kavak Palace**. Those played by the Whirling Dervishes are on display at the **Mevlevi Monastery**. Instruments can also be seen, and bought, in two shops situated near the entrance to Gülhane Park *(see p61)*. Traditional Turkish military instruments can be heard being played at the **Military Museum**.

MILITARIA

THE BEAUTIFUL barges in which the Ottoman sultans were rowed around the Golden Horn and the Bosphorus are among the exhibits at the **Naval Museum**. Its most fascinating collection, however, is of the beautiful maps created by the Ottoman cartographer Piri Reis. Weapons and armour from the 12th–20th centuries can be found in the **Military Museum**, along with a huge cannon, captured by the Turks during their European campaigns. There is a smaller selection of weaponry in the armoury of **Topkapı Palace**. The **Florence Nightingale**

Museum (in the Selimiye Barracks on the Asian Side) commemorates the work of the nurse during the Crimean War. It also has some interesting military exhibits.

PAINTING

CLOSE TO Dolmabahçe Palace is Istanbul's **Museum of Fine Arts**, which offers a collection of largely late 19th- and early 20th-century Turkish paintings. Those interested in more contemporary works of art may also like to visit the changing exhibitions at the **Taksim Art Gallery**.

SCIENCE AND TECHNOLOGY

LOCATED IN a converted warehouse in the heart of Istanbul's docks is the **Rahmi Koç Museum**. It is home to a selection of mechanical and scientific instruments dating from the early years of the Industrial Revolution, as well as an entire reconstructed bridge taken from an early 20th-century ship.

Celebrated Visitors and Residents

THE CITY OF ISTANBUL has attracted foreign visitors since time immemorial. As reports of its beauty, its architecture and the opulence of its court circulated, so it came to be included on the extended Grand Tour route of the 19th century, undertaken by those seeking a little exotic pleasure while broadening their education. Because of Istanbul's pivotal geographic position, the ambassadors of the great powers of Europe were important figures, rubbing shoulders with the sultans. Other visitors were brought here by war, as either participants or refugees.

Lord Byron
The itinerant British poet stayed in Pera in 1810–11. During this time he swam the Dardanelles (see p170) and met Sultan Mahmut II in Topkapı Palace (see pp54–9).

Pierre Loti
The Café Pierre Loti (see p120) in Eyüp is named after the 19th-century French romantic writer who spent much time there.

GOLDEN HORN

Gurdjieff
A refugee of the Russian Revolution, the mystic, wily businessman and sometime spy was a frequent visitor to the Mevlevi Monastery (see p104) in 1920–21.

THE BAZAAR
QUARTER

Le Corbusier
During his visit to Istanbul in 1911, the French modern architect made drawings of mosques, among them the Süleymaniye (see pp72–5), houses and boats.

Agatha Christie
Room 411 of the Pera Palas Hotel (see p104) preserves the memory of the thriller writer whose Murder on the Orient Express was inspired by her journeys on the train (see p66) in the 1920s–30s.

Adam Mickiewicz
The Polish national poet came to Istanbul from Paris in 1855, during the Crimean War. He hoped to quell factional squabbles in the Polish military forces, but caught typhus soon after his arrival and died the same year.

Kaiser Wilhelm II
The last Kaiser of Germany visited Istanbul in 1889 and 1898. The Şale Pavilion at Yıldız Palace (see pp124–5) and the fountain in the Hippodrome (see p80) were built in his honour.

BEYOĞLU

BOSPHORUS

Ernest Hemingway
Sent to Istanbul from Paris in 1922 by his newspaper, to cover the war between Greece and Turkey, Hemingway stayed at the Hotel de Londres (see p182).

Florence Nightingale
Modern nursing methods were pioneered by Florence Nightingale in 1855–6, during the Crimean War, as she tended the injured in the Selimiye Barracks (see p132).

SERAGLIO POINT

Lady Wortley Montagu
As wife of the British Ambassador, Lady Mary Wortley Montagu was in Istanbul from 1718. Her letters give an intimate and appreciative insight into the workings of Ottoman society, from the sultan and his harem downwards.

THE ASIAN SIDE

0 metres	500
0 yards	500

ISTANBUL THROUGH THE YEAR

ISTANBUL is at its best in late May and early September, when temperatures are mild and sunshine is plentiful. High season, from June to August, is the most expensive, crowded and hottest time to visit, but the summer arts and music festivals are highlights in the city's cultural calendar. From late November until April a grey smog can hang over the city. However, Istanbul is still mild in autumn

Independence Day in Istanbul

and winter and, with very few tour parties around, you can enjoy the sights in peace. As well as arts and sporting events, several public holidays and religious festivals punctuate the year. It is wise to be aware of these when planning an itinerary as some sights may be closed or else crammed with locals enjoying a day out. Some of these celebrations are also fascinating spectacles in their own right.

Tulips growing in Emirgan Park, scene of the spring Tulip Festival

SPRING

AS THE WINTER SMOG fades and sunshine increases, cafés and restaurants prepare for the first wave of alfresco dining. After a winter's diet of apples and oranges, a welcome crop of spring fruits, including fresh figs, strawberries and tart green plums, arrives in the shops. Toasted sweetcorn is sold from carts *(see p200)*, and a spring catch of sea bream, sea bass and turbot is on the menu. Tulips, hyacinths, daffodils and pansies fill parks and gardens, and the distinctive pink buds of the Judas tree are seen along the Bosphorus. Monuments and museums are generally uncrowded in spring, and discounts are available at many hotels. In May the popular son et lumière shows outside the Blue Mosque *(see pp78–9)* begin and continue until September.

EVENTS

Easter *(March or April)*. Pilgrimage to the Monastery of St George on Büyükada in the Princes' Islands *(see p159)*.
International Istanbul Film Festival *(late March–mid-April)*, selected cinemas. Screening of Turkish and foreign films, and related events.
Tulip Festival *(April)*, Emirgan Park *(see p141)*. Displays of springtime blooms.
Independence Day *(23 April)*. Public holiday marking the inauguration of the Turkish Republic in 1923 *(see pp28–9)*. Children take to the streets in folk costume.
Commemoration of the Anzac Landings *(25 April)*, Gallipoli. Britons, Australians and New Zealanders gather at the location of the Anzac landings at Gallipoli during World War I *(see pp170–71)*.

Spring Day and Workers' Day *(1 May)*. Unofficial public holiday when workers usually attend union-organized rallies.
Kakava Festival *(early May)*, Edirne. A celebration of gypsy music and dance.
Youth and Sports Day *(19 May)*. Public holiday in commemoration of the start of the War of Independence *(see p29)* in 1919, with sporting events and other activities held throughout the city in stadiums and on the streets.
International Istanbul Theatre Festival *(May–June)*, various venues. European and Turkish productions.
Conquest of Istanbul *(29 May)*, between Tophane and Karaköy and on the shores of the upper Bosphorus. Mehmet the Conqueror's taking of the city in 1453 *(see p24)* is re-enacted in street parades and mock battles.

Colourful evening son et lumière show at the Blue Mosque

AVERAGE DAILY HOURS OF SUNSHINE

Hours

10 — 8 — 6 — 4 — 2 — 0

Jan Feb Mar Apr May Jun Jul Aug Sep Oct Nov Dec

Sunshine Chart
One of Istanbul's attractions is its summer sunshine – there are about 2,500 hours each year. From May to October the city is bathed in light well into the evening, and a long Indian summer can some-times linger into November. Winter, by contrast, is notoriously deprived of sun.

SUMMER

IN CONTRAST to an all-too-brief spring, the warm weather and clear skies of summer can linger on in Istanbul until November. In July and August temperatures soar and although luxury hotels have air condi-tioning, cheaper ones do not. Popular sights are packed with tourists throughout the high season. Picturesque locations outside Istanbul may, on the other hand, be overrun by locals. At weekends city dwellers trek out to the Belgrade Forest and Black Sea beaches *(see p158)* or to health clubs along the Bospho-rus. Those who can afford it flee to their coastal summer homes until autumn.

For those who stay behind there is a strong summer cul-ture. This includes a wild nightlife in hundreds of bars and night spots *(see p213)*, and enthusiastic support for many arts festivals, which attract world-famous performers. Look out, too, for events tak-ing place in historical buildings. You may be able to listen to classical music in Haghia Eirene *(see p60)* or enjoy a pop concert in the Fortress of Europe on the Bosphorus *(see pp140–41)*. This is also the best time of year for out-door sports such as hiking, horse-riding, water sports, golf and parachuting.

In summer, the menu focuses more on meat than fish, but vegetables and fresh fruit – such

Silk Market in Bursa, which operates in June and July

as honeydew melons, cherries, mulberries, peaches and apri-cots – are widely available. In July and August many shops have summer sales *(see p203)*.

EVENTS

Silk Market *(June–July)*, Bursa. Special market for the sale of silk cocoons *(see p164)*.
International Istanbul Music and Dance Festival *(mid-June–July)*. Classical music, opera and dance performed in historic locations. Mozart's *Abduction from the*

Performance of Mozart's *Abduction from the Seraglio* in the Harem of Topkapı Palace

Seraglio is staged annually in Topkapı Palace *(see pp54–9)*.
Bursa Festival *(June–July)*, Bursa Park. Music, folk dancing, plays, opera and shadow puppetry.
Navy Day *(1 July)*. Parades of old and new boats along the Bosphorus.
International Istanbul Jazz Festival *(July)*, various venues. International event with a devoted following.
International Sailing Races *(July)*. Regatta held at the Marmara Islands *(see p169)*.
Grease Wrestling *(July)*, Kırkpınar, Edirne. Wrestlers smeared in olive oil grapple with each other *(see p154)*.
Hunting Festival *(3 days, late July)*, Edirne. Music, art and fishing displays.
Folklore and Music Festival *(late July)*, Bursa. Ethnic dances and crafts displays.
Festival of Troy *(August)*, Çanakkale. Re-enactment of the tale of Troy *(see p171)*.
Victory Day *(30 August)*. Public holiday commemorating victory over Greece in 1922.

AVERAGE MONTHLY RAINFALL

mm		Inches
150		6
120		5
90		4
60		3
30		2
		1
0		0

Jan Feb Mar Apr May Jun Jul Aug Sep Oct Nov Dec

Rainfall Chart
Winter is the wettest season in Istanbul. Heavy showers of rain can sometimes continue into April and May, making spring seem shorter. Sudden snowstorms are not uncommon in winter, but these are short-lived and snowfalls will usually melt away as quickly as they come.

AUTUMN

RESIDENTS of Istanbul often consider their city to be at its best in autumn. As the summer heat loses its grip, chestnut sellers appear on the streets *(see p200)*, pumpkins are sold in the markets, and fresh figs are eaten in abundance. In the surrounding countryside, cotton, wheat and sunflowers are harvested. Migratory grouper and bonito are among the tastiest types of fish which are caught at this time of year.

A popular beauty spot for its array of autumn colours is Lake Abant, 200 km (125 miles) east of Istanbul. Meanwhile, bird-watchers converge on the hills overlooking the Bosphorus to view great flocks of migratory birds heading for their warm wintering grounds in Africa *(see p141)*.

On the cultural agenda is a world-class arts biennial and an antiques fair which blends Turkish and Western aesthetics. Several public holidays reaffirm Turkey's commitment to secularism, including Republic Day in late October, during which flags are hung from balconies. The bridges over the Bosphorus *(see p138)* are hung with particularly huge flags.

Street-side roasting of seasonal chestnuts

EVENTS

Tüyap Arts Fair *(September)*, opposite the Pera Palas Hotel *(see p104)*. A showcase of Istanbul's artistic talent.
Yapı Kredi Festival *(September)*, various venues. A celebration of music and dance promoting young performers.

Republic Day *(29 October)*. Public holiday commemorating Atatürk's proclamation of the Republic in 1923 *(see p29)*. The Turkish flag adorns buildings in the city.
Akbank Jazz Festival *(October)*, various venues. Jazz music *(see p213)*.
International Istanbul Fine Arts Biennial *(October–November every two years)*. International and local avant-garde artists exhibit work in historic locations such as Haghia Eirene and the Imperial Mint *(see p60)*, and the Basilica Cistern *(see p76)*.
Anniversary of Atatürk's Death *(10 November)*. A minute's silence is observed at 9:05am, the precise time of Atatürk's death in Dolmabahçe Palace *(see pp128–9)* in 1938.
Tüyap Book Fair *(first week of November)*, opposite the Pera Palas Hotel. Symposia featuring prominent publishers and writers. Manuscripts, prints and books displayed.
Efes Pilsen Blues Festival *(early November)*, selected venues. Foreign and local blues bands play in popular music venues around the city.
Interior Design Fair *(first week of November)*, Çırağan Palace Hotel Kempinski *(see p123)*. Interior designers and antique dealers display up-market wares in this popular annual show.
Elit's Küsav Antiques Fair *(mid-November)*, Military Museum *(see p126)*. Sale of local and foreign paintings, furniture, carpets, maps, books, porcelain, textiles, silver, clocks and bronze statuary.

Crowds gathering to celebrate Republic Day on 29 October

AVERAGE MONTHLY TEMPERATURE

Temperature Chart
The temperature of the city rarely drops below freezing in winter, and even very cold snaps seldom last longer than three days. The heat of the long, humid summer is intensified by the lodos *wind, which blows in from the Sea of Marmara. However, the northerly* poyraz *occasionally provides a cooling breeze.*

WINTER

THERE ARE distinct bonuses to visiting Istanbul in the winter, when even major sights are uncrowded, although the rain, fog and pollution may be off-putting. Shops in the Akmerkez, Galleria, Capitol and Carousel malls *(see p203)* hold sales, making the city a shopper's paradise for leather, woollens and fashion.

Outside Istanbul, when enough snow has fallen on the mountains, the ski season begins in Uludağ *(see p169)*, one of Turkey's most important winter sports resorts. Meanwhile, tea with baklava and cream cakes is consumed in the cosy cafés along the Bosphorus and in the old quarter of Beyoğlu *(see pp100–7)*.

View of Bebek on the Bosphorus *(see pp136–49)* in winter

Multitude of lights to welcome in the New Year in Beyoğlu

EVENTS

Mevlana Festival *(17–24 December)*, Mevlevi Monastery *(see p104)*. Enthusiastic Istanbul devotees perform special dances in honour of the founder of the famous Whirling Dervishes.
Christmas *(late December)*. Though Christmas Day is not a public holiday, major hotels organize seasonal festivities.
New Year's Day *(1 January)*. Public holiday incorporating European Christmas traditions including eating turkey, decorating trees and partying. Strings of lights adorn the main roads.
Karadam Ski Festival *(second half of February)*, Uludağ Mountain. Competitions organized by local radio stations and the Uludağ Ski Instructors' Association.

MUSLIM HOLIDAYS

The dates of Muslim holidays vary according to the phases of the moon and therefore change from year to year. In the holy month of **Ramazan**, Muslims refrain from eating and drinking between dawn and dusk. Some restaurants are closed during the day, and tourists should be discreet when eating in public. Straight after this is the three-day **Şeker Bayramı** (Sugar Festival), when sweetmeats are prepared. Two months later the four-day **Kurban Bayramı** (Feast of the Sacrifice) commemorates the Koranic version of Abraham's sacrifice. This is the main annual public holiday in Turkey, and hotels, trains and roads are packed. Strict Muslims also observe the festivals of **Regaip Kandili**, **Miraç Kandili**, **Berat Kandili** and **Mevlid-i-Nebi**.

Festivities during Şeker Bayramı

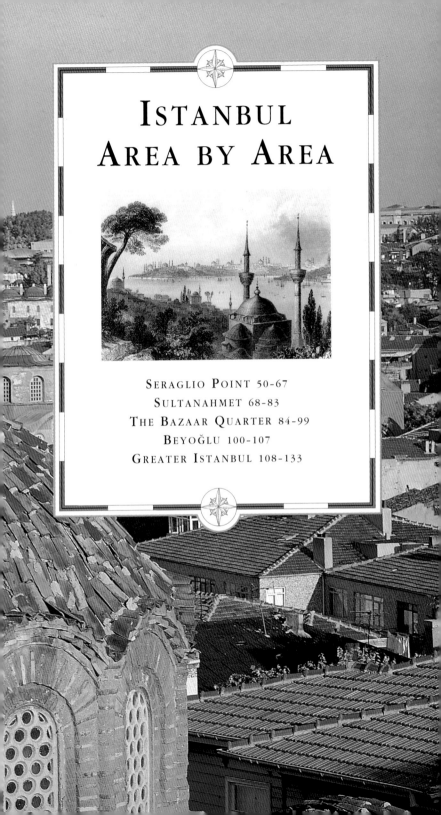

ISTANBUL
AREA BY AREA

SERAGLIO POINT

THE HILLY, wooded promontory that marks the meeting point of the Bosphorus and the Sea of Marmara occupies a natural strategic position. In Byzantine times, monasteries and public buildings stood on this incomparable site. Today it is dominated by the grandiose complex of buildings forming Topkapı Palace, the residence of the Ottoman sultans and the women of the harem for 400 years.

Lion relief from the Ishtar Gate

The palace is now open to the public as a rambling museum, with lavish apartments and glittering collections of jewels and other treasures. Originally the palace covered almost the whole of the area with its gardens and pavilions. Part of the grounds have now been turned into a public park. Adjacent to it is the Archaeological Museum, a renowned collection of finds from Turkey and the Near East.

SIGHTS AT A GLANCE

Museums and Palaces
Archaeological Museum pp62–5 ②
Topkapı Palace pp54–9 ①

Churches
Haghia Eirene ④

Historic Buildings and Monuments
Fountain of Ahmet III ⑤
Imperial Mint ③
Sirkeci Station ⑪
Sublime Porte ⑨

Streets and Courtyards
Cafer Ağa Courtyard ⑦
Soğukçeşme Sokağı ⑥

Parks
Gülhane Park ⑧

Turkish Baths
Cağaloğlu Baths ⑩

GETTING AROUND
With little traffic, this small area is easily explored on foot. Trams from the Grand Bazaar and the ferry piers at Eminönü stop outside Gülhane Park.

0 metres   400
0 yards   400

KEY

Street-by-Street map
See pp52–3

⚓ Ferry boarding point

🚉 Railway station

🚋 Tram stop

Tourist information

C Mosque

— Walls

◁ **The Circumcision Pavilion in the third courtyard of Topkapı Palace**

Street-by-Street: The First Courtyard of Topkapı

THE JUXTAPOSITION of Ottoman palace walls, intimately proportioned wooden houses and a soaring Byzantine church lends plenty of drama to the First Courtyard, the outer part of Topkapı Palace. This was once a service area, housing the mint, a hospital, college and a bakery. It was also the mustering point of the Janissaries *(see p127)*. Nowadays, the Cafer Ağa Courtyard and the Fatih Büfe, just outside the courtyard wall, offer unusual settings for refreshments. Gülhane Park, meanwhile, is one of the few shady open spaces in a city of monuments.

Gülhane Park
Once a rose garden in the outer grounds of Topkapı Palace, the wooded Gülhane Park provides welcome shade in which to escape from the heat of the city ❽

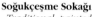

Soğukçeşme Sokağı
Traditional, painted wooden houses line this narrow street ❻

Museum of the Ancient Orient

Sublime Porte
A Rococo gate stands in place of the old Sublime Porte, once the entrance to (and symbol of) the Ottoman government ❾

Entrance to Gülhane Park

Gülhane tram stop

Alay Pavilion

0 metres 75
0 yards 75

KEY
— — — Suggested route

Zeynep Sultan Mosque
Resembling a Byzantine church, this mosque was built in 1769 by the daughter of Ahmet III, Princess Zeynep.

Fatih Büfe, a tiny ornate kiosk, sells drinks and snacks.

Otag Music Shop
sells traditional Turkish instruments.

Cafer Ağa Courtyard
The cells of this former college, ranged round a tranquil courtyard café, are now occupied by jewellers, calligraphers and other artisans selling their wares ❼

STAR SIGHTS

★ **Archaeological Museum**

★ **Topkapı Palace**

★ Archaeological Museum

Classical statues, dazzling carved sarcophagi, Turkish ceramics and other treasures from all over the former Ottoman Empire make this one of the world's great collections of antiquities ❷

Çinili Pavilion
(see p65)

LOCATOR MAP
See Street Finder maps 3 and 5

The Executioner's Fountain is so named because the executioner washed his hands and sword here after a public beheading.

★ Topkapı Palace

For 400 years the Ottoman sultans ruled their empire from this vast palace. Its fine art collections, opulent rooms and leafy courtyards are among the highlights of a visit to Istanbul ❶

Entrance to Topkapı Palace

Topkapı Palace ticket office

Imperial Mint

This museum houses exhibitions on the historical background to Istanbul ❸

Haghia Eirene
The Byzantine church of Haghia Eirene dates from the 6th century. Unusually, it has never been converted into a mosque ❹

Imperial Gate

Fountain of Ahmet III

Built in the early 18th century, the finest of Istanbul's Rococo fountains is inscribed with poetry likening it to the fountains of paradise ❺

Topkapı Palace ❶
Topkapı Sarayı

Süleyman I's *tuğra* over the main gate

Bᴇᴛᴡᴇᴇɴ 1459 and 1465, shortly after his conquest of Constantinople *(see p24)*, Mehmet II built Topkapı Palace as his principal residence. Rather than a single building, it was conceived as a series of pavilions contained by four enormous courtyards, a stone version of the tented encampments from which the nomadic Ottomans had emerged. Initially, the palace served as the seat of government and contained a school in which civil servants and soldiers were trained. In the 16th century, however, the government was moved to the Sublime Porte *(see p61)*. Sultan Abdül Mecit I abandoned Topkapı in 1853 in favour of Dolmabahçe Palace *(see pp128–9)*. In 1924 it was opened to the public as a museum.

★ Harem
The labyrinth of exquisite rooms where the sultan's wives and concubines lived can be visited on a guided tour (see pp58–9).

Exhibition of arms and armour *(see p56)*

Entrance to Harem

Harem ticket office

Gate of Salutations: entrance to the palace

Divan
The viziers of the imperial council met in this chamber, sometimes watched covertly by the sultan.

Second courtyard

The Gate of Felicity is also called the Gate of the White Eunuchs.

The kitchens contain an exhibition of ceramics, glass and silverware *(see p56).*

İftariye Pavilion

Standing between the Baghdad and Circumcision pavilions, this canopied balcony provides views down to the Golden Horn.

VISITORS' CHECKLIST

Babıhümayun Cad. **Map** 3 F3.
(0212) 512 04 80. Sultan-ahmet. 9:30am–5pm; public hols: midday–5pm Wed–Mon. **Harem** 10am–4pm Wed–Mon. (book early).

Baghdad Pavilion

In 1639 Murat IV built this pavilion to celebrate his capture of Baghdad. It has exquisite blue-and-white tilework.

Circumcision Pavilion

Exhibition of clocks *(see p57)*

Pavilion of the Holy Mantle *(see p57)*

Exhibition of miniatures and manuscripts *(see p57)*

Konyalı Restaurant *(see p194)*

The fourth courtyard is a series of gardens dotted with pavilions.

Third courtyard

Library of Ahmet III

Erected in 1719, the library is an elegant marble building. This ornamental fountain is set into the wall below its main entrance.

Exhibition of imperial costumes *(see p56)*

Throne Room

★ Treasury

This 17th-century jewel-encrusted jug is one of the precious objects exhibited in the former treasury (see p57).

STAR FEATURES

★ Harem

★ Treasury

Exploring the Palace's Collections

DURING THEIR 470-YEAR REIGN, the Ottoman sultans amassed a glittering collection of treasures. After the foundation of the Turkish Republic in 1923 *(see p29)*, this was nationalized and the bulk of it put on display in Topkapı Palace. As well as diplomatic gifts and articles commissioned from the craftsmen of the palace workshops, a large number of items in the collection were brought back as booty from successful military campaigns. Many such trophies date from the massive expansion of the Otto-man Empire during the reign of Selim the Grim (1512–20), when Syria, Arabia and Egypt were conquered.

Royal crib displayed in the Treasury

CERAMICS, GLASS AND SILVERWARE

THE KITCHENS contain the palace's collection of ce-ramics, glass and silverware. Turkish and European pieces are massively overshadowed here by the vast display of Chinese and, to a lesser extent, Japanese porcelain. This was brought to Turkey along the Silk Route, the overland trading link between the Far East and Europe. Topkapı's collection of Chinese porcelain is the world's second best after China itself.

The Chinese porcelain on display spans four dynasties: the Sung (10–13th centuries), followed by the Yüan (13–14th centuries), the Ming (14–17th centuries) and the Ching (17–20th centuries). Celadon, the earliest form of Chinese porcelain collected by the sultans, was made to look like jade, a stone believed by the Chinese to be lucky. The Ottomans prized it be-cause it was said to neutralize poison in food. More delicate than these are a number of exquisite blue-and-white pieces, mostly of the Ming era.

Chinese aesthetics were an important influence on Otto-man craftsmen, particularly in the creation of designs for their fledgling ceramics industry at İznik *(see p161)*. Although there are no İznik pieces in the Topkapı collection, many of the tiles on the palace walls originated there. These clearly show the influence of designs used for Chinese blue-and-white porcelain, such as stylized flowers and cloud scrolls. Much of the later porcelain, par-ticularly the Japanese Imari ware, was made specifically for the export mar-ket. The most ob-vious examples of this are some plates decorated with quo-tations from the Koran. A part of the kitchens, the old confectioners' pantry, has been preserved as it would have been when in use. On display are huge cauldrons and other utensils wielded by the palace's chefs as they prepared to feed its 12,000 residents and guests.

Japanese porcelain plate

ARMS AND ARMOUR

TAXES AND TRIBUTES from all over the empire were once stored in this chamber, which was known as the Inner Treasury. Straight ahead as you enter are a series of horse-tail standards. Carried in processions or displayed out-side tents, these proclaimed the rank of their owners. Viziers *(see p27)*, for example, merit-ed three, and the grand vizier five, while the sultan's banner would flaunt nine.

The weaponry includes or-nately embellished swords and several bows made by sultans themselves (Beyazıt II was a particularly fine craftsman). Seen next to these exquisite items, the huge iron swords used by European crusaders look crude by comparison. Also on view are pieces of 15th-century Ottoman chain-mail and colourful shields. The shields have metal centres surrounded by closely woven straw painted with flowers.

IMPERIAL COSTUMES

A COLLECTION of imperial costumes is displayed in the Hall of the Campaign Pages, whose task was to look after the royal wardrobe. It was a palace tradition that on the death of a sultan his clothes were carefully folded and placed in sealed bags. As a result, it is possible to see a perfectly preserved kaftan once worn by Mehmet the Conqueror *(see p24)*. The reforms of Sultan Mahmut II included a revolution in the dress code *(see p28)*. The end of an era came as plain grey serge replaced the earlier luxurious silken textiles.

Sumptuous silk kaftan once worn by Mehmet the Conqueror

TREASURY

O F ALL THE exhibitions in the palace, the Treasury's collection is the easiest to appreciate, glittering as it does with thousands of precious and semi-precious stones. The only surprise is that there are so few women's jewels here. Whereas the treasures of the sultans and viziers were owned by the state and reverted to the palace on their deaths, those belonging to the women of the court did not.

In the first hall stands a full, diamond-encrusted suit of chainmail, designed for Mustafa III (1757–74) for ceremonial use.

Diplomatic gifts include a fine pearl statuette of a prince seated beneath a canopy, which was sent to Sultan Abdül Aziz (1861–76) from India.

The Topkapı dagger

The greatest pieces are in the second hall. Foremost among these is the Topkapı dagger (1741). This splendid object was commissioned by the sultan from his own jewellers. It was intended to be a present for the Shah of Persia, but he died before it reached him. Among other exhibits here are a selection of the bejewelled aigrettes (plumes) which added splendour to imperial turbans.

In the third hall, the 86-carat Spoonmaker's diamond is said to have been discovered in a rubbish heap in Istanbul in the 17th century, and bought from a scrap merchant for three spoons. The gold-plated Bayram throne was given to Murat III (see p30) by the Governor of Egypt in 1574 and used for state ceremonies until early this century.

It was the throne in the fourth hall, given by the Shah of Persia, which was to have been acknowledged by the equally magnificent gift of the Topkapı dagger. In a cabinet near the throne is an unusual relic: a case containing bones said to be from the hand of St John the Baptist.

MINIATURES AND MANUSCRIPTS

I T IS POSSIBLE to display only a tiny fraction of Topkapı's total collection of over 13,000 miniatures and manuscripts at any one time. Highlights of it include a series of depictions of warriors and fearsome creatures known as *Demons and Monsters in the Life of Nomads*, which was painted by Mohammed Siyah Qalem, possibly as early as the 12th century. It is from this Eastern tradition of miniature painting, which was also prevalent in Mogul India and Persia, that the ebullient Ottoman style of miniatures developed.

Also on show are some fine examples of calligraphy (see p95), including copies of the Koran, manuscripts of poetry and several firmans, the imperial decrees by which the sultan ruled his empire.

Cover of a Koran, decorated in gold filigree work

CLOCKS

E UROPEAN CLOCKS given to, or bought by, various sultans form the majority of this collection, despite the fact that there were makers of clocks and watches in Istanbul from the 17th century. The clocks

A 17th-century watch made of gold, enamel and precious stones

range from simple, weight-driven 16th-century examples to an exquisite 18th-century English mechanism encased in mother-of-pearl and featuring a German organ which played tunes on the hour to the delight of the harem.

Interestingly, the only male European eyewitness accounts of life in the harem were written by the mechanics sent to service these instruments.

PAVILION OF THE HOLY MANTLE

S OME OF THE HOLIEST relics of Islam are displayed in these five domed rooms, which are a place of pilgrimage for Muslims. Most of the relics found their way to Istanbul as a result of the conquest by Selim the Grim (see p24) of Egypt and Arabia, and his assumption of the caliphate (the leadership of Islam) in 1517.

The most sacred treasure is the mantle once worn by the Prophet Mohammed. Visitors cannot actually enter the room in which it is stored; instead they look into it from an antechamber through an open doorway. Night and day, holy men continuously chant passages from the Koran over the gold chest in which the mantle is stored. A stand in front of the chest holds two of Mohammed's swords.

A glass cabinet in the anteroom contains hairs from the beard of the Prophet, a letter written by him and an impression of his footprint.

In the other rooms you can see some of the ornate locks and keys for the Kaaba (see p37) which were sent to Mecca by successive sultans.

Topkapı Palace: The Harem

THE WORD HAREM comes from the Arabic for "forbidden". It was the residence of the sultan's wives, concubines and children, who were guarded by black slave eunuchs. The sultan and his sons were the only other men allowed access to the Harem, which also included the Cage, a set of rooms where the sultan's brothers were confined to avoid succession contests. Topkapı's Harem was laid out by Murat III in the late 16th century and is a labyrinth of brilliantly tiled corridors and chambers. Visitors must take a guided tour. These last a little over half an hour and often get booked up early in the day.

Stained-glass window in the Paired Pavilions

LOCATOR MAP
See main illustration of the palace on pp54–5

Apartments and courtyard of the favourites

Sultan's bathroom

★ Paired Pavilions
These twin apartments, built in the 17th century for the crown prince, boast superb İznik tiles (see p161) and a dome lined with gilded canvas.

The Library of Ahmet I is pleasantly light and airy, with ivory-faced shutters.

The Salon of Murat III, built by Sinan *(see p91)*, has fine tiled walls, a handsome fountain and a large hearth.

★ Dining Room of Ahmet III
A sumptuous array of fruit and flowers is painted on to the walls of this 18th-century chamber, which is also known as the Fruit Room.

Imperial Hall
The largest room in the Harem, this hall was used for entertainments. Against one wall stands a large throne, from which the sultan would view the proceedings.

LIFE IN THE HAREM

The women of the Harem were slaves, gathered from the furthest corners of the Ottoman Empire and beyond. Their dream was to become a favourite of the sultan *(see p26)* and bear him a son, which on some occasions led to marriage. Competition was stiff, however, for at its height the Harem contained over 1,000 concubines, many of whom never rose beyond the service of their fellow captives. The last women eventually left in 1909.

A western view of Harem life in a 19th-century engraving

Salon of the Valide Sultan
The sultan's mother, the valide sultan (see p27), was the most powerful woman in the Harem and had some of the best rooms.

The Tower of Justice can be climbed after a tour of the Harem for a superb view of Topkapı's roof-tops and beyond.

Courtyard of the valide sultan

The Golden Way is so called because new sultans reputedly threw gold coins to their concubines here.

Exit

Entrance

Courtyard of the concubines

Valide sultan's bedchamber

The Harem baths were where the concubines bathed and relaxed.

Barracks of the black eunuchs

Valide sultan's prayer room

KEY

- – – Route of guided tour
- ☐ Rooms on guided tour
- ☐ Areas closed to the public

STAR FEATURES

★ **Paired Pavilions**

★ **Dining Room of Ahmet III**

Courtyard of the Black Eunuchs
Marble columns line this court-yard, which still has some old-fashioned, wrought-iron lamps.

Archaeological Museum **②**

See pp62–5.

Imperial Mint **③**
Darphane-i Amire

First courtyard of Topkapı Palace.
Map 3 E4 (5 F3). **〔** *(0212) 513 20
35.* 🚊 *Gülhane or Sultanahmet.*
🅾 *10am–7pm Wed–Sun.*

T HE OTTOMAN MINT opened
here in 1727, but most of
what can be seen today dates
from the reign of Mahmut II
(1808–39), when the complex
was extended. In 1967, the
mint moved to a new location.
The buildings are now used
for exhibitions on the history
of Istanbul. It is planned to
convert them into a museum
of social history.

Haghia Eirene **④**
Aya İrini Kilisesi

First courtyard of Topkapı Palace.
Map 3 E4 (5 F3). **〔** *(0212) 522 17
50.* 🚊 *Gülhane or Sultanahmet.*
🅾 *for concerts.*

T HOUGH THE present church
dates only from the 6th
century, it is at least the third
building to be erected on
what is thought to be the
oldest site of Christian worship
in Istanbul. Within a decade
of the Muslim conquest of the
city in 1453 *(see p24)* it had

One of the four elaborately decorated sides of the Fountain of Ahmet III

been included within the
Topkapı Palace complex and
pressed into use as an arsenal.
Today the building, which has
good acoustics, is the setting
for concerts during the Istanbul
Music Festival *(see p45).*

Inside are three fascinating
features that have not survived
in any other Byzantine church
in the city. The *synthronon,*
the five rows of built-in seats
hugging the apse, were
occupied by clergymen offi-
ciating during services. Above
this looms a simple black
mosaic cross on a gold background, which dates from the
iconoclastic period *(see p18),*
when figurative images were
forbidden. At the back of the
church is a cloister-like
courtyard where deceased
Byzantine emperors once lay
in their porphyry sarcophagi.
Most have been moved to the
Archaeological Museum.

Fountain of Ahmet III **⑤**
Ahmet III Çeşmesi

Junction of İshak Paşa Cad &
Babıhümayun Cad. **Map** 3 E4 (5 F4).
🚊 *Gülhane or Sultanahmet.*

B UILT IN 1728, the most
beautiful of Istanbul's
countless fountains survived
the violent deposition of
Sultan Ahmet III two years
later. Many of the other
monuments constructed by
the sultan during his reign,
which has become known as
the Tulip Period *(see p25),*
were destroyed. The fountain
is in the delicate Turkish
Rococo style, with five small
domes, mihrab-shaped niches
and dizzying floral reliefs.

Ottoman "fountains" do not
spout jets of water, but are
more like ornate public
taps. They sometimes incorporated a counter, or *sebil,*
from which refreshments
would be served.

In this case, each of the
fountain's four walls is equipped with a tap, or *çeşme,*
above a carved marble basin.
Over each tap is an elaborate
calligraphic inscription by the
18th-century poet Seyit Vehbi
Efendi. The inscription, in
gold on a blue-green background, is in honour of the
fountain and its founder. At
each of the four corners there
is a *sebil* backed by three
windows covered by ornate
marble grilles. Instead of the
customary iced water, passers-
by at this fountain would have
been offered sherbets and flavoured waters in silver goblets.

The apse of Haghia Eirene, with its imposing black-on-gold cross

Soğukçeşme Sokağı ⑥

Map 3 E4 (5 F3). 🚇 *Gülhane.*

CHARMING OLD wooden houses line this narrow, sloping cobbled lane ("the street of the cold fountain"), which squeezes between the outer walls of Topkapı Palace and the towering minarets of Haghia Sophia. Traditional houses like these were built in the city from the late 18th century onwards.

The buildings in the lane were renovated by the Turkish Touring and Automobile Club (TTOK, *see p175*) in the 1980s. Some of them now form the Ayasofya Pansiyonları *(see p180)*, a series of attractive pastel-painted guesthouses popular with tourists. Another building has been converted by the TTOK into a library of historical writings on Istanbul, and archive of engravings and photographs of the city. A Roman cistern towards the bottom of the lane has been converted into the Sarnıç restaurant *(see p194)*.

Traditional calligraphy on sale in Cafer Ağa Courtyard

Cafer Ağa Courtyard ⑦
Cafer Ağa Medresesi

Caferiye Sok. **Map** 5 E3. 🗎 *(0212) 245 11 60.* 🚇 *Gülhane.* ◻ *8:30am–8pm daily.*

THIS PEACEFUL courtyard at the end of an alley was built in 1559 by Sinan *(see p91)* for the chief black eunuch *(see p27)* as a *medrese* (theological college, *see p36)*. Sinan's bust presides over the café tables in the courtyard. The former students' lodgings

Restored Ottoman house on Soğukçeşme Sokağı

are now used to display a variety of craft goods typically including jewellery, silk prints, ceramics and calligraphy.

Gülhane Park ⑧
Gülhane Parkı

Alemdar Cad. **Map** 3 E3 (5 F2). 🚇 *Gülhane.* ◻ *daily.*

GÜLHANE PARK occupies what was the lower grounds of Topkapı Palace. Today it has a neglected air but it is still a shady place to stroll and it includes a couple of interesting landmarks.

Ignore the ill-kept zoo on the left of the road through the park, but seek out the aquarium by the disused cascade on the right. It is in the cavernous vaults of a Roman water cistern. At the far end of the park is the Goths' Column, a well-preserved 3rd-century victory monument, surrounded by a cluster of clapboard teahouses. Its name comes from the Latin inscription on it which reads: "Fortune is restored to us because of victory over the Goths".

Across Kennedy Caddesi, the main road running along the northeast side of the park, there is a viewpoint over the busy waters where the Golden Horn meets the Bosphorus.

OTTOMAN HOUSES

The typical, smart town house of 19th-century Istanbul had a stone ground floor above which were one or two wooden storeys. The building invariably sported a *çıkma*, a section projecting out over the street. This developed from the traditional Turkish balcony, which was enclosed in the northern part of the country because of the colder climate. Wooden lattice covers, or *kafesler*, over the windows on the upper storeys ensured that the women of the house were able to watch life on the street below without being seen themselves. Few wooden houses have survived. Those that remain usually owe their existence to tourism and many have been restored as hotels. While the law forbids their demolition, it is extremely hard to obtain insurance for them in a city that has experienced many devastating fires.

Sublime Porte ⑨
Bab-ı Ali

Alemdar Cad. **Map** 3 E3 (5 E2). 🚇 *Gülhane.*

FOREIGN AMBASSADORS to Ottoman Turkey were known as Ambassadors to the Sublime Porte, after this monumental gateway which once led into the offices and palace of the grand vizier. The institution of the Sublime Porte filled an important role in Ottoman society because it could often provide an effective counterbalance to the whims of sultans.

The Rococo gateway you see today was built in the 1840s. Its guarded entrance now shields the offices of Istanbul's provincial government.

Rococo decoration on the roof of the Sublime Porte

Archaeological Museum ❷
Arkeoloji Müzesi

ALTHOUGH THIS collection of antiquities was begun only in the mid-19th century, provincial governors were soon sending in objects from the length and breadth of the Ottoman Empire. Today the museum has one of the world's richest collections of classical artifacts, and also includes treasures from the pre-classical world. The main building was erected under the directorship of Osman Hamdi Bey (1881–1910), to house his finds. This archaeologist, painter and polymath discovered the exquisite sarcophagi in the royal necropolis at Sidon in present-day Lebanon. A new four-storey wing of the museum was opened in 1991.

Roman statue of Apollo

★ **Alexander Sarcophagus**
This fabulously carved marble tomb from the late 4th century BC is thought to have been built for King Abdalonymos of Sidon. It is called the Alexander Sarcophagus because Alexander the Great is depicted on it winning a victory over the Persians.

Sarcophagus of the Mourning Women

KEY

- ☐ Classical Archaeology
- ☐ Children's Museum
- ☐ Thracian, Bithynian and Byzantine Collections
- ☐ Istanbul Through the Ages
- ☐ Anatolia and Troy
- ☐ Anatolia's Neighbouring Cultures
- ☐ Turkish Tiles and Ceramics
- ☐ Museum of the Ancient Orient
- ☐ Non-exhibition space

The porticoes of the museum take their design from the 4th-century BC Sarcophagus of the Mourning Women.

GALLERY GUIDE

The 20 galleries of the main building house the museum's important collection of classical antiquities. The new wing has displays on the archaeology of Istanbul and nearby regions, and includes the Children's Museum. There are two other buildings within the grounds: the Çinili Pavilion, which contains Turkish tiles and ceramics, and the Museum of the Ancient Orient.

Çinili Pavilion

Outdoor café

STAR EXHIBITS

- ★ **Alexander Sarcophagus**
- ★ **Karaman Mihrab**
- ★ **Treaty of Kadesh**

★ **Karaman Mihrab**
This blue, richly tiled mihrab (see p36) comes from the city of Karaman in southeast Turkey, which was the capital of the Karamanid state from 1256–1483. It is the most important artistic relic of that culture.

Geometric Period Cypriot Jug
Stylized fish decorate this jug, in a design typical of the Geometric Period (1050–750 BC), when a vibrant ceramics culture flourished on Cyprus.

Stairs to main building

Third floor

Second floor

First floor

Ground floor of the new wing

Statue of Marsyas

Statue and bust of Alexander the Great

Entrance

VISITORS' CHECKLIST

Osman Hamdi Bey Yokuşu.
Map 3 E3 (5 F2). (0212) 520 77 40. Gülhane. 9:30am–4:30pm Tue–Sun. public hols.

Mosaic Icon of the Presentation
Dating from the 6th–7th centuries AD, this battered panel from Kalenderhane Mosque (see p92) is the only religious figurative mosaic to have survived Byzantium's iconoclastic period (see p18).

Porphyry Sarcophagi
These monumental purple sarcophagi (4th–5th centuries AD) are thought to have held the bodies of some of the early Byzantine emperors.

★ Treaty of Kadesh
This tablet constitutes the world's earliest surviving peace treaty, agreed between the Egyptians and Hittites in 1269 BC. Among its many clauses are provisions for the return of political refugees.

Exploring the Archaeological Museum

THIS ENORMOUS COLLECTION spans over 5,000 years, from figurines of the Mother Goddess modelled in the 3rd millennium BC to Turkish pottery thrown in the 19th century. To cover everything in one visit is impossible. Visitors with little time should not miss the breathtaking sarcophagi from the royal necropolis at Sidon. To learn more about the history of Istanbul itself you should head for the gallery exploring this theme, on the first floor of the new wing. Youngsters may enjoy the displays in the Children's Museum.

CLASSICAL ARCHAEOLOGY

MONUMENTAL BES, the ancient Egyptian god, greets visitors at the door to the main building. Hugely popular in the 1st–3rd centuries, Bes' comically grotesque appearance was an effective deterrent for evil spirits. Rooms 9 and 8 contain the highlights of the museum's entire collection: a group of sarcophagi unearthed in 1887 at Sidon (in present-day Lebanon). These are thought to have been made for a line of Phoenician kings who ruled in the 6th–4th centuries BC. Their decoration vividly shows the transition from Egyptian to Greek influence in the art of the Near East at that time.

Marble bust of Emperor Augustus

The latest and finest of them is the so-called Alexander Sarcophagus (late 4th century BC). Alexander the Great features in two decorative, high-relief friezes on the longest sides. These show a battle scene and a hunting scene. The friezes survive in almost perfect condition, showing traces of their original colouring, though the metal weapons of the soldiers and hunters have been lost.

The Sarcophagus of the Mourning Women is thought to have been made for King Straton (374–358 BC), who was known for his fondness for women. The grief-stricken females may have been members of his harem.

Rooms 14–20 contain some remarkable statues. Among them is a Roman copy of a 3rd century BC statue of Marsyas, depicting the satyr about to be flayed after daring to challenge Apollo's musical ability. A statue and bust of Alexander the Great (3rd–2nd centuries BC) show the conqueror as the perfect hero, with a meditative expression on his face. Room 18 contains realistic busts of Roman emperors.

CHILDREN'S MUSEUM

SPECIAL LOW CABINETS are used in this part of the museum, which is designed for visiting schoolchildren. Paper and coloured crayons are to hand in a bid to stimulate future archaeologists.

THRACIAN, BITHYNIAN AND BYZANTINE COLLECTIONS

THIS GALLERY on the ground floor of the new wing displays religious and other artifacts from the ancient civilizations of Thrace and Bithynia, and from Byzantium (see pp18–23) – including a statue of Byzantine Emperor Valens. This section of the museum also covers the architecture of the ancient world.

Bronze head of a snake from the Serpentine Column

ISTANBUL THROUGH THE AGES

WITH A FEW well-chosen pieces and explanatory texts in Turkish and English, this gallery brilliantly chronicles Istanbul's archaeological past.

The rare Mosaic Icon of the Presentation (c.AD 600) originally adorned the Kalenderhane Mosque (see p92). One of the three snakes' heads from the Serpentine Column, which has stood headless in the Hippodrome (see p80) since the 18th century, is also displayed here. Look out too for a section of the iron chains that the Byzantines hung across both the Bosphorus and the Golden Horn to stop hostile ships (see p21).

Frieze showing the battle of Issus (333 BC), on the side panel of the Alexander Sarcophagus

Reconstruction of a mausoleum discovered at Palmyra in Syria

ANATOLIA AND TROY

ONE SIDE OF this narrow, long hall chronicles the history of Anatolia (the Asiatic part of modern Turkey) from the Palaeolithic era to the Iron Age. It culminates in a room devoted to the Phrygian culture, which centred on the city of Gordion. The highlight is a recreation of an 8th-century BC royal tomb, which was housed beneath a tumulus in a juniper-wood chamber. As well as cooking utensils, the king was buried with furniture made of oak, box, yew and juniper.

The other side of the gallery traces the excavations of nine different civilizations at Troy (see p171), from 3000 BC to the time of Christ. On display are a few pieces of the gold hoard known as the Schliemann treasure, after the archaeologist who first discovered it in the late 19th century. Most of the pieces were smuggled out of Turkey, however, and are now in museums around the world.

ANATOLIA'S NEIGHBOURING CULTURES

THIS LONG GALLERY is also divided in two, with one side devoted to Cyprus and the other to Syria-Palestine. The Cypriot collection was assembled by the joint American and Russian consul to Cyprus, Luigi Palma di Cesnola, who systematically looted its tombs from 1865–73. Apart from some beautiful pots, the most interesting objects are the figures

of plump, naked temple boys (3rd century BC). They are thought to represent boy prostitutes at temples to Aphrodite, the Greek goddess of love.

Among the Syrian exhibits are funerary reliefs, the Gezer Calendar (925 BC) – a limestone tablet bearing the oldest known Hebrew inscription – and a reconstruction of a 1st–3rd-century mausoleum from the trading oasis of Palmyra.

16th-century İznik tiled lunette in the Çinili Pavilion

TURKISH TILES AND CERAMICS

APART FROM CARPETS, the most distinctive Turkish art form is ceramics. This is particularly seen in the sheets of tiles used to decorate the walls of mosques and pavilions such as the Çinili Pavilion, where the entrance archway is plastered with geometric and calligraphic tiles.

In the main room there is an exquisite early 15th-century tiled mihrab from central Anatolia. Rooms 3 and 4 contain tiles and mosque lamps from the famed İznik potteries, the hub

of Turkish ceramics production (see p161). With the decline in quality of İznik ceramics in the late 16th century, other centres took over. One of these, Kütahya, also produced pieces of beauty and high quality (rooms 5 and 6).

MUSEUM OF THE ANCIENT ORIENT

ALTHOUGH THIS collection contains antiquities of great rarity and beauty from the Egyptian and Hittite cultures, pride of place goes to the artifacts from the early civilizations of Mesopotamia (present-day Iraq).

The monumental glazed brick friezes from Babylon's main entrance, the Ishtar Gate, (rooms 3 and 9) date from the reign of Nebuchadnezzar II (605–562 BC), when the capital of Babylon experienced its final flowering. The elegant, 30-kg (65-lb) duck-shaped weight in Room 4 comes from a much earlier Babylonian temple (c.2000 BC).

Room 5 contains some of the earliest known examples of writing, in the form of cuneiform inscriptions on clay tablets, dating from 2700 BC. The famous Treaty of Kadesh (room 7), concluded around 1269 BC between the Egyptian and Hittite empires, was originally written on a sheet of silver. The one in this collection is a Hittite copy. The treaty includes many sophisticated clauses, including one providing for the return of a political refugee, who was "not to be charged with his crime, nor his house and wives and his children be harmed".

Glazed frieze of a bull from Ishtar Gate, Babylon

Cağaloğlu Baths ⑩
Cağaloğlu Hamamı

Prof Kazım İsmail Gürkan Cad 34,
Cağaloğlu. **Map** 3 E4 (5 D3).
📞 *(0212) 522 24 24.*
🚋 *Sultanahmet.* ⭘ *daily 8am–
9pm (women); 8am–10pm (men).*

AMONG THE city's more sumptuous Turkish baths, the
ones in Cağaloğlu were built
by Sultan Mahmut I in 1741.
The income from them was
designated for the maintenance
of Mahmut's library in Haghia
Sophia *(see pp72–5)*.
The city's smaller baths have
different times at which men
and women can use the same
facilities. But in larger baths,

**Corridor leading into the Cağaloğlu
Baths, built by Mahmut I**

such as this one, there are
entirely separate sections. In
the Cağaloğlu Baths the men's
and women's sections are at
right angles to one another and
entered from different streets.
Each consists of three parts: a
camekan, a *soğukluk* and the
main bath chamber or *hararet*,
which centres on a massive
octagonal massage slab.
The Cağaloğlu Baths are
popular with foreign visitors
because the staff are happy to
explain the procedure. Even
if you do not want to sweat it
out, you can still take a look
inside the entrance corridor and
camekan of the men's section.
Here you will find a small
display of Ottoman bathing
regalia, including precarious
wooden clogs once worn by
women on what would fre-
quently be their only outing
from the confines of the home.
You can also sit and have a
drink by the fountain in the
peaceful *camekan*.

Sirkeci Station ⑪
Sirkeci Garı

Sirkeci İstasyon Cad, Sirkeci. **Map** 3E3
(5 E1). 📞 *(0212) 527 00 50.*
🚋 *Sirkeci.* ⭘ *daily.*

THIS MAGNIFICENT railway
station was built to receive
the long-anticipated Orient
Express from Europe. It was
officially opened in 1890, even

**Sirkeci Station, final destination
of the historic Orient Express**

though the luxurious train had
been running into Istanbul for
a year by then. The design, by
the German architect Jasmund,
successfully incorporates features from the many different
architectural traditions of
Istanbul. Byzantine alternating
stone and brick courses are
combined with a Seljuk-style
monumental recessed portal
and Muslim horseshoe arches
around the windows.
The station café is a good
place in which to escape the
bustle of the city for a while.
Sirkeci serves Greece and
other destinations in Europe
as well as the European part
of Turkey. Istanbul's other
mainline railway station is
Haydarpaşa *(see p133)*, on
the Asian side of the city.

THE WORLD-FAMOUS ORIENT EXPRESS

The Orient Express made its first run from Paris to
Istanbul in 1889, covering the 2,900-km (1,800-mile)
journey in three days. Both Sirkeci Station and the
Pera Palas Hotel *(see p104)* in Istanbul were built
especially to receive its passengers. The wealthy and
often distinguished passengers of "The Train of
Kings, the King of Trains" did indeed include kings
among the many presidents, politicians, aristocrats
and actresses. King Boris III of Bulgaria even made a
habit of taking over from the driver of the train when
he travelled on it through his own country.
   A byword for exoticism and romance, the train was
associated with the orientalist view of Istanbul as a
treacherous melting pot of diplomats and arms dealers.
It inspired no fewer than 19 books – *Murder on the
Orient Express* by Agatha Christie and *Stamboul Train*
by Graham Greene foremost among them – six films
and one piece of music. During the Cold War
standards of luxury crashed, though a service of
sorts, without even a restaurant car, continued twice
weekly to Istanbul until 1977.

**A 1920s poster for the Orient Express,
showing a romantic view of Istanbul**

Turkish Baths

NO TRIP TO ISTANBUL is complete without an hour or two spent in a Turkish bath *(hamam)*, which will leave your whole body feeling rejuvenated. Turkish baths differ little from the baths of ancient Rome, from which they derive, except there is no pool of cold water to plunge into at the end.

A full service will entail a period of relaxation in the steam-filled hot room, punctuated by bouts of vigorous soaping and massaging. There is no time limit, but allow at least an hour and a half for a leisurely bath. Towels and soap will be provided, but you can take special toiletries with you. Two historic baths located in the old city, Çemberlitaş *(see p81)* and Cağaloğlu (illustrated below), are used to catering for foreign tourists. Some luxury hotels have their own baths *(see pp174–85)*.

Ornate wash basin

Choosing a Service
Services, detailed in a price list at the entrance, range from a self-service option to a luxury body scrub, shampoo and massage.

The camekan (entrance hall) is a peaceful internal courtyard near the entrance of the building. Bathers change clothes in cubicles surrounding it. The *camekan* is also the place to relax with a cup of tea after bathing.

Changing Clothes
Before changing you will be given a cloth (peştemal), *to wrap around you, and a pair of slippers for walking on the hot, wet floor.*

Corridor from street

Basin and tap for washing

Small, star-like windows piercing the domes

CAĞALOĞLU BATHS
The opulent, 18th-century Turkish baths at Cağaloğlu have separate, identical sections for men and women. The men's section is shown here.

The soğukluk (intermediate room) is a temperate passage between the changing room and the *hararet*. You will be given dry towels here on your way back to the *camekan*.

In the hararet (hot room), the main room of the Turkish bath, you are permitted to sit and sweat in the steam for as long as you like.

The Exfoliating Body Scrub
In between steaming, you (or the staff at the baths) scrub your body briskly with a coarse, soapy mitt (kese).

The Body Massage
A marble plinth (göbek taşı) *occupies the centre of the hot room. This is where you will have your pummelling full-body massage.*

SULTANAHMET

STANBUL's two principal monuments face each other across an area of gardens known informally as Sultanahmet Square. This part of the city gets its name from Sultan Ahmet I, who built the Blue Mosque. Opposite is Haghia Sophia, an outstanding example of early Byzantine architecture, and still one of the world's most remarkable churches. A neat oblong square

Mosaic of Empress Irene in Haghia Sophia

next to the Blue Mosque marks the site of the Hippodrome, a chariot-racing stadium built by the Romans in around AD 200. On the other side of the Blue Mosque, Sultanahmet slopes down to the Sea of Marmara in a jumble of alleyways. Here, traditional-style Ottoman wooden houses have been built over the remains of the Great Palace of the Byzantine emperors.

SIGHTS AT A GLANCE

Mosques and Churches
Blue Mosque pp78–9 ❼
Church of SS Sergius and
  Bacchus ⓮
Haghia Sophia pp72–5 ❶
Sokollu Mehmet Paşa
  Mosque ⓭

Museums
Mosaics Museum ❻
Museum of Turkish and
  Islamic Arts ❽
Vakıflar Carpet Museum ❺

Squares and Courtyards
Hippodrome ❾
Istanbul Crafts
  Centre ❸

Historic Buildings and Monuments
Basilica Cistern ❷
Baths of Roxelana ❹
Bucoleon Palace ⓯
Cistern of 1,001 Columns ❿
Constantine's Column ⓬
Tomb of Sultan Mahmut II ⓫

KEY

	Street-by-Street map See pp70–71
🚋	Tram stop
ℹ	Tourist information
C	Mosque
—	Walls

GETTING AROUND

Trams from Eminönü and Beyazıt stop in Sultanahmet by the Firuz Ağa Mosque on Divanyolu Caddesi. From there, most of the sights are easily reached on foot.

Street-by-Street: Sultanahmet Square

T WO OF ISTANBUL'S most venerable monuments, the Blue Mosque and Haghia Sophia, face each other across a leafy square, informally known as Sultanahmet Square (Sultanahmet Meydanı), next to the Hippodrome of Byzantium. Also in this fascinating historic quarter are a handful of museums, including the Mosaics Museum, built over part of the old Byzantine Great Palace (see pp82–3), and the Museum of Turkish and Islamic Arts. No less diverting than the cultural sights are the cries of the *simit* (bagel) hawkers and carpet sellers, and the chatter of children selling postcards.

Tomb of Sultan Ahmet I
Stunning 17th-century İznik tiles (see p161) adorn the inside of this tomb, which is part of the outer complex of the Blue Mosque.

★ Blue Mosque
Towering above Sultanahmet Square are the six beautiful minarets of this world-famous mosque. It was built in the early 17th century for Ahmet I ❼

Sultanahmet tram stop

Firuz Ağa Mosque

Fountain of Kaiser Wilhelm II

Museum of Turkish and Islamic Arts
Yurts, used by Turkey's nomadic peoples, and rugs are included in this impressive collection ❽

Egyptian Obelisk

Serpentine Column

Brazen Column

Hippodrome
This stadium was the city's focus for more than 1,000 years before it fell into ruin. Only a few sections, such as the central line of monuments, remain ❾

Vakıflar Carpet Museum
Part of the Blue Mosque complex, this museum displays fine antique carpets ❺

Mosaics Museum
Hunting scenes are one of the common subjects that can be seen in some of the mosaics from the Great Palace ❻

| 0 metres | 75 |
| 0 yards | 75 |

★ Basilica Cistern
This marble Medusa head is one of two classical column bases found in the Basilica Cistern. The cavernous cistern dates from the reign of Justinian (see p18) in the 6th century ❷

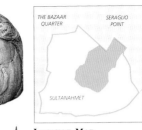

A stone pilaster next to the remains of an Ottoman water tower is all that survives of the Milion *(see p83)*, a triumphal gateway.

THE BAZAAR QUARTER	SERAGLIO POINT
SULTANAHMET	

LOCATOR MAP
See Street Finder, maps 3 and 5

★ Haghia Sophia
The supreme church of Byzantium is over 1,400 years old but has survived in a remarkably good state. Inside it are several glorious figurative mosaics ❶

Baths of Roxelana
Sinan (see p91) designed these beautiful baths in the mid-16th century. They no longer serve their original function, however, having been converted into a state-run carpet shop ❹

Yeşil Ev Hotel
(see p182)

Istanbul Crafts Centre
Visitors have a rare opportunity here to observe Turkish craftsmen practising a range of skills ❸

Cavalry Bazaar
Eager salesmen will call you over to peruse their wares – mainly carpets and handicrafts – in this bazaar. With two long rows of shops on either side of a lane, the bazaar was once a stable yard.

STAR SIGHTS

- **★ Blue Mosque**
- **★ Basilica Cistern**
- **★ Haghia Sophia**

Haghia Sophia ❶
Aya Sofya

T HE "CHURCH OF HOLY WISDOM", Haghia Sophia is among the world's greatest architectural achievements. More than 1,400 years old, it stands as a testament to the sophistication of the 6th-century Byzantine capital and was of paramount influence on architecture in the following centuries. The vast edifice was built over two earlier churches and inaugurated by Emperor Justinian in 537. In the 15th century the Ottomans converted it into a mosque: the minarets, tombs and fountains date from this period. To help support the structure's great weight, the exterior has been buttressed on numerous occasions, which has partly obscured its original shape.

Print of Haghia Sophia from the mid-19th century

Seraphims adorn the pendentives at the base of the dome.

Calligraphic roundel

Kürsü
(see p37)

Byzantine Frieze
Among the ruins of the monumental entrance to the earlier Haghia Sophia (dedicated in AD 415) is this frieze of sheep.

Buttresses

Imperial Gate

Entrance

Outer Narthex

Inner Narthex

The galleries were originally used by women during services.

HISTORICAL PLAN OF HAGHIA SOPHIA

Nothing remains of the first 4th-century church on this spot, but there are traces of the second one from the 5th century, which burnt down in AD 532. Earthquakes have taken their toll on the third structure, strengthened and added to many times.

KEY

☐ 5th-century church

▣ 6th-century church

☐ Ottoman additions

STAR FEATURES

★ **Nave**

★ **The Mosaics**

★ **Ablutions Fountain**

★ **Nave**
Visitors cannot fail to be staggered by this vast space which is covered by a huge dome reaching to a height of 56 m (184 ft).

VISITORS' CHECKLIST

Ayasofya Meydanı, Sultanahmet.
Map 3 E4 (5 F3). (0212) 522
17 50. Sultanahmet.
9:30am–4:30pm Tue–Sun.
ground floor only.

Brick minaret

★ **The Mosaics**
The church's splendid Byzantine mosaics include this one at the end of the south gallery. It depicts Christ flanked by Emperor Constantine IX and his wife, the Empress Zoe.

Sultan's loge

Müezzin mahfili
(see p36)

The Coronation Square served for the crowning of emperors.

Mausoleum of Mehmet III

Library of Sultan Mahmut I

The mausoleum of Murat III was used for his burial in 1599. Murat had by that time sired 103 children.

The Baptistry, part of the 6th-century church, now serves as the tomb of two sultans.

Exit

Mausoleum of Selim II
The oldest of the three mausoleums was completed in 1577 to the plans of Sinan (see p91). Its interior is entirely decorated with İznik tiles (see p161).

★ **Ablutions Fountain**
Built around 1740, this fountain is an exquisite example of Turkish Rococo style. Its projecting roof is painted with floral reliefs.

Exploring Haghia Sophia

Calligraphic roundel

DESIGNED AS AN EARTHLY mirror of the heavens, the interior of Haghia Sophia succeeds in imparting a truly celestial feel. The artistic highlights are a number of glistening figurative mosaics – remains of the decoration that once covered the upper walls but which has otherwise mostly disappeared. These remarkable works of Byzantine art date from the 9th century or later, after the iconoclastic era *(see p18)*. Some of the patterned mosaic ceilings, however, particularly those adorning the narthex and the neighbouring Vestibule of the Warriors, are part of the cathedral's original 6th-century decoration.

Interior as it looked after restoration in the 19th century

GROUND FLOOR

THE FIRST of the surviving Byzantine mosaics can be seen over the Imperial Gate. This is now the public entrance into the church, although previously only the emperor and his entourage were allowed to pass through it. The mosaic shows **Christ on a throne with an emperor kneeling beside him** ① and has been dated to between 886 and 912. The emperor is thought to be Leo VI, the Wise *(see p19)*.

The most conspicuous features at ground level in the nave are those added by the Ottoman sultans after the conquest of Istanbul in 1453, when the church was converted into a mosque. The **mihrab** ②, the niche indicating the direction of Mecca, was installed in the apse of the church directly opposite the entrance. The **sultan's loge** ③, on the left of the mihrab as you face it, was built by the Fossati brothers. These Italian-Swiss architects undertook a major restoration of Haghia Sophia for Sultan Abdül Mecit in 1847–9.

To the right of the mihrab is the **minbar** ④, or pulpit, which was installed by Murat III (1574–95). He also erected the four **müezzin mahfilis** ⑤, marble platforms for readers of the Koran *(see p37)*. The largest of these is adjacent to the *minbar*. The patterned marble **coronation square** ⑥ next to it marks the supposed site of the Byzantine emperor's throne, or omphalos (centre of the world). Nearby, in the south aisle, is the **library of Mahmut I** ⑦, which was built in 1739 and is entered by a decorative bronze door.

Across the nave, between two columns, is the 17th-century marble **preacher's throne** ⑧, the contribution of Murat IV (1623–40). Behind it is one of several **maqsuras** ⑨. These low, fenced platforms were placed beside walls and pillars to provide places for elders to sit, listen and read the Koran.

In the northwestern and western corners of the church are two **marble urns** ⑩, thought to date from the Hellenistic or early Byzantine period. A rectangular pillar behind one of the urns, the **pillar of St Gregory the Miracle-Worker** ⑪, is believed to have healing powers.

As you leave the church you pass through the Vestibule of the Warriors, so called because the emperor's bodyguards would wait here for him when he came to worship. Look behind you as you enter it at the wonderful mosaic of the **Virgin with Constantine and Justinian** ⑫ above the door. It shows Mary seated

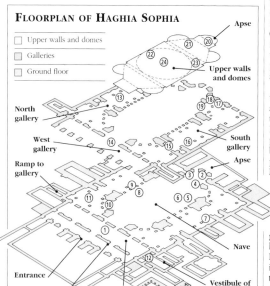

FLOORPLAN OF HAGHIA SOPHIA

- ☐ Upper walls and domes
- ☐ Galleries
- ☐ Ground floor

Apse

North gallery

West gallery

Ramp to gallery

South gallery

Apse

Upper walls and domes

Nave

Entrance

Outer narthex   Narthex

Vestibule of the Warriors

on a throne holding the infant Jesus and flanked by two of the greatest emperors of the city. Constantine, on her right, presents her with the city of Constantinople, while Justinian offers her Haghia Sophia. This was made long after either of these two emperors lived, probably in the 10th century, during the reign of Basil II *(see p19)*. Visitors exit the church by the door that was once reserved for the emperor due to its proximity to the Great Palace *(see pp82–3)*.

Figure of Christ, detail from the Deesis Mosaic in the south gallery

GALLERIES

A RAMP LEADS from the ground floor to the north gallery. Here, on the eastern side of the great northwest pier, you will find the 10th-century mosaic of **Emperor Alexander holding a skull** ⑬. On the west face of the same pier is a medieval drawing of a galleon in full sail. The only point of interest in the western

gallery is a green marble disk marking the location of the Byzantine **Empress's throne** ⑭.

There is much more to see in the south gallery. You begin by passing through the so-called **Gates of Heaven and Hell** ⑮, a marble doorway of which little is known except that it predates the Ottoman conquest *(see p24)*.

Around the corner to the right after passing through this doorway is the **Deesis Mosaic** ⑯ showing the Virgin Mary and John the Baptist with Christ Pantocrator (the All-Powerful). Set into the floor opposite it is the tomb of Enrico Dandalo, the Doge of Venice responsible for the sacking of Constantinople in 1204 *(see p22)*.

In the last bay of the southern gallery there are two more mosaics. The right-hand one of these is of the **Virgin holding Christ, flanked by Emperor John II Comnenus and Empress Irene** ⑰. The other shows **Christ with Emperor Constantine IX Monomachus and Empress Zoe** ⑱. The faces of the emperor and empress have been altered.

Eight great **wooden plaques** ⑲ bearing calligraphic inscriptions hang over the nave at the level of the gallery. An addition of the Fossati brothers, they bear the names of Allah, the Prophet Mohammed, the first four caliphs and Hasan and Hussein, two of the Prophet's grandsons who are revered as martyrs.

Mosaic depicting the archangel Gabriel, adorning the lower wall of the apse

UPPER WALLS AND DOMES

T HE APSE is dominated by a large and striking mosaic showing the **Virgin with the infant Jesus on her lap** ⑳. Two other mosaics in the apse show the archangels **Gabriel** ㉑ and, opposite him, Michael, but only fragments of the latter now remain. The unveiling of these mosaics on Easter Sunday 867 was a triumphal event celebrating victory over the iconoclasts *(see p19)*.

Three mosaic portraits of **saints** ㉒ adorn niches in the north tympanum and are visible from the south gallery and the nave. From left to right they depict: St Ignatius the Younger, St John Chrysostom and St Ignatius Theophorus.

In the four pendentives (the triangular, concave areas at the base of the dome) are mosaics of six-winged **seraphim** ㉓. The ones in the eastern pendentives date from 1346–55, but may be copies of much older ones. Those on the western side are 19th-century imitations that were added by the Fossati brothers.

The great **dome** ㉔ itself is decorated with Koranic inscriptions. It was once covered in golden mosaic and the tinkling sound of pieces dropping to the ground was familiar to visitors until the building's 19th-century restoration.

Mosaic of the Virgin with Emperor John II Comnenus and Empress Irene

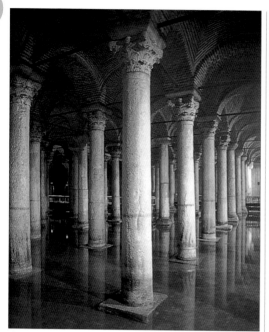

The cavernous interior of the Byzantine Basilica Cistern

Basilica Cistern ❷

Yerebatan Sarayı

13 Yerebatan Cad, Sultanahmet.
Map 3 E4 (5 E4). ☏ *(0212) 522 12 59.* 🚋 *Sultanahmet.* ◯ *9am–5:30pm daily.*

THIS VAST underground water cistern, a beautiful piece of Byzantine engineering, is the most unusual tourist attraction in the city. Although there may have been an earlier, smaller cistern here, this cavernous vault was laid out under Justinian in 532, mainly to satisfy the growing demands of the Great Palace *(see pp82–3)* on the other side of the Hippodrome *(see p80).* For a century after the conquest *(see p24),* the Ottomans did not know of the cistern's existence. It was rediscovered after people were found to be collecting water, and even fish, by lowering buckets through holes in their basements.

Visitors tread walkways, to the mixed sounds of classical music and dripping water. The cistern's roof is held up by 336 columns, each over 8 m (26 ft) high. Only about two thirds of the original structure is visible today, the rest having been bricked up in the 19th century.

In the far left-hand corner two columns rest on Medusa head bases. These bases are evidence of plundering by the Byzantines from earlier monuments. They are thought to mark a *nymphaeum,* a shrine to the water nymphs.

Istanbul Crafts Centre ❸

Mehmet Efendi Medresesi

Kabasakal Cad, Sultanahmet.
Map 3 E4 (5 E4). ☏ *(0212) 517 67 82.* 🚋 *Sultanahmet.* ◯ *9:30am–6:30pm daily.*

IF YOU ARE INTERESTED in Turkish craftwork, this former Koranic college is worth a visit. You can watch skilled artisans at work: they may be binding a book, executing an elegant piece of calligraphy or painting glaze onto ceramics. Items produced here are all for sale. Others include exquisite dolls, meerschaum pipes and jewellery based on Ottoman designs.

Next door is the Yeşil Ev Hotel *(see p182),* a restored Ottoman building with a pleasant café in its courtyard.

Baths of Roxelana ❹

Haseki Hürrem Hamamı

Ayasofya Meydanı, Sultanahmet.
Map 3 E4 (5 E4). ☏ *(0212) 638 00 35.* 🚋 *Sultanahmet.* ◯ *9am–5pm Wed–Mon.*

THESE BATHS were built for Süleyman the Magnificent *(see p24)* by Sinan *(see p91),* and are named after Roxelana, the sultan's scheming wife. They were designated for the

ROXELANA

Süleyman the Magnificent's power-hungry wife Roxelana (1500–58, Haseki Hürrem in Turkish), rose from being a concubine in the imperial harem to become his chief wife, or first *kadın (see p26).* Thought to be of Russian origin, she was also the first consort permitted to reside within the walls of Topkapı Palace *(see pp54–9).*

Roxelana would stop at nothing to get her own way. When Süleyman's grand vizier and friend from youth, İbrahim Paşa, became a threat to her position, she persuaded the sultan to have him strangled. Much later, Roxelana performed her *coup de grâce.* In 1553 she persuaded Süleyman to have his handsome and popular heir, Mustafa, murdered by deaf mutes to clear the way for her own son Selim *(see p24)* to inherit the throne.

The 16th-century Baths of Roxelana, now housing an exclusive carpet shop

use of the congregation of Haghia Sophia (see pp72–5) when it was used as a mosque. With the women's entrance at one end of the building and the men's at the other, their absolute symmetry makes them perhaps the most handsome baths in the city.

The building is now a government-run carpet shop, but the baths' original features are still clearly visible. A look around it is a must for those who have no intention of baring themselves in a public bath, but are curious about what the interior of a Turkish baths (see p67) is like.

Each end starts with a *camekan*, a massive domed hall which would originally have been centred on a fountain. Next is a small *soğukluk*, or intermediate room, which opens into a *hararet*, or steam room. The hexagonal massage slab in each *hararet*, the *göbek taşı*, is inlaid with coloured marbles, indicating that the baths are of imperial origin.

Vakıflar Carpet Museum 5
Vakıflar Halı Müzesi

Imperial Pavilion, Blue Mosque, Sultanahmet. **Map** 3 E5 (5 E4). *(0212) 518 13 30.* Sultanahmet. *9am–4pm Tue–Wed.*

A RAMP TO THE LEFT of the main doorway into the Blue Mosque (see pp78–9) leads up to the Vakıflar Carpet Museum. It has been installed

in what was formerly the mosque's imperial pavilion. This pavilion was built by Ahmet I and used on most Fridays by him and his successors when they attended prayers.

The carpets (see pp210–11) in this fine collection are hidden from potentially destructive sunlight by stained-glass windows. They date from the 16th to the 19th centuries and are mostly from the principal western Anatolian regions of Uşak, Bergama and Konya. For many years mosques have played a vital role in the preservation of early rugs: all the carpets in this museum lay inside mosques until recently.

Detail of a 5th-century mosaic in the Mosaics Museum

Mosaics Museum 6
Mozaik Müzesi

Arasta Çarşısı, Sultanahmet. **Map** 3 E5 (5 E5). *(0212) 518 12 05.* Sultanahmet. *9:30am–4:30pm Wed–Mon.*

T HIS MUSEUM was created simply by roofing over a part of the Great Palace of the Byzantine Emperors (see pp82–3) which was discovered in the 1930s. In its heyday the palace boasted hundreds of rooms, many of them glittering with gold mosaics.

The surviving mosaic floor shows a lively variety of wild and domestic beasts and includes some hunting and fighting scenes. It is thought to have adorned the colonnade leading from the royal apartments to the imperial enclosure beside the Hippodrome, and dates from the late 5th century AD.

Blue Mosque 7
See pp78–9.

Museum of Turkish and Islamic Arts 8
Türk ve İslam Eserleri Müzesi

Atmeydanı Sok, Sultanahmet. **Map** 3 D4 (5 D4). *(0212) 518 18 05.* Sultanahmet. *9:30am–5pm Tue–Sun.*

O VER 40,000 items are on display in the former palace of İbrahim Paşa (c.1493–1536), the most gifted of Süleyman's many grand viziers. The collection was begun in the 19th century and ranges from the earliest period of Islam, under the Omayyad caliphate (661–750), through to modern times.

Each room concentrates on a different chronological period or geographical area of the Islamic world, with detailed explanations in both Turkish and English. The museum is particularly renowned for its collection of rugs. These range from 13th-century Seljuk fragments to the palatial Persian silks that cover the walls from floor to ceiling in the palace's great hall.

On the ground floor, an ethnographic section focuses on the lifestyles of different Turkish peoples, particularly the nomads of central and eastern Anatolia. The exhibits include recreations of a round felt yurt (Turkic nomadic tent) and a traditional brown tent.

Recreated yurt interior, Museum of Turkish and Islamic Arts

Blue Mosque **❼**
Sultan Ahmet Camii

THE BLUE MOSQUE, which takes its name from the mainly blue İznik tilework (*see p161*) decorating its interior, is one of the most famous religious buildings in the world. Serene at any time, it is at its most magical when floodlit at night, its minarets circled by keening seagulls. Sultan Ahmet I (*see p31*) commissioned the mosque during a period of declining Ottoman fortunes, and it was built between 1609–16 by Mehmet Ağa, the imperial architect. The splendour of the plans provoked great hostility at the time, especially because a mosque with six minarets was considered a sacrilegious attempt to rival the architecture of Mecca itself.

A 19th-century engraving showing the Blue Mosque viewed from the Hippodrome (*see p80*)

Thick piers support the weight of the dome.

Mihrab

The loge (*see p37*) accommodated the sultan and his entourage during mosque services.

The Imperial Pavilion now houses the Vakıflar Carpet Museum (*see p77*).

Minbar
The 17th-century minbar is intricately carved in white marble. It is used by the imam during prayers on Friday (see pp36–7).

Prayer hall

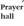

Exit for tourists

Müezzin mahfili (*see p36*)

Entrance to courtyard

★ İznik Tiles
No cost was spared in the decoration of the mosque. The tiles were made at the peak of tile production in İznik (see p161).

STAR FEATURES

★ İznik Tiles

★ Inside of the Dome

★ View of the Domes

★ **Inside of the Dome**
Mesmeric designs, employing flowing arabesques, are painted onto the interior of the mosque's domes and semidomes. The windows which pierce the domes no longer have their original 17th-century stained glass.

VISITORS' CHECKLIST

Sultanahmet Meydanı. **Map** 3 E5
(5 E5). 🅒 *(0212) 518 13 19.*
🚇 *Sultanahmet.* ⬤ *daily.*
⬤ *prayer times.* **Son et Lumière**
*May–Sep: daily just after dusk
(see board on Mimar Mehmet
Ağa Caddesi for details).*

★ **View of the Domes**
The graceful cascade of domes and semidomes makes a striking sight when viewed from the courtyard below.

Over 250 windows
allow light to flood
into the mosque.

Entrance

Ablutions Fountain
The hexagonal şadırvan is now purely ornamental since ritual ablutions are no longer carried out at this fountain.

Each minaret
has two or three
balconies.

**Exit to
Hippodrome**

Washing the Feet
The Muslim's ritual ablutions conclude with the washing of the feet (see p37). Taps outside the mosque are used by the faithful for this purpose.

The courtyard covers
the same area as the
prayer hall, balancing
the whole building.

Egyptian Obelisk and the Serpentine Column in the Hippodrome

Hippodrome ⑨

At Meydanı

Sultanahmet. **Map** 3 E4 (5 D4).
⊕ *Sultanahmet.*

LITTLE IS LEFT of the gigantic stadium which once stood at the heart of the Byzantine city of Constantinople (*see pp20–21*). It was originally laid out by Emperor Septimus Severus during his rebuilding of the city in the 3rd century. AD (*see p17*). Emperor Constantine (*see p18*) enlarged the Hippodrome and connected its *kathisma*, or royal box, to the nearby Great Palace (*see pp82–3*). It is thought that the stadium held

Relief carved on the base of the Egyptian Obelisk

up to 100,000 people. The site is now an elongated public garden, At Meydanı, the Square of the Horses. There are, however, enough remains of the Hippodrome to get a sense of its scale and importance.

The road running around the square almost directly follows the line of the chariot racing track. You can also make out some of the arches of the *sphendone* (the curved end of the Hippodrome) by walking a few steps down İbret Sokağı. Constantine adorned the *spina*, the central line of the stadium, with obelisks and columns from Ancient Egypt and Greece, importing a sense of history to his new capital. Conspicuous by its absence is the column which once stood on the spot where the tourist information office is now located. This was topped by four bronze horses which were pillaged during the Fourth Crusade (*see p22*) and taken to St Mark's in Venice. Three ancient monuments remain, however. The **Egyptian Obelisk**, which was built in 1500 BC, stood outside Luxor until Constantine had it brought to his city. This beautifully carved monument is broken and is probably only one third of its original height. It stands on a base, made in the 4th century AD, showing Theodosius I (*see p18*) and his family in the *kathisma*

watching various events. The four sides depict a chariot race; Theodosius preparing to crown the winner with a wreath of laurel; prisoners paying homage to the emperor; and the erection of the obelisk itself.

Next to it is the **Serpentine Column**, believed to date from 479 BC, which was shipped here from Delphi. The heads of the serpents were knocked off in the 18th century by a drunken Polish nobleman. One of them can be seen in the Archaeological Museum (*see pp62–5*).

Another obelisk still standing, but of unknown date, is usually referred to as the **Column of Constantine Porphyrogenitus**, after the emperor who restored it in the 10th century AD. It is also sometimes called the Brazen Column, because it is thought to have once been sheathed in a case of bronze. Its dilapidated state owes much to the fact that young Janissaries (*see p127*) would routinely scale it as a test of their bravery.

The only other structure in the Hippodrome is a domed fountain which commemorates the visit of Kaiser Wilhelm II to Istanbul in 1898 (*see p43*).

The Hippodrome was the scene of one of the bloodiest events in Istanbul's history. In 532 a brawl between rival chariot-racing teams developed into the Nika Revolt, during which much of the city was destroyed. The end of the revolt came when an army of mercenaries, under the command of Justinian's general Belisarius, massacred an estimated 30,000 people trapped in the Hippodrome.

Cistern of 1001 Columns ⑩

Binbirdirek Sarnıcı

Klodfarer Cad, Sultanahmet.
Map 3 D4 (5 D4). ☎ (0212) 638 22 38. ⊕ *Çemberlitaş.* ○ *8am–midnight daily.* ♿

THIS CISTERN, dating back to the 4th century AD, is the second largest underground Byzantine cistern in Istanbul after the Basilica Cistern (*see p76*). Spanning an area of

CEREMONIES IN THE HIPPODROME

Beginning with the inauguration of Constantinople on 11th May 330 *(see p18)*, the Hippodrome formed the stage for the city's greatest public events for the next 1,300 years. The Byzantines' most popular pastime was watching chariot racing in the stadium. Even after the Hippodrome fell into ruins following the Ottoman conquest of Istanbul *(see p24)*, it continued to be used for great public occasions. This 16th-century illustration depicts Murat III watching the 52-day-long festivities staged for the circumcision of his son Mehmet. All the guilds of Istanbul paraded before the Sultan displaying their crafts.

Sultan Murat III

Palace of İbrahim Paşa (Museum of Turkish and Islamic Arts, *see p77*)

Column of Constantine Porphyrogenitus — Serpentine Column — Egyptian Obelisk

---

64 m (210 ft) by 56 m (185 ft), the herring-bone brick roof vaults are held up by 264 marble columns – the 1,001 columns of its name is poetic exaggeration. Until not long ago, the cistern was filled with rubble and only explored by adventurous visitors. It has recently been transformed into an atmospheric shopping complex specializing in jewellery, carpets and tiles and other merchandise inspired by Ottoman culture.

Tomb of Sultan Mahmut II ⓫

Mahmut II Türbesi

Divanyolu Cad, Çemberlitaş.
Map 3 D4 (4 C3). **Ⓜ** *Çemberlitaş.*
◻ 9:30am–4:30pm daily.

THIS LARGE octagonal mausoleum is in the Empire style (modelled on Roman architecture), made popular by Napoleon. It was built in 1838, the year before Sultan Mahmut II's death and is shared by sultans Mahmut II, Abdül Aziz and Abdül Hamit II *(see pp30–31)*. Within, Corinthian pilasters divide up walls which groan with symbols of prosperity and victory. The huge tomb dominates a cemetery that has beautiful headstones, a fountain and, at the far end, a good café.

Constantine's Column ⓬

Çemberlitaş

Yeniçeriler Cad, Çemberlitaş.
Map 3 D4 (4 C3). **Ⓜ** *Çemberlitaş.*
Çemberlitaş Baths Vezirhanı Cad 8.
Ⓒ *(0212) 511 25 35.* ◻ *7am–11pm daily (8am–11pm for women).*

A SURVIVOR OF both storm and fire, this 35-m (115-ft) high column was constructed in AD 330 as part of the celebrations to inaugurate the new Byzantine capital *(see p18)*. It once dominated the magnificent Forum of Constantine *(see p21)*.

Made of porphyry brought from Heliopolis in Egypt, it was originally surmounted by a Corinthian capital bearing a statue of Emperor Constantine dressed as Apollo. This was brought down in a storm in 1106. Although what is left is relatively unimpressive, it has been carefully preserved. In the year 416 the 10 stone drums making up the column were reinforced with metal rings. These were renewed in 1701 by Sultan Mustafa III, and consequently the column is

Constantine's Column

known as Çemberlitaş (the Hooped Column) in Turkish. In English it is sometimes referred to as the Burnt Column because it was damaged by several fires, especially one in 1779 which decimated the Grand Bazaar *(see pp98–9)*.

A variety of fantastical holy relics were supposedly entombed in the base of the column, which has since been encased in stone to strengthen it. These included the axe which Noah used to build the ark, Mary Magdalen's flask of anointing oil, and remains of the loaves of bread with which Christ fed the multitude.

Next to Constantine's Column, on the corner of Divanyolu Caddesi, stand the Çemberlitaş Baths. This splendid *hamam* complex *(see p67)* was commissioned by Nur Banu, wife of Sultan Selim II, and built in 1584 to a plan by the great Sinan *(see p91)*. Although the original women's section no longer survives, the baths still have separate facilities for men and women. The staff are used to foreign visitors, so this is a good place for your first experience of a Turkish bath.

Sokollu Mehmet Paşa Mosque ⓭
Sokollu Mehmet Paşa Camii

Şehit Çeşmesi Sok, Sultanahmet. **Map** 3 D5 (4 C5). 🚇 Çemberlitaş or Sultanahmet. ⭘ daily.

BUILT BY THE ARCHITECT Sinan *(see p91)* in 1571–2, this mosque was commissioned by Sokollu Mehmet Paşa, grand vizier to Selim II *(see p30)*. The simplicity of Sinan's design solution for the mosque's sloping site has been widely admired. A steep entrance stairway leads up to the mosque courtyard from the street, passing beneath the teaching hall of its *medrese (see p36)*, which still functions as a college. Only the tiled lunettes above the windows in the portico give a hint of the jewelled mosque interior to come.

Inside, the far wall around the carved mihrab is entirely covered in İznik tiles *(see p161)* of a sumptuous greenblue hue. This tile panel, designed specifically for the space, is complemented by six stained-glass windows. The "hat" of the *minbar* is covered with the same tiles. Most of the mosque's other walls are of plain stone, but they are enlivened by a few more tile panels. Set into the wall over the entrance there is a small piece of greenish stone which is supposedly from the Kaaba, the holy stone at the centre of Mecca.

Interior of the 16th-century Sokollu Mehmet Paşa Mosque

The Byzantine Church of SS Sergius and Bacchus, now a mosque

SS Sergius and Bacchus' Church ⓮
Küçük Ayasofya Camii

Küçük Ayasofya Cad. **Map** 3 D5 (4 C5). 🚇 Çemberlitaş or Sultanahmet. ⭘ daily. ♿

COMMONLY REFERRED to as "Little Haghia Sophia", this church was built in 527, a few years before its namesake *(see pp72–5)*. It too was founded by Emperor Justinian *(see p18)*, together with his empress, Theodora, at the beginning of his long reign. Ingenious and highly decorative, the church gives a somewhat higgledy-piggledy impression both inside and out and is one of the most charming of all the city's architectural treasures.

Inside, an irregular octagon of columns on two floors supports a broad central dome composed of 16 vaults. The

RECONSTRUCTION OF THE GREAT PALACE

In Byzantine times, present-day Sultanahmet was the site of the Great Palace, which, in its heyday, had no equal in Europe and dazzled medieval visitors with its opulence. This great complex of buildings – including royal apartments, state rooms, churches, courtyards and gardens – extended over a sloping, terraced site from the Hippodrome to the imperial harbour on the shore of the Sea of Marmara. The palace was built in stages, beginning under Constantine in the 4th century. It was enlarged by Justinian following the fire caused by the Nika Revolt in 532 *(see p80)*. Later emperors, especially the 9th-century Basil I *(see p19)*, extended it further. After several hundred years of occupation, it was finally abandoned in the second half of the 13th century in favour of Blachernae Palace *(see p117)*.

The Mese was a colonnaded street lined with shops and statuary.

Hippodrome *(see p80)*

Hormisdas Palace

Church of SS Peter and Paul

Church of SS Sergius and Bacchus

mosaic decoration which once adorned some of the walls has long since crumbled away. However, the green and red marble columns, the delicate tracery of the capitals and the carved frieze running above the columns are original features of the church.

The inscription on this frieze, in boldly carved Greek script, mentions the founders of the church and St Sergius, but not St Bacchus. The two saints were Roman centurions who converted to Christianity and were martyred. Justinian credited them with saving his life when, as a young man, he was implicated in a plot to kill his uncle, Justin I. The saints supposedly appeared to Justin in a dream and told him to release his nephew.

The Church of SS Sergius and Bacchus was built between two important edifices to which it was connected, the Palace of Hormisdas and the Church of SS Peter and Paul, but has outlived them both. After the conquest of Istanbul in 1453 *(see p24)* it was converted into a mosque.

Bucoleon Palace ⓯

Bukoleon Sarayı

Kennedy Cad, Sultanahmet.
Map 3 E5. 🚋 *Sultanahmet.*

FINDING THE SITE of what remains of the Great Palace of the Byzantine emperors requires precision. It is not advisable to visit the ruins alone as they are usually inhabited by tramps.

Take the path under the railway from the Church of SS Sergius and Bacchus, turn left and walk beside Kennedy Caddesi, the main road along the shore of the Sea of Marmara for about 400 m (450 yards). This will bring you to a stretch of the ancient sea walls, constructed to protect the city from a naval assault. Within these walls you will find a creeper-clad section of stonework pierced by three vast windows framed in

marble. This is all that now survives of the Bucoleon Palace, a maritime residence that formed part of the sprawling Great Palace. The waters of a small private harbour lapped right up to the palace and a private flight of steps led down in to the water, allowing the emperor to board imperial caïques. The ruined tower just east of the palace was a lighthouse, called the Pharos, in Byzantine times.

Wall of Bucoleon Palace, the only part of the Byzantine Great Palace still standing

The Kathisma was the imperial box of the Hippodrome.

The Milion was the point from which road distances were measured *(see p71).*

Haghia Sophia *(see pp72–5)*

The Augusteum was a porticoed public square.

Chalke Gate was the main entrance to the palace.

Hall of Gold (site of Mosaics Museum, *see p77*)

Lighthouse

Magnaura Palace

The Bucoleon Palace had a magnificent façade looking out over the sea.

The Nea Ekklesia, erected by Basil I, set the style for all subsequent Byzantine churches.

Daphne Palace

THE BAZAAR QUARTER

RADE HAS always been important in a city straddling the continents of Asia and Europe. Nowhere is this more evident than in the warren of streets lying between the Grand Bazaar and Galata Bridge. Everywhere, goods tumble out of shops onto the pavement. Look through any of the archways in between shops and you will discover hidden courtyards or hans *(see p96)* containing feverishly industrious workshops. With its seemingly limitless range of goods, the labyrinthine Grand Bazaar is at the centre of all this commercial activity. The Spice Bazaar is equally colourful but smaller and more manageable.

Window from Nuruosmaniye Mosque

Up on the hill, next to the university, is Süleymaniye Mosque, a glorious expression of 16th-century Ottoman culture. It is just one of numerous beautiful mosques in this area.

SIGHTS AT A GLANCE

Mosques and Churches
Atik Ali Paşa Mosque ⑳
Bodrum Mosque ⑫
Church of St Theodore ⑥
Kalenderhane Mosque ⑩
Mahmut Paşa Mosque ㉒
New Mosque ❶
Nuruosmaniye Mosque ㉑
Prince's Mosque ⑨
Rüstem Paşa Mosque ❸
Sülemaniye Mosque pp90–91 ❺
Tulip Mosque ⑪

Bazaars, Hans and Shops
Book Bazaar ⑯
Grand Bazaar pp98–9 ⑱
Spice Bazaar ❷
Valide Hanı ⑰
Vefa Bozacısı ❽

Museums and Monuments
Forum of Theodosius ⑬
Museum of Calligraphy ⑭
Valens Aqueduct ❼

Squares and Courtyards
Beyazıt Square ⑮
Çorlulu Ali Paşa Courtyard ⑲

Waterways
Golden Horn ❹

KEY

▦	Street-by-Street map *See pp86–7*
🛥	Ferry boarding point
🚋	Tram stop
🚌	Main bus stop
C	Mosque

GETTING AROUND

Trams from Sultanahmet run down Yeniçeriler Caddesi, and stop outside the Grand Bazaar. Ferries from various destinations dock at Eminönü, opposite the Spice Bazaar.

0 metres   500

0 yards   500

◁ **The inside of the Grand Bazaar, always thronging with bargain-hunters**

Street-by-Street: Around the Spice Bazaar

THE NARROW STREETS around the Spice Bazaar encapsulate the spirit of old Istanbul. From here buses, taxis and trams head off across the Galata Bridge and into the interior of the city. The blast of ships' horns signals the departure of ferries from Eminönü to Asian Istanbul. It is the quarter's shops and markets, though, that are the focus of attention for the eager shoppers who crowd the Spice Bazaar and the streets around it, sometimes breaking for a leisurely tea beneath the trees in its courtyard. Across the way, and entirely aloof from the bustle, rise the domes of the New Mosque. On one of the commercial alleyways which radiate out from the mosque, an inconspicuous doorway leads up stairs to the terrace of the serene, tile-covered Rüstem Paşa Mosque.

★ Rüstem Pasa Mosque
The interior of this secluded mosque is a brilliant pattern-book made of İznik tiles (see p161) of the finest quality ❸

Nargile on sale near the Spice Bazaar

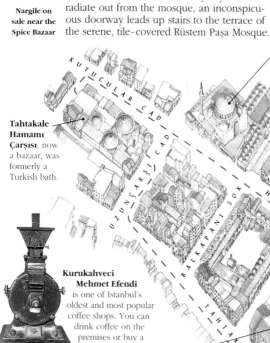

The *pastırma* shop
at 11 Hasırcılar Caddesi sells thin slices of dried beef, spiced with fenugreek – a Turkish delicacy.

Tahtakale Hamamı Çarşısı, now a bazaar, was formerly a Turkish bath.

Dolmuş and bus station

Kurukahveci Mehmet Efendi
is one of Istanbul's oldest and most popular coffee shops. You can drink coffee on the premises or buy a packet to take away with you *(see p205)*.

KUTUCULAR CAD

UZUNÇARŞILI CAD

BALKAPANI SOK

HASIRCILAR CAD

TAHTAKALE CAD

SABUNCUHANI SOK

MARPUÇCUL

0 metres		75
0 yards		75

STAR SIGHTS

- ★ Rüstem Pasa Mosque
- ★ New Mosque
- ★ Spice Bazaar

Stall holders
and street traders, such as this man selling garlic cloves, ply their wares in Sabuncuhanı Sokağı and the other narrow streets around the Spice Bazaar.

Eminönü is the port from which ferries depart to many destinations *(see p236)* and for trips along the Bosphorus *(see pp144–9)*. It bustles with activity as traders compete to sell drinks and snacks.

LOCATOR MAP
See Street Finder map 2

Galata Bridge

The royal pavilion, a suite of beautifully tiled private rooms, is linked by a passage to the sultan's loge inside the New Mosque.

Pandeli's Restaurant *(see p195)*

Eminönü sea bus boarding point

Eminönü tram stop

RESADIYE CAD

TAHMIS CAD

CAMI MEYDANI SOK

Cafés

ÇIÇEK PAZARI SOK

YENI CAMI CAD

★ New Mosque
This mosque, which dominates the Eminönü waterfront, was completed in the 17th century by the mother of Sultan Mehmet IV (see p31) ❶

Mausoleum of Turhan Hatice Valide Sultan, mother of Mehmet IV

Pet market and garden centre

CAD

KEY

– – – Suggested route

★ Spice Bazaar
This market was built in 1660 as part of the New Mosque complex, and it has always been associated with the sale of spices, though today there is much more on offer ❷

New Mosque ❶
Yeni Cami

Yeni Cami Meydanı, Eminönü.
Map 3 D2. 🚇 Eminönü. ⏱ daily.

Situated at the southern end of Galata Bridge, the New Mosque is one of the most prominent mosques in the city. It dates from the time when a few women from the harem became powerful enough to dictate the policies of the Ottoman sultans (see p25). The mosque was started in 1597 by Safiye, mother of Mehmet III, but building was suspended on the sultan's death as his mother then lost her position. It was not completed until 1663, after Turhan Hadice, mother of Mehmet IV, had taken up the project.

Though the mosque was built after the classical period of Ottoman architecture, it shares many traits with earlier imperial foundations, including a monumental courtyard. The mosque once had a hospital, school and public baths.

The turquoise, blue and white floral tiles decorating the interior are from İznik (see p161) and date from the mid-17th century, though by this time the quality of the tiles produced there was already in decline. More striking are the tiled lunettes and bold Koranic frieze decorating the porch between the courtyard and the prayer hall.

At the far left-hand corner of the upper gallery is the sultan's loge (see p37), which is linked to his personal suite of rooms (see p87).

A selection of nuts and seeds for sale in the Spice Bazaar

Spice Bazaar ❷
Mısır Çarşısı

Cami Meydanı Sok. **Map** 3 D2 (4 C1).
🚇 Eminönü. ⏱ 8am–7pm Mon–Sat.

This cavernous, L-shaped market was built in the early 17th century as an extension of the New Mosque complex. Its revenues once helped maintain the mosque's philanthropic institutions.

In Turkish the market is named the Mısır Çarşısı – the Egyptian Bazaar – because it was built with money paid as duty on Egyptian imports. In English it is usually known as the Spice Bazaar. From medieval times spices were a vital and expensive part of cooking and they became the market's main produce. The bazaar came to specialize in spices from the orient, taking advantage of Istanbul's site on the trade route between the East (where most spices were grown) and Europe.

Stalls in the bazaar stock spices, herbs and other foods such as honey, nuts, sweetmeats and pastırma (dried beef). Today's expensive Eastern commodity, caviar, is also available, the best variety being Iranian.

Nowadays an eclectic range of other items can be found in the Spice Bazaar, including everything from household goods, toys and clothes to exotic aphrodisiacs. The square between the two arms of the bazaar is full of commercial activity, with cafés, and stalls selling plants and pets.

Floral İznik tiles adorning the interior of Rüstem Paşa Mosque

Rüstem Paşa Mosque ❸
Rüstem Paşa Camii

Hasırcılar Cad, Eminönü.
Map 3 D2. 🚇 Eminönü. ⏱ daily.

Raised above the busy shops and warehouses around the Spice Bazaar, this mosque was built in 1561 by the great architect Sinan (see p91) for Rüstem Paşa, son-in-law of and grand vizier to Süleyman I (see p24). Rents from the businesses in the bazaar were intended to pay for the upkeep of the mosque.

The staggering wealth of its decoration says something about the amount of money that the corrupt Rüstem managed to salt away during his career. Most of the interior is covered in İznik tiles of the very highest quality.

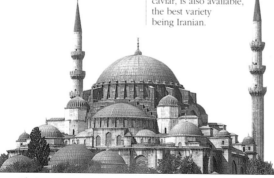

The New Mosque, a prominent feature on the Eminönü waterfront

The four piers are adorned with tiles of one design but the rest of the prayer hall is a riot of different patterns, from abstract to floral. Some of the finest tiles can be found on the galleries. All in all, there is no other mosque in the city adorned with such a magnificent blanket of tiles.

The mosque is also notable for its numerous windows: it was built with as many as the structure would allow.

Golden Horn **4**
Haliç

Map 3 D2. 🚊 *Eminönü.* 🚌 *55T, 99A.*

OFTEN DESCRIBED as the world's greatest natural harbour, the Golden Horn is a flooded river valley which flows southwest into the Bosphorus. The estuary attracted settlers to its shores in the 7th century BC and later enabled Constantinople to become a rich and powerful port. According to legend, the Byzantines threw so many valuables into it during the Ottoman conquest *(see p24)*, that the waters glistened with gold. Today, however, belying its name, the Golden Horn has become polluted by the numerous nearby factories.

For hundreds of years the city's trade was conducted by ships that off-loaded their goods into warehouses lining the Golden Horn. Nowadays, though, the great container ships coming to Istanbul use ports on the Sea of Marmara. Spanning the mouth of the Horn is the Galata Bridge, which joins Eminönü to Galata. The bridge, built in 1992, opens in the middle to allow access for tall ships. It is a good place from which to appreciate the complex geography of the city and admire the minaret-filled skyline. Fishermen's boats selling mackerel sandwiches are usually moored at each end.

The functional Galata Bridge replaced the raffish charm of a pontoon bridge with a busy lower level of restaurants. The old bridge has been reconstructed just south of the Rahmi Koç Museum *(see p127)*. There is another bridge, Atatürk, between these, and a fourth, Fatih, further up the Horn near the end of the city walls.

Süleymaniye Mosque **5**

See pp90–91.

Church of St Theodore **6**
Kilise Camii

Vefa Cad, Cami Sok, Vefa. **Map** 2 B2. 🚌 *28, 61B, 87.*

APART FROM ITS delightfully dishevelled ancient exterior, very little else remains of the former Byzantine Church of St Theodore. The elaborate church was built in the 12th–14th centuries, the last great era of Byzantine construction. It was converted into a mosque following the Ottoman conquest of the city in 1453 *(see p24)*.

One feature that is still evident in the south dome in its outer porch is a 14th-century mosaic of the Virgin Mary surrounded by the Prophets. The fluted minaret makes a sympathetic addition.

The 4th-century Valens Aqueduct crossing Atatürk Bulvarı

Valens Aqueduct **7**
Bozdoğan Kemeri

Atatürk Bulvarı, Saraçhane. **Map** 2 A3. 🚊 *Laleli.* 🚌 *28, 61B, 87.*

EMPEROR VALENS built this mighty aqueduct, supported by two imposing rows of arches, in the late 4th century AD. Part of the elaborate water system feeding the palaces and fountains of the Byzantine capital, it brought water from the Belgrade Forest *(see p158)* and mountains over 200 km (125 miles) away to a vast cistern which stood in the vicinity of what is now Beyazıt Square *(see p94)*.

The aqueduct supplied the city's water until the late 19th century, when it was made obsolete by a modern water distribution network. The original open channels, however, had by this stage already been replaced first by clay pipes and then by iron ones.

The structure was repaired many times during its history, latterly by sultans Mustafa II (1695–1703) and Ahmet III *(see p25)*. It was originally 1,000 m (3,300 ft) long, of which 625 m (2,050 ft) remain.

Fisherman on the modern Galata Bridge spanning the Golden Horn

Süleymaniye Mosque ❺

Süleymaniye Camii

ISTANBUL'S MOST IMPORTANT MOSQUE is both a tribute to its architect, the great Sinan, and a fitting memorial to its founder, Süleyman the Magnificent *(see p24)*. It was built above the Golden Horn in the grounds of the old palace, Eski Saray *(see p94)*, between 1550–57. Like the city's other imperial mosques, the Süleymaniye Mosque was not only a place of worship, but also a charitable foundation, or *külliye (see p36)*. The mosque is surrounded by its former hospital, soup kitchen, schools, caravanserai and bath house. This complex provided a welfare system which fed over 1,000 of the city's poor – Muslims, Christians and Jews alike – every day.

Courtyard
The ancient columns that surround the courtyard are said to have come originally from the kathisma, *the Byzantine royal box in the Hippo-drome (see p80).*

Muvakkithane Gateway
The main courtyard entrance (now closed) contained the rooms of the mosque astronomer, who determined prayer times.

Minaret

Tomb of Sinan

The caravanserai provided lodging and food for travellers and their animals.

İmaret Gate

Café in a sunken garden

İmaret
The kitchen – now a restaurant (see p195) – fed the city's poor as well as the mosque staff and their families. The size of the millstone in its courtyard gives some idea of the amount of grain needed to feed everyone.

★ Mosque Interior

A sense of soaring space and calm strikes you as you enter the mosque. The effect is enhanced by the fact that the height of the dome from the floor is exactly double its diameter.

VISITORS' CHECKLIST

Prof Sıddık Sami Onar Caddesi, Vefa. **Map** 2 C3 (4 A1).
((0212) 514 01 39. Beyazıt or Eminönü, then 10 mins walk.
daily.

The Tomb of Roxelana contains Süleyman's beloved wife *(see p76)*.

★ Tomb of Süleyman

Ceramic stars said to be set with emeralds sparkle above the coffins of Süleyman, his daughter Mihrimah and two of his successors, Süleyman II and Ahmet II.

Entrance

Graveyard

These marble benches were used to support coffins before burial.

"Addicts Alley" is so called because the cafés here once sold opium and hashish as well as coffee and tea.

The *medreses* *(see p36)* to the south of the mosque house a library containing 110,000 manuscripts.

Former hospital and asylum

SINAN, THE IMPERIAL ARCHITECT

Like many of his eminent contemporaries, Koca Mimar Sinan (c.1491–1588) was brought from Anatolia to Istanbul in the *devşirme*, the annual roundup of talented Christian youths, and educated at one of the elite palace schools. He became a military engineer but won the eye of Süleyman I, who made him chief imperial architect in 1538. With the far-sighted patronage of the sultan, Sinan – the closest Turkey gets to a Renaissance architect – created masterpieces which demonstrated his master's status as the most magnificent of monarchs. Sinan died aged 97, having built 131 mosques and 200 other buildings.

Bust of the great architect Sinan

STAR FEATURES

★ Mosque Interior

★ Tomb of Süleyman

Vefa Bozacısı ❽

Katip Çelebi Cad 102, Vefa.
Map 2 B2. 📞 *(0212) 519 49 22.*
🚌 *61B, 90.* 🕐 *8am–11pm daily.*

W ITH ITS wood-and-tile
interior and glittering
glass-mosaic columns, this
unusual shop and bar has
changed little since the 1930s.
It was founded in 1876 to sell
boza, a popular winter drink
made from bulgur (cracked
wheat, *see p191*). In summer
a slightly fermented grape
juice known as *şıra* is sold.
The shop's main trade throughout the whole year, however,
is in wine vinegar.

Inside the shop you will
see a glass from which Kemal
Atatürk *(see p29)* drank *boza*
in 1937, enshrined in a display
beneath a glass dome.

**Bottles of *boza*, a wheat-based drink, lining
the interior of Vefa Bozacısı**

Prince's Mosque ❾
Şehzade Camii

Şehzade Başı Cad 70, Saraçhane.
Map 2 B3. 🚇 *Laleli.* 🕐 *daily.*
Tombs 🕐 *9am–5pm Tue–Sun.*

T HIS MOSQUE complex was
erected by Süleyman the
Magnificent *(see p24)* in
memory of his eldest son by
Roxelana *(see p76)*, Şehzade
(Prince) Mehmet, who died of
smallpox at the age of 21. The
building was Sinan's *(see p91)*
first major imperial commission
and was completed in 1548.
The architect used a delightful
decorative style in designing
this mosque before abandon-
ing it in favour of the classical
austerity of his later work.
The mosque is approached

**Dome of the Prince's Mosque,
Sinan's first imperial mosque**

through an elegant porticoed
inner courtyard, while the
other institutions making up
the mosque complex, including a *medrese (see p36)*, are
enclosed within an
outer courtyard.
The interior of the
mosque is unusual and
was something of an
experiment in that it
is symmetrical, having
a semidome on each
of its four sides.
The three tombs
located to the rear of
the mosque, belonging
to Şehzade Mehmet
himself and grand vi-
ziers İbrahim Paşa and
Rüstem Paşa *(see p88)*,
are the finest in the
city. Each has beauti-
ful İznik tiles *(see
p161)* and lustrous original
stained glass. That of Şehzade
Mehmet also boasts the finest
painted dome in Istanbul.
On Fridays you will notice
a crowd of women flocking
to another tomb within the

complex, that of Helvacı
Baba, as they have done for
over 400 years. Helvacı Baba
is said to miraculously cure
crippled children, solve fertil-
ity problems and find husbands
or accommodation for those
who beseech him.

Kalenderhane
Mosque ❿
Kalenderhane Camii

16 Mart Şehitleri Cad, Saraçhane.
Map 2 B3. 🚇 *Üniversite.*
🕐 *prayer times only.*

S ITTING IN THE LEE of the
Valens Aqueduct *(see p89)*,
on the site where a Roman
bath once stood, is this Byzantine church with a chequered
history. It was built and rebuilt several times between
the 6th and 12th centuries,
before finally being converted
into a mosque shortly after
the conquest in 1453 *(see
p24)*. The mosque is named
after the Kalender brotherhood
of dervishes which used the
church as its headquarters for
some years after the conquest.
The building has the cruci-
form layout characteristic of
Byzantine churches of the
period. Some of the decoration remaining from its last
incarnation, as the Church
of Theotokos Kyriotissa (her
Ladyship Mary, Mother of
God), also survives in the
prayer hall with its marble
panelling and in the fragments of fresco in the narthex
(entrance hall). A series of
frescoes depicting the life of
St Francis of Assisi were removed in the 1970s and are
no longer on public view.

A shaft of light illuminating the interior of Kalenderhane Mosque

The Baroque Tulip Mosque, housing a marketplace in its basement

Tulip Mosque ⑪
Laleli Camii

Ordu Cad, Laleli. **Map** 2 B4.
🚇 Laleli. ⏰ prayer times only.

BUILT IN 1759–63, this
mosque complex is the
best example in the city of
the Baroque style, of which
its architect, Mehmet Tahir Ağa,
was the greatest exponent.
Inside the mosque, a variety
of gaudy, coloured marble
covers all of its surfaces.

More fascinating is the area
underneath the main body of
the mosque. This is a great
hall supported on eight piers,
with a fountain in the middle.
The hall is now used as a
subterranean marketplace,
packed with Eastern Europeans
and Central Asians haggling
over items of clothing.

The nearby Büyük Taş Hanı
(see p96), or Big Stone Han,
is likely to have been part of
the mosque's original complex
but now houses leather shops
and a restaurant. To get to the
mosque turn left outside the mosque
into Fethi Bey Caddesi and
then take the second left into
Çukur Çeşme Sokağı. The
main courtyard of the han is
at the end of a long passage
situated off this lane.

Bodrum Mosque ⑫
Bodrum Camii

Sait Efendi Sok, Laleli. **Map** 2 A4.
🚇 Laleli. ⏰ prayer times only.

NARROW COURSES of brick
forming the outside walls,
and a window-pierced dome,
betray the early origins of this
mosque as a Byzantine church.
It was built in the early 10th
century by co-Emperor Romanus I Lacapenus (919–44)
as part of the Monastery of
Myrelaion and adjoined a
small palace. The palace was
later converted into a nunnery
where the emperor's widow,
Theophano, lived out her
final years. She was eventually buried in a sanctuary
chapel beneath the church,
which is closed to the public.

In the late 15th century the
church was converted into
a mosque by Mesih Paşa, a
descendant of the Palaeologus
family, the last dynasty to rule

Byzantium. The building was
gutted by fire several times
and nothing remains of its
internal decoration. Today
it is still a working mosque
and is accessed via a stairway
which leads up to a raised
piazza filled with coat stalls.

Forum of Theodosius ⑬

Ordu Cad, Beyazıt. **Map** 2 C4 (4 A3).
🚇 Üniversite or Beyazıt.

CONSTANTINOPLE (see p18)
was built around several
large public squares or forums.
The largest of them stood on
the site of present-day Beyazıt
Square. It was originally known
as the Forum Tauri (the Forum
of the Bull) because of the
huge bronze bull in the middle of it in which sacrificial
animals, and sometimes even
criminals, were roasted.

After Theodosius the Great
enlarged it in the late 4th
century, the forum took his
name. Relics of the triumphal
arch and other structures can
be found lying and stacked
on either side of the tram
tracks along Ordu Caddesi.
The huge columns, decorated
with a motif reminiscent of a
peacock's tail, are particularly
striking. Once the forum had
become derelict, these columns were reused all over
the city. Some can be seen in
the Basilica Cistern (see p76).
Other fragments from the
forum were built into Beyazıt
Hamamı, a Turkish bath (see
p67) further west down Ordu
Caddesi, now a bazaar.

Peacock feather design on a column
from the Forum of Theodosius

Museum of Calligraphy ⑭

Türk Vakıf Hat Sanatları Müzesi

Beyazıt Meydanı, Beyazıt. **Map** 2 C4 (4 A3). 📞 *(0212) 527 58 51.* 🚇 *Üniversite.* ○ *9am–4pm Tue & Wed.* 🖼️ 🚻

The fortress-like entrance to Istanbul University, Beyazıt Square

THE DELIGHTFUL courtyard in which this museum has been installed was once a *medrese (see p36)* of Beyazıt Mosque, situated on the other side of the square.

Its changing displays are taken from the massive archive belonging to the Turkish Calligraphy Foundation. As well as some beautiful manuscripts there are also examples of calligraphy on stone and glass. There is also an exhibition of tools used in calligraphy. One of the cells in the *medrese* now contains a waxwork tableau of a master calligrapher with his pupils.

Beyazıt Tower, within the wooded grounds of Istanbul University

Beyazıt Square ⑮

Beyazıt Meydanı

Ordu Cad, Beyazıt. **Map** 2 C4 (4 A3). 🚇 *Beyazıt.*

ALWAYS FILLED with crowds of people and huge flocks of pigeons, Beyazıt Square is the most vibrant space in the old part of the city. Throughout the week the square is the venue for a flea market, where everything from carpets *(see pp210–11)* and Central Asian silks to general bric-a-brac can be purchased. When

you have tired of rummaging, you can choose between a number of cafés located beneath shady plane trees.

On the northern side of the square is the Moorish-style gateway leading into Istanbul University. The university's main building dates from the 19th century and once served as the Ministry of War. Within the wooded grounds rises Beyazıt Tower. This marble fire-watching station was built in 1828 on the site of Eski Saray, the palace first inhabited by Mehmet the Conqueror *(see p24)* after Byzantium fell to the Ottomans. A climb of 180 steps inside the tower leads to the top for a panoramic view over Istanbul.

On the square's eastern side is Beyazıt Mosque, which was commissioned by Beyazıt II and completed in 1506. It is the oldest surviving imperial mosque in the city. Behind the impressive outer portal is a harmonious courtyard with an elegant domed fountain at its centre. Around the courtyard are columns made of granite and green and red Egyptian porphyry, and a pavement of multi-coloured marble. The layout of the mosque's interior, with its central dome and surrounding semi-domes, is heavily inspired by the design of Haghia Sophia *(see pp72–5).*

Book Bazaar ⑯

Sahaflar Çarşısı

Sahaflar Çarşısı Sok, Beyazıt. **Map** 2 C4 (4 A3). 🚇 *Üniversite.* ○ *8am–8pm daily.* 🚻

THIS CHARMING booksellers' courtyard, on the site of the Byzantine book and paper market, can be entered either from Beyazıt Square or from inside the Grand Bazaar *(see pp98–9).* Racks are laden with all sorts of books, from tourist guides to academic tomes.

During the early Ottoman period *(see pp23–5)*, printed books were seen as a corrupting European influence and were banned in Turkey. As a result the bazaar only sold manuscripts. Then on 31 January 1729 İbrahim Müteferrika (1674–1745) produced the first printed book in the Turkish language, an Arabic dictionary. His bust stands in the centre of the market today. Note that book prices are fixed and cannot be haggled over.

Customers browsing in the Book Bazaar

The Art of Ottoman Calligraphy

CALLIGRAPHY IS one of the noblest of Islamic arts. Its skills were handed down from master to apprentice, with the aim of the pupil being to replicate perfectly the hand of his master. In Ottoman Turkey, calligraphy was used to ornament firmans (imperial decrees) as well as poetry and copies of the Koran. However, many examples are also to be found on buildings, carved in wood and applied to architectural ceramics. The art of the calligrapher in all cases was to go as far as possible in beautifying the writing without altering the sense of the text. It was particularly important that the text of the Koran should be accurately transcribed. With the text of a firman, made to impress as much as to be read, the calligrapher could afford to add more flourishes.

The Great Calligraphers of the Ottoman period were Şeyh Hamdullah (1436–1520), whose work is seen in this Koran, Hafiz Osman (1642–98) and Ahmet Karahisari (d.1556). Their pupils also achieved great renown.

Floral decorations

Ornamental loops

The sultan's tuğra *was his personal monogram, used in place of his signature. It would either be drawn by a calligrapher or engraved on a wooden block and then stamped on documents.*
The tuğra *incorporated the sultan's name and title, his patronymic and wishes for his success or victory – all highly stylized. This is the* tuğra *of Selim II (1566–74).*

Calligraphy *developed further in the 19th and early 20th centuries when artists explored more creative forms and worked with new media. There was greater freedom to depict human faces and animal forms. Calligraphers also began to practise the technique of découpage (cutting out the letters) and, as seen here, wrote inscriptions on delicate leaf skeletons.*

The later sultans *were taught calligraphy as part of their education and became skilled artists. This panel, from the 19th century, is by Mahmut II (1808–39).*

Breathing techniques *were probably practised by some calligraphers in order to achieve the steadiness of hand required for their craft.*

Burnisher

Knife for cutting pen nib

The calligrapher's tools *and materials included a burnisher, usually made of agate, which was used to prepare the paper. A knife was used to slit the reed nib of the pen before writing.*

Valide Han ⑰
Valide Hanı

Junction of Çakmakçılar Yokuşu & Tarakçılar Cad, Beyazıt. **Map** 2 C3 (4 B2). 🚇 *Beyazıt, then 10 mins walk.* ⏲ *9:30am–5pm Mon–Sat.*

IF THE GRAND BAZAAR *(see pp98–9)* seems large, it is sobering to realize that it is only the covered part of an huge area of seething commercial activity which reaches all the way to the Golden Horn *(see p89).* As in the Grand Bazaar, most manufacturing and trade takes place in hans, courtyards hidden away from the street behind shaded gateways.

The largest han in Istanbul is Valide Han. It was built in 1651 by Kösem, the mother of Sultan Mehmet IV. You enter it from Çakmakçılar Yokuşu through a massive portal. After passing through an irregularly shaped forecourt, you come out into a large courtyard centring on a Shiite mosque. This was built when the han became the centre of Persian trade in the city. Today, the han throbs to the rhythm of hundreds of weaving looms.

A short walk further down Çakmakçılar Yokuşu is Büyük Yeni Han, hidden behind another impressive doorway. This Baroque han, built in

Carpet shops in Çorlulu Ali Paşa Courtyard

1764, has three arcaded levels. The entrance is on the top level, where distinctive bird cages are among the wares.

In the labyrinth of narrow streets around these hans, artisans are grouped according to their wares: on Bakırcılar Caddesi, for instance, you will find metal workers, while the craftsmen of Uzunçarşı Caddesi make wooden items.

Grand Bazaar ⑱

See pp98–9.

HANS OF ISTANBUL
The innumerable hans that dot the centre of Istanbul originally provided temporary accommodation for travellers, their pack animals and their wares. The typical han was built as part of a mosque complex *(see pp36–7).* It consists of two- or three-storey buildings around a courtyard. This is entered via a large gateway which can be secured by a heavy wooden door at night. When vans and lorries replaced horses and mules, the city's hans lost their original function and most of them were converted into warrens of small factories and workshops. These working hans are frequently in bad repair, but in them you can still sense the entrepreneurial, oriental atmosphere of bygone Istanbul.

Café in Büyük Taş Han, near the Tulip Mosque *(see p93)*

Çorlulu Ali Paşa Courtyard ⑲
Çorlulu Ali Paşa Külliyesi

Yeniçeriler Cad, Beyazıt. **Map** 4 B3. 🚇 *Beyazıt.* ⏲ *daily.*

LIKE MANY OTHERS in the city, the *medrese (see p36)* of this mosque complex outside the Grand Bazaar has become the setting for a tranquil outdoor café. It was built for Çorlulu Ali Paşa, son-in-law of Mustafa II, who served as grand vizier under Ahmet III *(see p25).* Ahmet later exiled him to the island of Lésvos and had him executed there in 1711. Some years later his family smuggled his head back to Istanbul and interred it in the tomb built for him.

The complex is entered from Yeniçeriler Caddesi by two alleyways. Several carpet shops now inhabit the *medrese* and rugs are hung and spread all around, waiting for prospective buyers. The carpet shops share the *medrese* with a *kahve,* a traditional café *(see p200),* which is popular with locals and students from the nearby university. It advertises itself irresistibly as the "Traditional Mystic Water Pipe and Erenler Tea Garden". Here you can sit and drink tea, and perhaps smoke a nargile (bubble pipe), while deciding which carpet to buy *(see pp210–11).*

Situated across Bıleycıler Sokak, an alleyway off Çorlulu Ali Paşa Courtyard, is the Koca Sinan Paşa tomb complex, the courtyard of which is another tea garden. The charming *medrese*, mausoleum and *sebil* (a fountain where water was handed out to passers-by) were built in 1593 by Davut Ağa, who succeeded Sinan (*see p91*) as chief architect of the empire. The tomb of Koca Sinan Paşa, grand vizier under Murat III and Mehmet III, is a striking 16-sided structure.

Just off the other side of Yeniçeriler Caddesi is Gedik Paşa Hamamı, thought to be the oldest working Turkish baths (*see p67*) in the city. It was built around 1475 for Gedik Ahmet Paşa, grand vizier under Mehmet the Conqueror (*see p24*).

The dome and minaret of the mosque of Atik Ali Paşa, dating from 1496

Atik Ali Paşa Mosque ⓴
Atik Ali Paşa Camii

Yeniçeriler Cad, Beyazıt. **Map** 3 D4 (4 C3). 🚋 Çemberlitaş. 🚌 61B. ⬜ daily. 🚫

SECRETED BEHIND walls in the area north of the Grand Bazaar, this is one of the oldest mosques in the city. It was built in 1496 during the reign of Beyazıt II, the successor of Mehmet the Conqueror, by his eunuch grand vizier, Atik Ali Paşa. The mosque stands in a small garden. It is a simple rectangular structure entered through a deep stone porch. In an unusual touch, its mihrab

is contained in a kind of apse. The other buildings which formed part of the mosque complex – its kitchen (*imaret*), *medrese* and Sufi monastery (*tekke*) – have all but disappeared during the widening of the busy Yeniçeriler Caddesi.

Nuruosmaniye Mosque ⓴
Nuruosmaniye Camii

Vezirhanı Cad, Beyazıt. **Map** 3 D4 (4 C3). 🚋 Çemberlitaş. 🚌 61B. ⬜ daily. 🚫

NURUOSMANIYE CADDESI, a street lined with top-of-the-market carpet and antique shops, leads to the gateway of the mosque from which it gets its name. Mahmut I began the mosque in 1748, and it was finished by his brother, Osman III. It was the first in the city to exhibit the exaggerated traits of the Baroque, as seen in its massive cornices. Its most striking features, however, are the enormous unconcealed arches supporting the dome, each pierced by a mass of windows.

Light floods into the plain square prayer hall, allowing you to see the finely carved wooden calligraphic frieze which runs around the walls above the gallery.

On the other side of the mosque complex is the Nuruosmaniye Gate. This leads into Kalpakçılar Caddesi, the Grand Bazaar's street of jewellery shops (*see p204*).

The tomb of Mahmut Paşa, behind the mosque named after him

Mahmut Paşa Mosque ⓴
Mahmut Paşa Camii

Vezirhanı Cad, Beyazıt. **Map** 3 D3 (4 C3). 🚋 Çemberlitaş. 🚌 61B. ⬜ daily. 🚫

BUILT IN 1462, just nine years after Istanbul's conquest by the Ottomans, this was the first large mosque to be erected within the city walls. Unfortunately, it has been over-restored and much of its original charm lost.

The mosque was funded by Mahmut Paşa, a Byzantine aristocrat who converted to Islam and became grand vizier under Mehmet the Conqueror. In 1474 his disastrous military leadership incurred the sultan's fury, and he was executed. His tomb, behind the mosque, is unique in Istanbul for its Moorish style of decoration, with small tiles in blue, black, turquoise and green set in swirling geometric patterns.

Rows of windows illuminating the prayer hall of Nuruosmaniye Mosque

Grand Bazaar

Kapalı Çarşı

NOTHING CAN PREPARE YOU for the Grand Bazaar. This labyrinth of streets covered by painted vaults is lined with thousands of booth-like shops, whose wares spill out to tempt you and whose shopkeepers are relentless in their quest for a sale. The bazaar was established by Mehmet II shortly after his conquest of the city in 1453 *(see p24).* It can be entered by several gateways, two of the most useful being Çarşıkapı Gate (from Beyazıt tram stop) and Nuruosmaniye Gate (from Nuruosmaniye Mosque). It is easy to get lost in the bazaar in spite of the signposting. Many of the bazaar's goods are made behind the scenes in secluded hans *(see p96).*

Muhlis Günbattı is a well known textile and carpet shop *(see p204).*

Örücüler Gate

Spice Bazaar *(p88),* **Valide Han** *(p96)*

ASTARCI HANI

İÇ CEBECİ HAN

PERDAHÇILAR SOK

YORGANCILAR CAD

YAĞLIKÇILAR SOK

KAVAFLAR SOK

HACI HASAN SOK

ZENNECİLER SOK

FERACECİLER SOK

TAKKECİLER CAD

BODRUM HANI

FESÇİLER CAD

KALPAKÇILAR BAŞI CA

The Rooftops of the Grand Bazaar

Cafés, restaurants, toilets, banks, a post office, a police station and a mosque serve those who work and shop inside the bazaar.

Beyazıt Gate

Çadırcılar Caddesi, Book Bazaar *(see p94)*

Havuzlu Lokanta is the best restaurant in the bazaar *(see p194).*

Çarşıkapı Gate

Beyazıt tram stop

Şark Kahvesi

This traditional Turkish café is a popular choice with local bazaar traders.

Marble Fountain

Two copper and marble fountains once provided the bazaar with fresh water.

Zincirli Han

This is one of the prettiest hans in the bazaar. Here a piece of jewellery can be made to your own choice of design.

The İç Bedesten is the oldest part of the bazaar. Once a locked warehouse, it also served as a place where jewellers could make and sell their wares.

The Oriental Kiosk was built as a coffee house in the 17th century and is now a jewellery shop.

Rugs on Display

Carpets and kilims (see pp210–11) from all over Turkey and Central Asia are on sale in the bazaar.

Mahmut Paşa Gate

Money trading is conducted on mobile phones.

Gateway to the İç Bedesten

Though the eagle was a symbol of the Byzantine emperors (see p23), this eagle, like the bazaar itself, postdates the Byzantine era.

The Sandal Bedesteni dates from the 16th century and is covered by 20 brick domes supported on piers.

Nuruosmaniye Mosque *(see p97),* **Çemberlitaş tram stop**

Nuruosmaniye Gate

Kalpakçılar Başı Caddesi, the widest of the streets in the bazaar, is lined with the glittering windows of countless jewellery shops.

Souvenirs

Traditionally crafted items, such as this brass coffee pot, are for sale in the bazaar.

ZİNCİRLİ HAN

AYNACILAR SOK

HALICILAR ÇARŞISI CAD

AĞA SOK

İÇ BEDESTEN

MUHAFAZACILAR SOK

TERZİ BAŞI SOK

SANDAL BEDESTENI SOK

KESECİLER CAD

SANDAL BEDESTENI

| 0 metres | 40 |
| 0 yards | 40 |

KEY

— Suggested route

▨ Antiques and carpets

▨ Leather and denim

☐ Gold and silver

▨ Fabrics

☐ Souvenirs

☐ Household goods and workshops

▨ Boundary of the bazaar

BEYOĞLU

OR CENTURIES Beyoğlu, a steep hill north of the Golden Horn, was home to the city's foreign residents. First to arrive here were the Genoese. As a reward for their help in the reconquest of the city from the Latins in 1261 *(see p22)*, they were given the Galata area, which is now dominated by the Galata Tower. During the Ottoman period, Jews from

Monument of Independence, Taksim Square

Spain, Arabs, Greeks and Armenians settled in communities here. From the 16th century the great European powers established embassies in the area to further their own interests within the lucrative territories of the Ottoman Empire. The district has not changed much in character over the centuries and is still a thriving commercial quarter today.

SIGHTS AT A GLANCE

Historic Buildings and Monuments
Galata Tower ❸
Mevlevi Monastery ❷
Pera Palas Hotel ❶
Tophane Fountain ❾

Mosques and Churches
Arab Mosque ❺
Azap Kapı Mosque ❻
Church of SS Peter and Paul ❹
Kılıç Ali Paşa Mosque ❽

Nusretiye Mosque ❿
Yeraltı Mosque ❼

Quarters
Çukurcuma ⓫
Taksim ⓬

KEY

	Street-by-Street map *See pp102–3*
🚢	Ferry boarding point
Ⓜ	Metro or Tünel station
🚊	Tram stop
🚌	Bus stop
🛈	Tourist information
C	Mosque
✚	Church

GETTING AROUND

The Tünel underground railway climbs the hill between the bottom station on Yüzbaşı Sabahattin Evren Caddesi and the top station at the beginning of İstiklal Caddesi. An old-fashioned tram travels the length of İstiklal Caddesi but it is equally pleasant to walk. Taksim Square is a centre for buses, taxis and dolmuşes.

0 metres   500
0 yards   500

◁ **The Galata Tower and backstreets of Beyoğlu, seen from the mouth of the Golden Horn**

Street-by-Street: İstiklal Caddesi

Crest on top of the Russian Consulate gate

THE PEDESTRIANIZED İstiklal Caddesi is Beyoğlu's main street. Once known as the Grande Rue de Pera, it is lined by late 19th-century apartment blocks and European embassy buildings whose grandiose gates and façades belie their use as mere consulates since Ankara became the Turkish capital in 1923 *(see p29).* Hidden from view stand the churches which used to serve the foreign communities of Pera (as this area was formerly called), some still buzzing with worshippers, others just quiet echoes of a bygone era. Today, the once seedy backstreets of Beyoğlu, off İstiklal Caddesi, are taking on a new lease of life, with trendy jazz bars opening and shops selling hand-crafted jewellery, furniture and the like. Crowds are also drawn by the area's cinemas and numerous stylish restaurants.

★ **Pera Palas Hotel**
This hotel is an atmospheric period piece. Many famous guests, including Agatha Christie, have stayed here since it opened in 1892. Non-residents can enjoy a drink in the bar ❶

St Mary Draperis
is a Franciscan church dating from 1789. This small statue of the Virgin stands above the entrance from the street. The vaulted interior of the church is colourfully decorated. An icon of the Virgin, said to perform miracles, hangs over the altar.

Tünel underground railway to Karaköy

★ **Mevlevi Monastery**
A peaceful garden surrounds this small museum of the Mevlevi Sufi sect (see p104). On the last Sunday of every month visitors can see dervishes perform their famous swirling dance ❷

Tünel Square

Tünel/ Square

Swedish Consulate

Russian Consulate

MEŞR

ASMALI MESCİT SOK

İSTİKLAL CAD

TÜNEL MEYDANI

Galatasaray Fish Market
(Balık Pazarı) mainly sells
fresh fish, but inside you will
also discover numerous delica-
tessens offering everything
from meats and cheeses
through to delicious
sweetmeats and pickles.

LOCATOR MAP
See Street Finder map 7

**British
Consulate**

**Armenian
church**

H A M A L B A Ş I   C A D

İ Y E T   C A D

İ S T İ K L A L   C A D

Y E N İ   Ş A R Ş I   C A D

**Galatasaray
Lisesi School**

Çiçek Pasajı was originally a flower market. Its
stalls have now been
replaced by bars and
restaurants *(see p196)*,
which are particularly
lively in the evenings.

**Dutch
Consulate**

**The Church of St Anthony
of Padua**, Istanbul's largest
Catholic church, is identified
by a grand arcaded balcony
along its front façade.

KEY

– – – Suggested route

| 0 metres | 75 |
| 0 yards | 75 |

STAR SIGHTS

★ **Pera Palas Hotel**

★ **Mevlevi Monastery**

The Church of the Panaghia
serves the now much reduced
Greek Orthodox population
of Beyoğlu. Dedicated to the
Virgin Mary, it contains this
beautiful classical iconostasis.

The elegant Grand Orient bar in the Pera Palas Hotel

Pera Palas Hotel ❶
Pera Palas Oteli

Meşrutiyet Cad 98–100, Tepebaşı.
Map 7 D5. ☎ *(0212) 251 45 60.*
Ⓜ *Tünel.* ♿ *by arrangement.* 📷

THROUGHOUT the world there are hotels that have attained an almost legendary status. One such is the Pera Palas *(see p183)*. Relying on the hazy mystique of yester-year, it has changed little since it opened in 1892, principally to cater for travellers on the Orient Express *(see p66)*. It still evokes images of uniformed porters and exotic onward destinations such as Baghdad and Isfahan. The Grand Orient bar serves cocktails beneath its original chandeliers, while the patisserie still attracts customers with its irresistible cakes and genteel ambience.

Former guests who have contributed to the hotel's reputation include Mata Hari, Greta Garbo, Jackie Onassis, Sarah Bernhardt, Josephine Baker, and Atatürk *(see p29)*. A room used by the thriller writer Agatha Christie *(see p42)* can be visited on request.

SUFISM AND THE WHIRLING DERVISHES

Sufism is the mystical branch of Islam *(see pp36–7)*. The name comes from *suf*, the Arabic for wool, for Sufis were originally associated with poverty and self-denial, and often wore rough woollen clothes next to the skin. Sufis aspire to a personal experience of the divine. This takes the form of meditative rituals, involving recitation, dance and music, to bring the practitioner into direct, ecstatic communion with Allah. There are several sects of Sufis, the most famous of which are the Mevlevi, better known as the Whirling Dervishes on account of their ritual spinning dance.

Painting of the Whirling Dervishes (1837) at the Mevlevi Monastery

Mevlevi Monastery ❷
Mevlevi Tekkesi

Galip Dede Cad 15, Beyoğlu. **Map** 7 D5. ☎ *(0212) 243 50 45.* Ⓜ *Tünel.* ⏰ *9:30am–4:30pm Tue–Sun.*

ALTHOUGH SUFISM was banned by Atatürk in 1924, this monastery has survived as the Divan Edebiyatı Müzesi, a museum of *divan* literature (classical Ottoman poetry). The monastery belonged to the most famous sect of Sufis, who were known as the Whirling Dervishes. The original dervishes were disciples of the mystical poet and great Sufi master "Mevlana" (Our Leader) Jelaleddin Rumi, who died in Konya, in south central Anatolia in 1273.

Tucked away off a street named after one of the great poets of the sect, Galip Dede, the museum centres on an 18th-century lodge, within which is a beautiful octagonal wooden dance floor. Here, for the benefit of visitors, the *sema* (ritual dance) is performed by a group of latter-day Sufi devotees on the last Sunday of every month. Between 5pm and 7pm, a dozen or so dancers unfurl their great circular skirts to whirl round the room in an extraordinary state of ecstatic meditation, accompanied by haunting music.

Around the dance floor are glass cases containing a small exhibition of artifacts belonging to the sect, including hats, clothing, manuscripts, photographs and musical instruments. Outside, in the calm,

The peaceful courtyard of the Mevlevi Monastery

terraced garden, stand the ornate tombstones of ordinary members and prominent sheikhs (leaders) of the sect. Surrounding the elegantly carved tombs is a profusion of delicately scented roses.

Galata Tower ❸
Galata Kulesi

Büyük Hendek Sok, Beyoğlu.
Map 3 D1. 🎫 *(0212) 245 11 60.*
🚇 *Tünel.* ⬜ *9am–9pm daily.* 🅿
Restaurant & Nightclub ⬜
8pm–midnight daily.

THE MOST distinctive silhouette on the Galata skyline is a 62-m (205-ft) high round tower topped by a conical roof. It was built in 1348 by the Genoese *(see p23)* as part of their fortifications. Throughout the Ottoman period the building was used as a watchtower, but it has since been converted to cater for tourism. The top two floors, the 8th and 9th, are occupied by a restaurant and nightclub *(see p213)*. Sadly the interior decor no longer reflects the building's medieval origins.

You can reach the top of the tower either by lift or by way of a narrow spiral staircase. It is worth the climb simply to admire the fabulous panoramic view from the balcony, which encompasses the main monuments of Istanbul and, beyond, the Princes' Islands.

Doorway into the main courtyard of the Church of SS Peter and Paul

Church of SS Peter and Paul ❹
Sen Piyer Kilisesi

Galata Kulesi Sok 44, Karaköy.
Map 3 D1. 🎫 *(0212) 249 23 85.*
🚇 *Tünel.* ⬜ *9–11am & 4–6pm daily.*

WHEN THEIR original church was requisitioned as a mosque (to become the nearby Arab Mosque) in the early 16th century, the Dominican brothers of Galata moved to this site, just below the Galata Tower. The present building, dating from 1841, was built by the Fossati brothers, architects of Italian-Swiss origin who

also worked on the restoration of Haghia Sophia *(see pp72–5)*. The church's rear wall is built into a section of Galata's old Genoese ramparts.

According to Ottoman regulations, the main façade of the building could not be directly on a road, so the church is reached through a courtyard, the entrance to which is via a tiny door on the street. Ring the bell to gain admittance.

The church is built in the style of a basilica, with four side altars. The cupola over the choir is sky blue, studded with gold stars. Mass is said here in Italian every morning.

Set inside a large silver case is the revered icon of the Virgin Hodegetria ("the Guide") which is said to have been one of the protective icons of Byzantine Constantinople, and is attributed to St Luke. In support of this reputation, the icon miraculously survived a fire in 1731 that burned down the earlier church which stood on this site.

Arab Mosque ❺
Arap Camii

Kalyon Sok 1, Galata. **Map** 3 D1.
🚇 *Tünel.* ⬜ *prayer times only.*

THE ARABS after whom this mosque was named were Moorish refugees from Spain. Many settled in Galata after their expulsion from Andalusia following the fall of Granada in 1492. The church of SS Paul and Dominic, built in the first half of the 14th century by Dominican monks, was given to the settlers for use as a mosque. It is an unusual building for Istanbul: a vast, strikingly rectangular Gothic church with a tall square belfry which now acts as a minaret. The building has been restored several times, but of all the converted churches in the city it makes the least convincing mosque.

The distinctive Galata Tower, as seen from across the Golden Horn

Azap Kapı Mosque, built by the great architect Sinan

Azap Kapı Mosque **6**
Azap Kapı Camii

Tersane Cad, Azapkapı. **Map** 2 C1.
Ⓜ *Tünel.* 🚌 *46H, 61B.* ⬜ *prayer times only.*

D ELIGHTFUL though they are, this little mosque complex and fountain are somewhat overshadowed by the stream of traffic thundering over the adjacent Atatürk Bridge. The trees surrounding the mosque, however, help to screen it from the noise. It was built in 1577–8 by Sinan *(see p91)* for Grand Vizier Sokollu Mehmet Paşa and is considered to be one of Sinan's more attractive mosques. Unusually, the entrance is up a flight of internal steps leading to the porch and prayer hall. The building was rescued from ruin when the bridge was built in 1942 and its vanished İznik tiles were replaced with Kütahya tiles *(see p204)*.

The lavishly decorated Baroque fountain to the north of the mosque dates from 1732. It has been restored, too, although vagrants sometimes sleep in its water troughs.

Yeraltı Mosque **7**
Yeraltı Camii

Karantina Sok, Karaköy. **Map** 3 E1.
Ⓜ *Tünel.* ⬜ *daily.*

T HIS STRANGE, secluded sight, literally "the underground mosque", contains the shrines of two Muslim saints, Abu Sufyan and Amiri Wahibi, who died during the first Arab siege of the city in the 7th century *(see p19)*. It was the discovery of their bodies in the cellar of an ancient Byzantine fortification in 1640 that led to the creation of first a shrine on the site and later, in 1757, a mosque. The building may even have been part of the Galata Castle, from which one end of the chain protecting the Byzantine harbour on the Golden Horn was suspended *(see p21)*.

The tombs of the saints are behind grilles at the end of a low, dark prayer hall, the roof of which is supported by a forest of pillars. Adorning the entrance and mihrab are beautiful İznik tiles *(see p161)*.

Kılıç Ali Paşa Mosque **8**
Kılıç Ali Paşa Camii

Necatibey Cad, Tophane. **Map** 7 E5.
🚌 *25E, 56.* ⬜ *daily.*

T HIS MOSQUE WAS built in 1580 by Sinan, who was by then in his 90s. The church of Haghia Sophia *(see pp72–5)* provided the architect with his inspiration. Although the mosque's smaller proportions stop it from soaring heavenwards like Haghia Sophia, it is still a pleasing building, with İznik tiles around the mihrab and a delightful deep porch before the main

door. Above the entrance portal is an inscription giving the date when the mosque was established.

Kılıç Ali Paşa, who commissioned the mosque, had a colourful life. Born in Italy, he was captured by Muslim pirates and later converted to Islam in the service of Süleyman the Magnificent (1520–66). He served as a naval commander under three sultans and after retiring asked Murat III *(see p25)* where to build his mosque. The sultan is said to have replied "in the admiral's domain, the sea". Taking him at his word, Kılıç Ali Paşa reclaimed part of the Bosphorus for his complex. He died in 1587 at the age of 90, allegedly in the arms of a concubine, and was buried in the *türbe* (tomb) behind the mosque.

Detail of a carved panel on Tophane Fountain

Tophane Fountain **9**
Tophane Çeşmesi

Tophane İskele Cad, Tophane.
Map 7 E5. 🚌 *25E, 56.*

A CROSS the small road beside Kılıç Ali Paşa Mosque stands a beautiful but abandoned Baroque fountain, built in 1732 by Mahmut I. With its elegant roof and dome, it resembles the fountain of Ahmet III *(see p60)*. Each of the four walls is entirely covered in low-relief floral carving, which would once have been gaily painted.

Koranic inscription in İznik tiles at the Kılıç Ali Pasa Mosque

The name, meaning "cannon foundry fountain", comes from the brick and stone foundry building on the hill nearby. Established in 1453 by Mehmet the Conqueror *(see p24)* and rebuilt several times, the foundry no longer produces weapons but is still owned by the military.

Nusretiye Mosque ❿
Nusretiye Camii

Necatibey Cad, Tophane. **Map** 7 E5. 🚌 *25E, 56.* ⭕ *daily.*

THE BAROQUE "Mosque of Victory" was built in the 1820s by Kirkor Balyan *(see p128)*, who went on to found a dynasty of architects. This ornate building seems more like a large palace pavilion than a mosque, with its decorative out-buildings and marble terrace.

Commissioned by Mahmut II to commemorate his abolition of the Janissary corps in 1826 *(see p28)*, it faces the Selimiye Barracks *(see p132)*, across the Bosphorus, which housed the New Army that replaced the Janissaries. In the high-domed interior, the Empire-style swags and embellishments celebrate the sultan's victory. The marble panel of calligraphy around the interior of the mosque is particularly fine, as is the pair of *sebils* (kiosks for serving drinks) outside.

The window-filled dome and arches of Nusretiye Mosque

Fountain in the park at the centre of Taksim Square

Çukurcuma ⓫

Map 7 E4. Ⓜ *Tünel.*

THIS CHARMING OLD quarter of Beyoğlu, radiating from a neighbourhood mosque on Çukurcuma Caddesi, has become an important centre for Istanbul's furnishings and antiques trades. The old warehouses and houses have been converted into shops and showrooms, where modern upholstery materials are piled up in carved marble basins and antique cabinets. It is worth browsing here to discover anything from 19th-century Ottoman embroidery to 1950s biscuit boxes.

Suzani **textiles *(see p204)* on sale in Çukurcuma**

Taksim ⓬

Map 7 E3. 🚉 *Taksim.* Ⓜ *Taksim.* **Taksim Art Gallery** ☎ *(0212) 245 20 65.* ⭕ *11am–7pm daily.*

CENTRING ON THE vast, open Taksim Square (Taksim Meydanı), the Taksim area is the hub of activity in modern Beyoğlu. Taksim means "water distribution centre", and from the early 18th century it was from this site that water from the Belgrade Forest *(see p158)* was distributed throughout the modern city. The original stone reservoir, built in 1732 by Mahmut I, still stands at the top of İstiklal Caddesi. In the southwest of the square is the Monument of Independence, sculpted by the Italian artist Canonica in 1928. It shows Atatürk *(see pp28–9)* and the other founding fathers of the modern Turkish Republic.

Further up, on Cumhuriyet Caddesi, is the modern building of the **Taksim Art Gallery**. As well as temporary exhibitions it has a permanent display of Istanbul landscapes by some of Turkey's most important 20th-century painters.

At the far end of Taksim Park, to the north of Taksim Square, breathtaking views of Istanbul and the Bosphorus can be enjoyed from the bars on the top floor of the Inter-Continental Hotel *(see p183)*.

GREATER ISTANBUL

AWAY FROM the city centre there are many sights which repay the journey to visit them. Greater Istanbul has been divided into five areas shown on the map below; each also has its own map to help you get around. Closest to the centre are the mosques and churches of Fatih, Fener and Balat: most conspicuously the gigantic Fatih Mosque. Across the Golden Horn (see p89) from Balat

Tiles depicting Mecca, Cezri Kasım Paşa Mosque, Eyüp

are two sights worth seeing: Aynalı Kavak Palace and a fascinating industrial museum. The Theodosian Walls, stretching from the Golden Horn to the Sea of Marmara, are one of the city's most impressive monuments. Along these walls stand several ancient palaces and churches: particularly interesting is the Church of St Saviour in Chora, with its stunning Byzantine mosaics. Beyond the

walls, up the Golden Horn, is Eyüp, a focus of pilgrimage to Muslims, where you can visit a number of fine mausoleums and walk up the hill to the historic café associated with the French writer Pierre Loti (see p42). Following the Bosphorus northwards past Beyoğlu (see pp100–7) brings you to Dolmabahçe Palace, one of the top sights of Istanbul. This opulent fantasy created in the 19th century by Sultan Abdül Mecit I requires a lengthy visit. Beyond it is peaceful Yıldız Park containing yet more beautiful palaces and pavilions. Not all visitors to Istanbul make it to the Asian side, but if you have half a day to spare it is only a short ferry trip from Eminönü (see pp234–5). Its attractions include some splendid mosques, a handsome railway station and a small museum dedicated to Florence Nightingale.

KEY

� Central Istanbul	═ Motorway	— City Walls
Greater Istanbul	═ Main road	0 kilometres 1
⚓ Ferry boarding point	═ Other road	0 miles 1

◁ **Fountain in the grounds of the sumptuous Dolmabahçe Palace**

Fatih, Fener and Balat

A VISIT TO THESE NEIGHBOURHOODS is a reminder that for centuries after the Muslim conquest *(see p24)*, Jews and Christians made up around 40 per cent of Istanbul's population. Balat was home to Greek-speaking Jews from the Byzantine era onwards; Sephardic Jews from Spain joined them in the 15th century. Fener became a Greek enclave in the early 16th century and many wealthy residents rose to positions of prominence in the Ottoman Empire. Hilltop Fatih is linked to the city's radical Islamic tradition and you will see far more devout Muslims here than anywhere else in Istanbul. All three areas are residential, their maze of streets the preserve of washing lines and children playing.

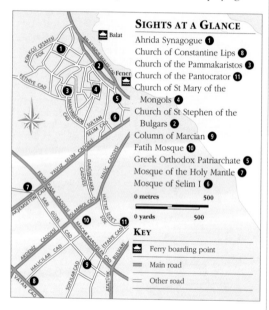

SIGHTS AT A GLANCE

Ahrida Synagogue ❶
Church of Constantine Lips ❽
Church of the Pammakaristos ❸
Church of the Pantocrator ⓫
Church of St Mary of the Mongols ❹
Church of St Stephen of the Bulgars ❷
Column of Marcian ❾
Fatih Mosque ❿
Greek Orthodox Patriarchate ❺
Mosque of the Holy Mantle ❼
Mosque of Selim I ❻

0 metres 500
0 yards 500

KEY

⛴ Ferry boarding point

▬ Main road

— Other road

Ahrida Synagogue ❶

Ahrida Sinagogu

Gevgili Sok, Balat. **Map** 1 C1.
🚌 55T, 99A. ◻ by appointment. ⬛

T HE NAME OF Istanbul's oldest and most beautiful synagogue is a corruption of Ohrid, a town in Macedonia from which its early congregation came. It was founded before the Muslim conquest of the city in 1453 and, with a capacity for up to 500 worshippers, has been in constant use ever since. However, tourists can only visit by prior arrangement with a guided tour company *(see p220)*. The synagogue's painted walls and ceilings, dating from the late 17th century, have been restored to their Baroque glory. Pride of place, however, goes to the central Holy Ark, covered in rich tapestries, which contains rare holy scrolls.

During an explosion of fervour that swept the city's Jewish population in the 17th century, the religious leader Shabbetai Zevi (1629–76), a self-proclaimed messiah, started preaching at this synagogue. He was banished from the city and later converted to Islam. However, a significant number of Jews held that Zevi's conversion was a subterfuge and his followers, the Sabbatians, exist to this day.

Church of St Stephen of the Bulgars ❷

Bulgar Kilisesi

Mürsel Paşa Cad 85, Balat.
Map 1 C1. 🚌 55T, 99A. ⛴ Balat.
◻ 9am–4pm daily.

A STONISHINGLY, this entire church was cast in iron, even the internal columns and galleries. It was created in Vienna in 1871, shipped all the way to the Golden Horn *(see p89)* and assembled on its shore. The church was needed for the Bulgarian community who had broken away from the authority of the Greek Orthodox Patriarchate just up the hill. Today, it is still used by this community, who keep the marble tombs of the first Bulgarian patriarchs permanently decorated with flowers. The church stands in a pretty little park that is dotted with trees and flowering shrubs and which runs down to the edge of the Golden Horn.

The Church of St Stephen of the Bulgars, wholly made of iron

Church of the Pammakaristos ❸

Fethiye Camii

Fethiye Cad, Draman. **Map** 1 C2. 🚌 90, 90B. ◻ prayer times only. 📷

T HIS BYZANTINE church is one of the hidden secrets of Istanbul. It is rarely visited despite the important role it has played in the history of the city and its breathtaking series of mosaics. For over 100 years after the Ottoman

Byzantine façade of the Church of the Pammakaristos

conquest it housed the Greek Orthodox Patriarchate, but was converted into a mosque in the late 16th century by Murat III *(see p30)*. He named it the Mosque of Victory to commemorate his conquests of Georgia and Azerbaijan.

The charming exterior is obviously Byzantine, with its alternating stone and brick courses and finely carved marble details. The main body of the building is the working mosque, while the extraordinary mosaics are in a side chapel. This now operates as a museum and officially you need to get permission in advance from Haghia Sophia *(see pp72–5)* to see it. However there is a chance that if the caretaker is around he may simply let you in.

Dating from the 14th century, the great Byzantine renaissance *(see p23)*, the mosaics show holy figures isolated in a sea of gold, a reflection of the heavens. From the centre of the main dome, Christ Pantocrator ("the All-Powerful"), surrounded by the Old Testament prophets, stares solemnly down. In the apse another figure of Christ, seated on a jewel-encrusted throne, gives his benediction. On either side are portraits of the Virgin Mary and John the Baptist beseeching Christ. They are overlooked by the four archangels, while the side apses are filled with other saintly figures.

Church of St Mary of the Mongols ❹
Kanlı Kilise

Tevkii Cafer Mektebi Sok, Fener. **Map** 1 C2. 【 *(0212) 521 71 39.* 🚌 *55T, 99A.* ◯ *9am–5pm daily.*

CONSECRATED in the late 13th century, the Church of St Mary of the Mongols is the only Greek Orthodox church in Istanbul to have remained continuously in the hands of the Greek community since the Byzantine era. Its immunity from conversion into a mosque was

Detail on Church of St Mary of the Mongols

decreed in an order signed by Mehmet the Conqueror *(see p24)*. A copy of this is kept by the church to this day.

The church gets its name from the woman who founded it, Maria Palaeologina, an illegitimate Byzantine princess who was married off to a Mongol khan, Abagu, and lived piously with him in Persia for 15 years. On her husband's assassination, she returned to Constantinople, built this church and lived out her days in it as a nun.

A beautiful Byzantine mosaic which depicts Theotokos Pammakaristos ("the All-Joyous Mother of God") is the church's greatest treasure.

Greek Orthodox Patriarchate ❺
Ortodoks Patrikhanesi

Sadrazam Ali Paşa Cad 35, Fener. 【 *(0212) 525 21 17.* 🚌 *55T, 99A.* ◯ *9am–5pm daily.* ☑

THIS WALLED COMPLEX has been the seat of the patriarch of the Greek Orthodox Church since the early 17th century. Though nominally head of the whole church, the patriarch is now shepherd to a diminishing flock in and around Istanbul.

As you walk up the steps to enter the Patriarchate through a side door you will see that the main door has been welded shut. This was done in memory of Patriarch Gregory V, who was hanged here for treason in 1821 after encouraging the Greeks to overthrow Ottoman rule at the start of the Greek War of Independence (1821–32). Antagonism between the Turkish and Greek communities worsened with the Greek occupation of parts of Turkey in the 1920s *(see p29)*. There were anti-Greek riots in 1955, and in the mid-1960s many Greek residents were expelled. Today the clergy here is protected by a metal detector at the entrance.

The Patriarchate centres on the basilica-style Church of St George, which dates back to 1720. Yet the church contains much older relics and furniture. The patriarch's throne, the high structure to the right of the nave, is thought to be Byzantine, while the pulpit on the left is adorned with fine Middle Eastern wooden inlay and Orthodox icons.

The ornate, gilded interior of the Church of St George in the Greek Orthodox Patriarchate

İznik tile panel capping a window in the Mosque of Selim I

Mosque of Selim I ❻

Selim I Camii

Yavuz Selim Cad, Fener. **Map** 1 C2.
🚌 55T, 90, 90B, 99A. ⭕ daily.

THIS MUCH-ADMIRED mosque is also known locally as Yavuz Sultan Mosque: Yavuz, "the Grim", being the nickname the infamous Selim acquired (see p24). It is idyllic in a rather off-beat way, which seems at odds with the barbaric reputation of the sultan.

The mosque, built in 1522, sits alone on a hill beside a vast sunken parking lot, once the Byzantine Cistern of Aspar. Sadly it is rarely visited and has an air of neglect, yet the mosque's intimate courtyard gives an insight into concept of paradise in Islam. At the centre of this lovely garden is an octagonal, domed fountain, surrounded by trees filled with chirruping birds.

The windows set into the porticoes in the courtyard are capped by early İznik tiles (see p161). These were made by the *cuerda seca* technique, in which each colour is separated during the firing process, thus affording the patterns greater definition.

Similar tiles lend decorative effect to the simple prayer hall, with its fine mosque furniture (see pp36–7) and original painted woodwork.

Mosque of the Holy Mantle ❼

Hırka-i Şerif Camii

Keçeciler Cad, Karagümrük. **Map** 1 B3.
🚌 28, 87, 90, 91. ⭕ daily.

BUILT IN the Empire Style in 1851, this mosque was designed to house a cloak (*hırka*) in the imperial collection which once belonged to and was worn by the Prophet Mohammed. This resides in a sanctuary directly behind the mihrab. The mosque's minarets are in the form of Classical columns, and its balconies styled like Corinthian capitals. The interior of the octagonal prayer hall, meanwhile, has a plethora of decorative marble. Abdül Mecit I, the mosque's patron, was jointly responsible for the design of its calligraphic frieze.

Knocker, Mosque of the Holy Mantle

Church of Constantine Lips ❽

Fenari İsa Camii

Vatan Cad, Fatih. **Map** 1 B4.
🚌 90B. ⭕ daily.

THIS 10TH-CENTURY monastic church, dedicated to the Immaculate Mother of God, was founded by Constantine Lips Dungarios, a commander of the Byzantine fleet. Following the Byzantine reconquest

Byzantine brickwork exterior of the Church of Constantine Lips

of the city in 1261 (see p22), Empress Theodora, wife of Michael VIII Palaeologus (see pp22–3), added a second church. She also commissioned a funerary chapel, where she and her sons were buried.

This unusual history has given the structure its present rambling appearance. In an idiosyncratic touch, there are also four tiny chapels perched on the roof around the main dome. Another highlight is the building's eastern exterior wall. This is decorated with a *tour de force* of brick friezes, of the kind that are a hallmark of Byzantine churches of this period. When the church was converted into a mosque in 1496, it adopted the name Fenari İsa, or the Lamp of Jesus. This was in honour of İsa (Turkish for Jesus), the leader of a Sufi brotherhood (see p104) who worshipped here at that time. Inside the mosque, which is still in use today, there are some well-restored capitals and decorated cornices.

Column of Marcian ❾

Kız Taşı

Kıztaşı Cad, Saraçhane. **Map** 1 C4 (2 A3). 🚌 28, 87, 90, 91.

STANDING IN a little square, this 5th-century Byzantine column was once surmounted by a statue of the Emperor Marcian (AD 450–57). On its base you can still see a pair of Nikes, Greek winged goddesses of victory, holding an inscribed medallion.

Interestingly, the column's Turkish name translates as the Maiden's Column, suggesting that it was mistaken for the famous Column of Venus. According to legend, this column was said to sway at the passing of an impure maid. It originally stood nearby and is thought to have been employed as one of the largest columns in the Süleymaniye Mosque (see pp90–91).

Chandelier hanging in the light and airy interior of Fatih Mosque

Fatih Mosque ❿
Fatih Camii

Macar Kardeşler Cad, Fatih. **Map** 1 C3.
🚌 28, 87, 90, 91. ⭕ daily.

A SPACIOUS OUTER courtyard surrounds this vast Baroque mosque, which is the third major structure on this site. The first was the Church of the Holy Apostles (see p21), the burial place of most of the Byzantine emperors. When Mehmet the Conqueror (see p24) came to construct a mosque here, the church's crumbling remains provided a symbolic location. But the first Fatih Mosque collapsed in an earthquake in 1766, and most of what you see today was the work of Mehmet Tahir Ağa, the chief imperial architect under Mustafa III. Many of the buildings he constructed around the prayer hall, including eight Koranic colleges (medreses) and a hospice, still stand.

The only parts of Mehmet the Conqueror's mosque to have survived are the three porticoes of the courtyard, the ablutions fountain, the

main gate into the prayer hall and, inside, the mihrab. Two exquisite forms of 15th-century decoration can be seen over the windows in the porticoes: İznik tiles made using the cuerda seca technique and lunettes adorned with calligraphic marble inlay.

Inside the prayer hall, stencilled patterns decorate the domes, while the lower level of the walls is revetted with yet more tiles – although these are inferior to those used in the porticoes.

The tomb of Mehmet the Conqueror stands behind the prayer hall, near that of his consort Gülbahar. His sarcophagus and turban are both appropriately large. It is a place of enormous gravity, always busy with supplicants. If you pay a visit to the mosque on a Wednesday, you will also see the weekly market (see p206) which turns the streets around it into a circus of commerce. From tables piled high with fruit and vegetables to lorries loaded with unspun wool, this is a real spectacle, even if you don't buy anything.

Church of the Pantocrator ⓫
Zeyrek Camii

İbadethane Sok, Küçükpazar.
Map 2 B2. 🚌 28, 61B, 87.
⭕ prayer times daily. ♿

E MPRESS IRENE, the wife of John II Comnenus (see p19), founded the Church of the Pantocrator ("Christ the Almighty") during the 12th century. This hulk of Byzantine masonry was once the centrepiece of one of the city's most important religious foundations, the Monastery of the Pantocrator. As well as a monastery and church, the complex included a hospice for the elderly, an asylum and a hospital. In this respect it prefigured the social welfare system provided by the great imperial mosque complexes that the Ottomans later built in the city (see p36).

The church, now a mosque, boasts a magnificent figurative marble floor. It is composed of three interlinked chapels. The one with the highest dome was built by Empress Irene. Emperor John II added another as a mortuary chapel when Irene died in 1124, and he later filled the area between with a third apsed chapel. The rest of the Comnenus dynasty and many of the Palaeologus imperial family were interred within these chapels.

Shortly after the Muslim conquest in 1453 (see p24), the building was converted into a mosque. A caretaker may let you in outside prayer times in the afternoons.

Church of the Pantocrator, built by Empress Irene in the 12th century

Along the City Walls

ISTANBUL'S LAND WALLS are one of the most impressive remains of the city's Byzantine past. Pierced by monumental gates and strengthened by towers, they encompass the city centre in a great arc, stretching all the way from Yedikule, on the Sea of Marmara, to Ayvansaray, on the Golden Horn (see p89). The suburbs that lie adjacent to the walls, particularly Edirnekapı and Topkapı, are mainly working-class, residential districts, interspersed with areas of wasteland which are unsafe to explore alone. Dotted around these suburbs, however, are important remnants of the city's past, particularly the Byzantine period. The outstanding sight here is the Church of St Saviour in Chora (see pp118–19), with its beautifully preserved mosaics and frescoes.

Silivrikapı, one of the gateways through the Theodosian Walls

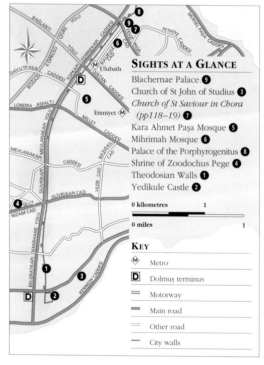

SIGHTS AT A GLANCE

Blachernae Palace **9**
Church of St John of Studius **3**
Church of St Saviour in Chora (pp118–19) **7**
Kara Ahmet Paşa Mosque **5**
Mihrimah Mosque **6**
Palace of the Porphyrogenitus **8**
Shrine of Zoodochus Pege **4**
Theodosian Walls **1**
Yedikule Castle **2**

0 kilometres   1
0 miles   1

KEY

Ⓜ	Metro
Ⓓ	Dolmuş terminus
═══	Motorway
▬▬	Main road
══	Other road
▬	City walls

The walls were built between AD 412–22, during the reign of Theodosius II (408–50). In 447 an earthquake destroyed 54 of the towers but these were immediately rebuilt, under threat of the advancing Attila the Hun. Subsequently the walls resisted sieges by Arabs, Bulgarians, Russians and Turks. Even the determined armies of the Fourth Crusade (see p22) only managed to storm the ramparts along the Golden Horn, while the land walls stood firm.

Mehmet the Conqueror finally breached the walls in May 1453 (see p24). Successive Ottoman sultans then kept the walls in good repair until the end of the 17th century.

Recently, large stretches of the walls, particularly around Belgratkapı (Belgrade Gate) have been rebuilt. Byzantine scholars have criticized the restoration for insensitive use of modern building materials, but the new sections do give you an idea of how the walls used to look. Many, although not all, of the gateways are still in good repair. Mehmet the Conqueror directed his heaviest cannon at the St Romanus and Charsius gates. Under the Ottomans, the former became known as Topkapı, the Gate

Theodosian Walls **1**

Teodos II Surları

From Yedikule to Ayvansaray. **Map 1** A1. 🚊 *Topkapı.* Ⓜ *Ulubatlı.*

WITH ITS 11 fortified gates and 192 towers, this great chain of double walls sealed Constantinople's landward side against invasion for more than a thousand years. Extending for a distance of 6.5 km (4 miles) from the Sea

of Marmara to the Golden Horn, they are built in layers of red tile alternating with cut limestone blocks. Different sections can be reached by metro, tram, train or bus; but to see their whole length you will need to take a taxi or dolmuş (see p230) along the main road that runs outside them.

Carving of the Byzantine eagle over Yedikule Gate

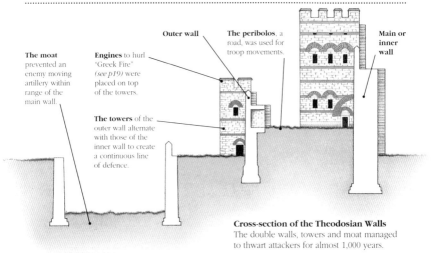

The moat prevented an enemy moving artillery within range of the main wall.

Engines to hurl "Greek Fire" *(see p19)* were placed on top of the towers.

Outer wall

The peribolos, a road, was used for troop movements.

Main or inner wall

The towers of the outer wall alternate with those of the inner wall to create a continuous line of defence.

Cross-section of the Theodosian Walls
The double walls, towers and moat managed to thwart attackers for almost 1,000 years.

---

of the Cannon (not to be confused with Topkapı Palace, *see pp54–9).* Unfortunately, a section of walls close to this gate was demolished in the 1950s to make way for a road, Millet Caddesi. The Charsius Gate (now called Edirnekapı), Silivrikapı, Yeni Mevlanakapı and other original gates still give access to the city. The Yedikule Gate (which stands beside the castle of the same name) has an imperial Byzantine eagle *(see p23)* carved above its main archway.

Yedikule Castle ②
Yedikule Müzesi

Yedikule Meydanı Sok, Yedikule.
🚌 80, 93T. ◯ 9am–5pm Tue–Sun.

Yedikule, the "Castle of the Seven Towers", is built on to the southern section of the Theodosian Walls. Its seven towers are connected by thick walls to make a five-sided fortification. One of the sides, with four towers spaced along it, is formed by a stretch of the land walls themselves.

The fortress as it is today incorporates both Byzantine and Ottoman features. The two stout, square marble towers built into the land walls once flanked the Golden Gate (now blocked up), the triumphal entrance into medieval Byzantium *(see p20)* built by Theodosius II. Imperial processions would enter the city

through this gate to mark the investiture of a new emperor or in celebration of a successful military campaign. When it was first built, the gate was covered in gold plate and the façade decorated with sculptures, including a statue of a winged Victory, four bronze elephants and an image of Emperor Theodosius himself.

In the 15th century, Mehmet the Conqueror added the three tall, round towers that are not part of the land walls, and the connecting curtain walls, to complete the fortress.

After viewing the castle from the outside, you can enter through a doorway in the northeastern wall. The tower immediately to your left as you enter is known as the *yazılı kule,* "the tower with inscriptions". This was used as a prison for foreign envoys

and others who fell foul of the sultan. These hapless individuals carved their names, dates and other details on the walls and some of these inscriptions are still visible.

Executions were carried out in Yedikule Castle, in the northern of the two towers flanking the Golden Gate. Among those executed here was the 17-year-old Osman II *(see p31).* In 1622 he was dragged to Yedikule by his own Janissaries *(see p127),* after four years of misrule, which included, it is alleged, using his own pages as targets for archery practice.

The walkway around the ramparts is accessible via a steep flight of stone steps. It offers good views of the land walls and nearby suburbs, and also of the cemeteries which lie outside the walls.

Aerial view of Yedikule Castle with the Sea of Marmara behind

Church of St John of Studius ❸

İmrahor Camii

İmam Aşir Sok, Yedikule. ▣ 80, 80B, 80T. 🚊 Yedikule.

I STANBUL'S OLDEST surviving church, St John of Studius, is now a mere shell consisting only of its outer walls. However, you can still get an idea of the original beauty of what was once part of an important Byzantine institution.

The church was completed in AD 463 by Studius, a Roman patrician who served as consul during the reign of Emperor Marcian (450–57). Originally connected to the most powerful monastery in the Byzantine Empire, in the late 8th century it was a spiritual and intellectual centre under the rule of Abbot Theodore, who was buried in the church's garden. The abbot is venerated today in the Greek Orthodox Church as St Theodore.

Until its removal by the soldiers of the Fourth Crusade (see p22), the most sacred relic housed in the church was the head of St John the Baptist. The emperor would visit the church each year for the Beheading of the Baptist feast on 29 August.

In the 15th century the church housed a university and was converted into a mosque. The building was abandoned in 1894 when it was severely damaged by an earthquake.

The church is a perfect basilica, with a single apse at the east end, preceded by a narthex and a courtyard. It has a magnificent entrance portal, with carved Corinthian capitals and a sculpted architrave and cornice. Inside, it is empty, apart from a colonnade of six columns of verdigris.

Ruins of the Church of St John of Studius

The Shrine of Zoodochus Pege, founded on a sacred spring

Shrine of Zoodochus Pege ❹

Balıklı Kilise

Seyit Nizam Cad 3, Silivrikapı. 📞 (0212) 582 30 81. 🚊 Seyitnizam. ▣ 93T. ◯ 8am–4pm daily.

T HE FOUNTAIN OF Zoodochus Pege ("Life-Giving Spring") is built over Istanbul's most famous sacred spring, which is believed to have miraculous powers. The fish swimming in it are supposed to have arrived though a miracle which occurred shortly before the fall of Constantinople (see p24). They are said to have leapt into the spring from a monk's frying pan on hearing him declare that a Turkish invasion of Constantinople was as likely as fish coming back to life.

The spring was probably the site of an ancient sanctuary of Artemis. Later, with the arrival of Christianity, a church was built around it, which was dedicated to the Virgin Mary. The spring was popular throughout the Byzantine era, especially on Ascension Day, when the emperor would visit it. The church was destroyed and rebuilt many times over the years by various Byzantine emperors, but the present one dates

from 1833. The inner courtyard is filled with tombs of bishops and patriarchs of the Greek Orthodox Church.

Kara Ahmet Paşa Mosque ❺

Kara Ahmet Paşa Camii

Undeğirmeni Sok, Fatma Sultan. ◯ Prayer times only. ⚐ Ulubatlı. 🚃 Topkapı. ▣ 93T.

O NE OF THE most worthwhile detours along the city walls is the Kara Ahmet Paşa Mosque, also known as Gazi Ahmet Paşa. This lovely building, with its peaceful leafy courtyard and graceful proportions, is one of Sinan's (see p91) lesser known achievements. He built it in 1554 for Kara Ahmet Paşa, a grand vizier of Süleyman the Magnificent (see p24).

The courtyard is surrounded by the cells of a *medrese* and a *dershane*, or main classroom. Attractive apple-green and yellow İznik tiles (see p161) grace the porch, while blue-and-white ones are found on the east wall of the prayer hall. These **Tilework over *medrese* doorway at** tiles date **Kara Ahmet Paşa Mosque** from the mid-16th century. Of the three galleries, the wooden ceiling under the west one is elaborately painted in red, blue, gold and black.

Outside the city walls, nearby, is tiny Takkeci İbrahim Ağa Mosque, which dates from 1592. Wooden-domed, it has some particularly fine İznik tile panels.

Mihrimah Mosque ❻

Mihrimah Camii

Sulukule Cad, Edirnekapı. **Map** 1 A2. ▣ 28, 87, 91. ◯ daily.

A N IMPOSING monument located just inside the city walls, the Mihrimah Mosque complex was built by Sinan between 1562 and 1565. Mihrimah, the daughter of Süleyman the Magnificent (see p24), was then the recently widowed wife of Rüstem Paşa, a grand vizier who gave his name to the tiled mosque near the Spice Bazaar (see pp88–9).

This mosque rests on a platform, occupying the highest point in the city. Its profile is visible from far away on the Bosphorus and also when approaching Istanbul from Edirne (see pp154–7).

The building is square in shape, with four strong turrets at its corners, and is surmounted by a 37-m (121-ft) high dome. The single minaret is tall and slender, so much so that it has twice been destroyed by earthquakes. On the second occasion, in 1894, the minaret crashed through the roof of the mosque. The 20th-century stencilling on the inside of the prayer hall was added following this accident.

The interior is illuminated by numerous windows, some of which have stained glass. The supporting arches of the sultan's loge (see p37) have been skilfully painted to resemble green-and-white marble. The carved marble *minbar* is also impressive.

Stained-glass window in the Mihrimah Mosque

now open to the elements, does, however, have an attractive three-storey façade in typically Byzantine style. This is decorated in red brick and white marble, with arched doorways at ground level and two rows of windows looking down on to a courtyard.

The palace dates from the late Byzantine era. Its exact age is debatable since the technique of alternating stone with three courses of brick is typical of the 10th century, whereas its geometrical designs were common in the 14th century. It was most likely constructed as an annexe of nearby Blachernae Palace. These two palaces became the principle residences of the imperial sovereigns during the last two centuries before the fall of Byzantium in 1453 (see p24).

During the reign of Ahmet III (1703–30, see p25) the last remaining İznik potters (see p161) moved to the palace and it became a centre for tile production. However, by this time their skills were in decline and the tiles made here never acquired the excellence of those created at the height of production in

İznik. Yet, some strong colours, including a rich red, were used. Cezri Kasım Paşa Mosque (see p121) in Eyüp has some fine examples of these tiles.

Blachernae Palace ❾
Anemas Zindanları

İvaz Ağa Cad, Ayvansaray.
🚌 55T, 99A.

AS THE CITY WALLS approach the Golden Horn you come to the scant remains of Blachernae Palace. These consist of a tower in the city wall, known as the Prison of Anemas, a terrace to the east (the present site of the İvaz Efendi Mosque), and another tower to the south of the terrace, known as the Tower of Isaac Angelus.

The origins of the palace date as far back as AD 500, when it was an occasional residence for imperial visitors to the shrine of Blachernae. It was the great Comnenus emperors (see p19) who rebuilt the structure in the 12th century, transforming it into a magnificent palace.

The remains of the marble decoration and wall frescoes in the Anemas tower indicate that this was probably an imperial residence. Although you can walk around the site, you will be unable to gain access into the towers unless the caretaker is there.

Church of St Saviour in Chora ❼

See pp118–19.

Palace of the Porphyrogenitus ❽
Tekfur Sarayı

Şişehane Cad, Edirnekapı. **Map** 1 B1.
🚌 87, 90, 126.

ONLY GLIMPSES of the former grandeur of the Palace of the Porphyrogenitus (Sovereign) during its years as an imperial residence are discernible from the sketchy remains. Its one extant hall,

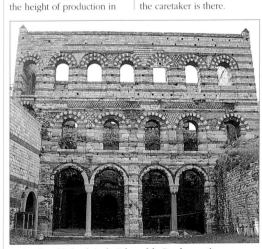

Brick and marble façade in the Palace of the Porphyrogenitus

Church of St Saviour in Chora ❼

Kariye Camii

Scene from the
Life of the Virgin

SOME OF THE VERY FINEST Byzantine mosaics and frescoes can be found in the Church of St Saviour in Chora. Little is known of the early history of the church, although its name "in Chora", which means "in the country", suggests that the church originally stood in a rural setting. The present church dates from the 11th century. Between 1315–21 it was remodelled and the mosaics and frescoes added by Theodore Metochites, a theologian, philosopher and one of the elite Byzantine officials of his day.

View of St Saviour in Chora

THE GENEALOGY OF CHRIST

THEODORE METOCHITES, who restored St Saviour, wrote that his mission was to relate how "the Lord himself became a mortal on our behalf". He takes the *Genealogy of Christ* as his starting point: the mosaics in the two domes of the inner narthex portray 66 of Christ's forebears.

The crown of the southern dome is occupied by a figure of Christ. In the dome's flutes are two rows of his ancestors: Adam to Jacob ranged above the 12 sons of Jacob. In the northern dome, there is a central image of the Virgin and Child with the kings of the House of David in the upper row and lesser ancestors of Christ in the lower row.

Mosaic showing Christ and his ancestors, in the southern dome of the inner narthex

THE LIFE OF THE VIRGIN

ALL BUT ONE of the 20 mosaics in the inner narthex depicting the *Life of the Virgin* are well preserved. This cycle is based mainly on the apocryphal Gospel of St James, written in the 2nd century, which gives an account of the Virgin's life. This was popular in the Middle Ages and was a rich source of material for ecclesiastical artists.

Among the events shown are the first seven steps of the Virgin, the Virgin entrusted to Joseph and the Virgin receiving bread from an angel.

THE INFANCY OF CHRIST

SCENES FROM the *Infancy of Christ*, based largely on the New Testament, occupy the semicircular panels of the outer narthex. They begin on

---

GUIDE TO THE MOSAICS AND FRESCOES

Outer narthex

Entrance

Inner narthex

Nave

Entrance to nave　　Parecclesion

Outer narthex looking east

KEY

☐ The Genealogy of Christ	☐ Christ's Ministry
☐ The Life of the Virgin	☐ Other Mosaics
☐ The Infancy of Christ	☐ The Frescoes

Outer narthex looking west

the north wall of the outer narthex with a scene of Joseph being visited by an angel in a dream. Subsequent panels include Mary and Joseph's *Journey to Bethlehem*, their *Enrolment for Taxation*, the *Nativity of Christ* and, finally, Herod ordering the *Massacre of the Innocents*.

The *Enrolment for Taxation*

CHRIST'S MINISTRY

WHILE MANY of the mosaics in this series are badly damaged, some beautiful panels remain. The cycle occupies the vaults of the seven bays of the outer narthex and some of the south bay of the inner narthex. The most striking mosaic is the portrayal of Christ's temptation in the wilderness, in the second bay of the outer narthex.

Theodore Metochites presents St Saviour in Chora to Christ

OTHER MOSAICS

THERE ARE three panels in the nave of the church, one of which, above the main door from the inner narthex, illustrates the *Dormition of the Virgin*. This mosaic, protected by a marble frame, is the best preserved in the church. The Virgin is depicted laid out on a bier, watched over by the Apostles, with Christ seated behind. Other devotional panels in the two narthexes include one, on the east wall of the south bay of the inner narthex, of the *Deësis*, depicting Christ with the Virgin Mary and unusually, without St John. Another, in the inner narthex over the door into the nave, is of Theodore Metochites himself, shown wearing a large turban, and humbly presenting the restored church as an offering to Christ.

THE FRESCOES

THE FRESCOES IN the parecclesion are thought to have been painted just after the mosaics were completed, probably in around 1320. The most engaging of the frescoes – which reflect the purpose of the parecclesion as a place of burial – is the *Anastasis*, in the semidome above the apse. In it, the central figure of Christ, the vanquisher of death, is shown dragging Adam and Eve out of their tombs. Under Christ's feet are the gates of hell, while Satan lies before him. The fresco in the vault overhead depicts *The Last Judgment*, with the souls of the saved on the right and those of the damned to the left.

Figure of Christ from the *Anastasis* fresco in the parecclesion

Inner narthex looking east

Parecclesion and outer narthex looking south

Inner narthex looking west

Parecclesion and outer narthex looking north

Eyüp

AS THE BURIAL PLACE of Eyüp Ensari, the standard bearer of the Prophet Mohammed, the village of Eyüp is a place of pilgrimage for Muslims from all over the world. Its sacrosanct status has kept it a peaceful place of contemplation, far removed from the squalid effects of industrialization elsewhere on the Golden Horn *(see p89)*. The wealthy elite established mosques and street fountains in the village but, above all, they chose Eyüp as a place of burial. Their grand mausoleums line the streets surrounding Eyüp Mosque, while the cypress groves in the hills above the village are filled with the gravestones of ordinary people.

Gateway to the Baroque Complex of Valide Sultan Mihrişah

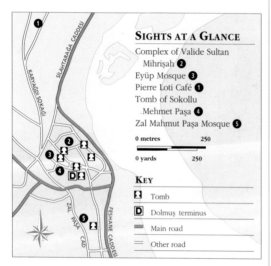

SIGHTS AT A GLANCE

Complex of Valide Sultan
 Mihrişah ❷
Eyüp Mosque ❸
Pierre Loti Café ❶
Tomb of Sokollu
 .Mehmet Paşa ❹
Zal Mahmut Paşa Mosque ❺

0 metres   250

0 yards   250

KEY

🗌 Tomb

🅳 Dolmuş terminus

━━ Main road

═══ Other road

Pierre Loti Café ❶
Piyer Loti Kahvesi

Gümüşsuyu Balmumcu Sok 1.
📞 *(0212) 581 26 96.* 🚌 *39, 55T, 99A.* ⏰ *8am–midnight daily.*

THIS FAMOUS CAFÉ stands at the top of the hill in Eyüp Cemetery, about 20 minutes' walk up Karyağdı Sokağı from Eyüp Mosque, from where it commands sweeping views down over the Golden Horn. It is named after the French novelist and Turkophile Pierre Loti, who frequented a café in Eyüp – claimed to be this one – during his stay here in 1876. Loti *(see p42)*, a French naval officer, fell in love with a married Turkish woman and wrote an autobiographical

novel, *Aziyade*, about their affair. The café is prettily decked out with 19th-century furniture and, to add to the atmosphere, the waiters wear period clothing.

The path up to the café passes by a picturesque array of tombstones, most of which date from the Ottoman era. Just before the café on the right, a few tall, uninscribed tombstones mark the graves of executioners.

Period interior of the Pierre Loti Café

Complex of Valide Sultan Mihrişah ❷
Mihrişah Valide Sultan Külliyesi

Seyit Reşat Cad. 🚌 *39, 55T, 99A.* ⏰ *9:30am–4:30pm Tue–Sun.*

MOST OF THE northern side of the street leading from Eyüp Mosque's northern gate is occupied by the largest Baroque *külliye (see p36)* in Istanbul, although unusually it is not centred on a mosque. Built for Mihrişah, mother of Selim III *(see p31)*, the *külliye* was completed in 1791.

The complex includes the ornate marble tomb of Mihrişah and a soup kitchen, which is still in use today. There is also a beautiful grilled fountain *(sebil)*, from which an attendant once served water and refreshing drinks of sweet sherbet to passers-by.

Eyüp Mosque ❸
Eyüp Camii

Cami-i Kebir Sok. 🚌 *39, 55T, 99A.* ⏰ *daily.*

MEHMET THE Conqueror built the original mosque on this site in 1458, five years after his conquest of Istanbul *(see p24)*, in honour of Eyüp Ensari. That building fell into ruins, probably as a result of an earthquake, and the present mosque was completed in 1800, by Selim III *(see p31)*.

The mosque's delightful inner courtyard is a garden in which two huge plane trees grow on a platform. This platform was the setting for the Girding of the Sword of

Osman, part of a sultan's inauguration from the days of Mehmet the Conqueror.

The mosque itself is predominantly covered in gleaming white marble, and inside there is a magnificent green carpet underfoot.

Opposite the mosque is the tomb of Eyüp Ensari himself, believed to have been killed during the first Arab siege of Constantinople in the 7th century (see p19). The tomb dates from the same period as the mosque and most of its decoration is in the Ottoman Baroque style. Both the outer wall of the tomb facing the mosque, and most of its interior, have an impressive covering of tiles, some of them from İznik (see p160).

Zal Mahmut Paşa Mosque, as viewed from its tomb garden

Visitors at the tomb of Eyüp Ensari, Mohammed's standard bearer

Tomb of Sokollu Mehmet Paşa ❹
Sokollu Mehmet Paşa Türbesi

Cami-i Kebir Sok. 🚌 39, 55T, 99A.
🕒 9:30am–4:30pm Tue–Sun.

GRAND VIZIER (see p27) Sokollu Mehmet Paşa commissioned his tomb around 1574, five years before he was assassinated by a madman in Topkapı Palace (see pp54–7). Of Balkan royal blood, he started his career as falconer royal and steadily climbed the social order until he became grand vizier to Süleyman the Magnificent (see p24) in 1565. He held this position through the reign of Selim II (see p25) and into that of Murat III. The architect Sinan (see p91)

built this elegantly proportioned octagonal tomb. It is notable for its stained glass, some of which is original. A roofed colonnade connects the tomb to what was formerly a Koranic school.

Zal Mahmut Paşa Mosque ❺
Zal Mahmut Paşa Camii

Zal Paşa Cad. 🚌 39, 55T, 99A.
🕒 daily.

HEADING SOUTH from the centre of Eyüp, it is a short walk to Zal Mahmut Paşa Mosque. The complex was built by Sinan for the man who assassinated Mustafa,

the first-born heir of Süleyman the Magnificent.

Probably erected some time in the 1560s, the mosque is notable for the lovely floral tiles around its mihrab, and for its carved marble *minbar* and *müezzin mahfili* (see p36). Proceeding down some stone steps to the north of the mosque you will come to a garden. In it stands the large tomb of Zal Mahmut Paşa and his wife, said to have both died on the same day.

On the same street, Cezri Kasım Paşa Mosque (1515) is a small mosque with a pretty portal and a tiled mihrab. Most of the tiles were produced at the Palace of the Porphyrogenitus (see p117) in the first half of the 18th century.

OTTOMAN GRAVESTONES

The Ottoman graveyard was a garden of the dead, where the living happily strolled without morbid inhibitions. The gravestones within it were often lavishly symbolic: from their decoration you can tell the sex, occupation, rank and even the number of children of the deceased. As the turban was banned in 1828 (see p28), only the fez appears on men's gravestones erected after that date.

Women's *graves have a flower for each child.*

***A turban's** size reflected a gentleman's status.*

This hat *indicates the grave of a member of a Sufi order.*

***A fez** was worn by a paşa, or public servant (see p27).*

Beyond Taksim

The area to the north of Taksim Square *(see p107)* became fashionable in the 19th century, when sultans built palaces along the Bosphorus and in the wooded hills above it. The extravagant Dolmabahçe Palace, built by Abdül Mecit I *(see p28)*, started the trend. High-ranking court officials soon followed, and the area achieved a glamour that it retains to this day. Two other sights worth seeing are on the northern shore of the Golden Horn. Aynalı Kavak Palace is the last surviving trace of a grand palace built by Ahmet III *(see p25)*, while the Rahmi Koç Museum, in nearby Hasköy, is an interesting industrial museum. Hasköy became a royal park in the 15th century and later supported fruit orchards, before dockyards brought industrialization to the area in the 19th century.

Ortaköy's fashionable waterfront square and ferry landing

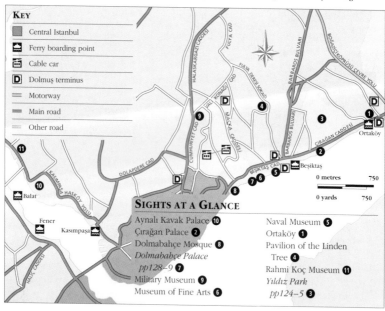

KEY

▮	Central Istanbul
🛳	Ferry boarding point
🚡	Cable car
Ⓓ	Dolmuş terminus
═══	Motorway
▬▬	Main road
═ ═	Other road

SIGHTS AT A GLANCE

Aynalı Kavak Palace ❿
Çırağan Palace ❷
Dolmabahçe Mosque ❽
*Dolmabahçe Palace
pp128–9* ❼
Military Museum ❾
Museum of Fine Arts ❻

Naval Museum ❺
Ortaköy ❶
Pavilion of the Linden
   Tree ❹
Rahmi Koç Museum ⓫
*Yıldız Park
pp124–5* ❸

Cobbled Ortaköy side street lined with cafés and shops

Ortaköy ❶

Map 9 F3. 🚌 *25E, 40.*

Crouched at the foot of Bosphorus Bridge *(see p138)*, the suburb of Ortaköy has retained a village feel. Life centres on İskele Meydanı, the quayside square, which was until recently busy with fishermen unloading the day's catch. Nowadays, though, Ortaköy is better known for its lively Sunday market *(see p207)*, which crowds out the square and surrounding streets, and its shops selling the wares of local artisans. It is also the

location for a thriving bar and café scene, which in the summer especially is the hub of Istanbul's nightlife *(see p213)*.

Mecidiye Mosque, Ortaköy's most impressive landmark, is located on the waterfront. It was built in 1855 by Nikoğos Balyan, who was responsible for Dolmabahçe Palace *(see pp128–9)*. A simple structure, it has grace and originality, with window-filled tympanum arches and corner turrets.

Ortaköy also has a Greek Orthodox church, Haghios Phocas, and a synagogue, Etz Ahayim. The origins of both date from the Byzantine era.

Çırağan Palace ❷
Çırağan Sarayı

Çırağan Cad 84, Beşiktaş. **Map** 9 D3.
((0212) 258 33 77. **▤** 25E, 40.

SULTAN ABDÜL MECİT I started
work on Çırağan Palace in
the 1850s, but it was not completed until 1874, during the
reign of Abdül Aziz (see p28).
It replaced an earlier wooden
palace where torch-lit processions were held during the
Tulip Period (see p25).

The palace was designed
by Nikoğos Balyan. At the
sultan's request he added
Arabic touches from sketches
of Moorish buildings such as
the Alhambra at Granada in
Spain. Externally this is evi-
denced in the honeycomb
capitals over its windows. The
sultan entered Çırağan Palace
directly from the Bosphorus,
through the ornate ceremonial
gates along its shoreline.

Çırağan Palace had a sad,
short history as an imperial
residence. Abdül Aziz died
here in 1876, supposedly
committing suicide – although
his friends believed he had
been murdered. His successor,
Murat V (see p31), was imprisoned in the palace for a year
after a brief reign of only three
months. He died in the Malta
Pavilion (see p125) 27 years
later, still a prisoner. The palace was eventually destroyed
by fire in 1910. It remained a
burnt out shell for many years,

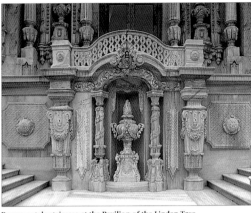

Baroque-style staircase at the Pavilion of the Linden Tree

before being restored in 1990
as the Çırağan Palace Hotel
Kempinski (see p184), one of
Turkey's most luxurious hotels.

Yıldız Park ❸

See pp124–5.

Pavilion of the Linden Tree ❹
Ihlamur Kasrı

Ihlamur Teşvikiye Yolu, Beşiktaş.
Map 8 B2. **(** (0212) 259 50 86.
▤ 26 (from Eminönü). **◯** 9:30am–
5pm Tue–Wed & Fri–Sun. **◪ ◪**

THIS ONE-TIME residence of
sultans, dating from the
mid-19th century, stands in
beautiful, leafy gardens
planted with magnolias
and camellias, and
decorated with
ornamental fountains.
The gardens are
separated by walls from
the neighbouring mod-
ern suburb of Ihlamur,
in which they are left
as a somewhat incon-
gruous remnant of the
city's Ottoman past.

As the pavilion's
name suggests, the
area was once a grove
of lime (linden) trees,
and the gardens are all
that remain of what
was previously a vast
wooded park. This
park was a favourite
retreat and hunting
ground of the Ottoman

sultans. In the early 19th
century, Abdül Mecit I (see
p28) often came here and
stayed in the original pavilion
on this site. That building was
so unassuming that the French
poet Alphonse de Lamartine
(1790–1869) expressed great
surprise that a sultan should
have entertained him in a
humble cottage, with a gar-
dener working in plain view
through the windows.

In 1857 Abdül Mecit chose
Nikoğos Balyan, who had by
then finished the Dolmabahçe
Palace with his father, to design another residence here.
Two separate pavilions were
built, the grander of which is
the Ceremonial Pavilion, or
Mabeyn Köşkü, used by the
sultan and his guests. The
Entourage Pavilion, or Maiyet
Köşkü, a short distance away,
was reserved for the sultan's
retinue, including the women
of the harem. Both buildings
are open to visitors – the
Entourage Pavilion is currently
a café and bookshop.

The pavilions are constructed mainly of sandstone and
marble. Their façades are in
the Baroque style, with double
stairways, many decorative
embellishments and hardly a
single straight line to be seen.
The ornate interiors of the
buildings reflect 19th-century
Ottoman taste, incorporating
a mixture of European styles.
With their mirrors, lavish furnishings and gilded details,
they are similar to but less
ostentatious than those of
Dolmabahçe Palace.

**Çırağan Palace, notable for the Moorish-
style embellishments above its windows**

Yıldız Park **4**
Yıldız Parkı

Y ILDIZ PARK WAS ORIGINALLY laid out as the garden of the first Çırağan Palace *(see p123)*. It later formed the grounds of Yıldız Palace, an assortment of buildings from different eras now enclosed behind a wall and entered separately from Ihlamur-Yıldız Caddesi. Further pavilions dot Yıldız Park, which, with its many ancient trees and exotic shrubs, is a favourite spot for family picnics. The whole park is situated on a steep hill and, as it is a fairly long climb, you may prefer to take a taxi up to the Şale Pavilion and walk back down past the other sights.

Fountain, Yıldız Palace Theatre

Bridge over the lake in the grounds of Yıldız Palace

Yıldız Palace

The palace is a collection of pavilions and villas built in the 19th and 20th centuries. Many of them are the work of the eccentric Sultan Abdül Hamit II (1876–1909, *see p31*), who made it his principal residence as he feared a sea-borne attack on Dolmabahçe Palace *(see pp128–9)*.

The main building in the entrance courtyard is the **State Apartments** (Büyük Mabeyn), dating from the reign of Sultan Selim III (1789–1807, *see p31*), but not presently open to the public. Around the corner, the **City Museum** (Şehir Müzesi) has a display of Yıldız porcelain. The Italianate building opposite it is the former armoury, or Silahhane. Next door to the City Museum is the **Yıldız Palace Museum**, housed in what was once the Marangozhane, Abdül Hamit's carpentry workshop. This has a changing collection of art and objects from the palace.

A monumental arch leads from the first courtyard to the harem section of the palace.

The Italianate Silahhane, the former armoury of Yıldız Palace

On the left beside the arch is a pretty greenhouse, the Limonluk Serası (Lemon House).

Further on, **Yıldız Palace Theatre** is now a museum. It was completed in 1889 by Abdül Hamit, who encouraged all forms of Western art. The decor of the theatre's restored interior is mainly blue and gold. The stars on the domed ceiling are a reference to the name of the palace: *yıldız* means "star" in Turkish.

Abdül Hamit sat alone in a box over the entrance. Since no one was allowed to sit with his back to the sultan, the stalls were not used. Backstage, the former dressing rooms are given over to displays on the theatre, including costumes and playbills.

The lake in the palace grounds is shaped like Abdül Hamit's *tuğra (see p95)*. A menagerie was kept on the islands in the lake where 30 keepers tended tigers, lions, giraffes and zebras.

Salon in the lavish Şale Pavilion

Şale Pavilion
The single most impressive building in the park, the Şale Pavilion (Şale Köşkü) was among those erected by Abdül Hamit II. Although its façade appears as a whole, it was in fact built in three stages.

The first, left-hand section of the buildling was designed to resemble a Swiss chalet. It probably dates from the 1870s. Winston Churchill, Charles de Gaulle and Nicolae Ceauşescu have all stayed in its rooms.

The second section was added in 1889, to accommodate Kaiser Wilhelm II on the first ever state visit of a foreign monarch to the Ottoman capital. The 14-room suite includes a dining room known as the Mother-of-Pearl Salon (Sedefli Salon) after the delicate inlay that covers almost all of its surfaces.

The third section was also built for a visit by Kaiser Wilhelm II, this time in 1898. Its reception chamber is the grandest room in the whole pavilion. The vast silk Hereke carpet *(see p210)* covering its floor was painstakingly hand-knotted by 60 weavers.

Malta and Çadır Pavilions
These two lovely pavilions were built in the reign of Abdül Aziz (1861–76, *see p28*). Both formerly served as prisons but are now open as cafés. Malta Pavilion, also a

restaurant, has a superb view and on Sunday is a haunt for locals wanting to relax and read the newspapers.

Midhat Paşa, reformist and architect of the constitution, was among those imprisoned in Çadır Pavilion, for instigating the murder of Abdül Aziz. Meanwhile, Murat V and his mother were locked away in Malta Pavilion for 27 years after a brief incarceration in Çırağan Palace *(see p123)*.

Façade of Çadır Pavilion, which has now been refurbished as a café

Imperial Porcelain Factory
In 1895 this factory opened to feed the demand of the upper classes for European-style ceramics to decorate their homes. The unusual building was designed to look like a stylized European medieval castle, complete with turrets and portcullis windows.

The original sugar bowls, vases and plates produced here depict idealized scenes of the Bosphorus and other local beauty spots; they can be seen in museums and palaces all over Istanbul. The mass-produced china made today is on sale in the shop and the factory is open to visitors.

Park entrance

Imperial Porcelain Factory

PALANGA CADDESI

ÇIRAĞAN CADDESI

CADDESI

0 metres 250

0 yards 250

KEY

◻ Buildings of palace

— Park wall/Palace wall

🅿 Parking

Naval Museum ⑤
Deniz Müzesi

Hayrettin Paşa İskelesi Sok, Beşiktaş.
Map 8 B4. ⓒ (0212) 361 01 30.
🚌 25E, 28, 40, 56. ◯ 1:30–5pm
Fri–Tue. 📷 ✗

T HIS MUSEUM is located in
two buildings next to the
ferry landing in Beşiktaş. One
of them is the Caïques Gallery
which is devoted to huge imperial rowing boats, or caïques
(some of them manned by
replica oarsmen), dating from
the 17th century. The largest
of these, at 40 m (130 ft), was
used by Mehmet IV and powered by 144 oarsmen. The
rowing boats used by Atatürk
(see p28) look

tiny in compar-
ison: it is re-
markable to
think that he
entertained
heads of state
in them.
The exhibits in
the neighbouring

**Rowing boat
used by
Atatürk**

main museum
include a 16th-
century map of
America by Turk-
ish cartographer Piri Reis, oil
paintings of various military
scenes, ship figureheads, naval
uniforms and objects from
Atatürk's yacht, the Savarona.

Museum of Fine Arts ⑥
Resim ve Heykel Müzesi

Hayrettin Paşa İskelesi Sok, Beşiktaş.
Map 8 B4. ⓒ (0212) 261 42 98.
🚌 25E, 28, 40, 56. ◯ 10:30am–
4:30pm Wed–Sun.

F ORMERLY THE Crown Prince
Pavilion, this building, adjacent to Dolmabahçe Palace
(see pp128–9), houses a fine
collection of 19th- and 20th-
century paintings and sculpture. In the 19th century, the
westernization of the Ottoman
Empire (see pp28–9) led
artists such as Osman Hamdi
Bey (1842–1910, see p62) to
experiment with Western-
style painting. While their
styles rely heavily on European art forms, the subject
matter of their work gives a
glimpse into the oriental

**Woman with Mimosas by Osman
Hamdi Bey, Museum of Fine Arts**

history of the city. Look out
for Woman with Mimosas,
Portrait of a Young Girl and
Man with a Yellow Robe, all
by Osman Hamdi Bey, Sultan
Ahmet Mosque by Ahmet Ziya
Akbulut (1869–1938) and
Âşık, a statue of a poet by
İsa Behzat (1867–1944).

Dolmabahçe Palace ⑦

See pp128–9.

Dolmabahçe Mosque ⑧
Dolmabahçe Camii

Meclis-i Mebusan Cad, Kabataş.
Map 8 A5. 🚌 25E, 40. ◯ daily.

C OMPLETED AT THE same
time as Dolmabahçe
Palace, in 1853, the mosque
standing beside it was also
built by the wealthy Balyan
family. Its slim minarets were
constructed in the form of

Corinthian columns, while
great arching windows lighten
the interior. Inside, the decoration includes fake marbling
and trompe l'oeil painting,
two highly fashionable effects
in the mid-19th century.

Military Museum ⑨
Askeri Müze

Vali Konağı Cad, Harbiye. **Map** 7 F1.
ⓒ (0212) 233 71 15. 🚌 46H.
◯ 9am–5pm Wed–Sun. **Mehter
Band performances** 3–4pm
Wed–Sun. 📷 ✗

O NE OF ISTANBUL'S most
impressive museums, the
Military Museum traces the
history of the country's con-
flicts from the conquest of
Constantinople in 1453 (see
p24) through to modern warfare. The building used to be
the military academy where
Atatürk studied from 1899–
1905. His classroom has been
preserved as it was then.
The museum is also the
main location for performances
by the Mehter Band, which
was first formed in the 14th-
century during the reign of
Osman I (see p23). From then
until the 19th century, the
band's members were Janissaries, who would accompany
the sultan into battle and perform songs about Ottoman
hero-ancestors and battle
victories. The band had much
influence in Europe, and is
thought to have provided
some inspiration for Mozart
and Beethoven.
Some of the most striking
weapons on display on the
ground floor are the curved

Dolmabahçe Mosque, a landmark on the Bosphorus shoreline

Cembiyes – Ottoman curved daggers – on display in the Military Museum

daggers *(cembiyes)* carried at the waist by foot soldiers in the 15th century. These are ornamented with plant, flower and geometric motifs in relief and silver filigree. Other exhibits include 17th-century copper head armour for horses and Ottoman shields made from cane and willow covered in silk thread.

A moving portrayal of trench warfare, commissioned in 1995, is included in the section concerned with the ANZAC landings of 1915 at Chunuk Bair on the Gallipoli peninsula *(see p28)*.

Upstairs, the most spectacular of all the exhibits are the tents used by sultans on their campaigns. They are made of silk and wool with embroidered decoration.

Not far from the museum, from the station on Taşkışla Caddesi, you can take the cable car across Maçka Park to Abdi İpekçi Caddesi in Teşvikiye. Also, some of the city's best designer clothes, jewellery, furniture and art shops are to be found in this area *(see pp204–5)*.

Aynalı Kavak Palace ⑩
Aynalı Kavak Kasrı

Kasımpaşa Cad, Hasköy. **Map** 6 A3.
🔲 *(0212) 250 40 94.* 🚌 *47, 54.*
🕘 *9am–5pm Tue, Wed, Fri–Sun.* 📷

AYNALI KAVAK PALACE is the last vestige of a large Ottoman palace complex on the once lovely Golden Horn *(see p89)*. Originally it stood in extensive gardens covering an area of 7,000 sq m (75,300 sq ft). Inscriptions dated 1791 can be found all over the palace, but it is thought to have been built earlier by Ahmet III during the Tulip Period *(see p25)*, because of traces around the building of an older style of architecture.

The palace is built on a hill and as a result has two storeys on the southwest side and a single storey to the northeast. It retains some beautiful Ottoman features. These include the upper windows on the southwest façade, which are decorated with stained glass set in curvilinear stucco tracery. Particularly striking is the composition room, which Sultan Selim III (1789–1807) is thought to have used for writing music.

The audience chamber is adorned with an inscription in gold on blue which describes the activities of Selim III while he stayed at the palace. Restoration of Aynalı Kavak in 1984 has enabled it to be opened to the public. There is also a superb exhibition of archaic Turkish musical instruments permanently on show, in honour of Selim III, who contributed a great deal to Turkish classical music.

Audience chamber of Aynalı Kavak Palace on the Golden Horn

Rahmi Koç Museum ⑪
Rahmi Koç Müzesi

Hasköy Cad, Hasköy. 🔲 *(0212) 256 71 53.* 🚌 *47.* 🕘 *10am–5pm Tue–Sun.* 📷

SITUATED IN Hasköy, this old 19th-century factory, which once produced anchors and chains, now houses an eclectic collection named after its industrialist founder, Rahmi Koç. The building itself, with its four small domes, vaulted passageways and original wooden fittings, is one of the museum's highlights.

The theme of the industrial age loosely connects exhibitions on aviation, transport, steam engines and scientific instruments. Exhibits range from mechanical toys and scale models of transport and machinery to an entire recreated ship's bridge, an operational coin press and an old tram.

JANISSARIES

The Janissary (New Army) corps was formed in the 14th century to serve as the sultan's elite fighting force. Its ranks were filled by *devşirme*, the levy of Christian youths brought to Istanbul to serve the sultan. A highly professional and strong army, it was instrumental in the early expansion of the Ottoman Empire and, as well as a fighting force, it acted as the sultan's personal guard. However, discipline eventually began to weaken, and by 1800 the Janissaries had become a destabilizing element in society. They mutinied and overthrew many sultans until their final demise under Mahmut II in 1826 *(see p28)*.

Janissaries depicted in a 16th-century miniature

Dolmabahçe Palace ❼

Dolmabahçe Sarayı

Sèvres vase at the foot of the Crystal Staircase

SULTAN ABDÜL MECİT *(see p31)* built Dolmabahçe Palace in 1856. As its designers he employed Karabet Balyan and his son Nikoğos, members of the great family of Armenian architects who lined the Bosphorus *(see pp137–49)* with many of their creations in the 19th century. The extravagant opulence of the Dolmabahçe belies the fact that it was built when the Ottoman Empire was in decline. The sultan financed his great palace with loans from foreign banks. The palace can only be visited on a guided tour, of which two are on offer. The best tour takes you through the Selamlık (or Mabeyn-i Hümayun), the part of the palace that was reserved for men and which contains the state rooms and the enormous Ceremonial Hall. The other tour goes through the Harem, the living quarters of the sultan and his entourage. If you only want to go on one tour, visit the Selamlık.

★ **Crystal Staircase**
The apparent fragility of this glass staircase stunned observers when it was built. In the shape of a double horseshoe, it is made from Baccarat crystal and brass, and has a polished mahogany rail.

Imperial Gate
Once used only by the sultan and his ministers, this gate is now the main entrance to the palace. The Mehter, or Janissary, Band (see pp126–7) performs in front of the gate every Tuesday afternoon throughout the summer.

The Süfera Salon, where ambassadors waited for an audience with the sultan, is one of the most luxurious rooms in the palace.

Entrance

Swan Fountain
This fountain stands in the Imperial Garden. The original 16th-century garden here was created from recovered land, hence the palace's name, Dolmabahçe, meaning "Filled-in Garden".

Selamlık

The Red Room was used by the sultan to receive ambassadors.

★ **Ceremonial Hall**
This magnificent domed hall was designed to hold 2,500 people. Its chandelier, reputedly the heaviest in the world, was bought in England.

VISITORS' CHECKLIST

Dolmabahçe Cad, Beşiktaş.
Map 8 B4. (0212) 227 34 42.
25E, 40. 9am–4pm
(last adm) Tue, Wed & Fri–Sun
(Oct–Feb: last adm 3pm).
New Year's Day & some
religious festivals.

The Zülvecheyn, or Panorama Room

Blue Salon
On religious feast days the sultan's mother would receive his wives and favourites in the Harem's principal room.

Harem

The Rose-coloured salon was the assembly room of the Harem.

Reception room of the sultan's mother

Main shore gate

Sultan Abdül Aziz's bedroom had to accommodate a huge bed built especially for the 150-kg (23-stone) amateur wrestler.

Atatürk's Bedroom
Atatürk (see pp28–9) died in this room at 9:05am on 10 November 1938. All the clocks in the palace, such as this one near the crystal staircase, are stopped at this time.

★ **Main Bathroom**
The walls of this bathroom are revetted in finest Egyptian alabaster, while the taps are solid silver. The brass-framed bathroom windows afford stunning views across the Bosphorus.

STAR FEATURES

★ Crystal Staircase

★ Ceremonial Hall

★ Main Bathroom

The Asian Side

THE ASIAN SIDE of Istanbul comprises the two major suburbs of Üsküdar and Kadıköy, which date from the 7th century BC *(see p17)*. Üsküdar (once known as Scutari after the 12th century Scutarion Palace which was located opposite Leander's Tower) was the starting point of Byzantine trade routes through Asia. It retained its importance in the Ottoman period and today is renowned for its many classical mosques.

A number of residential districts radiate from Üsküdar and Kadıköy. Moda is a pleasant leafy suburb famous for its ice cream, while there is a lighthouse and an attractive park at Fenerbahçe. From there it is a short walk up to Bağdat Caddesi, one of Istanbul's best-known shopping streets *(see p204)*.

Leander's Tower, on its own small island

SIGHTS AT A GLANCE

Atik Valide Mosque ❺
The Great Hill of Pines ❿
Haydarpaşa Station ❾
İskele Mosque ❸
Karaca Ahmet Cemetery ❼
Leander's Tower ❶
Selimiye Barracks ❽
Şemsi Paşa Mosque ❷
Tiled Mosque ❻
Yeni Valide Mosque ❹

| 0 kilometres | 1 |
| 0 miles | 1 |

KEY

🚢	Ferry boarding point
🚉	Railway station
D	Dolmuş terminus
══	Motorway
──	Main road
──	Other road

Leander's Tower ❶

Kız Kulesi

Üsküdar. **Map** 10 A3. 🚢 *Üsküdar.*

LOCATED OFFSHORE from Üsküdar, the tiny, white Leander's Tower is a well-known Bosphorus landmark. The islet on which this 18th-century tower stands was the site of a 12th-century Byzantine fortress built by Manuel I Comnenus. In more recent years the tower has served as a quarantine centre during a cholera outbreak, a lighthouse, a customs control point and a maritime toll gate. It is currently used by the Turkish navy to monitor shipping and is not open to the public.

The tower is known in Turkish as the "Maiden's Tower" after a legendary princess, said to have been confined here after a prophet foretold that she would die from a snake-bite. The snake duly appeared from a basket of figs and struck the fatal blow. The English name of the tower derives from the Greek myth of Leander, who swam the Hellespont (the modern-day Dardanelles, *see p170*) to see his lover Hero.

Şemsi Paşa Mosque ❷

Şemsi Paşa Camii

Sahil Yolu, Üsküdar. **Map** 10 A2. 🚢 *Üsküdar.* 🔘 *daily.*

THIS IS ONE OF the smallest mosques to be commissioned by a grand vizier *(see p27)*. Its miniature dimensions combined with its picturesque waterfront location make it one of the most attractive mosques in the city.

Şemsi Ahmet Paşa succeeded Sokollu Mehmet Paşa *(see p82)* as grand vizier, and may have been involved in his murder. Sinan *(see p91)* built this mosque for him in 1580.

The garden, which overlooks the Bosphorus, is surrounded on two sides by the *medrese (see p36)*, with the mosque on the third side and the sea wall on the fourth. The mosque itself is unusual in that the tomb of Şemsi Ahmet is joined to the main building, divided from the interior by a grille.

Şemsi Paşa Mosque, built by Sinan for Grand Vizier Şemsi Ahmet Paşa

İskele Mosque ❸
İskele Camii

Hakimiyeti Milliye Cad, Üsküdar.
Map 10 B2. 🚊 *Üsküdar.* ◯ *daily.*

O NE OF ÜSKÜDAR'S most prominent landmarks, the İskele Mosque (also known as Mihrimah Sultan Mosque), takes its name from the ferry landing where it stands. A massive structure on a raised platform, it was built by Sinan between 1547 and 1548 for Mihrimah Sultan, favourite daughter of Süleyman the Magnificent and wife of Grand Vizier Rüstem Paşa *(see p88)*.

Without space to build a courtyard, Sinan constructed a large protruding roof which extends to cover the *şadırvan* (ablutions fountain) in front of the mosque. The porch and interior are rather gloomy as a result. This raised portico is an excellent place from which to look down on the main square below, in which stands the Baroque Fountain of Ahmet III, built in 1726.

Fountain set into the platform below the İskele Mosque

Yeni Valide Mosque ❹
Yeni Valide Camii

Hakimiyeti Milliye Cad, Üsküdar.
Map 10 B2. 🚊 *Üsküdar.* ◯ *daily.*

A CROSS THE main square from İskele Mosque, the Yeni Valide Mosque, or New Mosque of the Sultan's Mother, was built by Ahmet III between 1708 and 1710 to

The *mektep* (Koranic school) over the gate of Yeni Valide Mosque

honour his mother, Gülnuş Emetullah. The complex is entered through a large gateway, with the *mektep* (Koranic school) built above it. This leads into a spacious courtyard. The buildings in the complex date from an important turning point in Ottoman architecture. The mosque is in the classical style, yet there are Baroque embellishments on the tomb of the Valide Sultan, the neighbouring *sebil* (kiosk from which drinks were served) and the *şadırvan*.

Atik Valide Mosque ❺
Atik Valide Camii

Çinili Camii Sok, Üsküdar. **Map** 10 C3.
🚌 *12C (from Üsküdar).* ◯ *prayer times only.*

T HE ATİK VALİDE MOSQUE, set on the hill above Üsküdar, was one of the most extensive mosque complexes in Istanbul. The name translates as the Old Mosque of the Sultan's Mother, as the mosque was built for Nur Banu, the Venetian-born wife of Selim II ("the Sot") and the mother of Murat III. She was the first of the sultans' mothers to rule the Ottoman Empire from the harem *(see p25)*.

Dome in the entrance to Atik Valide Mosque

Sinan completed the mosque, which was his last major work, in 1583. It has a wide shallow dome which rests on five semidomes, with a flat arch over the entrance portal.

The interior is surrounded on three sides by galleries, the undersides of which retain the rich black, red and gold stencilling typical of the period. The mihrab apse is almost completely covered with panels of fine İznik tiles *(see p161)*, while the mihrab itself and the *minbar* are both made of beautifully carved marble. Side aisles were added to the north and south in the 17th century, while the grilles and architectural trompe l'oeil paintings on the royal loge in the western gallery date from the 18th century.

Outside, a door in the north wall of the courtyard leads down a flight of stairs to the *medrese*, where the *dershane* (classroom) projects out over the narrow street below, supported by an arch. Of the other buildings in the complex, the *şifahane* (hospital) is the only one which has been restored and is open to the public. Located just to the east of the mosque, it consists of 40 cells around a courtyard and was in use well into the 20th century.

Women attending an Islamic class in the Tiled Mosque

Tiled Mosque ➏
Çinili Camii

Çinili Camii Sok, Üsküdar. **Map** 10 C3.
🚢 Üsküdar, then 20 mins walk.
🕐 prayer times only.

THIS PRETTY little mosque is best known for the fine tiles from which it takes its name. It dates from 1640 and is noticeably smaller than other royal foundations of the 17th century. This is partly because by the middle of the century much of Istanbul's prime land had already been built on, and the size of the plot did not allow for a larger building. There was also a trend away from endowing yet more enormous mosque complexes in the city.

The mosque was founded by Mahpeyker Kösem Sultan. As the wife of Sultan Ahmet I *(see p31)*, and mother of sultans Murat IV and İbrahim the Mad, she wielded great influence. Indeed, she was one of the last of the powerful harem women *(see p25)*.

In the courtyard is a massive, roofed ablutions fountain. The adjacent *medrese (see p36)*, however, is tiny. The façade and interior of the mosque are covered with İznik tiles *(see p161)* in turquoise, white, grey and a range of blues. There are none of the red and green pigments associated with the heyday of İznik tile production, but the designs are still exquisite. Even the conical cap of the marble *minbar* is tiled, and the carving on the *minbar* itself is picked out in green, red and gold paint.

The mosque's Turkish bath is on Çinili Hamam Sokağı. It has been renovated and is used by local residents.

Karaca Ahmet Cemetery ➐
Karaca Ahmet Mezarlığı

Nuh Kuyusu Cad, Selimiye. **Map** 10 C4. 🚌 12. 🕐 8:30am–5:30pm daily. **Tomb** 🕐 9:30am–4:30pm daily.

SPRAWLING OVER a large area, this cemetery is a pleasant place in which to stroll among old cypress trees and look at ancient tombstones. The earliest dated stone is from 1521, although the cemetery itself, one of the largest in Turkey, is thought to date from 1338.

The carvings on each tombstone tell a story *(see p121)*. A man's tomb is indicated by a fez or a turban. The style of the turban denotes the status of the deceased. Women's stones are adorned with carved flowers, hats and shawls.

Crimean War memorial in the British War Cemetery

Standing on the corner of Gündoğumu Caddesi and Nuh Kuyusu Caddesi is the tomb of Karaca Ahmet himself. This warrior died fighting in the Turkish conquest of the Byzantine towns of Chrysopolis and Chalcedon (Üsküdar and Kadıköy) in the mid-14th century. The tomb and monument to his favourite horse date from the 19th century.

Selimiye Barracks ➑
Selimiye Kışlası

Çeşme-i Kebir Cad, Selimiye.
Map 10 B5. 📞 *(0216) 343 73 10.*
🏛 *Harem.* 🚌 *12.* 🕐 *by appointment only.*

THE SELİMİYE BARRACKS were originally built by Selim III in 1799 to house his New Army, with which he hoped to replace the Janissaries *(see p127)*. He failed in his attempt, and was deposed and killed in a Janissary insurrection in 1807–8 *(see p28)*. The barracks burnt down shortly afterwards. The present building, which dominates the skyline of the Asian shore, was started by Mahmut II in 1828, after he had finally disbanded the Janissary corps. Abdül Mecit I added three more wings between 1842 and 1853.

The barracks were used as a military hospital during the Crimean War (1853–6). They became famously associated with Florence Nightingale *(see p43)*, who lived and worked in the northeast tower from 1854. The rooms she occupied are now a museum, and are the only part of the barracks open to the public. They contain their original furniture, copies of some of the pamphlets she wrote on military nursing, and the lamp from which she gained the epitaph "Lady of the Lamp".

Visitor praying at the tomb of the warrior Karaca Ahmet

Haydarpaşa Station, terminus for trains arriving from Anatolia

The Great Hill of Pines ⓾

Büyük Çamlıca

Çamlıca. 🚌 11F, KÇ1; then 30 mins walk. **Park** ⬚ 9am–midnight daily.

O N A CLEAR DAY the view from the top of this hill takes in the Princes' Islands, the Sea of Marmara, the Golden Horn and Beyoğlu, and the Bosphorus as far as the Black Sea. It is even possible to see snow-capped Mount Uludağ near Bursa (see p169) to the south. The Great Hill of Pines, 4 km (2.5 miles) east of Üsküdar, is the highest point in Istanbul, at 261 m (856 ft) above sea level. Even the forest of radio and TV masts further down the slopes of the hill does not obscure the view.

The park at the summit, created by the Turkish Touring and Automobile Club (see p175) in 1980, is laid out with gardens, marble kiosks and two 18th-century-style cafés.

Neighbouring Küçük Çamlıca (Small Hill of Pines), located to the south, is rather less cultivated and consequently attracts fewer tourists to its little tea garden. It is another lovely place for a stroll, again with beautiful views.

Two other sites near the barracks – the Selimiye Mosque and the British War Cemetery – are both worth seeing. Built in 1804, the mosque is in a lovely garden courtyard. The interior is filled with light from tiers of windows set in high arches. It is simply decorated with a classically painted dome and grey marble *minbar*. The royal pavilion in the northwest corner of the mosque compound is flanked by graceful arches.

The British War Cemetery is a short walk south, on Burhan Felek Caddesi. It contains the graves of men who died in the Crimean War, in World War I at Gallipoli (see p170) and in World War II in the Middle East. There is no sign outside and opening hours vary, but the caretaker will usually be there to let you in.

Haydarpaşa Station ⑨

Haydarpaşa Garı

Haydarpaşa İstasyon Cad, Haydarpaşa. 🕾 (0216) 336 04 75. 🚆 Haydarpaşa or Kadıköy. ⬚ daily.

T HE WATERFRONT location and grandeur of Haydarpaşa Station, together with the neighbouring tiled jetty, make it the most impressive point of arrival or departure in Istanbul. The first Anatolian railway line, which was built in 1873, ran from here to İznik (see p160). The extension of this railway was a major part of Abdül Hamit II's drive to modernize

the Ottoman Empire. Lacking sufficient funds to continue the project, he applied for help to his German ally, Kaiser Wilhelm II (see p43). The Deutsche Bank agreed to invest in the construction and operation of the railway. In 1898 German engineers were contracted to build the new railway lines running across Anatolia and beyond into the far reaches of the Ottoman Empire. At the same time a number of stations were built. Haydarpaşa, the grandest of these, was completed in 1908. Trains run from Haydarpaşa into the rest of Asia.

FLORENCE NIGHTINGALE

A 19th-century painting of Florence Nightingale in Selimiye Barracks

The British nurse Florence Nightingale (1820–1910) was a tireless campaigner for hospital, military and social reform. During the Crimean War, in which Britain and France fought on the Ottoman side against the Russian Empire, she organized a party of 38 British nurses. They took charge of medical services at the Selimiye Barracks in Scutari (Üsküdar) in 1854. By the time she returned to Britain in 1856, at the end of the war, the mortality rate in the barracks had decreased from 20 to 2 percent, and the fundamental principles of modern nursing had been established. On her return home, Florence Nightingale opened a training school for nurses.

BEYOND
ISTANBUL

DENİZ KUŞU

THE BOSPHORUS

I F THE NOISE and bustle of the city get too much, nothing can beat a trip up the Bosphorus *(see pp144–9)*, the straits separating Europe and Asia, which join the Black Sea and the Sea of Marmara. The easiest way to travel is by boat. An alternative is to explore the sights along the shores at your own pace. For much of their length the shores are lined with handsome buildings: wooden waterside villas known as yalis, graceful mosques and opulent 19th-century palaces. The grander residences along the

Sait Halim Paşa Yali on the Bosphorus

Bosphorus have waterfront entrances. These date from the days when wooden caïques, boats powered by a strong team of oarsmen, were a popular form of transport along the straits among the city's wealthier inhabitants. Interspersed between the monumental architecture are former fishing villages, where you will find some of Istanbul's finest clubs and restaurants. The Bosphorus is especially popular in summer, when the cool breezes off the water provide welcome relief from the heat of the city.

SIGHTS AT A GLANCE

Museums and Palaces
Aşiyan Museum ❺
Beylerbeyi Palace ❷
Khedive's Palace ❿
Küçüksu Palace ❹
Maslak Pavilion ❾
Sadberk Hanım Museum ⓬

Towns and Villages
Bebek ❸
Beykoz ⓫
Kanlıca ❼
Rumeli Kavağı ⓭

Historic Buildings
Bosphorus Bridge ❶
Fortress of Europe ❻

Parks
Emirgan Park ❽

KEY

▢	Central Istanbul
▢	Greater Istanbul
⛴	Ferry stops on Bosphorus trip
═	Motorway
▬	Main road

0 kilometres   5

0 miles   5

THE BOSPHORUS TRIP

This vital navigational channel is 33 km (20 miles) long and varies between 700 m (2,300 ft) and 3.6 km (2 miles) wide. The trip has been divided into three stages, indicated by the boxes on this map.

Black Sea

Kilyos

Rumeli Feneri

See pp148–9

D016

See pp146–7

O-2 (E80)

O-1(E5)

D020

O-3

See pp144–5

D100

O-4 (E80)

D020

O-2 (E80)

Sea of Marmara

◁ **Anadolu Hisarı, the Fortress of Asia, on the Asian shore of the Bosphorus**

The Bosphorus suspension bridge between Ortaköy and Beylerbeyi

Bosphorus Bridge ❶
Boğaziçi Köprüsü

Ortaköy and Beylerbeyi. **Map** 9 F2.
🚌 200 (double decker, from Taksim).

SPANNING the Bosphorus between the districts of Ortaköy and Beylerbeyi, this was the first bridge to be built across the straits that divide Istanbul. Known also as Atatürk Bridge, it was finished on 29 October 1973, the 50th anniversary of the inauguration of the Turkish Republic (see p29). It is the world's sixth longest suspension bridge, at a length of 1,560 m (5,120 ft), and it reaches 64 m (210 ft) above water level.

Beylerbeyi Palace ❷
Beylerbeyi Sarayı

Çayırbaşı Cad, Asian side. 📞 (0216) 321 93 20. 🚌 15 (from Üsküdar).
🚇 from Üsküdar. ⏰ 9:30am–5pm Tue–Wed & Fri–Sun. 📷 📹

DESIGNED IN the Baroque style by Sarkis Balyan, Beylerbeyi Palace seems fairly restrained compared to the excesses of the earlier Dolmabahçe (see pp128–9) or Küçüksu (see p140) palaces. It was built by Sultan Abdül Aziz (see p28) in 1860–65 as a summer residence and a place to entertain visiting heads of state. Empress Eugénie of France visited Beylerbeyi on her way to the opening of the Suez Canal in 1869 and had her face slapped by the sultan's

mother for daring to enter the palace on the arm of Abdül Aziz. Other regal visitors to the palace included the Duke and Duchess of Windsor.

The palace looks its most attractive from the Bosphorus, from where its two bathing pavilions – one for the harem and the other for the selamlık (the men's quarters) – can best be seen.

The most attractive room is the reception hall, which has a pool and fountain. Running water was popular in Ottoman houses for its pleasant sound and cooling effect in the heat. Egyptian straw matting covers the palace's floors as a form of insulation. The crystal chandeliers are mostly Bohemian and the carpets (see pp210–11) are from Hereke.

Ornate landing at the top of the stairs in Beylerbeyi Palace

Beylerbeyi impressed many visiting dignitaries, including the Empress Eugénie of France, who was so delighted by the palace that she had a copy of the window in the guest room made for her bedroom in Tuileries Palace, in Paris.

Bebek ❸

European side. 🚌 25E, 40.

BEBEK IS ONE OF the most fashionable villages along the Bosphorus. It is famous for its marzipan (badem ezmesi, see p205), and for the cafés which line its waterfront. It was once a favourite location for summer residences and palaces of Ottoman aristocrats, and at the end of the 19th century, caïques (see p126) of merrymakers would set off on moonlit cruises from the bay, accompanied by a boat of musicians. The women in the party would trail pieces of velvet or satin edged with silver fishes in the water behind them while the musicians played to the revellers.

Detail of the gate of the Egyptian Consulate, Bebek

One of the hosts of these parties was the mother of the last Khedive of Egypt (see p27), Abbas Hilmi II. Built in the late 19th century, the only remaining monumental architecture in Bebek is the Egyptian Consulate, which, like the Khedive's Palace (see p142), was commissioned by Abbas Hilmi II. The steep, mansard roof of this yalı is reminiscent of 19th-century northern French architecture. There are lighter Art Nouveau touches including the railings draped in wrought-iron vines and a rising sun between the two turrets, symbolizing the beginning of the new century.

The Khedive used the yalı as a summer palace until he was deposed by the British in 1914. From then on to the present day it has been used as the Egyptian Consulate.

Yalis on the Bosphorus

At the end of the 17th century, *paşas*, grand viziers and other distinguished citizens of Ottoman Istanbul began to build themselves elegant villas – yalis – along the shores of the Bosphorus. These served as summer residences, and the styles employed reflected their owners' prestige. Since then, the

Old yali at Kandilli, Asian side

yalis that have been built have become larger and more elaborate, adopting Baroque, Art Nouveau and modern styles of architecture. Most of them still conform to a traditional plan, making maximum use of the waterfront and, inside, having a large sitting room surrounded by bedrooms.

Köprülü Amcazade Hüseyin Paşa Yali (see p147), near Anadolu Hisarı, was built in 1698 and is the oldest building on the shores of the Bosphorus. Early yalis, like this one, were built at the water's edge, but in later years they were constructed a little way inland.

A cumba, or bay window, projects over the water.

Traditional wooden yalis were normally painted rust red, a colour known as "Ottoman rose".

Later yalis, built from the 18th century, were painted in pastel shades.

A bracket supports the projecting upstairs rooms.

Fethi Ahmet Paşa Yali (see p145), or Mocan Yali, at Kuzguncuk, was built in the late 18th century. Among visitors were the composer Franz Liszt and the architect Le Corbusier (see p42). Famous as the "Pink Yali", after its boldly decorated exterior, the house is almost invisible from the land.

Ethem Pertev Yali (see p147), at Kanlıca, is a prime example of the so-called "cosmopolitan period" of yali building, between 1867 and 1908. It has a boat house below and combines intricate wood carving, a later development, with the more traditional features of a yali.

Baroque influence is clearly visible in the ornately carved balcony.

Boat house under the yali

The Egyptian Consulate (see p146) at Bebek clearly shows the influence of Art Nouveau, with its wrought iron railings worked into a leaf design. It was commissioned by the Khedive of Egypt (see p138) around 1900.

A narrow quay often separates 19th-century yalis from the shore.

French-style mansard roof

Ornamental details were inspired by Austrian Art Nouveau designs.

Küçüksu Palace
Küçüksu Kasrı

Küçüksu Cad, Asian side. ☎ (0216) 332 02 37. 🚌 15 (from Üsküdar) or 101 (from Beşiktaş). ◯ 9:30am–5pm Tue, Wed & Fri–Sun.

MARBLE-FRONTED Küçüksu Palace has one of the prettiest façades on the shores of the Bosphorus. Particularly attractive is the curving double staircase which leads up to its main waterside entrance.

Sultan Abdül Mecit I *(see p28)* employed court architect Nikoğos Balyan *(see p128)* to build this palace to accommodate his entourage on their visits to the Sweet Waters of Asia. This was the romantic name European visitors gave to the Küçüksu and Göksu rivers. For centuries the Ottoman nobility liked to indulge in picnics in the meadows between the streams.

On the completion of Küçüksu Palace in 1856, the sultan complained that it was too plain and demanded more ornamentation, including his monogram engraved on the façade. Later, in the reign of Abdül Aziz *(see p28)*, the façade was further embellished, with the result that it is hard to follow the lines of the original architecture.

The room arrangement is typically Ottoman, with a large central salon opening on to four corner rooms on each floor. The interior decor was carried out by Séchan, the decorator of the Paris Opera, soon after the palace was finished. The carpets are fine examples from Hereke *(see pp210–11)* and the chandeliers Bohemian crystal.

Küçüksu Palace, an ornate Bosphorus residence built in 1856

On the shore near Küçüksu Palace is the picturesque, turreted Fountain of the Valide Sultan Mihrişah. Dating from 1796, it is in the Baroque style.

Kıbrıslı Yali, just south of the palace, was built in 1760. At over 60 m (200 ft), its brilliant white façade is the longest of any yali *(see p139)* along the Bosphorus. A little further south again is Kırmızı Yali, the Red Yali, so called for its distinctive crimson colour. This yali was constructed around 1790 for an aristocratic European family, the Ostrorogs.

Aşiyan Museum ❺
Aşiyan Müzesi

Aşiyan Yolu, Asian side. ☎ (0212) 263 69 86. 🚌 25E, 40. ◯ 9am–5pm Tue, Wed & Fri–Sun.

AŞIYAN, OR BIRD'S NEST, is the former home of Tevfik Fikret (1867–1915), a teacher, utopian visionary and one of Turkey's leading poets. The wooden mansion, built by Fikret himself in 1906, is an attractive example of Turkish vernacular architecture. The views from its upper-storey balcony are stunning.

On show are the poet's possessions and *Sis* (Fog), a painting·by Caliph Abdül Mecit (1922–24), inspired by Fikret's poem of that name.

Fortress of Europe ❻
Rumeli Hisarı

Yahya Kemal Cad, European side. ☎ (0212) 263 53 05. 🚌 25E, 40. ◯ 9:30am–4:30pm Tue–Sun. 🖻

THIS FORTRESS was built by Mehmet the Conqueror in 1452 as his first step in the conquest of Constantinople *(see p24)*. Situated at the narrowest point of the Bosphorus, the fortress controlled a major Byzantine supply route. Across the straits is Anadolu Hisarı, or the Fortress of Asia, which was built in the 14th century by Beyazıt I.

The Fortress of Europe's layout was planned by Mehmet himself. While his grand vizier

The Fortress of Europe, built by Mehmet the Conqueror to enable him to capture Constantinople

(see p27) and two other viziers were each responsible for the building of one of the three great towers, the sultan took charge of the walls. In the spirit of competition which evolved, the fortress was completed in four months.

The new fortress was soon nicknamed Boğazkesen – meaning "Throat-cutter" or "Strait-cutter". It was garrisoned by a force of Janissaries *(see p127)*. These troops trained their cannons on the straits to prevent the passage of foreign ships. After they had sunk a Venetian vessel, this approach to Constantinople was cut off. Following the conquest of the city, the fortress lost its importance as a military base and was used as a prison, particularly for out-of-favour foreign envoys and prisoners-of-war.

The structure was restored in 1953. Open-air theatre performances are now staged here during the Istanbul Music and Dance Festival *(see p45)*.

Café serving the yoghurt for which Kanlıca is famous

Kanlıca ❼

Asian side. 🚌 *15, 101.*

A DELICIOUS, creamy type of yoghurt is Kanlıca's best known asset. You will find this on the menu at cafés in the village square next to the ferry landing. The İskender Paşa Mosque, overlooking this square, is a minor work by Sinan *(see p91)*, built for Sultan Süleyman's vizier İskender Paşa in 1559–60. There have been changes to the original building: the wooden dome has been

replaced by a flat roof, and the porch was added later.

There are a number of yalis in and around Kanlıca, including the Köprülü Amcazade Hüseyin Paşa Yali *(see p139)*, the oldest surviving Bosphorus yali, just south of the village. This was built in 1698 by Mustafa II's grand vizier Hüseyin Paşa, the fourth grand vizier from the Köprülü family. The Treaty of Karlowitz, in which the Ottomans acknowledged the loss of territory to Austria, Venice, Poland and Russia, was signed here in 1699 *(see p25)*. All that remains of the yali, which is not open to visitors, is a T-shaped salon, its dome only saved by wooden props.

Emirgan Park ❽
Emirgan Parkı

Emirgan Sahil Yollu, European side.
🔲 *(0212) 277 57 82.* 🚌 *25E, 40.*
🔵 *8am–8pm daily.*

E MIRGAN PARK IS the location of some famous tulip gardens, which are at their finest for the annual Tulip Festival in April *(see p44)*. Tulips originally grew wild on the Asian steppes and were first propagated in large quantities in Holland. They were later reintroduced to Turkey by

Pembe Köşk in Emirgan Park

Mehmet IV (1648–87). The reign of his son Ahmet III is known as the Tulip Period *(see p25)* because of his fascination with the flowers.

In the late 19th century Sultan Abdül Aziz gave the park to the Egyptian Khedive *(see p27)*, İsmail Paşa, and its three pavilions date from that era. They are known by their colours. The Sarı Köşk (Yellow Pavilion), built in the style of a Swiss chalet, suffered fire damage in 1954 and was rebuilt in concrete with a façade resembling the original. The Beyaz Köşk (White Pavilion) is a Neo-Classical style mansion, while the Pembe Köşk (Pink Pavilion), whose terrace affords beautiful views of the Bosphorus, is in the style of a traditional Ottoman house. The pavilions have been refurbished and are due to reopen shortly as cafés.

BIRDS OF THE BOSPHORUS

In September and October, thousands of white storks and birds of prey fly over the Bosphorus on their way from their breeding grounds in eastern Europe to wintering regions in Africa. Large birds usually prefer to cross narrow straits like the Bosphorus rather than fly over an expanse of open water such as the Mediterranean. Among birds of prey on this route you can see the lesser spotted eagle and the honey buzzard. The birds also cross the straits in spring on their way to Europe but, before the breeding season, they are fewer in number.

The white stork, which migrates over the straits

Hot-house plants in the conservatory at Maslak Pavilions

retains an Oriental feel, with a low sofa and a central coal-burning brazier.

Behind the small but elegant Mabeyn-i Hümayun (the Private Apartments) is a large conservatory full of camellias, ferns and banana plants. Nearby, at the edge of the forest stands a tiny octagonal folly with an ornate balcony called the Çadır Köşkü, or Tent Pavilion, which now serves as a bookshop. The Paşalar Dairesi (the Apartments of the Paşa) are located at the other side of the complex.

Maslak Pavilions ❾
Maslak Kasırları

Büyükdere Cad, Maslak. █ (0212) 276 10 22. ▥ 40S (from Taksim). ◐ 9am–5pm Tue, Wed & Fri–Sun (closes at 4pm in winter).

THIS SMALL GROUP of buildings was a royal hunting lodge and country residence, much prized for its leafy setting and glorious views. The pavilions were built in the early and mid-19th century, when the focus of Istanbul court life moved away from Topkapı Palace (see pp54–9), in the centre of the city, to the sultans' lavish estates along the shore of the Bosphorus. The buildings are

thought to date mainly from the reign of Abdül Aziz (1861–76). He gave Maslak to his son Abdül Hamit in the hope that the crown prince would then stop sailing at Tarabya (see p148), which his father regarded as unsafe.

The four main buildings are less ornate than other 19th-century pavilions in Istanbul. This is possibly due to the austere character of Abdül Hamit. He personally crafted the balustrades of the beautiful central staircase in the Kasr-ı Hümayun (the Pavilion of the Sultan) during his stay here. His initials in Western script – AH – can also be seen in the headpieces over the mirrors. The pavilion's lounge

Khedive's Palace ❿
Hıdiv Kasrı

Hıdiv Kasrı Yolu 32, Çubuklu. █ (0216) 425 06 03. ▥ 15 (from Üsküdar) or 221 (from Taksim), then 30 mins walk. ◐ 9am–11pm daily. ▣

BUILT IN 1900 by the last khedive (the hereditary viceroy of Egypt, see p27), Abbas Hilmi II, this summer palace is one of the most striking buildings of its era in Istanbul. Its tower is an imposing landmark for those travelling up the Bosphorus.

The Italian architect Delfo Seminati based the design of the palace on an Italianate villa, throwing in Art Nouveau and vernacular Ottoman elements. Most impressive of all is the circular entrance hall. This is entered through Art Nouveau glass doors and features a stained-glass skylight above a central fountain surrounded by eight pairs of elegant columns.

Renovated by the Turkish Touring Club (TTOK, see p237), the palace is now open to visitors as a luxury hotel and restaurant (see p198).

Beykoz ⓫

Asian shore. ▥ 15 (from Üsküdar) or 221 (from Taksim).

BEYKOZ IS FAMOUS for its walnuts (beykoz means "prince's walnut") and for the glass produced here in the 19th century. The distinctive, mainly opaque, Beykoz glass (see p205), with its rich colours

JASON AND THE SYMPLEGADES

The upper Bosphorus features in the Greek myth of Jason's search for the Golden Fleece. The Argonauts, Jason's crew, helped a local king, Phineus, by ridding him of the harpies (female demons) sent by Zeus to torment him. In return, the king advised them on how to tackle the Symplegades, two rocks at the mouth of the Bosphorus which were reputed to clash together, making passage impossible. His advice was to send a dove in advance of the ship; if it went through safely, so would the ship. This the Argonauts duly did, and the rocks clipped the dove's tail feathers. The Argo then went through with only some damage to its stern.

Jason and the Argonauts making their way through the Symplegades

Fountain in the village square at Beykoz

and graceful designs, can be seen in museums all over Turkey. Nowadays, the village's main attraction is its fish restaurants *(see pp192–3)*, which serve excellent turbot.

A fine 18th-century fountain stands in the central square. Built on the orders of Sultan Mahmut I *(see p31)*, it is called the İshak Ağa Çeşmesi, after the customs inspector who inaugurated it in 1746. It has a large domed and colonnaded loggia, and 10 conduits spouting a constant stream of water.

Industrialization, particularly in the form of bottling and leather factories, has taken its toll on the village. Only a few buildings hint at its former splendour. The attractive 19th-century waterside mansion, Halil Ethem Yali, is an interesting mixture of Neo-Classical and Neo-Baroque styles. It stands on İbrahim Kelle Caddesi, south of the ferry landing.

Attic vase, Sadberk Hanım Museum

Sadberk Hanım Museum ⓬

Sadberk Hanım Müzesi

Piyasa Cad 25–29, Büyükdere,
📞 *(0212) 242 38 13.* 🚌 *25E.* ⭕
10:30am– 6pm Thu–Tue. 📷 🚫

OCCUPYING TWO archetypal wooden Bosphorus yalis *(see p139)*, the Sadberk Hanım Museum was the first private museum to open in Turkey,

in 1981. The larger of these yalis, the Azaryan Yali, is the former summer house of the wealthy Koç family. A four-storey mansion, it was built in 1911 and, like many buildings of the time, was inspired by European architecture. The distinctive criss-crossed wooden slats on its façade distinguish it from the neighbouring buildings. It contains some fine ethnographic artifacts collected by Sadberk Hanım, wife of the industrialist Vehbi Koç, to whom the museum is dedicated. She found many of them in the Grand Bazaar *(see pp98–9)* and in Istanbul's other markets. A number of exhibits are laid out in tableaux depicting 19th-century Ottoman society. These include a henna party, at which the groom's female relatives would apply henna to the hands of his bride; and a circumcision bed, with a young boy dressed in traditional costume. Also worth seeking out in this section is a display of infinitely delicate *oya*, Turkish embroideries. These remarkably life-like pieces imitate garlands of flowers, such as carnations, roses, hyacinths and lilies and were used to fringe scarves and petticoats. Some of the examples on show were made in palace harems in the 18th century.

The neighbouring building is called the Sevgi Gönül Wing. Also dating from the early 20th century, it was bought to house the archaeological collection of Hüseyin Kocabaş, a friend of the Koç family. Displays are ordered chronologically, ranging from the late Neolithic period (5400 BC) to the Ottoman era. Exhibits are changed from time to time, but typically include Assyrian cuneiform tablets dating from the second millennium BC, Phrygian metalwork and Greek pottery from the late Geometric Period (750–680 BC). Among the other items usually on display are a large selection of Roman gold jewellery and Byzantine reliquary and pendent crosses.

Rumeli Kavağı ⓭

European shore. 🚌 *25A (from Beşiktaş)* ⛴ Rumeli Kavağı.

THIS PRETTY VILLAGE has a broad selection of restaurants specializing in fish and fried mussels. They are clustered around the harbour from where there are views of the wild, rocky shores on the approach to the Black Sea. On the hill above Rumeli Kavağı are the scant remains of a castle, İmros Kalesi, built by Manuel I Comnenus *(see p19)* in the 12th century to guard his customs point.

Further up the Bosphorus, the shore road leads from Rumeli Kavağı to Altın Kum beach. This small strip of sand backed by restaurants is popular with local people.

The fishing village of Rumeli Kavağı, on the upper Bosphorus

The Bosphorus Trip

Ceremonial gate, Çırağan Palace

ONE OF THE GREAT PLEASURES of a visit to Istanbul is a cruise up the Bosphorus. You can go on a pre-arranged guided tour or take one of the small boats that tout for passengers at Eminönü. But there is no better way to travel than on the official trip run by Turkish Maritime Lines (TDİ, *see pp234–5*), which is described on the following pages. Laden with sightseers, the TDİ ferry makes a round-trip to the upper Bosphorus two or three times daily, stopping at six piers along the way, including a leisurely stop at Anadolu Kavağı for lunch. You can return to Eminönü on the same boat or make your way back to the city by bus, dolmuş or taxi.

LOCATOR MAP

Naval Museum (see p126)

Dolmabahçe Palace

This opulent 19th-century palace (see pp128–9) has a series of ornate gates along the waterfront. These were used by the sultan to enter the palace from his imperial barge.

Barbaros Hayrettin Paşa   **Beşik**

İnönü Stadium

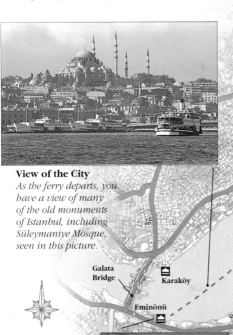

Kabataş

Museum of Fine Arts (see p126)

View of the City

As the ferry departs, you have a view of many of the old monuments of Istanbul, including Süleymaniye Mosque, seen in this picture.

Dolmabahçe Mosque was completed in 1853 at the same time as the palace (see p126).

Galata Bridge

Karaköy

Eminönü

Eminönü Port

The official Bosphorus ferry departs from Istanbul's busiest ferry terminal.

Leander's Tower

One the landmarks of the city, this white tower stands prominently in mid-channel, a short way off the Asian shore (see p130).

See pages 146–7

Kuleli Military School has a pretty wooden mosque beside it.

Arnavutköy

Galatasaray Island is a private sports complex.

Çengelköy

Mecidiye Mosque
Sultan Abdül Mecit I ordered the construction of this Baroque mosque on a promontory near the ferry pier at Ortaköy (see p122).

Sadullah Paşa Yali, built in the 1760s, is painted red-brown, as are many old yalis *(see p139).*

Beylerbeyi

Ortaköy *(see p122)*

Yıldız Park *(see pp124–5)*

Bosphorus Bridge *(see p138)*

Fethi Ahmet Paşa Yali *(see p139)*

Çırağan Palace dates from 1874, but had to be rebuilt after a devastating fire in 1910. It is now a luxury hotel *(see p123).*

Kuzguncuk

İskele Mosque *(see p131)*

Üsküdar

Beylerbeyi Palace
The palace grounds contain two shore-side bathing pavilions: one for men and the other for the women of the harem (see p138).

```
0 metres        750
0 yards         750
```

KEY

	Motorway
	Main road
	Other road
	Built-up area
	Ferry boarding point
– –	Route of Bosphorus trip
	Yali *(see p139)*
	Viewpoint

Şemsi Paşa Mosque
The circular windows of this 16th-century mosque by Sinan (see p130) are an allusion to Şemsi Paşa, whose name derives from the word "shams", meaning "sun" in Arabic.

arem

The Middle Bosphorus

Paşabahçe glass vase

NORTH OF ARNAVUTKÖY, the outskirts of Istanbul give way to attractive towns and villages, such as Bebek with its popular bars and cafés. The Bosphorus flows fast and deep as the channel reaches its narrowest point – 700 m (2,300 ft) across – on the approach to the Fatih Sultan Mehmet suspension bridge. It was at this point that the Persian emperor Darius and his army crossed the Bosphorus on a pontoon bridge in 512 BC, on their way to fight the Greeks. Two famous old fortresses face each other across the water near here. Several elegant yalis are also found in this part of the strait, particularly in the region known to Europeans as the Sweet Waters of Asia.

LOCATOR MAP

İstinye Bay
This huge natural bay, the largest inlet on the Bosphorus, has been used as a dock for centuries. There is a fish market along the quay every morning.

Emirgan Park
Situated above the pretty village of Emirgan, this park is famous for its tulips in spring (see p44). The grounds contain pleasant cafés and pavilions (see p141).

The Bosphorus University, one of the most prestigious in Turkey, enjoys spectacular views. Almost all teaching here is in English.

Bebek
(*see p138*)

Egyptian Consulate
(*see p138*)

Kandilli

Fortress of Europe
Situated at the narrowest point on the Bosphorus, this fortress (see p140) was built by Mehmet II in 1452, as a prelude to his invasion of Constantinople (see p24).

Arnavutköy

See pages 144–5

See pages
148–9

Yeniköy
Handsome 19th-century villas define the waterfront of this village dating from Byzantine times.

Yeniköy

Paşabahçe

Sait Halim Paşa Yali

İstinye

The Paşabahçe Glass Works
produce Turkey's finest glassware *(see p205).*

Kanlıca is a pretty village *(see p141)* with a mosque built by Sinan *(see p91).* It is also known for its delicious yoghurt.

Çubuklu

Karlıca

Ethem Pertev Yali *(see p139)*

Khedive's Palace
Above Çubuklu stands the palace built by the last viceroy of Egypt (see p27), Abbas Hilmi Paşa, in around 1900. It is now a hotel and restaurant (see p142).

Fortress of Asia
Fifty years older than the Fortress of Europe, this fortress was built by Beyazıt I just before the failed Ottoman siege of Constantinople in 1396–7.

Fatih Sultan
Mehmet
Bridge

Köprülü
mcazade
üseyin
aşa Yali
see p141)

Anadolu
Hisarı

üçüksu
alace
ee p140)

mızı
(see
0)

Göksu River
This pretty little river and the Küçüksu River south of it are together known as the Sweet Waters of Asia (see p140).

KEY

▨	Motorway
▨	Main road
▨	Other road
🌿	Built-up area
⛴	Ferry boarding point
– –	Route of Bosphorus trip
⊞	Yali *(see p139)*
✣	Viewpoint

0 metres   750

0 yards   750

The Upper Bosphorus

Black Sea mussels

IN THE 19TH CENTURY ambassadors to Turkey built their summer retreats between Tarabya and Büyükdere, on the European side of the Bosphorus. As the hills fall more steeply towards the shore along the upper reaches of the straits, the built-up area peters out. The public ferry pauses for lunch at Anadolu Kavağı on the Asian side before heading back to Istanbul. You can also catch a bus or dolmuş back to the city. The Bosphorus itself continues for another 8 km (5 miles) or so to meet the Black Sea, but the land on both sides of this stretch is now under military control.

LOCATOR MAP

Sadberk Hanım Museum

This museum, housed in two wooden yalıs, has variety of interesting exhibits. These include antiquities from Greece and Rome, and Ottoman craftwork (see p143).

Sarıyer

Büyükdere

Tarabya Bay

The small village set within a lovely bay first attracted wealthy Greeks in the 18th century. The bay still thrives as an exclusive resort with up-market fish restaurants.

Huber Köşkü is a 19th century yalı owned by the Turkish president.

FISHING ON THE BOSPHORUS

A multitude of fishing vessels ply the waters of the Bosphorus, ranging from large trawlers returning from the Black Sea to tiny rowing boats from which a line is cast into the water. On a trip up the Bosphorus you often see seine nets spread out in circles, suspended from floats on the surface. The

Fishing boats at Sarıyer, the main fishing port on the Bosphorus

main types of fish caught are mackerel, mullet, *hamsi* (similar to anchovy, *see p188*) and sardine. Much of the fish caught is sold at Istanbul's principal fish market in Kumkapı.

Rumeli Kavağı
This village is the most northerly ferry stop on the European side (see p143). From here the Bosphorus widens out to meet the Black Sea.

Anadolu Kavağı

Anadolu Kavağı
A short climb from this village – the last stop on the trip – brings you to a ruined 14th-century Byzantine fortress, the Genoese Castle, from which there are great views over the straits.

Beykoz
Beykoz is the largest fishing village along the Asian shore. Close to its village square, which has this fountain dating from 1746, are several fish restaurants which are very popular in summer (see p142).

Beykoz

0 metres 750

0 yards 750

Halil Ethem Yali
(see p143)

See pages 146–7

KEY

▩	Main road
	Other road
▨	Built-up area
⚓	Ferry boarding point
– –	Route of Bosphorus trip
⌗	Yali *(see p139)*
☀	Viewpoint

EXCURSIONS FROM ISTANBUL

*S*TANDING AT A NATURAL CROSSROADS, *Istanbul makes a good base for excursions into the neighbouring areas of Thrace and Anatolia – European and Asian Turkey respectively. Whether you want to see great Islamic architecture, immerse yourself in a busy bazaar, relax on an island or catch a glimpse of Turkey's rich birdlife, you will find a choice of destinations within easy reach of the city.*

On public holidays and weekends nearby resorts become crowded with Istanbul residents taking a break from the noisy city. For longer breaks, they head for the Mediterranean or Aegean, so summer is a good time to explore the Marmara and western Black Sea regions while they are quiet.

The country around Istanbul varies immensely from lush forests to open plains and, beyond them, impressive mountains. The Belgrade Forest is one of the closest green areas to the city if you want a short break. The Princes' Islands, where the pine forests and monasteries can be toured by a pleasant ride in a horse-and-carriage, are also just a short boat trip away from the city.

Window, Selimiye Mosque, Edirne

Further away, through rolling fields of bright yellow sunflowers, is Edirne, the former Ottoman capital. The town stands on a site first settled in the 7th century BC. It is visited today for its fine mosques, especially the Selimiye.

South of the Sea of Marmara is the pretty spa town of Bursa, originally a Greek city which was founded in 183 BC. Another early Ottoman capital, it has some fine architecture. Near the mouth of the straits of the Dardanelles (which link the Sea of Marmara to the Aegean) lie the ruins of the legendary city of Troy, dating from as early as 3600 BC. North of the Dardanelles are cemeteries commemorating the battles which were fought over the Gallipoli peninsula during World War I.

Boats in Burgaz Harbour on the Princes' Islands, a short ferry ride from Istanbul

◁ **The Green Tomb of Mehmet I in Bursa, one of the city's best-known landmarks**

Exploring Beyond Istanbul

W ITHIN A RADIUS of 250 km (150 miles) of Istanbul
there are many destinations worth visiting. To
the northwest is Edirne, an attractive riverside town
and the location of several fine mosques. South
of Istanbul is Bursa, which lies at the foot
of Uludağ, a mountain famed for its
skiing. Closer to Istanbul are the Black
Sea resorts of Şile and Kilyos, and the
Princes' Islands, popular in summer,
which are easily reached by ferry.
The war cemeteries of the Dardanelles and the site of ancient
Troy require a longer trip.

**The 15th-century Beyazıt II
Mosque in Edirne**

KEY

▦	Motorway
▦	Main road
░	Other road
▦	Scenic route
➤	River
☆	Viewpoint

0 kilometres 25

0 miles 25

SIGHTS AT A GLANCE

One of the main ski runs in Uludağ National Park

GETTING AROUND

The road network around Istanbul is steadily improving, and modern, cheap and efficient coaches (*see p236*) will get you to most places. Ferries and sea buses (*see p236*) cross the Sea of Marmara to ports on its southern shore and reach both the Princes' and Marmara Islands.

View over the picturesque city of Bursa

Edirne **❶**

STANDING ON THE RIVER TUNCA near the border with Greece, Edirne is a provincial university town which is home to one of Turkey's star attractions, the Selimiye Mosque *(see pp156–7)*. As this huge monument attests, Edirne was historically of great importance. It dates back to AD 125, when the Roman Emperor Hadrian joined two small towns to form Hadrianopolis, or Adrianople. For nearly a century, from when Murat I *(see p23)* took the city in 1361 until Constantinople was conquered in 1453 *(see p24)*, Edirne was the Ottoman capital. The town has one other claim to fame – the annual grease wrestling championships in July.

Entrance arch, Mosque of the Three Balconies

The colonnaded inner mosque courtyard, unlike most later examples, covers three times the area of the mosque itself. Inside, the mosque's impressive dome is supported on sweeping pendentives which arise just above head height.

Entrance to Beyazıt II Mosque viewed from its inner courtyard

❼ Beyazıt II Mosque
Beyazıt II Külliyesi
Yeni Maharet Cad. ⬤ *daily.* **Health Museum** ⓘ *(0284) 212 09 22.* ⬤ *8:30am–5:30pm daily.* ✦✦

Beyazıt II Mosque stands in a peaceful location on the northern bank of the Tunca River, 1.5 km (1 mile) from the town centre. It was built in 1484–8, soon after Beyazıt II *(see p30)* succeeded Mehmet the Conqueror *(see p24)* as sultan.

The mosque and its courtyards are open to the public. Of the surrounding buildings in the complex, the old hospital, which incorporated an asylum, has been converted into the **Health Museum**. Disturbed patients were treated in the asylum – a model of its time – with water, colour and flower therapies. The Turkish writer Evliya Çelebi (1611–84) reported that singers and instrumentalists would play soothing music here three times a week. Overuse of hashish was one of the commonest afflictions.

❼ Mosque of the Three Balconies
Üç Şerefeli Camii
Hükümet Cad. ⬤ *daily.* ✦

Until the fall of Constantinople, this was the grandest building in the early Ottoman state. It was finished in 1447 and takes its name from the three balconies adorning its southeast minaret, at the time the tallest in existence. In an unusual touch, the other three minarets of the mosque are each of a different design and height. Unlike its predecessors in

Bursa *(see pp162–8)*, the mosque has an open courtyard, setting a precedent for the great imperial mosques of Istanbul. The plan of its interior was also innovative. With minimal obstructions, the mihrab and *minbar* can both be seen from almost every corner of the prayer hall. Like the minarets, the dome, too, was the largest of its time.

❼ Old Mosque
Eski Cami
Talat Paşa Asfaltı. ⬤ *daily.* ✦

The oldest of Edirne's major mosques, this is a smaller version of the Great Mosque in Bursa *(see p164)*. The eldest son of Beyazıt I *(see p30)*, Süleyman, began the mosque in 1403, but it was his youngest son, Mehmet I, who completed it in 1414.

A perfect square, the mosque is divided by four massive piers into nine domed sections. On either side of the prayer hall entrance there are massive Arabic inscriptions proclaiming "Allah" and "Mohammed".

GREASE WRESTLING

The Kırkpınar Grease Wrestling Championships take place annually in July, on the island of Sarayiçi in the Tunca River. The event is famed throughout Turkey and accompanied by a week-long carnival. Before competing, the wrestlers dress

Grease wrestlers parading before they fight

in knee-length leather shorts *(kispet)* and grease themselves from head to foot in diluted olive oil. The master of ceremonies, the *cazgır*, then invites the competitors to take part in a high-stepping, arm-flinging parade across the field, accompanied by music played on a deep-toned drum *(davul)* and a single-reed oboe *(zurna)*. Wrestling bouts can last up to two hours and involve long periods of frozen, silent concentration interspersed by attempts to throw down the opponent.

🛏 Rüstem Paşa Caravanserai

Rüstem Paşa Kervansarayı
Çilingirler Cad 57.
🔲 (0284) 212 61 19.

Sinan (see p91) designed this caravanserai for Süleyman's most powerful grand vizier, Rüstem Paşa (see p88), in 1560–61. It was constructed in two distinct parts. The larger courtyard, or han (see p96), which is now the Rüstem Paşa Kervansaray Hotel (see p184), was built for the merchants of Edirne, while the smaller courtyard, now a student hostel, was an inn for other travellers.

A short walk away, on the other side of Saraçlar Caddesi, is the Semiz Ali Paşa Bazaar, where Edirne's merchants still sell their wares. This is another work of Sinan, dating from 1589. It consists of a long, narrow street of vaulted shops.

🏛 Museum of Turkish and Islamic Arts

Türk ve İslam Eserleri Müzesi
Kıyık Cad. 🔲 (0284) 225 11 20.
🔘 8am–5pm Tue–Sun. 🖼

Edirne's small collection of Turkish and Islamic works of art is attractively located in the *medrese* of the Selimiye Mosque (see pp156–7).

The museum's first room is devoted to the local sport of grease wrestling. It includes enlarged reproductions of miniatures depicting 600 years of the sport. These show the wrestling stars resplendent in their leather shorts, their skin glistening with olive oil.

Other objects on display in the museum include the original doors of the Beyazıt II Mosque. There are also military exhibits. Among them are some beautiful 18th-century Ottoman shields, with woven silk exteriors, and paintings of military subjects.

The tranquil 15th-century Muradiye Mosque

VISITORS' CHECKLIST

210 km (130 miles) NW of Istanbul. 🏠 398,000. 🚌 Londra Asfaltı, (0284) 235 26 73. 🚌 Talat Paşa Cad, (0284) 225 19 79. 🚇 Serhat Cad. 🛈 Hürriyet Meydanı 17, (0284) 213 92 08. 🛒 Mon, Wed, Thu, Sat. 🎪 Grease Wrestling Championships (early Jul); Liberation Day (25 Oct).

🔲 Muradiye Mosque

Muradiye Camii
Küçükpazar Cad. 🔘 prayer times only. 🚫

This mosque was built as a *zaviye* (dervish hospice) in 1421 by Murat II (see p30), who dreamt that the great dervish leader Jelaleddin Rumi (see p104) asked him to build one in Edirne. Only later was it converted into a mosque. Its interior is notable for its massive inscriptions, similar to those in the Old Mosque, and for some fine early 15th-century İznik tiles (see p161).

EDİRNE CITY CENTRE

Beyazıt II Mosque ①
Mosque of the Three Balconies ②
Muradiye Mosque ⑦
Museum of Turkish and Islamic Arts ⑥
Old Mosque ③
Rüstem Paşa Caravanserai ④
Selimiye Mosque ⑤ (see pp156–7)

KEY

🅓 Dolmuş terminus
🛈 Tourist information
🔲 Mosque

0 metres   750
0 yards   750

Edirne: Selimiye Mosque
Selimiye Camii

THE SELIMIYE IS THE GREATEST of all the Ottoman mosque complexes, the apogee of an art form and the culmination of a lifetime's ambition for its architect, Sinan *(see p91)*. Built on a slight hill, the mosque is a prominent landmark. Its complex includes a *medrese (see p36)*, now housing the Museum of Turkish and Islamic Arts *(see p155)*, a school and the Kavaflar Arasta, a covered bazaar.

Selim II *(see p25)* commissioned the mosque. It was begun in 1569 and completed in 1575, a year after his death. The dome was Sinan's proudest achievement. In his memoirs, he wrote: "With the help of Allah and the favour of Sultan Selim Khan, I have succeeded in building a cupola six cubits wider and four cubits deeper than that of Haghia Sophia". In fact, the dome is of a diameter comparable to and slightly shallower than that of the building *(see pp72–5)* Sinan had so longed to surpass.

★ Minarets
The mosque's four slender minarets tower to a height of 84 m (275 ft). Each one has three balconies. The two northern minarets contain three intertwining staircases, each one leading to a different balcony.

Ablutions Fountain
Intricate, pierced carving decorates the top of the 16-sided open şadırvan (ablutions fountain), which stands in the centre of the courtyard. The absence of a canopy helps to retain the uncluttered aspect of the courtyard.

STAR FEATURES

★ **Minarets**

★ **Dome**

★ **Minbar**

The columns supporting the arches of the courtyard are made of old marble, plundered from Byzantine architecture.

Courtyard Portals
Alternating red and honey-coloured slabs of stone were used to build the striking arches above the courtyard portals. This echoes the decoration of the magnificent arches running around the mosque courtyard itself.

★ **Dome**
The dome masterfully dominates the entire interior of the mosque. Not even the florid paintwork – the original 16th-century decoration underwent restoration in the 19th century – detracts from its effect.

★ **Minbar**
Many experts claim that the Selimiye's minbar, with its conical tiled cap, is the finest in Turkey. Its lace-like side panels are exquisitely carved.

Mihrab, cut from Marmara marble

VISITORS' CHECKLIST

Mimar Sinan Cad, Edirne.
((0284) 213 97 35.
○ daily. ● prayer times.

The Interior
The mosque is the supreme achievement of Islamic architecture. Its octagonal plan allows for a reduction in the size of the buttresses supporting the dome. This permitted extra windows to be incorporated, making the mosque exceptionally light inside.

The *müezzin mahfili*
(see p36) still retains original, intricate 16th-century paintwork on its underside. Beneath it is a small fountain.

Entrance from Kavaflar Arasta

Sultan's Loge
The imperial loge is supported on green marble columns. They are connected by pointed arches, whose surrounds are adorned with floral İznik tiles (see p161). Unusually, its ornately decorated mihrab contains a shuttered window, which opened on to countryside when the mosque was first built.

Main entrance

Kilyos ❷

27 km (17 miles) N of Istanbul.
🏛 *1,665.* 🇩 *from Sarıyer.*

K ILYOS, on the shore of the
Black Sea, is the closest
seaside resort to Istanbul and
very popular. It has a long,
sandy beach and temptingly
clear water, but visitors should
not swim here in the absence
of a lifeguard because there
are dangerous currents beneath the calm surface.

A 14th-century Genoese
castle perches on a cliff top
overlooking the town but
it is not open to visitors.
The three ruined towers on
the left of the main approach
road into the village were formerly water control towers.
They were part of the system
that once brought water here
from the Belgrade Forest.

Belgrade Forest ❸
Belgrad Ormanı

20 km (12 miles) N of Istanbul. 🚌 *405
from Taksim to Çayırbaşı, then 42 to
Bahçeköy.* **Park** 📞 *(0212) 226 23
35.* 🕐 *Apr–Oct: 6am–8:30pm daily;
Nov–Mar: 8am–4pm daily.* 🅿 🔥

O NE OF THE most popular
escapes from the city,
the Belgrade Forest is the only
sizeable piece of woodland
in the immediate vicinity of
Istanbul. The forest is made
up of pines, oaks, beeches,
chestnuts and poplars, beneath which a profusion of
wild flowers grow in spring.
Within it is a huge woodland
park, best visited during the
week, since it attracts hordes
of picnickers at weekends.
The main entrance to the park
is near the village of
Bahçeköy and the
popular Neşetsuyu
picnic area is a half-
hour stroll from this
gate. Beautiful
walks through the
forest start here.

The park's other
attractions are the
relics of the dams,
reservoirs and aque-
ducts used for over
1,000 years to trans-
port spring water in
to Istanbul. The

Büyük Bent, a Byzantine dam and reservoir in the Belgrade Forest

oldest structure, Büyük Bent
(Great Reservoir), dates back
to the early Byzantine era. It
is a pleasant half-hour walk
from Neşetsuyu picnic area.
Meanwhile, the Sultan Mahmut
Dam, outside the park's gate,
is a fine curve of marble which
dates from 1839.

Eğri Kemer (Crooked Aque-
duct) and Uzun Kemer (Long
Aqueduct) are on the 016
road between Levent and Kısır-
mandıra and are best reached
by taxi. Both have impressive
rows of arches. The former
probably dates from the 12th
century, while Sinan *(see p91)*
built the latter for Süleyman
the Magnificent *(see p24).*

Şile ❹

72 km (45 miles) NE of Istanbul.
🏛 *25,372.* 🚌 *from Üsküdar.*

T HE QUINTESSENTIAL Black
Sea holiday village of Şile
has a number of fine, sandy
beaches and a black-and-
white striped cliff-top light-

**The village of Şile, a holiday resort and centre
for cotton production**

house. In antiquity, the village,
then known as Kalpe, was a
port used by ships sailing east
from the Bosphorus.

Şile's lighthouse, the largest
in Turkey, was built by the
French for Sultan Abdül Aziz
(see p28) in 1858–9; it can be
visited after dusk. Apart from
tourism, the main industry
is now the production of a
coarse cotton which is made
into clothing and sold in
shops along Üsküdar Caddesi.

Polonezköy ❺

25 km (16 miles) NE of Istanbul. 🏛
500. 🚌 *221 from Taksim to Beykoz,
then dolmuş.* 📞 *(0216) 432 31 61.*

P OLONEZKÖY WAS originally
called Adampol, after the
Polish Prince Adam Czartoryski
who bought prime arable
land here in 1842 for Polish
emigrants settling in Turkey.
Soon after, in 1853, the Poles
formed a band of Cossack soldiers to fight for Abdül Mecit I
(see p28) in the Crimea. After
this he granted them the land
as a tax-free haven.

Polonezköy's rustic charm
is now big business, and a
number of health spas and
villas have sprung up. A couple
of restaurants *(see p199)* still
serve the pork for which the
town was once famous.

The surrounding beech
forest, which offers pleasant
walks, has now been protected
from further development. As
part of this scheme, the locals
have even waived their rights
to collect firewood.

Princes' Islands ❻

Kızıl Adalar

12 km (7 miles) SE of Istanbul. ▨
19,413. ⛴ from Sirkeci or Kabataş
(sea bus). ⓘ (0126) 382 70 71.

THE PINE-FORESTED Princes'
Islands provide a welcome
break from the bustle of the
city and are just a short ferry
ride southeast from Istanbul.
Most ferries call in turn at the
four largest of the nine islands:
Kınalıada, Burgazada, Heybeliada and finally Büyükada.

Easily visited on a day trip,
the islands take their name
from a royal palace built
by Justin II on Büyük-
ada, then known as
Prinkipo (Island of the
Prince) in 569. During
the Byzantine era the
islands became infa-
mous as a place of
exile. Members of the
royal family and public
figures were often
banished to the mon-
asteries here.

In the latter half of
the 19th century, with
the inauguration of
a steamboat service from
Istanbul, several wealthy ex-
patriates settled on the islands.
Among the foreign exiles to
live here was Leon Trotsky.
From 1929–33 he lived at 55
Çankaya Caddesi, one of the
finest mansions on Büyükada.

Büyükada is the largest
island and attracts the most
visitors with its sandy beaches,
ice creams and fin-de-siècle
elegance. Its 19th-century
atmosphere is enhanced by

**Door to the
Monastery of
St George**

the omnipresence of horse-
drawn phaetons. These quaint
carriages are in fact the only
form of public transport on
Büyükada (and Heybeliada)
since motorized transport is
banned. At the top of Büyükada's wooded southern hill,
in a clearing, stands the
Monastery of St George. It is
a 20th-century structure, built
on Byzantine foundations.

To the left of the ferry pier
on Heybeliada, the second
largest island, is the imposing
former Naval High School
(Deniz Harp Okulu), built
in 1942. The island's
northern hill is the
stunning location of
the Greek Orthodox
School of Theology
(built in 1841). The
school is now closed
but its library, famous
among Orthodox
scholars, is still open.
The island also has a
pleasant beach on its
south coast at Çam
Limanı Köyü.

The smaller islands
of Kınalıada and
Burgazada are less
developed and are peaceful
places to stop off for a meal.

Termal ❼

38 km (24 miles) SE of Istanbul.
▨ 5,018. ⛴ from Kabataş to Yalova.
ⓘ Iskele Meyd 5, (0226) 814 21 08.

THIS SMALL SPA buried deep
in a wooded valley has
been patronized by ruling
elites since the Roman era.

**Ornamental fountain at Atatürk's
former house at Termal**

Termal is situated 12 km (7
miles) from the port of Yalova.
Its popularity was revived by
Sultan Abdül Hamit II (see p31)
in the early 20th century, when
he refurbished the Kurşunlu
Baths, now part of the **Turban
Termal** complex. Comprising
four baths and a couple of
hotels, facilities include Turkish baths (see p67), a sauna
and a swimming pool.

Atatürk enjoyed taking the
waters here. The small chalet-
style house he built at the
bottom of the valley, now the
Atatürk Museum, preserves
some of his possessions.

🛁 Turban Termal
Termal. ☎ (0226) 675 74 00.
🕐 8:30am–5pm daily.
🏛 Atatürk Museum
Atatürk Köşkü, Termal.
☎ (0226) 675 70 28.
🕐 9:30am–5pm Tue, Wed, Fri–Sun.

The harbour of Burgazada, one of the relaxed and picturesque Princes' Islands near Istanbul

İznik

87 km (54 miles) SE of Istanbul.
🚏 17,200. 🚌 Yeni Mahalle, (0224)
757 25 83. 🛈 Belediye İşhane,
Kılıçaslan Cad, (0224) 757 19 33.
🛒 Wed. 🎪 İznik Fair (5–10 Oct);
İznik Festival (late Nov).

A CHARMING lakeside town, İznik gives little clue now of its former glory as, at one point, the capital of the Byzantine Empire. Its most important legacy dates, however, from the 16th century, when its kilns produced the finest ceramics ever to be made in the Ottoman world.

The town first reached prominence in AD 325, when it was known as Nicaea. In that year Constantine *(see p18)* chose it as the location of the first Ecumenical Council of the Christian Church. At this meeting, the Nicene Creed, a statement of doctrine on the nature of Christ in relation to God, was formulated.

The Seljuks *(see p19)* took Nicaea in 1081 and renamed it İznik. It was wrested back from them in 1097 by the First Crusade on behalf of Emperor Alexius I Comnenus. After the capture of Constantinople in 1204 *(see p24)*, the city was capital of the 'Empire of Nicaea', a remaining fragment of the Byzantine Empire, for half a century. In 1331, Orhan Gazi *(see p30)* captured İznik and incorporated it into the Ottoman Empire.

Grand domed portico fronting the Archaeological Museum

İznik still retains its original layout. Surrounded by the **city walls**, its two main streets are in the form of a cross, with minor streets running out from them on a grid plan. The walls still more or less delineate the town's boundaries. They were built by the Greek Lysimachus, then ruler of the town, in 300 BC, but they were frequently repaired by both the Byzantines and later the Ottomans. They cover a total of 3 km (2 miles) in circumference and are punctuated by huge gateways. The main one of these, Istanbul Gate (İstanbul Kapısı), is at the city's northern limit. It is decorated with a carved relief of fighting horsemen and is flanked by Byzantine towers.

Istanbul Gate from within the city walls

One of the town's oldest surviving monuments, the ruined church of **Haghia Sophia**, stands at the intersection of the main streets, Atatürk Caddesi and Kılıçaslan Caddesi. An earlier version of the church was the principal place of worship in Byzantine Nicaea. The current building was erected after an earthquake in 1065. The remains of a fine mosaic floor, and also of a Deësis, a fresco that depicts Christ, the Virgin and John the Baptist, are protected from damage behind glass screens.

Just off the eastern end of Kılıçaslan Caddesi, the 14th-century **Green Mosque** (Yeşil Cami) is named after the tiles covering its minaret. Unfortunately, the originals have been replaced by modern copies of an inferior quality.

Opposite the mosque, the Kitchen of Lady Nilüfer (Nilüfer Hatun İmareti), one of İznik's loveliest buildings, now houses the town's **Archaeological Museum**. This *imaret* was set up in 1388 by Nilüfer Hatun, wife of Orhan Gazi, and also served as a hospice for wandering dervishes. Entered through a spacious five-domed portico, the central domed area is flanked by two further domed rooms. The museum has displays of Roman antiquities and glass as well as some recently discovered examples of Seljuk and Ottoman tiles.

🕌 **Haghia Sophia**
Atatürk Cad. 📞 (0224) 757 10 24.
⏰ Tue–Sun. 🎫
📞 **Green Mosque**
Müze Sok. ⏰ daily.
🏛 **Archaeological Museum**
Müze Sok. 📞 (0224) 757 10 27.
⏰ daily. 🎫

Green Mosque, İznik, named after the green tiles adorning its minaret

İznik Ceramics

16th-century İznik mosque lamp

Towards the end of the 15th century, the town of İznik began to produce large quantities of ceramic bowls, jars and, later, tiles for the many palaces and mosques of Istanbul. Drawing on local deposits of fine clay and inspired by imported Chinese ceramics, the work of the craftsmen of İznik soon excelled both technically and aesthetically. İznik pottery is made from hard, white "fritware", which is akin to porcelain. This style of pottery was invented in Egypt in around the 12th century. It is covered by a bright, white slip (a creamy mixture of clay and water) and a transparent glaze. Early İznik pottery is brilliant blue and white. Later, other colours, especially a vivid red, were added. The potteries of İznik reached their height in the late 16th and early 17th centuries but shortly after fell into decline.

Chinese porcelain, which was imported into Turkey from the 14th century and of which there is a large collection in Topkapı Palace (see pp54–9), often inspired the designs used for İznik pottery. During the 16th century, İznik potters produced imitations of pieces of Chinese porcelain such as this copy of a Ming dish.

Rock and wave border pattern

Damascus ware was the name erroneously given to ceramics produced at İznik during the first half of the 16th century. They had fantastic floral designs in the new colours of turquoise, sage green and manganese. When such tiles were discovered at Damascus, the similar İznik pots were wrongly assumed to have been made there.

Cobalt blue and white was the striking combination of colours used in early İznik pottery (produced between c.1470–1520). The designs used were a mixture of Chinese and Arabesque, as seen on this tiled panel on the wall of the Circumcision Chamber in Topkapı Palace. Floral patterns and animal motifs were both popular at this time.

Armenian bole, an iron-rich red colour, began to be used in around 1550, as seen in this 16th-century tankard. New, realistic tulip and other floral designs were also introduced, and İznik ware enjoyed its heyday, which lasted until around 1630.

Wall tiles were not made in any quantity until the reign of Süleyman the Magnificent (1520–66). Süleyman used İznik tiles to refurbish the Dome of the Rock in Jerusalem. Some of the best examples are seen in Istanbul's mosques, notably in the Süleymaniye (see pp90–91), Rüstem Paşa Mosque (pp88–9) and, here, in this example from the Blue Mosque (pp78–9).

Miniature depicting potters

Bursa

Basin, Museum of Turkish and Islamic Arts

BURSA EXTENDS in a swathe along the northern foothills of Mount Uludağ *(see p169)*. A settlement known as Prusa was reputedly established here in the 3rd century BC by Prusias I of Bithynia. However, it was the Romans who first spotted the potential of Bursa's mineral springs: today there are an estimated 3,000 baths in the city. In 1326 Bursa became the first capital of the Ottoman Empire, following its capture by Osman Gazi *(see p23)*.

View over the rooftops of the city of Bursa

Today Bursa is a provincial capital whose status as one of Turkey's foremost centres of commerce and industry is evident in its broad boulevards and busy shops and bazaars. Apart from the central market area *(see pp164–5)*, the most frequented sightseeing area is Yeşil, on the eastern side of the Gök River, where the Green Mosque and Green Tomb are the main attractions.

C Yıldırım Beyazıt Mosque
Yıldırım Beyazıt Camii
Yıldırım Cad. ◯ *daily.*

This Mosque is named after Beyazıt I *(see p30)*, whose nickname was "Yıldırım", meaning "thunderbolt". This referred to the speed with which he reacted to his enemies. Built in 1389, just after Beyazıt became sultan, the mosque at first doubled as a lodge for Sufi dervishes *(see p104)*. It has a lovely portico with five domed bays.

Inside, the interior court (a covered "courtyard" in Bursa mosques, which prefigures the open courtyards preferred by later Ottoman architects) and prayer hall are divided by an impressive arch. This rises from two mihrab-like niches. The walls of the prayer hall itself are adorned with several bold and attractive pieces of calligraphic design *(see p95)*.

☲ Green Tomb
Yeşil Türbe
Yeşil Cad. ◯ *daily.* ◪ *donation.*

The tomb of Mehmet I *(see p30)*, which stands elevated above the mosque among tall cypress trees, is one of the city's most prominent landmarks. It was built between 1414 and 1421. The tomb is much closer to the Seljuk *(see p19)* style of architecture than Classical Ottoman. Its exterior is covered in green tiles, although these are mainly 19th-century replacements for the original faïence. However, a few older tiles survive around the entrance portal.

The interior, entered through a pair of superbly carved wooden doors, is simply dazzling. The space is small and the ornamentation, covering a relatively large surface area, is breathtaking in its depth of colour and detail. The mihrab has especially intricate tile panels, including a representation of a mosque lamp hanging from a gold chain between two candles.

The sultan's magnificent sarcophagus is covered in exquisite tiles and adorned by a long Koranic inscription. Nearby sarcophagi contain the remains of his sons, daughters and nursemaid.

C Green Mosque
Yeşil Cami
Yeşil Cad. ◯ *daily.*

Bursa's most famous monument was commissioned by Mehmet I in 1412, but it remained unfinished at his death in 1421 and still lacks a portico. Nevertheless, it is the finest Ottoman mosque built before the conquest of Constantinople *(see p24)*.

The main portal is tall and elegant, with an intricately carved canopy. It opens into the entrance hall. Beyond this is an interior court, with a carved fountain at its centre. A flight of three steps leads up from here into the prayer hall. On either side of the steps are niches where worshippers once left their shoes *(see p37)*. Above the entrance to the court is the sultan's loge, resplendent in richly patterned tiles created using the *cuerda seca* technique. They are in beautiful greens, blues and yellows, with threads of gold which were added after firing.

The Green Tomb and Green Mosque, Bursa's most distinctive monuments

The tiling of the prayer hall was carried out by Ali Ibn İlyas Ali, who learnt his art in Samarkand. It was the first time that tiles were used extensively in an Ottoman mosque and set a precedent for the later widespread use of İznik tiles *(see p161)*. The tiles covering the walls of the prayer hall, which is well lit by floor-level windows, are simple, green and hexagonal. Against this plain backdrop, the effect of the mihrab is especially glorious. Predominantly turquoise, deep blue and white, with touches of gold, the mihrab's tiles depict flowers, leaves, arabesques and geometric patterns. The mosque's exterior was also once clad in tiles, but they have since disappeared.

🏛 Museum of Turkish and Islamic Arts

Türk ve Islam Eserleri Müzesi
Yeşil Cad. 🄲 (0224) 327 76 79.
🕙 Tue–Sun. 🖼

This museum is housed in a fine Ottoman building, the former *medrese (see p36)* of the Green Mosque. A colon-nade surrounds its courtyard on three sides and the cells leading off from it, formerly used by the students, are now exhibition galleries. At the far end of the courtyard is the large, domed hall which was originally the main classroom.

Exhibits dating from the 12th–20th centuries include Seljuk and Ottoman ceramics, elaborately decorated Korans and costumes ranging from linen dervish robes to ornate wedding gowns. A display on Turkish baths *(see p67)* features embroidered towels and exotic high-heeled silver bath clogs. There is also a recreated setting of a traditional circumcision room, complete with a four-poster bed.

VISITORS' CHECKLIST

90 km (60 miles) S of Istanbul.
🏘 1,995,000. ✈ 20 km (12 miles) NW. 🚌 Kıbrıs Şehitler Cad, (0224) 251 18 34. 🄳 Atatürk Cad; Osman Gazi Cad.
🄸 Koza Parkı, Orhangazi Altgeçidi (0224) 220 18 48.
🎪 Textiles Fair (3rd week of May); Bursa Festival (12 Jun–12 Jul).

Façade of the Museum of Turkish and Islamic Arts

BURSA CITY CENTRE

Alaeddin Mosque ⑦
Archaeological Museum ⑩
Green Mosque ③
Green Tomb ②
Hüsnü Züber House ⑨

Muradiye Mosque ⑧
Museum of Turkish
  and Islamic Arts ④
Osman Gazi Tomb ⑥
Tophane Citadel ⑤
Yıldırım Beyazıt Mosque ①

KEY

▨	Street-by-Street area *See pp164–5*
🚌	Coach station
🄳	Dolmuş terminus
🄸	Tourist information
🄲	Mosque

Bursa: The Market Area

BURSA'S CENTRAL MARKET AREA is a warren of streets and ancient Ottoman courtyards (hans). The area is still central to Bursa's commercial activity and is a good place to experience the life of the city. Here too you can buy the local fabrics for which the town is famous, particularly handmade lace, towelling and silk. The silkworm was introduced to the Byzantine Empire in the 6th century and there is still a brisk trade in silk cocoons carried out in Koza Han in June and July. Among the many other items on sale today are the lovely hand-painted, camel-skin Karagöz puppets *(see p168)*.

★ **Covered Bazaar**
The great bazaar, built by Mehmet I in the 15th century, consists of a long hall with four domed bays, adjoined by a high, vaulted hall. The Bedesten is home to jewellers' shops.

★ **The Great Mosque**
A three-tiered ablutions fountain stands beneath the central dome of this monumental mosque, which was erected in 1396–9.

Şengül Hamamı Turkish baths

FEVZİ ÇAKMAK CAD

Bey Han (also called Emir Han) was built as part of the Orhan Gazi Mosque complex, to provide revenue for the mosque's upkeep.

Cafés

KOZA PARKI

ATATÜRK CAD

The Bey Hamamı (1339) is the oldest Turkish baths building in the world. It now houses workshops.

Koza Park
The gardens in front of Koza Han, with their fountains, benches and shaded café tables, are a popular meeting place for locals and visitors throughout the day.

★ Koza Han
This is the most attractive and fascinating building in the market area. Since it was built in 1491 by Beyazıt II, it has been central to the silk trade.

Geyve Han is also known as İvaz Paşa Han.

Fidan Han dates from around 1470, when it was built by a grand vizier of Mehmet the Conqueror.

İçkoza Han

Flower Market
The numerous bunches of flowers for sale in the streets around the town hall make a picturesque sight in the midst of Bursa's bustling market area.

BORSA SOK

UZUN ÇARŞI CAD

ÇÖMLEK SOK

BELEDİYE CAD

| 0 metres | 40 |
| 0 yards | 40 |

STAR SIGHTS
★ **Great Mosque**

★ **Covered Bazaar**

★ **Koza Han**

The Belediye, Bursa's town hall, is a Swiss chalet-style, half-timbered building that forms a surprising landmark in the centre of the town.

Tourist information

KEY
– – – Suggested route

Orhan Gazi Mosque
Built in 1339, just 13 years after the Ottoman conquest of Bursa, this mosque is the oldest of the city's imperial mosques.

Bursa: Tophane and Muradiye

TOPHANE, the most ancient part of Bursa, is distinguished by its clock-tower which stands on top of a hill. This area was formerly the site of the citadel and is bounded by what remains of the original Byzantine walls. It is also known as Hisar, which means "fortress" in Turkish. If you continue westwards for 2 km (1 mile), crossing the Cılımboz River, you come to the historic district of Muradiye. The 15th-century Muradiye Mosque, from which this suburb takes its name, is one of the most impressive royal mosque and tomb complexes in the city.

The clocktower in Tophane

Exploring Tophane

Tophane's northern limit is marked by the best preserved section of the citadel walls, built on to an outcrop of rock. At the top is a pleasant park filled with cafés, which also contains the imposing clock-tower and the tombs of the founders of the Ottoman dynasty. From here you can look down on the lower part of Tophane, where archetypal Ottoman houses still line many of the twisting streets. Pınarbaşı Kapısı, at Tophane's southern point, is the gate through which Orhan Gazi entered Bursa in 1326 *(see p23)*.

🏛 Tophane Citadel
Hisar
Osman Gazi Cad. ◯ *daily.* ♿

The citadel walls can be viewed from a set of steps which lead uphill from the intersection of Cemal Nadir Caddesi and Atatürk Caddesi. These steps end at the tea gardens above. The citadel fell into Turkish hands when Orhan Gazi's troops broke through its walls. Later, he built a wooden palace inside the citadel and had the old Byzantine ramparts refortified. The walls had until this era delimited the entire circumference of the ancient city. However, Orhan began to encourage Bursa's expansion and developed the present-day commercial heart of the city further to the east.

South of Hastalaryurdu Caddesi is an area notable for its old Ottoman houses *(see p61)*. Most of these have overhanging upper storeys. They consist of a timber frame filled in with adobe and plastered over, then painted in bright colours. Kaleiçi Sokağı, which can be reached down Karadut Sokağı from Hastalaryurdu Caddesi, is one of the best streets of such houses.

🔲 Tombs of Osman and Orhan Gazi
Osman & Orhan Gazi Türbeleri
Ulu Cami Cad. ◯ *daily.* 📷 *donation.*

Osman Gazi began the process of Ottoman expansion in the 13th century *(see p23)* and attempted to capture Bursa. But it was his son, Orhan, who took the city just before his father died. Orhan brought his father's body to be buried in the baptistry of a converted church and he himself was later buried in the nave. The tombs that can be seen today date from 1868. They were rebuilt after the destruction of the church and the original tombs in an earthquake in 1855. Fragments of the church's mosaic floor survive inside the tomb of Orhan Gazi.

Tomb of Osman Gazi, the first great Ottoman leader

🔲 Alaeddin Mosque
Alaeddin Camii
Alaeddin Mahallesi. ◯ *prayer times only.* 🚫

Further exploration in the Tophane area reveals the Alaeddin Mosque, the oldest in Bursa, built within 10 years of the city's conquest. It is in the form of a simple domed square, fronted by a portico of four Byzantine columns with capitals. The mosque was commissioned by Alaeddin Bey, brother of and vizier *(see p37)* to Orhan Gazi.

Exploring Muradiye
Muradiye is a leafy, largely residential district. Close to the Muradiye Mosque are the Hüsnü Züber House and the Ottoman House, two fine examples of traditional Turkish homes. To the north is a park, among the attractions of which are a boating lake and the Archaeological Museum.

🔲 Muradiye Mosque
Muradiye Külliyesi
Murat II Cad. ◯ *daily.* 📷 *donation.*

This mosque complex was built by Murat II, father of Mehmet the Conqueror *(see p24)*, in the early 15th century. The mosque itself is preceded by a graceful domed portico.

Popular café in the park above the ancient citadel walls in Tophane

Octagonal tomb of Mustafa in the grounds of Muradiye Mosque

Its wooden door is finely carved and the interior decorated with early İznik tiles *(see p161)*. The *medrese*, beside the mosque, now serves as a dispensary. It is a perfectly square building, with cells surrounding a central garden courtyard. Its *dershane*, or main classroom, is richly tiled and adorned with an ornate brickwork façade.

The mosque garden, with its cypresses, well-tended flower beds and fountains, is one of Bursa's most tranquil retreats. Murat II was the last Ottoman sultan to be buried in Bursa and his mausoleum, standing in the garden beside the mosque and *medrese*, was completed in 1437. His earth-filled sarcophagus lies beneath an opening in the roof. The eaves above the tomb's 16th-century porch still retain their original painted decoration.

Muradiye Mosque, constructed by Murat II

There are 11 other tombs in the garden, several of which were built for murdered princes. One such is the tomb of Mustafa, a son of Süleyman the Magnificent, who was ruthlessly disposed of to clear the way for his younger brother, Selim II, "the Sot", to inherit the throne *(see p76)*. According to an inscription, Selim had the octagonal mausoleum built for his brother. The interior is decorated with some particularly beautiful İznik tile panels depicting carnations, tulips and hyacinths. The tiles date from the best İznik period, the late 16th century.

🕌 Hüsnü Züber House
Hüsnü Züber Evi
Uzunyol Sok 3, Muradiye. **C** (0224) 221 35 42. ☐ Tue–Sun. 🏛 🗹
Ottoman House temporarily closed.
Among the numerous well-preserved houses in the Muradiye district is the Hüsnü Züber House. This 150-year-old mansion has been opened as a museum by its present owner, the artist Hüsnü Züber. It was originally a guest house for visiting dignitaries, later becoming the Russian Consulate and, most recently, a private residence.

The house is an interesting example of vernacular architecture. The upper storey projects over the street in the traditional manner of Ottoman houses *(see p63)*. Overlooking the interior

courtyard, which has rooms arranged around it on three sides, there is a loggia. Originally this would have been open, but it is now glazed. Meanwhile, inside the house, the decorative wooden ceilings (some with hand-painted borders) are particularly attractive.

Hüsnü Züber's private collection of carved wooden objects is now displayed here. These include spoons, musical instruments and even farming utensils. They are all decorated with Anatolian motifs by a unique technique of engraving by burning known as pyrogravure.

The 18th-century **Ottoman House** (Osmanlı Evi) stands on the square in front of the Muradiye Mosque. It is another fine house, but is closed to the public at present. The upper storey is adorned with elaborately patterned brickwork. Shutters and grilles hide the windows.

Hüsnü Züber House, dating from the mid-19th century

🏛 Archaeological Museum
Arkeoloji Müzesi
Inside Kültür Parkı. **C** (0224) 234 49 18. ☐ Tue–Sun. 🏛
Finds dating from the third millennium BC up to the Ottoman conquest of Bursa are collected in this museum. In the first hall there are clasps, vessels and an inscription from the Phrygian period. Other exhibits include Roman and Hellenistic jewellery and ceramics, a number of Roman statues of Cybele, goddess of nature, and a Roman bronze of the god Apollo with strange, lifelike eyes. There are also displays of Byzantine religious objects and coins.

Bursa: Çekirge

WITH A NAME WHICH TRANSLATES literally as "Realm of the Cicadas", Çekirge still earns Bursa the tag of Yeşil, or "Green", by which it is known in Turkey. This leafy western spa suburb of the city has attracted visitors to its mineral springs since Roman times. In the 6th century the Emperor Justinian *(see p18)* built a bathhouse here and his wife Theodora later arrived with a retinue of 4,000. Çekirge is also the location of most of the city's finest hotels and the area's hillside setting affords some spectacular views.

Çekirge's Old Spa, dating back to the 14th-century reign of Murat I

🕌 New Spa

Yeni Kaplıca
Yeni Kaplıca Cad 6, Osmangazi.
☎ *(0224) 236 69 68.*
🕐 *5am–11pm daily.*
Despite their name, the New Spa baths have a substantial pedigree. They were rebuilt in 1522 by Rüstem Paşa, grand vizier *(see p27)* to Süleyman the Magnificent *(see p24)*. The sultan is said to have ordered their rebuilding in gratitude after his recovery from gout when bathing in the Byzantine baths that stood on this site.

The present baths have a central pool surrounded with bays adorned with beautiful but damaged İznik tiles *(see p161)*. They are not open to women. Within the same complex there are two other baths: the modern Kaynarca baths for women and the Karamustafa baths for couples.

🏨 Çelik Palas Hotel

Çelik Palas Otel
Çekirge Cad 79.
☎ *(0224) 233 38 00.*
This five-star hotel *(see p185)* stands on one of Bursa's main thoroughfares. Built in 1933, it is the city's oldest, most prestigious spa hotel. Atatürk *(see pp28–9)* frequented its baths. Open to both sexes, their centrepiece is an attractive circular pool in a domed marble room.

🕌 Old Spa

Eski Kaplıca
Çekirge Meydanı, Kervansaray.
☎ *(0224) 233 93 00.*
🕐 *7am–11pm daily.*
The Old Spa baths were established by Murat I in the late 14th century and renovated in 1512, during the reign of Beyazıt II. Remnants of an earlier building, said to date from the reign of Emperor Justinian *(see p18)*, are also visible. These include some Byzantine columns and capitals in the *hararet* (steam room) of the men's section *(see p67)*. You enter the baths through the new Kervansaray Termal Hotel. Spring water, said to cure skin diseases and rheumatism, bubbles into the central pool of both the men's and women's sections at 45 °C (113 °F). The women's baths are not as old or grand, but are still the most attractive women-only ones in Bursa.

🕌 Murat I Hüdavendigar Mosque

Murat I Hüdavendigar Camii
I. Murat Cad, Çekirge. 🕐 *daily.*
Bursa's most unusual mosque was built for Murat I, self-styled Hüdavendigar, meaning "Creator of the Universe", in 1385. It is unlike any other mosque in the Ottoman world: its prayer hall is on the ground floor, with the *medrese* built around a second storey.

The façade looks more like that of a palace than a mosque, with a five-arched portico surmounted by a colonnade. This colonnade in turn has five sets of double-arched windows divided by Byzantine columns. Inside, the domed court and prayer hall rise through both storeys. The upper storey colonnade leads to the cells of the *medrese*. On this level, passageways lead around both sides of the mosque to a mysterious room, located over the mihrab, whose original purpose is unknown.

KARAGÖZ SHADOW PUPPETS

Suspended above Çekirge Caddesi is an imposing monument to the town's two famous scapegoats, Karagöz and Hacıvat. According to legend, these local clowns were executed in the 14th century for distracting their fellow workers while building the Orhan Gazi Mosque *(see p165)*. It is said that Sultan Orhan *(see p30)* created a shadow play about them in remorse.

In fact, shadow puppet theatre arrived in Turkey later and is thought to have originated in southeast Asia. Selim I is reported to have brought it back to Istanbul after his Egyptian campaign in 1517. The camel-skin puppets are 35–40 cm (14–16 in) high, brightly dyed and oiled to aid translucency.

Cadi, a witch in the Karagöz puppet shows

They are still made today and can be purchased in an antique shop in the Bedesten run by Şinasi Çelikkol, who also occasionally puts on shows.

Uludağ National Park, a popular ski resort in winter

Uludağ National Park ⑩

Uludağ Milli Parkı

100 km (60 miles) S of Istanbul.
☎ (0224) 271 51 68. 🚡 Teleferik to Sarıalan, then dolmuş. ☐ daily.
🚗 only for vehicles.

ONE OF A NUMBER of Turkish mountains to claim the title of Mount Olympus, Uludağ was believed by the Bithynians (of northwest Asia Minor) to be the home of the gods. In the Byzantine era, it was home to several monastic orders. After the Ottoman conquest of Bursa, Muslim dervishes (see p104) moved into their abandoned monasteries. Nowadays, however, no traces of Uludağ's former religious communities remain.

A visit to Uludağ National Park is especially enjoyable in spring or summer, when its alpine heights are relatively cool and it becomes a popular picnic area. The park includes 27,000 acres (67,000 hectares) of woodland. As you ascend, the deciduous beech, oak and hazel gradually give way to juniper and aspen, and finally to dwarf junipers. In spring, hyacinths and crocuses blanket the wooded slopes.

In winter, Uludağ is transformed into Turkey's most fashionable ski resort. The industry centres on the Oteller region, which has good alpine-style hotels.

Osman Gazi (see p23) is supposed to have founded seven villages for his seven sons and their brides in the Bursa region. **Cumalıkızık**, on the lower slopes of Uludağ, is the most perfectly preserved of the five surviving villages and is now registered as a national monument. Among its houses are many 750-year-old semi-timbered buildings. The village can be reached by minibus from Bursa.

Bird Paradise National Park ⑪

Kuşcenneti Milli Parkı

115 km (70 miles) SW of Istanbul.
☎ (0266) 735 54 22. 🅳 from Bandırma. ☐ 8am till sunset daily.
🚗 🚻 ♿ to park only.

AN ESTIMATED 255 species of birds visit Bird Paradise National Park at the edge of Kuş Gölü, the lake formerly known as Manyas Gölü. Located on the great migratory paths between Europe and Asia, the park is a happy combination of plant cover, reed beds and a lake that supports at least 20 species of fish.

At the entrance to the park, there is a small museum with displays about the many

Spoonbill wading in the lake at Bird Paradise National Park

different birds. Binoculars are provided at the desk and visitors make their way to an observation tower.

Two main groups of birds visit the lake: those that come here to breed (March–July), and those which pass by during migration, either heading south (November) or north (April–May). Among the numerous different birds that breed around the lake are the endangered Dalmatian pelican, the great crested grebe, cormorants, herons, bitterns and spoonbills. The migratory birds, which can be seen in spring and autumn, include storks, cranes, pelicans and birds of prey such as sparrowhawks and spotted eagles.

Sandy beach on Avşa, the most popular of the Marmara Islands

Marmara Islands ⑫

Marmara Adaları

120 km (75 miles) SW of Istanbul.
🚢 from Sirkeci. 🛈 Neyire Cad 31/3, Erdek, (0266) 835 11 69.

THIS BEAUTIFUL archipelago in the Sea of Marmara is a popular destination with Turkish holiday-makers, particularly with residents of Istanbul.

The loveliest of the islands is Avşa, whose sandy beaches and regular summer ferry from Istanbul make it popular with Turks and, increasingly, foreign tourists. The ferry arrives at Türkeli on the west coast. Transport to the most popular beach, at Maviköy, is by a tractor-pulled train.

Marmara, the largest island, has one beach, north of Marmara village at Çınarlı. It is famous for producing the prized Proconnesian marble.

The Dardanelles 🔞
Çanakkale Boğazı

200 km (125 miles) SW of Istanbul.
🚢 Çanakkale–Eceabat car ferry.
🚌 Çanakkale. 🛈 Çanakkale İskele
Meydanı 67, (0286) 217 11 87.

Named after Dardanus, an ancient king of Çanakkale, the Dardanelles are the straits that link the Aegean Sea to the Sea of Marmara, and which separate European Turkey from Asia. Some 40 km (25 miles) long and narrowing to little more than a kilometre (half a mile) wide, they are steeped in legend and have been of strategic importance for thousands of years. In modern times they are probably best known as the setting for a disastrous Allied campaign during World War I.

The classical name for this channel of water was the Hellespont. According to legend, the Greek goddess Helle fell into the straits from the back of a golden winged ram. In another tale, the lovelorn Leander swam nightly across the Hellespont to meet his lover, Hero, until one night he drowned. The English Romantic poet Byron swam across the straits in 1810, in emulation of Leander, and remarked on the hazardous nature of the currents.

Çanakkale, the old town at the mouth of the Dardanelles, has two museums. The **Military and Naval Museum** is a short walk from the ferry docks. Its collection includes a pocket watch that saved the

The Çanakkale Şehitleri Memorial, honouring the Turkish dead

life of Atatürk *(see pp28–9)* when he was hit by shrapnel. The **Archaeological Museum**, south of the town centre, has exhibits from ancient Troy.

To the west is the beautiful **Gallipoli** (Gelibolu) **Peninsula**. Part of this land is a national park, with an information centre near Eceabat. The peninsula still bears the scars of the horrific battles that took place here in 1915. The objectives of the Allied forces' invasion of Gallipoli were to capture Istanbul, force Turkey into submission and open a new supply route to Russia. The campaign began on 25 April 1915 with the landings of British and French troops at **Cape Helles**, and the Anzacs (Australian and New Zealand forces) at what they thought was the beach at Kabatepe. But currents had swept the Anzac force about 1.5 km (1 mile) to the north, to a place now known as **Anzac Cove**, near Arı Burnu. Here they were faced with unknown and tough terrain, including a cliff.

The Turks, led by Atatürk, managed to retain the high ground of **Chunuk Bair**. The battle here lasted three days, during which 28,000 men were killed. When the Allied

Statue of Allied soldiers near Anzac Cove

forces failed to make headway, more British troops landed at **Suvla Bay** on 6 August. This new offensive might have been successful, but there was incompetence among the Allied commanders who continually underestimated the Turks and the difficult ground. The slaughter of deadlocked trench warfare continued until the Allies were finally evacuated on 19 December. According to official estimates 160,000 Allied soldiers and 90,000 Turkish troops were killed at Gallipoli. Of the former, only 30,000 lie in marked graves. The whole peninsula is scattered with battlefield sites and war memorials.

The best place to begin a tour of the war memorials and cemeteries is at the **Kabatepe Visitors' Centre**, which houses a small collection of memorabilia including weapons, uniforms and soldiers' poignant letters home. North of here, near Anzac Cove, are several cemeteries and monuments. Chunuk Bair, now a peaceful pine grove above the beaches, has a memorial to the New Zealanders who died and some reconstructed Turkish trenches. The British Memorial is at Cape Helles, on the peninsula's tip.

Further east along the coast stand both the French Memorial and the vast Çanakkale Şehitleri Memorial to the Turks who died defending Gallipoli.

🏛 **Military and Naval Museum**
Gimenlik Kalesi, Çanakkale.
📞 *(0286) 217 24 60.*
🕐 *Tue, Wed & Fri–Sun.* 🖼

🏛 **Archaeological Museum**
Atatürk Cad, Çanakkale.
📞 *(0286) 217 32 52.* 🕐 *daily.* 🖼

🛈 **National Park Information Centre**
Near Eceabat. 📞 *(0286) 814 11 28.*
🕐 *daily.*

🛈 **Kabatepe Visitors' Centre**
Near Kabatepe. 📞 *(0286) 814 12 97.*
🕐 *daily.* 🖼

Troy ⑭
Truva

350 km (220 miles) SW of Istanbul.
🚌 *from Çanakkale.*
🕐 *8am–5:30pm daily.* 🖼

Model of the legendary wooden horse at Troy

I N HOMER'S epic poem, the *Iliad*, the city of Troy is besieged by the Greeks for ten years. For centuries Troy was assumed by many to be as mythical as Achilles, Hector and the other heroes in the tale. But a handful of 19th-century archaeologists were convinced that Homer had based his story on the events that happened to a real city and that traces of it could be found by searching near the Dardanelles. In 1865 British Consul Frank Calvert began investigating some ruins in Hisarlık. This interested the German archaeologist Heinrich Schliemann who soon found evidence of an ancient city resembling the layout of Homer's Troy. Over the last hundred years most historians have come to accept that this city must at least have inspired Homer, and was possibly even called Troy and besieged at the time specified in the story.

The settlement mound in fact has nine distinct levels (labelled Troy I–IX) representing 3,000 years of habitation. Sadly, the remains are sparse, and it takes some imagination to evoke an image of a city. Many structures were made of mud bricks and obviously levelled before new settlements were built on top.

The city Homer refers to is probably Troy VI (1800–1250 BC), while the Greek and Roman levels, when the city was known as Ilion, are Troy VIII (700–300 BC) and Troy IX (300 BC–AD 1) respectively.

What has survived includes a defence wall, palaces and houses from various periods, two sanctuaries (probably 8th century BC) and a Roman theatre. The grandest dwelling is the Pillar House, near the southern gate. Some believe this is the Palace of King Priam mentioned in the *Iliad*.

More conspicuous is a re-creation of the wooden horse, inside which a small group of the Greeks supposedly hid as a way of tricking the Trojans into letting them into their city. There is also a visitors' centre with a video and a scale model of the site.

SCHLIEMANN'S SEARCH FOR ANCIENT TROY

Heinrich Schliemann used a fortune amassed in business to realize his life-long dream of discovering ancient Troy. He began excavating some likely sites in the 1860s and started

Schliemann's wife wearing some of the excavated treasure

on the ruins at Hisarlık in 1870. An amateur, Schliemann drove a great trench through the mound, destroying some walls in his haste. He soon claimed to have found Troy, though he knew not all his findings pointed to this. His greatest find – a hoard of gold and silver jewellery that he smuggled to Germany, calling it "Priam's Treasure" *(see p64)* – pre-dates Homer's Troy by 1,000 years. Some of the treasure disappeared after World War II only to reappear spectacularly in Moscow in August 1993.

TRAVELLERS' NEEDS

WHERE TO STAY

WHETHER YOU feel like staying in an Ottoman palace, taking a room in a restored mansion or traditional wooden house, or even spending a night in a converted prison, you will find the hotel of your choice in Istanbul. Following a recent boom in tourism, the city's hotels and guesthouses now cater for every taste, as well as all budgets. Hotels tend to be clustered around Istanbul's main sightseeing areas. Sultanahmet contains most of the city's historic hotels and guesthouses.

Doorman at Hilton (p184)

Beyoğlu, across the Golden Horn, is a good place to look for three- and four-star hotels, including the grand old hotels of the 19th century. Most of Istanbul's five-star hotels are located in the Taksim area, on the slopes above the Bosphorus. Use the chart on pages 178–9 to find a hotel in your preferred price range which has the facilities you need. Fuller details of each hotel are given on pages 180–85. Information on other types of accommodation can be found on pages 176–7.

CHOOSING A HOTEL

MOST HOTELS in Istanbul are rated by the Ministry of Tourism according to a star system. They range from comfortable but basic one-star hotels to five-star luxury hotels. Other types of accommodation licensed by the Ministry of Tourism are the converted buildings known as Special Licence hotels, and guesthouses *(pansiyons)*. A further category is the non-graded accommodation licensed by the Greater Istanbul Municipality. These hotels provide only spartan facilities, with communal toilets and washing facilities, and shared rooms.

Accommodation is available in most central areas of the city. The Sultanahmet district is conveniently situated within walking distance of most of the city's major sights. Many of the Special Licence hotels in this area are tucked away on residential side streets. There

The luxurious Four Seasons Hotel, formerly a prison (see p182)

are guesthouses along Divanyolu Caddesi, the main through road, and on the slopes leading down to the Sea of Marmara. There are also middle-range hotels in central Sultanahmet.

A short tram ride west from Sultanahmet are the Beyazıt, Laleli and Aksaray districts, which are packed with one-, two- and three-star hotels. The cheaper hotels here are used mostly by Central Asian and Russian traders, while many of the three-star hotels cater for package tour groups.

Beyoğlu and Taksim, the old European centre of Istanbul, are within easy reach of the best sights in the city. Both have innumerable cheap hotels that are comfortable and dependable, as well as international chain hotels.

The Asian side of Istanbul is a mainly residential area and has few hotels, most of them very basic. There are, however, better hotels in Kadıköy, used more by Turks than foreigners.

Lounge of the Ceylan Inter-Continental Hotel in Taksim (see p183)

LUXURY HOTELS

THERE HAS been a rapid growth in the number of luxury hotels in the city, and most international chains are now represented in Istanbul. Almost all five-star hotels boast spectacular Marmara or Bosphorus views, and between them they have some of the best international restaurants in the city. All the major hotels have swimming pools and health clubs, which are open to non-residents for a fee. Many of them also have Turkish baths. Conference facilities are provided, and many hotels have casinos and extensive entertainment facilities. Most can also arrange tours of Istanbul and nearby places through local companies. Some of the largest hotels have floors where smoking is forbidden. They also provide facilities for the disabled and put on special activities for children (see p176).

◁ **Freshly fried fish sandwiches being prepared on a boat in Eminönü (see p200)**

SPECIAL LICENCE HOTELS

IN RECENT YEARS, a number of old buildings have been renovated and transformed into hotels. However, due to the nature of the buildings in which they are housed, most of these hotels cannot provide facilities such as lifts or air conditioning, and therefore do not meet the requirements of the official star-rating system. Instead, they belong to a separate category, the Special Licence hotel. Some are under private management, while others are owned and run by the Municipality.

The Special Licence hotels constitute some of Istanbul's most interesting and attractive hotels. They are often located in the residential streets of historic areas, and range from small, modestly priced traditional wooden houses to luxury Ottoman mansions. Even though they lack some modern conveniences, Special Licence hotels, whether large or small, are generally of a high standard. The authentic period decor of many of them gives even the larger ones a cosy atmosphere. Many Special Licence hotels exist only as a result of the efforts of the

Latticed window of a Special Licence hotel

Turkish Touring and Automobile Club (the TTOK, *see p237*). Led by its crusading director, Çelik Gülersoy, it has successfully preserved the Ottoman atmosphere of parts of the city by saving old buildings from demolition and restoring them. Its work can be seen particularly in the Special Licence hotels of Soğukçeşme Sokağı (*see p61*). The Club produces books, maps and other publications in several languages on places of interest in Istanbul and on the history of the city. It also runs cafés and tea gardens at Büyük Çamlıca (*see p133*), in the park at Fenerbahçe on the Asian side (*see p130*), and at other locations.

CHEAPER HOTELS

ISTANBUL HAS plenty of cheap, comfortable accommodation which meets the standards of the Turkish Ministry of Tourism. When choosing a cheaper hotel, however, do not base your decision on the façade or lobby, which may look brand new; it is always best to see a room.

One-star hotels provide the most basic facilities, but often have rooms with a private shower and toilet. Two- and three-star hotels have more comfortable rooms and usually a café or bar. Many three-star hotels offer rooms with a TV and mini-bar.

Guesthouses vary in terms of facilities. Most provide bed-linen and towels, and the better ones will have rooms with ensuite bathrooms. All should have communal cooking

Hotel roof terrace overlooking Sultanahmet

facilities. While cheaper hotels usually have central heating they are unlikely to have air conditioning, but an electric fan may be provided. Some small hotels may not provide hot water 24 hours a day.

WHAT TO EXPECT

ALL HOTELS listed in this book are comfortable, welcoming and secure. Front desk staff usually speak English, and will be able to give information on sights and travel.

Hotel rooms in Istanbul generally have two single beds, and enough space to add a third one if need be. If you want a double bed you should make this clear when booking or checking in.

Most hotels with three or more storeys will have a lift. There may not be a lift in a Special Licence hotel, however, because of the problems of installing one in an older building. Facilities for wheelchair users are usually found only in luxury hotels.

Noise can be a problem even in some smart hotels, so in busy areas choose a room that doesn't face on to a main street. If you are not satisfied with your room, you can always ask for another.

Breakfast (*see p188*) is usually included in the price of the room and typically consists of fresh bread, butter, jam, soft white cheese, tomatoes and black olives, served with tea or instant coffee (not Turkish coffee). Four- and five-star hotels provide a much wider choice, including cold meats, fruits, cereals and yoghurt. Only larger hotels will have restaurants that serve buffet or à la carte meals other than breakfast.

Yeşil Ev (see p182), a Special Licence hotel

Reception desk at the Istanbul Hilton *(see p184)*

PRICES AND DISCOUNTS

Hotel prices are usually quoted in US dollars, as exchange rates change daily. However, staff are always willing to quote in Turkish lira, or any hard currency. All prices usually include breakfast, and tax. Apart from top-class hotels, which have standard prices throughout the year, tariffs differ according to the season. The busy season, when hotel prices tend to be at their highest, is from April to the end of October. From the end of October until April prices fall by 40% or more. During the brief Christmas and New Year period, the higher summer tariffs are applied. There are no single rooms, but all hotels offer a single room rate of slightly more than half the price of a double room.

You should always bargain with hotels, and expect to get a discount of at least 15%. For longer stays of a week or more you can easily get a larger reduction. The price of a room usually varies according to its location in the hotel. Do not expect a room with a view if you have got it at a discount.

BOOKING A ROOM

While you will always be able to find a room of a reasonable standard, it is advisable to book in advance for the best hotels or those of

Lounge area of the Empress Zoe *(see p180)*

your choice during the busy season. You can book any hotel listed in this guide directly, by telephone or fax. You will probably be asked to give your credit card details, which will guarantee your reservation. This does not necessarily mean that you will be able to pay by credit card when you check out. If you cannot find a place in any of the hotels that fall in your preferred price range, you could try booking a room through one of the established travel companies based in Istanbul, such as **Meptur**, **Plan Tours** *(see p220)* or **Vip Tourism**. If you arrive without having reserved a room, the tourist information offices *(see p221)* in the airport, Sirkeci Station, Sultanahmet Square or Karaköy International Maritime Terminal will help you find a hotel, but they will not make a reservation for you.

CHECKING OUT AND PAYING

Guests are expected to check out by midday, but hotels will usually keep luggage for collection later. Most hotels accept the major credit cards, as well as Turkish lira and hard currency cash (preferably US dollars) for payment. Some also accept Euro and traveller's cheques. VAT and service are always included in the room price although since junior staff and cleaners are usually underpaid, it is customary to tip them. Leave a few dollars, or its equivalent, in the room for the cleaner, or give a larger sum to the receptionist to be divided among the staff. Phone calls and minibar drinks can add to the size of your bill.

CHILDREN

In most hotels, children up to six years are not charged for accommodation, and many hotels offer a 50% discount for those between 12 and 15 years old staying in their parents' room. Some of the larger hotels have cots for babies. A handful of hotels, including the Ceylan Intercontinental *(see p183)*, provide a babysitting service, usually hiring English-speaking sitters from agencies.

Some hotels arrange special entertainment for children. The Merit Antique *(see p182)* organizes Sunday brunches with children's menus, while the Swissôtel *(see p184)* offers a weekend-stay package which includes complimentary museum and cinema tickets.

Double room in the Special Licence Kariye Hotel *(see p183)*

Guests in the Yücelt Interyouth Hostel

HOSTELS

UNFORTUNATELY FOR those on a tight budget, Istanbul is short of decent youth hostels. The best known, in existence since the early 1970s, is the **Yücelt Interyouth Hostel** in Sultanahmet. On a peaceful, tree-lined street beside Haghia Sophia, Yücelt was often the first choice of travellers on the hippy trail in the 1970s. It is still a popular and friendly hostel, offering beds in dormitories, or in more expensive, but less crowded rooms. All rooms have heating. Yücelt is a member of the International Youth Hostel Federation (IYHF) and offers a discount for holders of an International Youth Hostel Card. The hostel has hot-water showers at certain hours of the day, a laundry, a safe, a luggage room and a cafeteria. Nearby, in Çemberlitaş, the **Cordial** is a newer, more attractive youth hostel with better facilities.

The tour operator Gençtur *(see p220)* is also affiliated to the IYHF and can give further information on hostels.

CAMPING

ONE OF Istanbul's main camp sites, **Ataköy Tatil Köyü** (Ataköy Holiday Village), occupies a large site on the sea shore, not far from the airport and the Galleria shopping mall *(see p203)*. It is open all year round and has toilets, hot showers and a communal cooking area. Other facilities include a bar, restaurant, swimming pool and children's playground. The **Doğa Karavanı** company, on the grounds of Ataköy Tatil Köyü, rents comfortable, air-conditioned caravans for four or more, to use on or off the site. Nearby, **Londra Kamping** is also open all year. It has washing and cooking facilities, a fast food restaurant, bar, pool table and football pitch. It has two-room bungalows for rent. The **Kilyos Turban Tatil Köyü**, just behind the beach at Kilyos *(see p158)*, is open in the summer months only, and provides toilets and hot showers, but no facilities for cooking. There is also a campsite at **Kumbaba Moteli**, 2 km outside Şile *(see p158)*. Open between May and September, it has hot showers and cooking facilities.

View over Dolmabahçe Mosque from the Swissôtel (see p184)

SELF-CATERING

ISTANBUL HAS a number of apartment hotels located near central business and residential districts, providing fully furnished apartments for those who prefer more homely surroundings. The **Akmerkez Residence Apart Hotel**, which is mostly used by businessmen, is in the up-market Akmerkez shopping mall in Etiler *(see p203)*. Its luxuriously decorated flats have air-conditioning and all domestic appliances. The **Family House Apart Hotel**, near Taksim, lets three-room flats. Meals can be provided upon request. The **Swissôtel** *(see p184)* also has fully-serviced, luxury flats.

Many travel agents can help to find flats of all sizes to rent for long or short stays.

DIRECTORY

DIRECTORY

TRAVEL AGENTS

Meptur
☎ (0212) 275 02 50.
FAX (0212) 275 40 09.

Vip Tourism
☎ (0212) 241 65 14.
FAX (0212) 230 64 25.

YOUTH HOSTELS

Cordial
Peykhane Sok 29, Çemberlitaş.
Map 3 D4 (4 C4).
☎ (0212) 518 05 76.
FAX (0212) 516 41 08

Yücelt Interyouth Hostel
Caferiye Sok 6/1, Sultanahmet.
Map 3 E4 (5 E3).
☎ (0212) 513 61 50.
FAX (0212) 512 76 28.

CAMPING

Ataköy Tatil Köyü
Ataköy Sahil Yolu, Ataköy.
☎ (0212) 559 60 00.

Doğa Karavanı
☎ (0212) 661 41 43.
FAX (0212) 661 41 44.

Kilyos Turban Tatil Köyü
Kilyos.
☎ (0212) 201 14 80.

Kumbaba Moteli
☎ (0216) 711 50 38.

Londra Kamping
Londra Asfaltı, Bakırköy.
☎ (0212) 560 42 00.

SELF-CATERING

Akmerkez Residence
Akmerkez Shopping & Business Centre, Etiler.
☎ (0212) 282 01 20.
FAX (0212) 282 06 12.

Family House
Kutlu Sok 53, Gümüşsuyu, Taksim. **Map** 7 F4.
☎ (0212) 249 73 51.
FAX (0212) 249 96 67.

Swissôtel Apartments
Bayıldım Cad 2, Maçka.
Map 8 A4.
☎ (0212) 259 01 01.
FAX (0212) 259 01 05.

Choosing a Hotel

THIS CHOOSING CHART is a quick reference to selected hotels in Istanbul, many of which offer charming decor and surroundings, even in lower price categories. The hotels are described in more detail in the listings on the following pages. For information about other types of accommodation, see page 177.

Hotel	Price	Number of Rooms	Restaurant	Swimming Pool	Attractive Views	Quiet Location	Special Licence	Business Facilities
SERAGLIO POINT (see p180)								
Barut's Guesthouse	TL	22			●	●		
Kybele	TL	16	●			●	●	
Ayasofya Pansiyonları	TL TL	53	●		●	●	●	
İshakpaşa Konağı	TL TL	18	●			●	●	
Konuk Evi	TL TL	12	●		●	●	●	
SULTANAHMET (see pp180–82)								
Karasu Green	TL	15	●			●		
Nomade	TL	15				●	●	
Şebnem	TL	7				●		
Alzer	TL TL	21	●		●	●	●	
Ayasofya	TL TL	21	●			●		
Empress Zoe	TL TL	19				●	●	
Historia	TL TL	27	●		●	●	●	
İbrahim Paşa	TL TL	19				●	●	
Sidera	TL TL	14	●			●	●	
Pierre Loti	TL TL	35	●					
Antea	TL TL TL	45	●			●		■
Armada	TL TL TL	110	●		●	□	●	■
Avicenna	TL TL TL	49	●		●	●		
Citadel	TL TL TL	29	●		●			
Festival	TL TL TL	113	●	■		●		
Obelisk	TL TL TL	41	●		●	●	●	
Sarı Konak	TL TL TL	17	●			●	●	
Sokullu Paşa	TL TL TL	37	●		●	●	●	
Valide Sultan Konağı	TL TL TL	17	●		●	●	●	
Kalyon	TL TL TL TL	103	●		●			■
Yeşil Ev	TL TL TL TL	18	●		●	●	●	
Four Seasons	TL TL TL TL	65	●		●	●	●	■
THE BAZAAR QUARTER (see p182)								
President	TL TL TL TL	204	●	■	●			■
Merit Antique	TL TL TL TL	274	●	■			●	■
BEYOĞLU (see pp182–3)								
Elan	TL	44	●					
Gezi	TL	50	●		●			
Plaza	TL	30	●		●	●		
Büyük Londra	TL TL	54	●		●		●	
Vardar	TL TL	40	●				●	
Emperyal	TL TL TL	52	●	■				■
Sed	TL TL TL	50	●		●	●		
Dilson	TL TL TL	112	●					■
Mercure	TL TL TL	197	●	■	●			■
Pera Palas	TL TL TL	144	●		●			■
Richmond	TL TL TL	109	●		●			■
Ceylan Inter-Continental	TL TL TL TL	335	●	■	●			■
Marmara	TL TL TL TL	410	●	■	●			■

ATTRACTIVE VIEWS
Many hotels have beautiful views over the Bosphorus, while others have terraces overlooking the domes and rooftops of historic areas.

QUIET LOCATION
Noisy streets can be a problem in Istanbul. This column indicates a hotel on a side street or other location away from heavy traffic.

SPECIAL LICENCE
These are hotels housed in restored historic buildings (see p175). They range from luxurious establishments to simple guesthouses, and include some of Istanbul's most charming hotels.

BUSINESS FACILITIES
The hotel can provide at least a meeting or conference room with audiovisual equipment.

		Price	NUMBER OF ROOMS	RESTAURANT	SWIMMING POOL	ATTRACTIVE VIEWS	QUIET LOCATION	SPECIAL LICENCE	BUSINESS FACILITIES
GREATER ISTANBUL AND THE BOSPHORUS (see pp183–4)									
Kariye	*Along the City Walls*	(TL)(TL)(TL)	27	●		●	■	●	
Lamartine	*Beyond Taksim*	(TL)(TL)(TL)	66	●					■
Golden Age	*Beyond Taksim*	(TL)(TL)(TL)(TL)	180	●	■				■
Green Park	*Beyond Taksim*	(TL)(TL)(TL)(TL)	81	●					■
Maçka	*Beyond Taksim*	(TL)(TL)(TL)(TL)	180	●		●	■		■
Çırağan Palace Hotel Kempinski	*Beyond Taksim*	(TL)(TL)(TL)(TL)(TL)	322	●	■	●	■		■
Divan	*Beyond Taksim*	(TL)(TL)(TL)(TL)(TL)	180	●		●			■
Istanbul Hilton	*Beyond Taksim*	(TL)(TL)(TL)(TL)(TL)	501	●	■	●	■		■
Swissôtel	*Beyond Taksim*	(TL)(TL)(TL)(TL)(TL)	585	●	■	●	■		■
Eysan	*The Asian Side*	(TL)(TL)	52	●		●			
Bebek	*The Bosphorus*	(TL)(TL)	30	●		●	■		
Bosphorus Paşa	*The Bosphorus*	(TL)(TL)(TL)(TL)	14	●		●	■	●	
OUTSIDE ISTANBUL (see pp184–5)									
Rüstempaşa Kervansaray	*Edirne*	(TL)	79	●				●	
Şile Resort	*Şile*	(TL)(TL)	52	●	■	●	■		
Polka Country	*Polonezköy*	(TL)(TL)(TL)	15	●		●	■	●	
Büyükada Princess	*Princes' Islands*	(TL)(TL)	24	●	■	●		●	
Splendid Palace	*Princes' Islands*	(TL)(TL)	70	●	■	●	■	●	
Halki Palace	*Princes' Islands*	(TL)(TL)(TL)	43	●	■	●	■	●	■
Atlas Termal	*Bursa*	(TL)	26					●	
Safran	*Bursa*	(TL)(TL)	10	●				●	
Çelik Palas	*Bursa*	(TL)(TL)(TL)	173	●		●	■		■
En Ön	*Marmara Islands*	(TL)	30	●		●			
Çınar	*Marmara Islands*	(TL)	52	●		●			
Anzac	*The Dardanelles*	(TL)	27						

USING THE LISTINGS

The hotels on pages 180–85 are listed according to area and price category. These symbols summarize the facilities in each hotel.

🚿 bath or shower in all rooms
🛏 rooms for more than two people available
24 24-hour room service
📺 TV in all rooms
🍸 mini-bar in all rooms
🗄 air conditioning in all rooms
🏋 gym or fitness facilities in the hotel
🏊 swimming pool
📊 business facilities available
🧒 caters for children (can provide at least a cot)
♿ wheelchair access
🛗 lift
🅿 hotel parking available
🍸 bar
🍴 restaurant
♨ Turkish bath in the hotel
💳 credit cards accepted:
AE American Express
DC Diners Club
JCB Japanese Credit Bureau
MC MasterCard (Access)
V Visa
🔓 open (for hotels outside Istanbul which are only open in summer months)

Price categories for a standard double room per night, including breakfast, tax and service:
(TL) under US$60
(TL)(TL) US$60–US$100
(TL)(TL)(TL) US$100–US$150
(TL)(TL)(TL)(TL) US$150–US$200
(TL)(TL)(TL)(TL)(TL) over US$200

Barut's Guesthouse

İshakpaşa Cad 8, Sultanahmet.
Map 3 E4 (5 F4). 【 *(0212) 517 68
41.* FAX *(0212) 516 29 44.* **Rooms:** *22.*
🛏 🏨 🖛 *MC, V.* ⓣ

A short walk downhill from the
entrance to Topkapı Palace, this
popular guesthouse has plain but
comfortable rooms. The manager,
Hikmet Bey, is skilled in the art of
making *ebru* (marbled paper and
fabric). Examples of his work
hang on the hotel walls and can
be bought in the lobby shop.

Kybele

Yerebatan Cad 35, Cağaloğlu.
Map 3 E4 (5 E3). 【 *(0212) 511 77
67.* FAX *(0212) 513 43 93.* **Rooms:** *16.*
🛏 🏨 🖼 📺 ⓨ ⓨ 🍴 🖛 *AE,
DC, MC, V.* ⓣ

A tiny, family-run hotel, the Kybele
is full of character, its public areas
filled with Turkish antiques and
handicrafts. The rooms are cosy
and attractive, most with brass
bedsteads. The little patio at the
back, where breakfast is served
in summer, is designed to resemble an Ottoman street. Advance
booking is essential.

Ayasofya Pansiyonları

Soğukçeşme Sok, Sultanahmet.
Map 3 E4 (5 F3). 【 *(0212) 513 36
60.* FAX *(0212) 514 02 13.* **Rooms:** *53.*
🛏 🏨 🖼 ⓨ 🍴 🖛 *AE, MC, V.*
ⓣⓣ

The half-dozen pastel-coloured
wooden buildings on the cobbled
street behind Haghia Sophia *(see
pp72–5)* were among the first of the
Special Licence hotels *(see p175)*.
Ayasofya Pansiyonları is a now a
row of top quality guesthouses. It
has elegant and peaceful rooms
decorated with antiques in late
19th-century Turkish style. Some
rooms are opulent, others under-
stated and simple, but all are
comfortable and full of character.

İshakpaşa Konağı

İshakpaşa Cad 15, Sultanahmet.
Map 3 E4 (5 F4). 【 *(0212) 638 62
67.* FAX *(0212) 638 18 70.* **Rooms:** *18.*
🛏 🏨 🖼 📺 ⓨ ⓨ 🍴 🖛 *V.*
ⓣⓣ

This reddish-brown wooden
building was opened as a Special
Licence hotel in 1996. Its rooms
are simply furnished with iron
bedsteads and white furniture.
The garden, where you can have
breakfast in summer, backs on to
the high walls which surround
Topkapı Palace *(see pp54–9)*.

Konuk Evi

Soğukçeşme Sok, Sultanahmet.
Map 3 E4 (5 E3). 【 *(0212) 513 36
60.* FAX *(0212) 514 02 13.* **Rooms:** *12.*
🛏 🏨 🖼 ⓨ 🍴 🖛 *AE, MC, V.*

The Konuk Evi hotel is a restored
Ottoman mansion across the street
from Ayasofya Pansiyonları. It, too,
is under the management of the
Turkish Touring and Automobile
Club *(see p175)*. This handsome
white wooden building has large
rooms, individually furnished in
the luxurious Ottoman style. It
also has a conservatory restaurant
in an attractive garden, ideal for
peaceful breakfasts.

Karasu Green

Akbıyık Cad 5, Sultanahmet.
Map 3 E4 (5 F4). 【 *(0212) 638 66
01.* FAX *(0212) 638 66 02.* **Rooms:** *15.*
🛏 🏨 🖼 🍴 🖛 *V.* ⓣ

The rooms in this friendly budget
hotel are plainly furnished and
airy. Like so many other hotels in
the area, the Karasu Green has a
large rooftop terrace with views of
the waterways around the city and
the major sights of Sultanahmet.
Downstairs, there is a restaurant,
serving kebabs, *pide* and *lahmacun*
(see p186). Although run by the
hotel, it has a separate entrance.

Nomade

Ticarethane Sok 15, Cağaloğlu.
Map 3 E4 (5 D3). 【 *(0212) 511 12
96.* FAX *(0212) 513 24 04.* **Rooms:** *15.*
🛏 🏨 🖼 🖛 *MC, V.* ⓣ

Tucked away on a rather shabby
sidestreet, Nomade comes as a
refreshing surprise. The tiny lobby
also serves as a sitting room. It
is furnished with sofas covered in
colourful ethnic textiles, and kilim-
covered parquet floors surround
the fireplace. The rooms are simple
but charmingly decorated, with
wooden wardrobes, Turkoman
bedspreads and iron bedsteads.

Şebnem

Adliye Sok 1, Sultanahmet.
Map 3 E4 (5 F4). 【 *(0212) 517 66
23.* FAX *(0212) 638 10 56.* **Rooms:** *7.*
🛏 🖛 *AE, V.* ⓣ

A tiny guesthouse, the Şebnem has
a large rooftop terrace with exceptional sea views. The hotel's pretty
little rooms are equipped with
simple wooden furniture. All of
them have central heating. In the
small lobby you can find a cosy
resting place to browse through a
variety of foreign periodicals.

Alzer

Atmeydanı Sok 72, Sultanahmet.
Map 3 D4 (5 D4). 【 *(0212) 516 62
62.* FAX *(0212) 516 00 00.* **Rooms:** *21.*
🛏 🏨 🖼 📺 🖛 ⓨ ⓨ 🍴 🖛
AE, JCB, MC, V. ⓣⓣ

The Alzer is a friendly, busy hotel
which could not be better situated.
The front rooms look out over the
monuments of the Hippodrome
and the Blue Mosque. The hotel
has a pavement café and restaurant for summer dining, and a
covered, top-floor restaurant overlooking Sultanahmet.

Ayasofya

Demirci Reşit Sok 28, Sultanahmet.
Map 3 D5 (4 C5). 【 *(0212) 516 94
46.* FAX *(0212) 518 07 00.* **Rooms:** *21.*
🛏 🏨 🖼 ⓨ 🍴 🖛 *AE, MC, V.*
ⓣⓣ

This Special Licence hotel, not to
be confused with the Ayasofya
Pansiyonları, is a restored 19th-
century wooden mansion. The
floors of its comfortable rooms are
covered with Turkish carpets.
Some rooms have air conditioning.
The hotel has a small "winter
garden" which serves as a café-
bar. The Ayasofya's experienced
staff are welcoming and gracious.

Empress Zoe

Adliye Sok 10, Sultanahmet.
Map 3 E4 (5 F4). 【 *(0212) 518 25
04.* FAX *(0212) 518 56 99.* **Rooms:** *19.*
🛏 🏨 ⓨ ⓨ 🖛 *MC, V.* ⓣⓣ

Offering modest comforts in a
compact space, the Empress Zoe
is one of the most interesting and
striking hotels in Istanbul. The
hotel's reception is decorated with
modern murals inspired by the
mosaics of Haghia Sophia and all
the rooms are uniquely decorated.
The beds, which include some four-
posters, are covered with boldly
coloured Asiatic textiles. All the
rooms, with the exception of two,
are small. The hotel has a tiny
garden and terrace.

Historia

Amiral Tafdil Sok 23, Sultanahmet.
Map 3 E5 (5 F5). 【 *(0212) 517 74
72.* FAX *(0212) 516 81 69.* **Rooms:** *27.*
🛏 🏨 🖼 🖼 🖛 📇 ⓨ 🍴 🖛
MC, V. ⓣ

This is a pretty wooden hotel with
beautiful views of the Sea of Marmara and its Asiatic shore in the
distance. The rooms are plain but
comfortably equipped. Ask for one
of the three rooms with balconies
that open on to the back gardens
of the neighbourhood. The Historia
has a small ivy-decked breakfast
patio, which is open in the summer.

İbrahim Paşa

Terzihane Sok 5, Sultanahmet.
Map 3 D4 (5 D4). (*(0212) 518 03
94.* FAX *(0212) 518 44 57.* **Rooms:** 19.
▦ ▦ TV 目 Y Y 凸 AE, DC,
MC, V. ⓉⓁⓉⓁ

The İbrahim Paşa is a charming
hotel housed in a small stone building. The individually decorated
rooms are uniquely stylish, with
furniture ranging from traditional
Turkish to Art Deco. Old family
photos hang in the breakfast room,
while a fireplace in the sitting
room warms winter evenings. The
tiny rooftop terrace is especially
pleasant after dark, when the
surrounding buildings of Sultanahmet are floodlit.

Sidera

Dönüş Sok 14, Sultanahmet.
Map 3 D5 (4 B5). (*(0212) 638 34
60.* FAX *(0212) 518 72 62.* **Rooms:** 14.
▦ ▦ ㉔ Y ⅰ 凸 AE, MC, V.
ⓉⓁⓉⓁ

A converted 19th-century wooden
house, the green-painted Sidera
feels like a family home. Although
it is small, it offers most hotel
facilities. Its location in an old
residential area, on a narrow street
lined with crooked wooden
homes, adds to its charm. Patch-
work-patterned bedspreads
brighten up the rooms.

Pierre Loti

Piyerloti Cad 5, Çemberlitaş.
Map 3 D4 (4 C4). (*(0212) 518 57
00.* FAX *(0212) 516 18 86.* **Rooms:** 35.
▦ ▦ ㉔ TV 目 凸 Y ⅰ ◐
凸 AE, MC, V. ⓉⓁⓉⓁ

Named after the 19th-century novelist and lover of Istanbul, Pierre Loti
(see p42), this is an attractive hotel
in the heart of the most historic
part of the city. Its summer garden,
next to the busy Divanyolu Caddesi,
where you can watch the trams
and people pass by, is surprisingly
peaceful thanks to a screen of
green plants. The rooms are small
and plainly furnished, but modern
and comfortable.

Antea

Piyerloti Cad 21, Çemberlitaş.
Map 3 D4 (4 C4). (*(0212) 638 11
21.* FAX *(0212) 517 79 49.* **Rooms:** 45.
▦ ▦ ㉔ TV Y 目 凸 凸 P
Y ⅰ 凸 DC, MC, V. ⓉⓁⓉⓁ

Overlooking a small square shaded
by tall trees just off the main road
through Sultanahmet, the Antea is
a peaceful hotel housed in a plain
restored stone building. Its rooms
are modern and well furnished.
The spacious restaurant serves
Turkish and international dishes.

Armada

Ahır Kapı Sok, Sultanahmet. **Map** 3
E5 (5 F5). (*(0212) 638 13 70.*
FAX *(0212) 518 50 60.* **Rooms:** 110.
▦ ▦ ㉔ 目 凸 目 凸 凸
P Y ⅰ 凸 AE, MC, V. ⓉⓁⓉⓁⓉⓁ

This modern but atmospheric hotel
is distinguished by its luxury accommodation and dining facilities. It is
located just off the road along the
shore of the Sea of Marmara, and
some of the front rooms have sea
views. The hotel prides itself on
using environmentally friendly
products such as herbal soaps and
recycled paper. There is a large
glassed-in terrace with views of
Sultanahmet and the sea. The restaurant *(see p194)* and bar have a
convivial atmosphere.

Avicenna

Amiral Tafdil Sok 31, Sultanahmet.
Map 3 E5 (5 E5). (*(0212) 517 05
53.* FAX *(0212) 516 65 55.* **Rooms:** 49.
▦ ▦ ㉔ TV P Y ⅰ 凸 AE,
MC, V. ⓉⓁⓉⓁ

Occupying two handsomely
renovated historic buildings, the
Avicenna is one of the more expensive Special Licence hotels. It has
luxurious interiors and parquet
floors covered with beautiful rugs.
The 13 rooms in the back building
are the largest and most elegant.
They also have air-conditioning, but
are right beside the railway line
and can be noisy. The Avicenna
has several attic rooms with
private balconies, complete with
chaise longues and umbrellas,
overlooking superb sea views.

Citadel

Kennedy Cad, Sultanahmet.
Map 3 E5 (5 F5). (*(0212) 516 23
13.* FAX *(0212) 516 13 84.* **Rooms:** 29.
▦ ▦ ㉔ TV Y 目 Y ⅰ 凸
AE, MC, V. ⓉⓁⓉⓁ

Located right on the busy coastal
road beneath Sultanahmet, the
Citadel is a pleasant hotel with
luxuriously comfortable rooms.
Those at the front of the building
have sea views. It has an attractive
restaurant and a nightclub which
features belly-dancing shows.

Festival

Piyerloti Cad 62, Çemberlitaş.
Map 3 D4 (4 B4). (*(0212) 638 22
00.* FAX *(0212) 518 50 65.* **Rooms:**
113. ▦ ▦ ㉔ TV Y 目 目
凸 Y ⅰ ◐ 凸 MC, V. ⓉⓁⓉⓁⓉⓁ

Despite an unremarkable exterior,
the interior of the Festival is among
the prettiest to be found in this
area. The pleasant corner café on
the mezzanine floor, for example,
is a miniature version of the Fruit

Room *(see p58)* in the Harem of
Topkapı Palace. The bedrooms,
meanwhile, are elegantly furnished.
In the tiled lobby café the wait-
resses wear Ottoman dress. There
is a tiny rooftop swimming pool.

Obelisk

Amiral Tafdil Sok 17, Sultanahmet.
Map 3 E5 (5 F5). (*(0212) 517 71
73.* FAX *(0212) 517 68 61.* **Rooms:** 41.
▦ ▦ ㉔ TV 凸 Y ⅰ 凸 AE,
MC, V. ⓉⓁⓉⓁⓉⓁ

The Obelisk is one of several
converted 19th-century wooden
mansions on this street. Its interior
is lavishly furnished in Ottoman
style. A number of rooms have
elegant brass bedsteads, and almost
all back rooms have spectacular
views of the Sea of Marmara, as
does the splendid terrace restaurant.

Sarı Konak

Mimar Mehmet Ağa Cad 42–46,
Sultanahmet. **Map** 3 E5 (5 E5).
(*(0212) 638 62 58.* FAX *(0212) 517
86 35.* **Rooms:** 17. ▦ ▦ ㉔ 凸
P Y ⅰ 凸 MC, V. ⓉⓁⓉⓁⓉⓁ

This converted Ottoman mansion
is one of the most attractive hotels
in Sultanahmet. The Sarı Konak has
a lovely patio with a small marble
fountain, and an equally charming
roof terrace. Ask for one of the
three bay-windowed rooms and lie
back on the sofa to watch the street
from behind latticed windows, just
as Ottoman women once did.

Sokullu Paşa

Şehit Mehmet Paşa Sok 5–7, Sultanahmet. **Map** 3 D5 (4 C5). (*(0212)
518 17 90.* FAX *(0212) 518 17 93.*
Rooms: 37. ▦ ▦ ㉔ Y ⅰ ◐
凸 AE, DC, JCB, MC, V. ⓉⓁⓉⓁⓉⓁ

What distinguishes the Sokullu Paşa
hotel is its intimate back garden
filled with plants, flowers and small
antique fountains. Interior decoration is in Art Deco style, and some
of the rooms have views of the
Sea of Marmara. The Sokullu's
small tiled Turkish bath occupies
part of a wine cellar dating back
many centuries.

Valide Sultan Konağı

Kutlugün Sok 1, Sultanahmet.
Map 3 E4 (5 F4). (*(0212) 638 06
00.* FAX *(0212) 638 14 60.* **Rooms:** 17.
▦ ▦ ㉔ TV Y 目 凸 Y ⅰ 凸
AE, MC, V. ⓉⓁⓉⓁ

Close to Topkapı Palace, the Valide
Sultan is a large corner building
with surprisingly few rooms. The
interior is lavishly decorated in the
style of late Ottoman mansions. It
has a rooftop restaurant *(see p194)*,
and a summer terrace from which
there are panoramic views.

Kalyon

Kennedy Cad, Sultanahmet.
Map 3 E5 (5 F5). 【 (0212) 517
44 00. **FAX** (0212) 638 11 11.
Rooms: 103. 🛏 🛗 24 TV Y 🗐
🗒 🗄 P Y 🔢 🗢 AE, MC, V.
℡℡℡℡

The Kalyon, a large four-star hotel
which is a perennial favourite, is
located on the main coastal road
below Sultanahmet. The restaurant
and bars are set in the hotel's green,
spacious grounds, and are popular
with locals as well as guests.

Yeşil Ev

Kabasakal Cad 5, Sultanahmet.
Map 3 E4 (5 E4). 【 (0212) 517 67
85. **FAX** (0212) 517 67 80. **Rooms:** 18.
🛏 🛗 24 Y 🔢 🗢 AE, MC, V.
℡℡℡℡

The pioneer of Special Licence
hotels, Yeşil Ev (the "Green House")
has been a favourite since its conversion in the early 1980s. Rooms
are decorated in period style and
service is attentive. Room 31, the
Pasha Room, even has its own *en
suite* Turkish bath. The tranquil rear
garden is charming in every season
with its birds, plants and fountain.
Advance booking is essential.

Four Seasons

Tevfikhane Sok 1, Sultanahmet.
Map 3 E4 (5 F4). 【 (0212) 638 82
00. **FAX** (0212) 638 82 10. **Rooms:** 65.
🛏 🛗 24 TV Y 🗐 🗒 🗄 🗢
🗄 P Y 🔢 🗢 AE, DC, JCB, MC,
V. ℡℡℡℡℡

The only reminders that this luxury
hotel was once a prison are a
marble pillar with an inscription
carved by a convict, dated 1935,
and the iron grilles on some windows. Neo-Classical in style, it is
the only five-star hotel in Sultanahmet. The rectangular building,
with watchtowers on each corner,
encloses an inner courtyard which
has been turned into a beautiful
garden with a conservatory restaurant. The impeccable rooms have
spectacular marble bathrooms.

THE BAZAAR QUARTER

President

Tiyatro Cad 25, Çarşıkapı. **Map** 2 C4
(4 A4). 【 (0212) 516 69 80.
FAX (0212) 516 69 98. **Rooms:** 204.
🛏 🛗 24 TV Y 🗢 🗄 🗒
P Y 🔢 🗢 AE, DC, MC, V.
℡℡℡℡℡

The President is one of the few
recommendable hotels in Beyazıt,
an area busy with traders from the

former Soviet Union and eastern
Europe. Most of the rooms in this
large modern hotel have views of
the Sea of Marmara, over the domes
of mosques and ancient churches.
The hotel has several restaurants
and bars, a renowned belly-dance
nightclub, Orient House *(see p213),*
and an "English pub". There is
also a tiny rooftop pool and sun-
bathing deck, and an indoor pool.

Merit Antique

Ordu Cad 226, Laleli. **Map** 2 B4.
【 (0212) 513 93 00. **FAX** (0212) 512
63 90. **Rooms:** 274. 🛏 🛗 24 TV
Y 🗐 🗢 🗄 🗒 🔢 🗢 🗢
AE, DC, MC, V. ℡℡℡℡℡

The four large buildings enclosing
several courtyards that the Merit
Antique occupies today were built
in 1918. It is one of the most attractive examples of early 20th-century
civil building in Istanbul. When it
became a hotel in 1987, glass roofs
were put over the courtyards, turning them into elegant lobbies and
dining rooms, complete with birds,
plants, marble fountains and graceful chandeliers. Grand spiral
staircases in every corner lead up
to the rooms. The Merit Antique
has gourmet Chinese and Turkish
restaurants, and the only Jewish
kosher restaurant in the city.
Rooms, however, tend to be small
and dark. Ask for one overlooking
the Tulip Mosque *(see p93).*

BEYOĞLU

Elan

Meşrutiyet Cad 213, Tepebaşı.
Map 7 D5. 【 (0212) 252 54 49.
FAX (0212) 252 61 17. **Rooms:** 44.
🛏 24 TV Y 🗐 🗒 Y 🔢 🗢
AE, DC, MC, V. ℡

The Elan is a modest but comfortable hotel for budget travellers,
with small, well-furnished rooms.
The upper front rooms have views
of the Golden Horn. The small bar
and the basement restaurant both
have decorative pools.

Gezi

Mete Cad 42, Taksim. **Map** 7 F3.
【 (0212) 251 74 30. **FAX** (0212) 251
74 73. **Rooms:** 50. 🛏 24 🗒 🔢
🗢 AE, MC, V. ℡

Despite the shabby exterior of this
downtown hotel, inside you will
find comfortable rooms at budget
prices, and attentive service. Above
all, this hotel has exceptional views
of the Bosphorus from all its back
rooms and from the dining area.
The view from the front rooms,
overlooking Taksim Park, is equally
pleasing. The Gezi is close to entertainment and shopping areas.

Plaza

Arslanyatağı Sok 19–21, Beyoğlu.
Map 7 E4. 【 (0212) 245 32 73.
FAX (0212) 293 70 40. **Rooms:** 30.
🛗 24 TV 🗒 🔢 🗢 MC, V. ℡

This inexpensive hotel is an old
apartment building on an atmospheric back street in Cihangir,
near central Taksim. It has excellent views of the Bosphorus and
the Asian shore from its back
rooms. Most rooms, however, are
rather spartan, and only 18 of
them have *en suite* showers.

Büyük Londra

Meşrutiyet Cad 117, Tepebaşı.
Map 7 D5. 【 (0212) 245 06 70.
FAX (0212) 245 06 71. **Rooms:** 54.
🛏 🛗 24 TV 🗒 Y 🔢 🗢 AE,
JCB, MC, V. ℡℡

Built in 1850 as the mansion of a
wealthy Greek merchant family,
this building was converted into the
Grand Hotel de Londres in 1892.
Since then only the name of this
museum-like building seems to
have changed. It is full of dusty
antique furniture and still impressive in its 19th-century grandeur.
Ernest Hemingway *(see p42)* was
one of the famous residents here
after World War I, when he was a
newspaper reporter. Sadly, although
the rooms are large, the furniture
and facilities are now worn out
and shabby. But the Golden Horn
view from the upper front rooms
helps to compensate for this.

Vardar

Sıraselviler Cad 54–56, Taksim.
Map 7 E4. 【 (0212) 252 28 88.
FAX (0212) 252 15 27. **Rooms:** 40.
🛏 🛗 24 TV 🗒 Y 🔢 🗢 AE,
MC, V. ℡℡

A dignified-looking 19th-century
stone building, the Vardar is
situated in the heart of the city's
entertainment district, close to
Taksim Square. The rooms are
comfortable, but those facing on
to the main street can be noisy
until well after midnight. Rooms at
the back are quiet but rather dark.

Emperyal

Meşrutiyet Cad 38, Tepebaşı.
Map 7 D4. 【 (0212) 293 39 55.
FAX (0212) 252 43 70. **Rooms:** 52.
🛏 🛗 24 TV Y 🗐 🗒 🗢 🗄 🗒
Y 🔢 🗢 AE, MC, V. ℡℡℡

This hotel stands on the site of the
Grand Imperial Hotel, one of the
great hotels of mid-19th century
Istanbul. It was destroyed by a fire
at the end of the 19th century, but
the façade of the present hotel was
built in the style of the original.
The Emperyal is a modern, com-

fortable hotel. The front rooms overlook a busy street, while the back rooms look out on to the pretty, peaceful garden of the British Consulate *(see p103)*.

Sed

Beşaret Sok 14, Kabataş. **Map** 7 F4.
(*(0212) 252 27 10.* FAX *(0212) 252 42 74.* **Rooms:** *50.* 🖥 🛏 📺 📺 🍽 🗐 🍴 🗑 **P** 🍷 🚻 🗐 *AE, MC, V.* 🗑🗑🗑

Tucked away in a peaceful residential street south of Taksim, the Sed has a familiar, homely atmosphere in spite of its size. But above all, most of the upper rooms offer delightful views of the Bosphorus. The hotel has a glass-roofed terrace which serves as a bar-restaurant.

Dilson

Sıraselviler Cad 49, Taksim. **Map** 7 E4.
(*(0212) 252 96 00.* FAX *(0212) 249 70 77.* **Rooms:** *112.* 🖥 🛏 📺 📺 🍽 🗐 🗐 🔧 🍷 🚻 🗐 *AE, DC, MC, V.* 🗑🗑🗑🗑

A stone's throw from Taksim Square, on one of the busiest streets for nightlife, the Dilson is a large hotel which provides four-star facilities in spacious surroundings. Most of its upper back rooms have views of the sea and the Asian side of Istanbul.

Mercure

Meşrutiyet Cad, Tepebaşı. **Map** 7 D5.
(*(0212) 251 46 46.* FAX *(0212) 249 80 33.* **Rooms:** *197.* 🖥 🛏 📺 📺 🍽 🗐 🍴 🔧 🍷 🚻 🗐 *AE, DC, JCB, MC, V.* 🗑🗑🗑

Situated opposite the historic Pera Palas Hotel, the tall modern Mercure stands in stark contrast to it. Most of the rooms have breathtaking views over the rooftops of the Galata district, the Golden Horn, the old city and the Sea of Marmara. The tiny swimming pool on the roof and the large breakfast salon also offer panoramic views. Café Opera in the lobby serves excellent Turkish and international food. There is also a patisserie there. Some of the rooms are reserved for non-smokers. All are rather small, but comfortable.

Pera Palas

Meşrutiyet Cad 98-100, Tepebaşı.
Map 7 D5. (*(0212) 251 45 60.*
FAX *(0212) 251 40 89.* **Rooms:** *144.* 🖥 📺 📺 🍷 🗐 🔧 🔧 **P** 🍷 🚻 🗐 *AE, DC, MC, V.* 🗑🗑🗑🗑

Built in 1892 to accommodate the passengers of the Orient Express, the Pera Palas is the most famous hotel in Istanbul *(see p104)*. It has hosted celebrities from all over the world, but its fame is due, in the main, to Agatha Christie, who stayed here several times between 1924 and 1933. It is said that she wrote her *Murder on the Orient Express* in Room 411, which is still available to visitors at no extra charge and is decorated with her books and pictures. The room Atatürk *(see pp28–9)* stayed in is preserved as a small museum. Today the Pera's faded beauty is still witness to its days of glory. Many of the fixtures are original, from the plumbing to the door handles, worn period furniture and the shaky wood and wrought iron lift. The salon, with its marble columns and lavish decorations, exudes a majestic atmosphere. The Pera's back rooms have enchanting views of the Golden Horn.

Richmond

İstiklal Cad 445, Beyoğlu. **Map** 7 D5.
(*(0212) 252 54 60.* FAX *(0212) 252 97 07.* **Rooms:** *109.* 🖥 🛏 📺 📺 🍽 🗐 🍴 🚻 🗐 *AE, MC, V.* 🗑🗑🗑🗑

The Richmond offers a choice of views from its modern comfortable rooms. Back rooms look out over the garden of the Russian Consulate, down to Seraglio Point and the Sea of Marmara. The front rooms face İstiklal Caddesi, with its colourful crowds and tinkling red trams. When the hotel is not fully occupied, one floor is allocated to non-smokers. Within the Richmond is one of the oldest cafés in Istanbul, the attractive, French-style Lebon *(see p201)*. There is also a Turkish restaurant which stages belly-dancing shows.

Ceylan Inter-Continental

Asker Ocağı Cad 1, Taksim. **Map** 7 F3.
(*(0212) 231 21 21.* FAX *(0212) 231 21 80.* **Rooms:** *335.* 🖥 🛏 📺 📺 🍽 🗐 🍴 🎭 🔧 🗑 🔧 **P** 🍷 🚻 🗐 *AE, DC, JCB, MC, V.* 🗑🗑🗑

This landmark skyscraper, previously the Sheraton, is one of the top international hotels in the city. The imposing lobby is decorated in the style of a fairy-tale Arabian palace, with striking golden staircases, over-size chandeliers and palm trees. The dining facilities and rooms are more sober. The Ceylan has one of the most beautiful and expansive views of Istanbul in all four directions, dazzling at any time of day. The top floor houses a French/Thai restaurant, Citronelle *(see p196)*, a quality Turkish restaurant, Safran, and the glitzy City Lights Bar. Amenities include an outdoor pool and a high-tech fitness centre.

Marmara

Taksim Meydanı, Taksim. **Map** 7 E4.
(*(0212) 251 46 96.* FAX *(0212) 244 05 09.* **Rooms:** *410.* 🖥 🛏 📺 📺 🍽 🗐 🍴 🎭 🔧 🔧 **P** 🍷 🚻 🗑 🔧 *AE, DC, JCB, MC, V.* 🗑🗑🗑

Few other hotels can beat the breathtaking views from the Marmara's rooftop restaurant and lounge bar. This towering luxury hotel in the middle of Taksim Square serves as the headquarters of the nearly 1,500 performers who appear in the International Istanbul Festival every summer *(see pp44–5)*. In the ground-level Café Marmara, which spills out on to the pavement in summer, you can have a late evening snack surrounded by the festival's celebrities. The Marmara's top-class facilities include a small terrace pool and the Brasserie Restaurant, which serves a variety of international dishes at its buffet lunches on Sundays.

ALONG THE CITY WALLS

Kariye

Kariye Camii Sok 18, Edirnekapı.
Map 1 B1. (*(0212) 534 84 14.*
FAX *(0212) 521 66 31.* **Rooms:** *27.* 🖥 🛏 📺 🍷 **P** 🍷 🚻 🗑 *AE, DC, MC, V.* 🗑🗑🗑

Set in the shadow of the Church of St Saviour in Chora *(see pp118–9)*, the Kariye is a wooden mansion, lovingly renovated by the Turkish Touring and Automobile Club *(see p175)*. The comfortable rooms are decorated in pale pastel colours, with wooden floors and latticed windows. Outside, there is a lovely tree-shaded summer garden. The hotel has an atmospheric restaurant, Asitane *(see p196)*, which serves excellent Turkish food.

BEYOND TAKSIM

Lamartine

Lamartin Cad 25, Taksim.
Map 7 E3. (*(0212) 254 62 70.*
FAX *(0212) 256 27 76.* **Rooms:** *66.* 🖥 🛏 📺 📺 🍷 🗐 🔧 🍷 🚻 🗐 *AE, MC, V.* 🗑🗑🗑

This is one of the numerous four-star hotels situated in Taksim, preferred for their convenient location close to the central shopping and entertainment areas of the city. The Lamartine's rooms are both comfortable and spacious. The Ming Garden Chinese Restaurant, located next door, is also run by the hotel.

For key to symbols *see p179*

Golden Age

Topçu Cad 22, Taksim. **Map** 7 E3.
((0212) 254 49 06. **FAX** (0212) 255
13 68. **Rooms:** 180. ▢ ▢ 24 TV
▢ ▢ ▢ ▢ ▢ ▢ ▢ ▢
▢ AE, DC, MC, V. ⓉⓁⓉⓁⓉⓁ

A massive, modern hotel in one of
the busy side streets near Taksim
Square, the Golden Age has a large
roof terrace with a small swimming pool and panoramic views
of the city. Its spacious rooms are
comfortably furnished in pastel
shades, with wall-to-wall carpets.

Green Park

Abdülhak Hamit Cad 50, Taksim.
Map 7 E3. **(** (0212) 238 05 05.
FAX (0212) 237 76 46. **Rooms:** 81.
▢ ▢ 24 TV ▢ ▢ ▢ ▢ ▢
▢ ▢ ▢ AE, DC, MC, V.
ⓉⓁⓉⓁⓉⓁ

Opened in 1996, the four-star Green
Park is one of the most pleasant
hotels in the area. It has comfortable, well-decorated rooms, and
several suites equipped with business facilities. The restaurant is
large and luxurious, and there is a
rooftop bar. Staff can arrange car
and boat hire, and tours of the city.

Maçka

Eytam Cad 35, Maçka. **Map** 8 A3.
((0212) 234 32 00. **FAX** (0212) 240
76 94. **Rooms:** 180. ▢ ▢ 24 TV
▢ ▢ ▢ ▢ ▢ ▢ ▢ ▢
AE, DC, MC, V. ⓉⓁⓉⓁⓉⓁ

This large, well-established hotel,
close to the business and conven-
tion centres of uptown Istanbul, is
on a pleasant boulevard with little
traffic. The Maçka is also close to
the shopping districts of Nişantaşı
and Teşvikiye. Many of the rooms
have balconies overlooking Maçka
Park, one of the largest parks in
the city, and the Bosphorus. The
leisure facilities include a sauna.

Çırağan Palace Hotel Kempinski

Çırağan Cad 84, Beşiktaş. **Map** 9 D3.
((0212) 258 33 77. **FAX** (0212) 259
66 86. **Rooms:** 322. ▢ ▢ 24 TV
▢ ▢ ▢ ▢ ▢ ▢ ▢ ▢
▢ AE, DC, MC, V. ⓉⓁⓉⓁⓉⓁⓉⓁ

Originally an Ottoman palace on
the Bosphorus, the Çırağan Palace
(see p123) is now one of the most
luxurious hotels in Istanbul, and
probably the most enchanting. It
was restored and converted in the
early 1990s, when new buildings
were added. The dining and entertainment areas are decorated in
arabesque style, supposedly resembling that of the original palace.
The Çırağan has an exceptionally
good Ottoman-cuisine restaurant,

Tuğra, and an Italian restaurant.
It is also famous for its outdoor
swimming pool, located right at
the edge of the palatial garden,
giving one the impression of
swimming in the Bosphorus.

Divan

Cumhuriyet Cad 2, Elmadağ.
Map 7 F3. **(** (0212) 231 41 00.
FAX (0212) 248 85 27. **Rooms:** 180.
▢ ▢ 24 TV ▢ ▢ ▢ ▢ ▢
▢ ▢ ▢ ▢ AE, DC, MC, V.
ⓉⓁⓉⓁⓉⓁⓉⓁ

Located on a tree-lined boulevard
a short walk from Taksim Square,
the Divan is one of the oldest five-
star hotels in the city. Opened in
1956, it is owned by the Koç family
(see p127), who head the biggest
industrial and commercial empire
in Turkey. Many of the rooms
overlook gardens. The front rooms
facing on to the street are noisy
when windows are open, but
otherwise well insulated. The hotel
has a good patisserie (see p200).

Istanbul Hilton

Cumhuriyet Cad, Taksim. **Map** 7 F2.
((0212) 231 46 50. **FAX** (0212) 240
41 65. **Rooms:** 501. ▢ ▢ 24 TV
▢ ▢ ▢ ▢ ▢ ▢ ▢ P
▢ ▢ ▢ ▢ AE, DC, JCB, MC, V.
ⓉⓁⓉⓁⓉⓁⓉⓁ

All the rooms in the towering
Istanbul Hilton have balconies
offering marvellous sweeping
views of either the Bosphorus or
the spacious gardens in which the
hotel stands. Non-smoking rooms
are available. Extensive leisure
facilities include squash and tennis
courts and a swimming pool. The
hotel also offers the most up-to-
date business services, such as
internet access, and personal com-
puter connection points in rooms.

Swissôtel

Bayıldım Cad 2, Maçka. **Map** 8 A4.
((0212) 259 01 01. **FAX** (0212) 259
01 05. **Rooms:** 585. ▢ ▢ 24 TV
▢ ▢ ▢ ▢ ▢ ▢ ▢ P
▢ ▢ ▢ ▢ AE, DC, JCB, MC, V.
ⓉⓁⓉⓁⓉⓁⓉⓁ

On a hill overlooking Dolmabahçe
Palace, the Swissôtel commands
expansive views which extend
from Seraglio Point along the Bosphorus. These can be enjoyed
from most of its rooms. Besides its
elegance and luxury, the Swissôtel
is noted for its variety of gourmet
restaurants (see p197), specializing
in Swiss, Turkish, Japanese,
Chinese and French food. Outside,
the hotel has lush gardens and
various sports facilities. For evening
entertainment there are several
bars and nightclubs. The Swissôtel
also has a non-smoking floor.

Eysan

Rihtim Cad 26, Kadıköy. **(** (0216)
346 24 40. **FAX** (0216) 347 23 29.
Rooms: 52. ▢ ▢ 24 TV ▢ ▢
P ▢ ▢ ▢ MC, V. ⓉⓁⓉⓁ

Standing opposite Kadıköy pier,
the Eysan is one of the better
hotels clustered in this colourful
area. The front rooms have views
of the Sea of Marmara and Seraglio
Point in the distance, but can be
noisy. The hotel is conveniently
located for sights and shopping
areas on the Asian side, and for
transport over to European Istanbul.

Bebek

Cevdetpaşa Cad 113-115, Bebek,
European side. **(** (0212) 263 30 00.
FAX (0212) 263 26 36. **Rooms:** 30.
▢ ▢ 24 ▢ ▢ ▢ ▢ AE, DC,
MC, V. ⓉⓁⓉⓁ

Located right on the waterfront, the
Bebek is an unassuming but
charming hotel. Front rooms have
lovely views of Bebek Bay. The
first-floor terrace bar is a popular
spot to have an early evening
drink while listening to live jazz.

Bosphorus Paşa

Yaliboyu Cad 64, Beylerbeyi, Asian
side. **(** (0216) 422 00 03.
FAX (0216) 422 00 12. **Rooms:** 14.
▢ ▢ 24 TV ▢ ▢ ▢ ▢ ▢
▢ AE, DC, MC, V. ⓉⓁⓉⓁⓉⓁⓉⓁ

The Bosphorus Paşa is a handsome
Special Licence hotel on the shores
of the Bosphorus. First built as a
yali (see p139) in 1890, it has been
carefully restored and retains its
original simple but elegant form.
The rooms are large, with high
ceilings, and are furnished with
period Italian pieces. In the basement there is a gourmet Italian
restaurant, Cecconi's, where waves
from the Bosphorus splash right
up against the windows.

Rüstempaşa Kervansaray

Eski Camii Yanı, Edirne. **(** (0284)
212 61 18. **FAX** (0284) 212 04 62.
Rooms: 79. ▢ ▢ 24 TV P ▢
▢ ▢ MC, V. ⓉⓁ

An ancient caravanserai, built
by the architect Sinan in the 16th
century (see p155), houses the

oldest hotel in Edirne. It has been skilfully renovated to retain something of the atmosphere of the old inn. The bedrooms are thick-walled and cell-like, with some of their original fixtures, like the fireplaces, but little furniture. Only half the caravanserai, the Büyük Han (Great Hall), is in use as a hotel; the other half, the Küçük Han (Small Hall), is a student hostel. In term time the students congregate in the courtyard and pool hall below the hotel and practise their English on willing guests. The restaurant is open in summer only.

ŞİLE

Şile Resort

Uzunkum, Şile. **(** (0216) 711 36 27.
FAX (0216) 711 40 03. **Rooms:** 52.
🛏 🎴 📺 📺 📺 🎴 📺 🎴 📺
🅿 📺 🍴 📧 MC, V. ⓣⓛ ⓣⓛ

This brand-new hotel is the most luxurious in Şile. It is located 5 km (3 miles) out of town, but frequent dolmuşes connect it to Şile town centre. The rooms are spacious and well furnished, with sea views from their balconies. The hotel has a private beach and an outdoor pool with a children's section. It also has a play room. The price includes breakfast and an evening meal.

POLONEZKÖY

Polka Country

Cumhuriyet Yolu 36, Polonezköy.
((0216) 432 32 20. **FAX** (0216) 432 30 42. **Rooms:** 15. 🛏 🍴 ⓣⓛ ⓣⓛ ⓣⓛ

Standing in a lush green garden in the peaceful village of Polonezköy (see p158), the interior of the Polka Country is decorated with walnut furniture throughout. The rooms are very comfortable and the hotel also has a sauna for the use of its guests.

THE PRINCES' ISLANDS

Büyükada Princess

İskele Cad 2, Büyükada. **(** (0216) 382 16 28. **FAX** (0216) 382 19 49.
Rooms: 24. 🛏 🎴 📺 📺 📋 📺
🎴 📺 🍴 📧 MC, V. ⓣⓛ ⓣⓛ

The Princess occupies an elegant Neo-Classical stone building in the town square on the largest of the Princes' Islands. Its rooms are comfortable and some have balconies overlooking the sea. The hotel has an outdoor swimming pool and facilities for children, including a playground.

Splendid Palace

Yirmiüç Nisan Cad 71, Büyükada.
((0216) 382 69 50. **FAX** (0216) 382 67 75. **Rooms:** 70. 🛏 🎴 📺 🍴
📧 AE, MC, V. 🕐 Apr–Oct. ⓣⓛⓣⓛ

Built in 1908, this wooden mansion set high on a hill is one of the most beautiful buildings on the island of Büyükada. The Splendid Palace has a large garden and an enticing outdoor swimming pool. Its balconied rooms have magnificent sea views. Sadly, the interiors have been somewhat neglected.

Halki Palace

Refah Şehitleri Cad 88, Heybeliada.
((0216) 351 88 90. **FAX** (0216) 351 84 83. **Rooms:** 43. 🛏 🎴 📺 📺
📺 📋 🎴 📺 📺 🍴 📧 MC, V. ⓣⓛⓣⓛ

Set in a large, terraced garden, the Halki Palace was built in the mid-19th century. The interior of the white wooden building has been lavishly decorated with a combination of classic and modern furniture, glittering chandeliers and antique pendulum clocks, one of which shows the ferry timetable from the island to the city. The Halki commands breathtaking views of the other islands and the Asian shore of Istanbul.

BURSA

Atlas Termal

Hamamlar Cad 35, Çekirge, Bursa.
((0224) 234 41 00. **FAX** (0224) 236 46 05. **Rooms:** 26. 🛏 🎴 📺 🎴
🍴 📺

The Atlas Termal is a small, intimate hotel with a pleasant open courtyard where breakfast is served. The interior is attractively decorated with modern stained glass, and a glass-walled lift gives access to the upper floors. In the basement, as in many of the hotels in Çekirge, there are two well-kept marble Turkish baths, fed by natural hot spring water.

Safran

Ortapazarı Cad, Arka Sok 4, Bursa.
((0224) 224 72 16. **FAX** (0224) 224 72 19. **Rooms:** 10. 🛏 🎴 📺 📺
📺 🅿 🍴 📧 AE, MC, V. ⓣⓛ ⓣⓛ

This attractively renovated, half-timbered building is over one hundred years old. It is located in an atmospheric part of town renowned for its old buildings. The rooms are small and furnished in a disappointingly modern style, but the restaurant is excellent, serving a variety of hot and cold meat and vegetable dishes.

Çelik Palas

Çekirge Cad 79, Çekirge, Bursa.
((0224) 233 38 00. **FAX** (0224) 236 19 10. **Rooms:** 173. 🛏 🎴 📺 📺
📺 📋 🎴 🅿 🎴 📺 🍴 📧
AE, DC, MC, V. ⓣⓛⓣⓛⓣⓛ

This renowned spa hotel (see p168) is situated high on the hillside above Bursa. From the front rooms there are spectacular views over Bursa, while back rooms look out towards the mountains that rise up behind the city. The hotel's luxurious Turkish bath is unusual in having a plunge pool (usually a feature of Roman baths) filled by a constant flow of hot spring water.

MARMARA ISLANDS

En Ön

En Ön Tatil Köyü, Marmara Island.
((0266) 885 50 32. **Rooms:** 30.
🛏 🎴 📺 🍴 🕐 Jul–Sep. ⓣⓛ

There are few activities for tourists on Marmara Island. Instead, visitors come for its relaxed, village way of life. This small family-run hotel is right on the beach, 20 minutes' walk from the town of Marmara. It has only simple facilities but the inexpensive price includes full board. To liven things up there is a discotheque in the hotel every weekend.

Çınar

Türkeli, Avşa Island. **(** (0266) 896 10 14. **FAX** (0266) 896 10 52. **Rooms:** 52. 🛏 🎴 🎴 📺 🅿 🍴 📧 MC, V
🕐 Jun–Sep. ⓣⓛ

This popular family hotel is situated on the seafront of Türkeli, the main resort on Avşa Island, and has a private beach. The water sports centre next door offers reduced rates for guests. As well as two- and three-bed rooms, the Çınar has several larger family rooms. The price includes breakfast and an evening meal.

THE DARDANELLES

Anzac

Saat Kulesi Meydanı 8, Çanakkale.
((0286) 217 77 77. **FAX** (0286) 217 20 18. **Rooms:** 27. 🛏 🎴 📺 📺
🎴 🅿 ⓣⓛ

In Çanakkale town centre, the Anzac is extremely clean and well maintained, with comfortable, light and spacious rooms and a rooftop terrace. The price is competitive compared with the larger, more conspicuous hotels around the ferry landing. The hotel has a laundry for the use of guests.

For key to symbols see p179

RESTAURANTS, CAFÉS AND BARS

ISTANBUL'S RESTAURANTS range from the informal *lokanta* and kebab house, which are found on almost every street corner, to the gourmet restaurants *(restoran)* of large hotels. There are also many international restaurants in the city offering a choice of almost every other kind of cuisine, from French to Japanese. Pages 188–91 illustrate the most typical Turkish dishes and the phrase book on pages 271–2 will help you tackle the menu. On page 191

Simit seller

you will find a guide to drinks available. The key features of the restaurants reviewed in the guide are summarized on pages 192–3 in the *Choosing a Restaurant* section, and a detailed description of each of the selected restaurants is provided on pages 194–9. These have been chosen from the best that Istanbul can offer across all price ranges. Light meals and snacks sold by street vendors and served in cafés and bars are described on pages 200–1.

WHERE TO LOOK

ISTANBUL'S SMARTEST and most expensive restaurants are concentrated in the European parts of the city: in and around Taksim; in the chic shopping districts of Nişantaşı, Maçka and Teşvikiye; and in the modern residential suburbs of Levent and Etiler, west of the Bosphorus. The best gourmet restaurants for both Western and Turkish food are usually in five-star hotels.

Beyoğlu district has several inexpensive restaurants, cafés and fast-food eateries, particularly around İstiklal Caddesi *(see pp102–3)*, which cater for a young and lively crowd.

Sultanahmet, and the neighbouring districts of Sirkeci, Eminönü and Beyazıt, are full of cheap restaurants serving the local population. In recent years, however, some stylish restaurants with modern decor have opened in these areas.

Further afield, in areas such as Fatih, Fener, Balat and Eyüp, there are plenty of cheap restaurants, cafés and pudding shops.

TYPES OF RESTAURANT

THE MOST COMMON type of restaurant is the traditional *lokanta*. This is an ordinary restaurant offering a variety of dishes, often listed by the entrance. *Hazır yemek* (precooked food) is usually served. This comprises hot meat and vegetable dishes displayed in steel containers. Other dishes on the menu may be *sulu yemek* (a broth or stew) and *et* (meat – meaning grilled meat and kebabs).

Equally ubiquitous is the Turkish kebab house *(kebapçı* or *ocakbaşı)*. As well as grilled meats, almost every kebab house serves *lahmacun*, a very thin dough base with minced meat, onions and

Pierre Loti café in Eyüp *(see p200)*

tomato sauce on top *(see p188)*. Cheaper restaurants and kebab houses also serve *pide*, a flattened bread base, served with various toppings such as eggs or lamb. There are also a few specialist *pide* restaurants *(pideci)*.

If you have had too much to drink you may welcome a tripe soup *(işkembe)*, a Turkish cure for a hangover, before going to bed. *İşkembe* restaurants stay open until the early hours of the morning.

FISH RESTAURANTS AND MEYHANES

THE ATMOSPHERE is always informal and lively in Istanbul's innumerable fish restaurants *(balık lokantası)*. The best of these are located on the shores of the Bosphorus *(see pp198–9)* and in Kumkapı, on the Sea of Marmara, which is like one large open-air restaurant in summer. A typical fish restaurant will offer a large variety of mezes *(see p190)*

Körfez, a luxury restaurant overlooking the Bosphorus *(see p199)*

Diners eating at the Konyalı Restaurant in Topkapı Palace *(see p194)*

before you order your main course from the day's catch. Baby tuna *(palamut)*, fresh sardines *(sardalye)* and sea bass *(levrek)* are the most popular fish. They are served fried or grilled and often accompanied by a large plate of salad and a bottle of raki *(see p191)*. The majority of fish restaurants in these busy and popular areas will not accept reservations. However, if you cannot find a table at one restaurant, you will find one at another nearby.

Meyhanes (taverns) serve the same kind of food as fish restaurants. The difference is that in a *meyhane* Turkish music is performed either by visiting musicians or by the customers themselves in an impromptu gathering.

In *meyhanes* and fish restaurants, you will seldom see a menu. Instead the waiters will bring a large tray of mezes to your table from which to make your choice. The day's fish will usually be displayed on large wooden trays. You can order your fish by pointing to it. The daily prices of fish, given per kilogram, should be displayed by the door. If not, simply ask the waiter to weigh the one you want. If you choose a small fish, ask how many fish there are in one portion. Bear in mind that even in the most modest restaurants, fish will always cost more than a meat dish, especially if you choose something out of the ordinary or not in season.

A selection of pastries

OPENING HOURS

TURKS EAT LUNCH between 12:30 and 2pm and have dinner around 8pm. Ordinary restaurants and kebab houses are open from about 11am to 11pm, while fish restaurants serve all day but stay open later. International restaurants have strict opening hours, usually from noon to 3:30pm and 7:30pm to midnight. *Meyhanes* will be open from 7pm until well after midnight. Most restaurants are open seven days a week, but some are closed on either Sunday or Monday. During Ramazan *(see p47)*, when Muslims fast from sunrise to sunset, many restaurants are closed. Some only shut during daylight hours and then serve special Ramazan meals, while others, especially in religious areas such as Fatih and Eyüp, will close altogether for the whole month. In sightseeing areas, however, you will always be able to find somewhere open.

WHAT TO EXPECT

FEW RESTAURANTS in Istanbul cater for special requirements such as vegetarian food or high chairs. However, staff are generally helpful and with some ingenuity and good will a solution can often be found.

When choosing a place to eat, bear in mind that many cheaper restaurants and kebab houses do not serve alcoholic drinks. Only international hamburger and pizza chains, however, have a no-smoking section. No restaurant in the city is equipped for wheelchairs but most are on the ground floor making easy access possible. While vegetarian main courses are rare, most restaurants will have vegetable mezes, which can make a filling main course, and you can always ask for an omelette. In local Turkish restaurants women should look for the *aile salonu* sign. This denotes a separate area for women and families from which solitary men are barred. A single woman will be just as unwelcome in the main restaurant with the men.

No restaurant in Istanbul requires customers to wear jacket and tie, but in luxurious establishments it is more acceptable to be smartly dressed.

SERVICE AND PAYING

IN SMALLER RESTAURANTS the waiter will recite the dishes from memory and possibly forget half your order instead of writing it down. Yet the friendliness of staff will make up for such shortcomings.

The major credit cards are widely accepted, except in kebab houses and cheaper restaurants. Tax and a service charge are included in the bill, but Turks always leave a 10% tip, regardless.

Delicious fried and grilled mackerel sold on Eminönü quayside *(see p200)*

What to Eat in Istanbul

F OR ALMOST FIVE CENTURIES, the different cultures under
Ottoman rule – territories ranging from the Balkans
to North Africa – contributed to the sophisticated cuisine
which was created in the kitchens of Topkapı Palace
(see pp54–9). As well as drawing on this palace tradition, the food of Istanbul today includes diverse
specialities from Anatolia (the Asian part of Turkey).
Many of today's staple dishes originated in central Asia
and were brought by the nomadic Turks as they spread
westwards. Turkish cuisine is sometimes ranked as one
of the world's top three, together
with French and Chinese.

*Breakfast in Turkey consists
of feta-type cheese, tomatoes,
olives and cucumber, as well
as honey, jam, butter and
bread, all served with tea.*

Yoğurt çorbası *is a yoghurt
soup made with pulses or
rice. Soups are eaten at any
time of the day in Istanbul.*

**Palamut
(Bonito)**

**Hamsi
(Anchovies)**

**Uskumru
(Mackerel)**

**Levrek
(Sea bass)**

**Kalkan
(Turbot)**

Hamsi pilavı *is a Black Sea
dish made with a mixture of
anchovies and rice. It is one
of many Turkish rice dishes.*

Levrek pilakisi *is a stew
made with a combination of
sea bass, onions and potatoes,
flavoured with garlic.*

*Fish is widely available in
Istanbul, due to the city's
proximity to the sea. During
the winter months, oil-rich
varieties of fish such as
bluefish and mackerel are
particularly plentiful in
restaurants. The method
of cooking can vary, but in
most cases the fish is served
either grilled or stewed.*

ANATOLIAN DISHES

The dishes of Anatolia are
as varied as the regions they
originate from. They are
traditional and simple, but
nonetheless often colourful
and spicy in taste.

Gözleme

Lahmacun

**Lahmacun and
gözleme** *are bread-
based snacks. The
first is a thin pizza-
style snack. The
second is folded
over or rolled up.*

Fırında mantı *is a dish of
noodle-dough parcels filled
with meat. Other mantı
dishes use the same dough.*

Karides güveç, *prawns with
peppers and tomatoes topped
with cheese, is just one of
many kinds of güveç (stew).*

Bamya bastısı *is a popular
okra and tomato stew which
can be made with or
without chunks of lamb.*

Doner kebab

Adana kebab

Şiş kebab

İskender kebab

Kebabs *may be meat, fish or vegetables. The most popular varieties are doner (sliced roast meat), şiş (cubes of meat grilled on a skewer), Adana (minced meat grilled on a skewer) and İskender, or Bursa kebab (doner meat on bread with a rich tomato and yoghurt sauce).*

PALACE SPECIALITIES

The cooks of the Topkapı Palace kitchens created elaborate dishes during the days of the Ottoman Empire. Vegetables were stuffed or cooked in olive oil. Meat was grilled or roasted, seasoned and sometimes served with either a cream or tomato sauce.

İmam bayıldı, *literally "the imam fainted," is a dish of aubergines stuffed with tomatoes and onions.*

Pomegranate *(nar)*

Apricot *(kayısı)*

Cherries *(kiraz)*

Fig *(incir)*

Water melon *(karpuz)*

Hünkar beğendili köfte *is meatballs "with sultan's delight": a purée of smoked aubergine with cheese.*

Karnıyarık *is a dish of aubergines, split open and stuffed with minced lamb, pine nuts and currants.*

Fresh fruit *in season is the ideal way to round off a Turkish meal. Water melons, figs, pomegranates and apricots are among the most popular choices.*

SWEETS

Sweets are eaten throughout the day in Turkey, not just after a meal. They are sold in shops, on stalls and by street vendors. Some sweets are linked to religious feasts. Istanbul is renowned for its baklava.

Varieties of baklava

Turkish pastries are sticky sweets made from various types of pastry, coated with syrup and sometimes filled with nuts.

Tulumba

Tavuk göğsü kazandibi is a milk pudding made with shredded chicken breasts.

Aşure, also known as "Noah's pudding", is made with a combination of dried fruit and beans.

Fırında sütlaç, an oven-baked rice pudding which is served cold, is popular in Istanbul.

Mezes

MOST TURKISH MEALS begin with mezes, Turkish starters, of which there are hundreds of different kinds with new ones being created all the time. They range from simple combinations, such as plain white cheese with melon, to elaborately stuffed vegetables. Mezes are served in all Turkish restaurants and are often accompanied by raki. *Meyhane* restaurants *(see p187)* specialize in mezes from Anatolia and you may be offered a selection on a tray. Most mezes are served cold and very few of them contain fish or meat, making them ideal for vegetarians.

Turşu, pickles

Ekmek

Pide | *Simit*

Turkish bread *includes* ekmek *(white loaves) and* pide *(flat bread), which is often served with kebabs, and also eaten during religious festivals.* Simit *is a crisp, ring-shaped, savoury bread covered with sesame seeds.*

Cigar-shaped **Sigara böreği**

Triangular **Muska böreği**

Yalancı yaprak dolması (**stuffed vine leaves**)

Midye dolması (**mussel shells stuffed with rice**)

Böreks and Dolmas

Anything that can be stuffed is made into a dolma. The most common are made with vine leaves, peppers and mussels. Börek *(or* böreği*), a filled savoury pastry which is deep fried, can be stuffed with mince, spinach, or cheese with herbs.*

Circassian chicken

(Çerkez tavuğu) *is a cold dish consisting of strips of meat dressed in a creamy walnut and bread sauce.*

COLD MEZES

Several mezes come in the form of purées and dips, often using yoghurt as a base. They are served with fresh, warm bread. Some of the most popular include *patlıcan salatası* (smoked aubergine salad), *haydari* (mint, garlic and yoghurt) and *tarama* (fish roe).

Patlıcan salatası (**smoked aubergine salad**)

Fava (**purée of broad beans**)

Tarama (**purée of fish roe**)

Haydari (**a dip made with mint and garlic**)

Çoban salatası (**tomato, onion and cucumber salad**)

Lakerda, *finely sliced smoked tuna served with lemon, is a popular fish meze from the Black Sea.*

Fasulye piyazı *is a salad of haricot beans with olive oil and lemon juice. It is sometimes topped with boiled egg.*

Zeytinyağlı enginar, *artichoke hearts, is one of many choice vegetable dishes cooked in olive oil.*

What to Drink in Istanbul

THE MOST COMMON DRINK in Istanbul is tea *(çay)*, which is normally served black in small, tulip-shaped glasses. It is offered to you wherever you go: in shops and bazaars, and even in banks and offices. Breakfast is usually accompanied by tea, whereas small cups of strong Turkish coffee *(kahve)* are drunk mid-morning and also at the end of meals. Cold drinks include a variety of fresh fruit juices, such as orange and cherry, and refreshing syrup-based sherbets. Although Turkey does produce its own wine and beer, the most popular alcoholic drink in Istanbul is raki, which is usually served to accompany mezes.

Fruit juice seller

SOFT DRINKS

BOTTLED mineral water *(su)* is sold in corner shops and served in restaurants everywhere. If you are feeling adventurous, you may like to try a glass of *ayran*, salty liquid yoghurt. *Boza*, made from bulgur wheat, is another local drink to sample *(see p92)*. There is always a variety of refreshing fruit and vegetable juices available. They include cherry juice *(vişne suyu)*, turnip juice *(şalgam suyu)* and *şıra*, a juice made from fermented grapes.

Vişne suyu   **Ayran**

COFFEE AND TEA

Traditional samovar for tea

TURKISH COFFEE is dark and strong and is ordered according to the amount of sugar required: *az* (little), *orta* (medium), or *çok şekerli* (a lot). You may have to ask for it especially, as some restaurants may give you instant coffee. The ubiquitous daily drink is tea with sugar but without milk. It is often served from a samovar, a large metal urn. Alternatives include herb teas, such as limeflower *(ıhlamur)*. In winter, *sahlep*, a hot milky drink, is a popular choice.

ALCOHOLIC DRINKS

THE NATIONAL alcoholic drink in Turkey is raki – "lion's milk" – a clear, anise-flavoured spirit, which turns cloudy when water is added. It is drunk with fish and mezes. The Turkish wine industry produces some good reds and whites, served in many restaurants. Doluca and Kavaklıdere are the leading brands. Wines from other countries are generally only available in the best foreign restaurants. Turkey's own Efes Pilsen beer is widely sold. Note that alcohol is not served in some of the cheaper restaurants and kebab houses.

Raki   **Beer**   **Red wine**   **White wine**

Turkish coffee is a very strong drink and an acquired taste for most people.

Sahlep is a hot, winter drink made from powdered orchid root.

Apple tea

Limeflower tea

Choosing a Restaurant

THIS IS A QUICK reference chart to restaurants in Istanbul, highlighting the aspects that might influence your choice. They have been grouped according to the main type of food that each specializes in. More details are given on the following pages.

		Page Number	Outdoor Tables	Air Conditioning	Vegetarian Food	Attractive Location	Alcohol not Served	Suitable for Children	Live Entertainment
TURKISH RESTAURANTS									
Bolkepçe	(TL)	197			●			■	
Cennet	(TL)	194						■	
Havuzlu	(TL)	194			●	■		■	
Sultanahmet Köftecisi	(TL)	194							
Birtat	(TL)(TL)	199	●		●	■		■	
Borsa	(TL)(TL)	195		■	●			■	
Çamlık Moteli	(TL)(TL)	199	●		●	■			
Darüzziyafe	(TL)(TL)	195	●		●	■	●	■	●
Hıdiv Kasrı	(TL)(TL)	198	●		●	■	●	■	
Hünkar	(TL)(TL)	196		■	●			■	
Kanaat	(TL)(TL)	198		■	●		●	■	
Karaca	(TL)(TL)	195	●		●	■			
Lades	(TL)(TL)	195		■	●		●	■	
Lalezar	(TL)(TL)	199	●			■		■	●
Leonardo	(TL)(TL)	199	●		●	■		■	
Moda Park	(TL)(TL)	198	●		●	■		■	
Nature and Peace	(TL)(TL)	195		■	●	■		■	
Safran Hotel Restaurant	(TL)(TL)	199		■	●			■	
Şayan	(TL)(TL)	198	●	■	●			■	
Sedef	(TL)(TL)	196	●	■				●	■
Subaşı	(TL)(TL)	195	●					●	■
Sümengen	(TL)(TL)	194			●	■			
A la Turka	(TL)(TL)	197			●	■	●	■	
Türkistan Aşevi	(TL)(TL)	194	●		●	■	●	■	
Ahırkapı	(TL)(TL)(TL)	194	●	■	●			■	●
Asitane	(TL)(TL)(TL)	197	●	■	●			■	●
Çatı	(TL)(TL)(TL)	196		■	●				●
Hacı Baba	(TL)(TL)(TL)	196	●		●	■			
Hasır Beykoz	(TL)(TL)(TL)	198	●	■		■		■	●
Huzur	(TL)(TL)(TL)	198			●	■			
Kathisma	(TL)(TL)(TL)	194	●	■	●	■		■	
Mercan	(TL)(TL)(TL)	199	●	■	●	■		■	●
Pandeli	(TL)(TL)(TL)	195			●	■			
Rami	(TL)(TL)(TL)	194			●	■			
Valide Sultan Konağı	(TL)(TL)(TL)	194	●	■	●	■			
Les Ambassadeurs	(TL)(TL)(TL)(TL)	199		■	●	■			
Four Seasons	(TL)(TL)(TL)(TL)	196		■		■			
Konyalı	(TL)(TL)(TL)(TL)	194	●		●	■		■	
Park Şamdan	(TL)(TL)(TL)(TL)	197		■	●				
Şark Sofrası	(TL)(TL)(TL)(TL)	197			●	■			●
Divan	(TL)(TL)(TL)(TL)(TL)	197		■	●			■	
Körfez	(TL)(TL)(TL)(TL)(TL)	199	●		●	■			
Panorama	(TL)(TL)(TL)(TL)(TL)	196		■	●	■			●
Sarnıç	(TL)(TL)(TL)(TL)(TL)	194			●	■			●
KEBAB HOUSES									
Develi	(TL)(TL)	196	●	■				■	
Hacıbey	(TL)(TL)	197		■				■	
Kebab's Ocakbaşı	(TL)(TL)	198		■		■		■	
He-De	(TL)(TL)(TL)	198	●	■		■		■	

OUTDOOR TABLES
The restaurant has outdoor tables, either on a terrace or the pavement.

VEGETARIAN FOOD
Restaurant serving either vegetarian dishes or a range of vegetable mezes (see p190) which can be eaten as a main course.

ALCOHOL NOT SERVED
Many Turkish restaurants, especially cheaper ones, do not serve alcohol.

SUITABLE FOR CHILDREN
This denotes a restaurant which will welcome parents with young children, and will not be too smoky or noisy.

		Page Number	Outdoor Tables	Air Conditioning	Vegetarian Food	Attractive Location	Alcohol Not Served	Suitable for Children	Live Entertainment
FISH RESTAURANTS									
Yakup 2	₺₺	195			●				
Yedigül	₺₺	198	●		●	■		■	
Ali Baba	₺₺₺	198	●		●	■		■	
Façyo	₺₺₺	198			●	■		■	
Karaca Han	₺₺₺	198	●		●	■		■	
Pafuli	₺₺₺	198	●		●	■			
Deniz Park	₺₺₺₺	199	●		●	■		■	
Karafaki	₺₺₺₺	196		■	●				
Yeni Güneş	₺₺₺₺	199	●		●	■		■	
Pescatore	₺₺₺₺₺	199	●	■	●	■		■	
MEYHANES									
Bekriya	₺₺	198				■			
Çiçek Pasajı	₺₺	195	●		●	■			●
Deniz Kızı	₺₺	196	●		●	■			●
Refik	₺₺	195			●				
Hasır	₺₺₺	196			●				●
Ece Bar	₺₺₺₺₺	199			●	■			●
INTERNATIONAL RESTAURANTS									
The China	₺₺	197		■	●				
Fischer	₺₺	195		■					
Rejans	₺₺	195							
Great Hong Kong	₺₺₺	196		■	●			■	
Mezzaluna	₺₺₺	197		■	●			■	
Rock House Café	₺₺₺	197		■	●			■	●
Dynasty Asian	₺₺₺₺	195		■	●				
Yeşil Ev	₺₺₺₺	194	●		●	■		■	●
Café du Levant	₺₺₺₺₺	197		■				■	
Citronelle	₺₺₺₺₺	196		■		■			
La Corne d'Or	₺₺₺₺₺	197		■			■		●
Miyako	₺₺₺₺₺	197		■	●	■			
Spasso	₺₺₺₺₺	198		■	●	■		■	
Süreyya	₺₺₺₺₺	199		■					

USING THE LISTINGS

The restaurants on pages 194–9 are listed according to area and price category. These symbols summarize the key features of each restaurant.

🍴 fixed-price menu
V vegetarian dishes/mezes

🚸 suitable for children
♿ wheelchair access
▤ air conditioning
🔲 outdoor tables
♪ live entertainment, usually in the evening
🍷 recommended wine list
💳 credit cards accepted:
AE American Express
DC Diners Club
JCB Japanese Credit Bureau

MC MasterCard (Access)
V VISA

Price categories for a three-course meal for one, including tax and service:
₺ under US$8
₺₺ US$8–15
₺₺₺ US$15–25
₺₺₺₺ US$25–35
₺₺₺₺₺ over US$35

SERAGLIO POINT

Konyalı

Topkapı Palace, Sultanahmet.
Map 3 F3. **(** *(0212) 513 96 96*.
🕐 *9:30am–5pm Wed–Mon.* 🍴
V ♿ 🏬 🗺 *AE, DC, MC, V.*
🍸🍸🍸🍸

In business since 1897, Konyalı is a gastronomic landmark, serving various mezes and fish, as well as international dishes. It is extremely popular, not just for its outstanding food but also for its privileged setting in the grounds of Topkapı Palace, with splendid views over the Sea of Marmara. Because of its incomparable location, it can get crowded in summer.

Sarnıç

Soğukçeşme Sok, Cağaloğlu.
Map 3 E4 (5 F3). **(** *(0212) 512 42 91*. 🕐 *8am–midnight.* 🌑 *Mon and all of June.* **V** 🎵 🗺 *AE, MC, V.*
🍸🍸🍸🍸🍸

Converted from a Byzantine cistern with lofty columns and a domed ceiling, Sarnıç is dimly lit by wrought-iron chandeliers, candles and a fireplace. In the evening there is live piano music. The menu offers an assortment of options, but prices reflect the atmosphere rather than the quality of the food. Thanks to its underground setting, Sarnıç is always cool in summer and yet well heated in winter.

SULTANAHMET

Cennet

Divanyolu Cad 90, Çemberlitaş.
Map 3 D4 (5 C3). **(** *(0212) 513 14 16*. 🕐 *11am–10pm daily.* ♿ ♿
🗺 *V.* 🍸

Cennet specializes in the cuisine of southeastern Turkey, such as *mantı* (meat-filled ravioli), *gözleme* (filled pancakes) and *börek (see p190)*. Village women prepare pastry dishes in view of the guests, and the waiters wear embroidered Ottoman waistcoats and red hats.

Sultanahmet Köftecisi

Divanyolu Cad 12, Sultanahmet.
Map 3 E4 (5 E4). **(** *(0212) 513 14 38*. 🕐 *11am–11pm daily.* ♿ 🍸

Modest but highly recommended, this establishment is famous for its *köfte* (meatballs), *piyaz* (beans served with a vinegar dressing) and *pilav* (rice). This busy *lokanta* has become so popular that other restaurants on the street have taken its name, but this is the original one, in business since 1920.

Sümengen

Amiral Tafdil Sok 21, Sultanahmet.
Map 3 E5 (5 F5). **(** *(0212) 517 68 75*. 🕐 *7am–11pm daily.* 🍴 **V** 🏬
🗺 *AE, MC, V.* 🍸🍸

The intimate restaurant of the pretty Sümengen hotel looks out over the Sea of Marmara. It serves an assortment of cold mezes, cheese and meat pastries, grilled meats and a number of international dishes such as *filet mignon*, schnitzel, beef stroganoff and chicken with curry sauce. In summer you can dine outdoors on the small terrace.

Türkistan Aşevi

Tavukhane Sok 36, Sultanahmet.
Map 3 E5 (5 D5). **(** *(0212) 638 65 25*. 🕐 *11am–11pm daily.* 🍴
♿ 🏬 🗺 *JCB, MC, V.* 🍸🍸

A converted Ottoman house, Türkistan Aşevi is furnished with exquisite carpets and textiles, copper trays which serve as tables and low, comfortable sofas. Guests are asked to take off their shoes and are given slippers. Central Asian-style *mantı* (ravioli), *gözleme (see p188)* and baklava dessert are some of the creations. The cold yoghurt soup (made from chickpeas and peppermint) is refreshing. Alcoholic drinks are not served.

Ahırkapı

Armada Hotel, Ahır Kapı Sok, Sultanahmet. **Map** 3 E5 (5 F5). **(** *(0212) 638 13 70*. 🕐 *7am–midnight daily.*
🍴 **V** ♿ 🗒 🏬 🎵 🗺 *AE, MC, V.* 🍸🍸🍸

Aiming to recreate the atmosphere of a 1930s Turkish tavern, Ahırkapı has live *fasıl* music *(see p213)* performed by a female singer accompanied by lute, violin and drums. The cuisine is strictly Turkish with delicious mezes and main dishes such as *yoğurtlu yaprak dolması* (minced meat in vine leaves with yoghurt). From the rooftop terrace, you can see the illuminated monuments in Sultanahmet.

Kathisma

Akbıyık Cad 26, Sultanahmet.
Map 3 E5 (5 F5). **(** *(0212) 518 97 10*. 🕐 *11:30am–midnight daily.* 🍴
V ♿ 🗒 🏬 🗺 *MC, V.* 🍸🍸🍸

This stylish restaurant gets its name from the Byzantine emperor's loge which once overlooked the Hippodrome *(see p80)*. Turkish dishes include *mücver* (fried courgettes), *fırında kuzu* (oven-cooked lamb) and traditional desserts, such as *sakızlı sütlaç* (rice pudding with mastic) and fig and apricot puddings. Some foreign food is also served. In summer a guitarist may entertain diners on the terrace.

Rami

Utangaç Sok 6, Sultanahmet.
Map 3 E4 (5 E4). **(** *(0212) 517 65 93*. 🕐 *11am–midnight daily.*
V 🍴 🗺 *MC, V.* 🍸🍸🍸

Dedicated to a 20th-century Impressionist painter, Rami Uluer, this romantic restaurant is owned by his son. It is housed in a restored wooden house and is arguably one of the prettiest restaurants in the area. Ottoman specialities include *hünkar beğendi* (meat with an aubergine sauce) and oven-cooked dishes served in terracotta terrines. Evening diners can watch the sound and light show at the Blue Mosque *(see pp78–9)* from the terrace.

Valide Sultan Konağı

Kutlugün Sok 1, Sultanahmet.
Map 3 E4 (5 F4). **(** *(0212) 638 06 00*. 🕐 *11am–midnight daily.* **V** 🗒
🏬 🗺 *AE, MC, V.* 🍸🍸🍸

The semicircular rooftop restaurant of the Valide Sultan Konağı Hotel *(see p181)* commands stunning views of the sea and the area's historic sights. The well balanced menu of meat and vegetable dishes includes mezes, doner and şiş kebabs, aubergine stews, dolmas (vegetables stuffed with rice and meat), seafood and pizzas.

Yeşil Ev

Kabasakal Cad 5, Sultanahmet.
Map 3 E4 (5 E4). **(** *(0212) 517 67 86*. 🕐 *noon–3pm, 7–10:30pm daily.*
V ♿ 🏬 🎵 🗺 *AE, MC, V.*
🍸🍸🍸🍸

An elegant and formal hotel and restaurant, Yeşil Ev is furnished with antiques in late 19th-century Ottoman style. The food it serves is both Turkish and international, including mezes, şiş kebabs, *köfte* (meatballs), steaks, a cheese platter and desserts. Live piano and violin music add to the delightful atmosphere. In summer, meals are served in the shady garden.

THE BAZAAR QUARTER

Havuzlu

Gani Çelebi Sok 3, Grand Bazaar, Beyazıt. **Map** 3 C4 (4 B3). **(** *(0212) 527 33 46*. 🕐 *noon–6pm Mon–Sat.*
V ♿ 🗺 *AE, MC, V.* 🍸

When hunger strikes on a shopping spree in the labyrinths of the Grand Bazaar, Havuzlu makes an excellent stop. Named after the Ottoman fountain in the middle of the restaurant, this is a simple, authentic *lokanta* that serves soups, dolmas, şiş kebab and grilled meats.

Borsa

Yalı Köşkü Cad, Yalı Köşkü Han
60–62, Sirkeci. **Map** 3 D2 (5 D1).
[*(0212) 527 23 50.*] *7am–
10pm daily.* V X & 目 🞹🞹

This traditional Turkish *lokanta* has
a self-service section, making it
ideal for a quick lunch as well as
for more leisurely meals. Borsa
has a varied menu, ranging from
plain doner kebabs and grilled
chicken to stews and traditional
Turkish dishes such as *beğendili
kebab* (meat with an aubergine
sauce). All its dishes are of a
consistently high quality.

Darüzziyafe

Şifahane Cad 6, Beyazıt. **Map** 2 B2.
[*(0212) 511 84 14.*] *noon–
3pm, 6pm–11pm daily.* V X 🞹
🎵 🞹 *AE, DC, MC, V.* 🞹🞹

The former kitchens of the 16th-
century Süleymaniye Mosque *(see
pp90–91)* have been converted
into this stunning restaurant. In
summer there is outdoor seating
in a large courtyard with a fountain
at its centre. Darüzziyafe serves
elaborate, Ottoman-inspired food,
including Süleymaniye soup (with
lentils, spinach, seasonal vegetables and meatballs), *hünkar
beğendi* (an aubergine and meat
dish), *köfte* (meatballs), mezes, and
desserts such as *keşkül* (custard
with pistachios and almonds).
Service can be rather slow.
Darüzziyafe does not serve alcohol.

Karaca

Gazi Sinan Paşa Sok 1/A, Cağaloğlu.
Map 3 D4 (4 C3). [*(0212) 512 90
94.*] *11:30am–6pm Mon–Sat.* V
🞹 🞹🞹

This cavernous restaurant is part
of an old caravanserai. The food
is typically Turkish and includes
pazı (stuffed chard leaves
with yoghurt) and *islim kebabı*
(lamb with aubergine). For dessert
there is *sütlaç* (rice pudding) or
kabak tatlısı (stewed pumpkin).
In winter, fish is also served. Karaca
is popular with local shopkeepers
from the Grand Bazaar.

Subaşı

Nuruosmaniye Cad 48, Çarşıkapı.
Map 3 D4 (4 C3). [*(0212) 522
47 62.*] *10:30am–5pm Mon–Sat.*
X & 🞹 🞹🞹

Conveniently located near the
Nuruosmaniye Gate of the Grand
Bazaar, Subaşı is a simple restaur-
ant on two floors. The menu,
which changes daily, offers basic
Turkish fare displayed in large
steel containers at the entrance.
With friendly and speedy service,
Subaşı is a convenient lunch stop.

Pandeli

Mısır Çarşısı 1, Eminönü. **Map** 3 D2
(4 C1). [*(0212) 527 39 09.*]
] *11:30am–4pm Mon–Sat.* 🍴
V 🞹 *AE, DC, MC, V.* 🞹🞹🞹

Pandeli is one of Istanbul's oldest
restaurants and something of an
institution. Located in the Spice
Bazaar, the restaurant's interior
is decorated with blue İznik-style
tiles. It is popular with locals for
its famous aubergine *börek* (stuffed
pastry), *kağıtta levrek* (sea bass
cooked in waxed paper) and *kılıç
şiş* (swordfish on a skewer).
Reserving a table is essential.

Dynasty Asian

Hotel Merit Antique, Ordu Cad 226,
Laleli. **Map** 2 B4. [*(0212) 513
93 00.*] *7–11pm Mon–Sat.* 🍴
V 目 🍴 🞹 *AE, DC, JCB, MC, V.*
🞹🞹🞹🞹

In the sumptuous setting of a five-
star hotel, this Chinese restaurant is
decorated with paper lanterns, giant
fans and dragons. Local gourmets
agree that this is one of the best
Chinese restaurants in Istanbul.
The Peking duck, dressed with
soy sauce and slices of orange,
is highly recommended.

BEYOĞLU

Çiçek Pasajı

İstiklal Cad, Galatasaray. **Map** 7 D4.
] *11am–midnight daily.* 🍴 V
& 🞹 🎵 🍴 🞹🞹

This glassed-over alleyway *(see
p103)* has numerous down-to-earth
meyhanes along its length. They
are all much the same and the street
is renowned more for its lively, convivial atmosphere than for any one
restaurant. However, two especially
popular choices are Çınar and
Mahzen. A typical meal begins with
kokoreç (charcoal-grilled tripe) or
midye tava (fried mussels) and continues with mezes, fish and raki.
Tables are nearly always available
so there is no need to book. Few
restaurants here accept credit cards.

Fischer

İnönü Cad 51/1, Taksim. **Map** 7 F4.
[*(0212) 245 25 76.*] *noon–3pm,
7–10pm daily.* 目 🞹 *DC, MC, V.*
🞹🞹

Since 1931 Fischer has been
serving middle and eastern European specialities to a loyal clientele.
The decoration is rather austere,
but the food is of a consistently
high quality. Among the staple
items on the menu are borscht, an
excellent Viennese schnitzel and
apple strudel for dessert.

Lades

Ahuduhu Sok 14, Beyoğlu. **Map** 7 E4.
[*(0212) 251 32 03.*] *11am–
9:30pm daily.* V X & 目 🞹🞹

Lades is an attractive little *lokanta*
serving simple, tasty home-style
food in a clean and cosy atmosphere. It is ideal for a quick lunch
while sightseeing in Beyoğlu.
There is a limited menu of meat
dishes, but make sure you try the
lahana dolması (stuffed cabbage),
accompanied by homemade yoghurt. Alcohol is not served.

Nature and Peace

Büyükparmakkapı Sok 21, Beyoğlu.
Map 7 E4. [*(0212) 252 86 09.*]
] *11am–midnight Mon–Sat.* 🍴
V X 目 🞹 *MC, V.* 🞹🞹

Nature and Peace is one of the
best health food restaurants in
Istanbul, offering a selection of
vegetable, chicken and fish dishes
but no red meat. Cakes and pastries
are available all day, accompanied
by delicious fruit juices.

Refik

Sofyalı Sok 10–12, Tünel. **Map** 7 D5.
[*(0212) 243 28 34.*] *noon–
3pm, 6:30pm–midnight Mon–Sat.*
V 🞹🞹

Refik is a cosy *meyhane*, named
after its friendly owner whom the
locals fondly call "baba" (father).
This popular restaurant serves
meat and vegetable dishes, including *karalahana dolması* (black
cabbage stuffed with minced meat,
served with home-made yoghurt).

Rejans

Emir Nevruz Sok 17, Beyoğlu.
Map 7 D4. [*(0212) 244 16 10.*]
] *noon–3pm, 7–11pm Mon–Sat.*
🞹 *MC, V.* 🞹🞹

This is one of the oldest restaurants
in Istanbul, established in the early
1920s by Russian immigrants. It is
still popular among locals for its
Russian specialities, such as beef
strogonoff, *kievsky* (deep-fried
chicken in breadcrumbs with
garlic), *piroshki* (vegetables in
pastry) and potent lemon vodka.

Yakup 2

Asmalı Mescit Cad 35–7, Tünel.
Map 7 D5. [*(0212) 249 29 25.*]
] *noon–2am daily.* V & 🍴 🞹
AE, MC, V. 🞹🞹

The amiable owner of this restaurant Yakup Aslan got his culinary
education from his uncle Refik
(who owns Refik, *see above*). This is
a connoisseur's eating and drinking
spot, with a friendly and informal
atmosphere and a memorable
selection of mezes and fish.

Çatı

Orhan Apaydın Sok 20, Beyoğlu.
Map 7 D5. 📞 *(0212) 251 00 00.*
⏱ *6pm–1am Mon–Sat.* 🍽 🍷
🍴 🍲 🍷 🍷 *MC, V.*

Çatı is a popular rendezvous with local writers, poets and actors, and its walls are covered with their caricatures, photographs and paintings. Turkish and international dishes are on offer. There is piano music in the evenings and sometimes belly-dancing shows.

Great Hong Kong

İnönü Cad 18, Taksim. **Map** 7 F4.
📞 *(0212) 252 42 68.* ⏱ *noon–3pm, 6–11:30pm daily.* 🍽 🍷 🎿
🍴 🍷 🍲 *AE, MC, V.* 🍷🍷🍷

Decorated in rich reds with hanging lanterns and a pagoda-shaped door, the Great Hong Kong is one of Istanbul's best gourmet Chinese restaurants. The house specialities are its spicy Szechuan dishes, such as the excellent beef with pickles. The menu also includes tasty *goba* (fried rice) dishes eaten with seafood or beef sauce. Chinese wine is available by the glass to accompany meals.

Hacı Baba

İstiklal Cad 49, Beyoğlu. **Map** 7 E4.
📞 *(0212) 244 18 86.* ⏱ *noon–11pm daily.* 🍷 🍲 🍷 *AE, V.*
🍷🍷🍷

This busy and popular *lokanta* serves traditional Turkish food such as mezes, kebabs and other meat specialities. Recommended items on the menu include *hünkar beğendi* (meat with an aubergine sauce), *elbasan tava* (an oven-cooked meat dish) and *imam bayıldı (see p189)*. Customers choose their meal from a selection of dishes behind a glass counter. Hacı Baba's interior is somewhat characterless but the terrace is charming and overlooks the courtyard of the Church of Aya Triada.

Hasır

Kalyoncu Kulluk Cad 94, Beyoğlu.
Map 7 D4. 📞 *(0212) 250 05 57.*
⏱ *1pm– midnight daily.* 🍷 🎵 🍷
🍷🍷🍷

Although its official name has been changed to Asır, this smoky, convivial *meyhane* is still known as Hasır, a reference to its straw-matted walls. As well as fresh fish, Hasır serves over 50 mezes, some of which are no longer available elsewhere. Try *topik* (an Armenian delicacy made with chickpeas, chicken and pistachio) or *bomba* (large kidney beans). Later in the evening musicians may stop by to perform *fasıl* music *(see p213)*.

Four Seasons

İstiklal Cad 509, Beyoğlu. **Map** 7 D5.
📞 *(0212) 293 39 41.* ⏱ *noon–3pm, 6pm–midnight, Mon–Sat.* 🍽
🍴 🍷 🍲 *AE, DC, MC, V.*
🍷🍷🍷🍷

This highly acclaimed restaurant, run by a British woman, offers Turkish, French and other international cuisines in a formal setting. It is a favourite with businessmen and staff from the nearby consulates. Chateaubriand and onion soup are two of its specialities. Its discreet and quiet atmosphere makes it an excellent rendezvous for romantic evenings.

Karafaki

Meşrutiyet Cad 100–102, Tepebaşı.
Map 7 D5. 📞 *(0212) 293 80 24.*
⏱ *7–11pm Mon–Sat.* 🍷 🍴 🍷 🍲
AE, DC, MC, V. 🍷🍷🍷🍷

In the basement of the Pera Palas Hotel *(see p104)*, Karafaki is a hidden treasure trove of Turkish regional cuisine. The rather dim surroundings are brightened up by trompe l'oeil windows and candle-lit tables. The restaurant's cooking is innovative and original, taking the food of the Aegean region as its inspiration. The emphasis is on seafood (try the sushi-like raw fish), vegetables and various different herbs. The dried fig dessert is especially recommended.

Citronelle

Ceylan Inter-Continental Hotel, Taksim.
Map 7 F3. 📞 *(0212) 231 21 21.*
⏱ *7–11pm Mon–Sat.* 🍴 🍷 🍲 *AE, DC, JCB, MC, V.* 🍷🍷🍷🍷🍷

Citronelle blends the subtle tastes of modern French cuisine with Thai flavours such as galingale, lemon grass and delicious curries. All this is in a stylish setting with large modern paintings, red velvet chairs and sweeping views of the city. A reservation is essential.

Panorama

Marmara Hotel, Taksim Square.
Map 7 E4. 📞 *(0212) 251 46 96.*
⏱ *6:30–11:30pm daily.* 🍽 🍷
🍴 🎵 🍲 *AE, DC, JCB, MC, V.*
🍷🍷🍷🍷

An elegant restaurant on the top floor of the high-rise Marmara hotel, Panorama has stunning views of the Bosphorus, the Sea of Marmara and the Golden Horn, and serves a gourmet selection of Turkish, French and Italian food. The rich decor is inspired by the Ottoman period: framed kilims blend with luxurious furnishings and candle-lit tables. On Fridays and Saturdays a trio performs jazz, and dance music is played after 9:30pm.

Denizkızı

Çakmaktaşı Sok 3/5, Kumkapı.
Map 2 C5 (4 A5). 📞 *(0212) 518 86 59.* ⏱ *8pm–12.30am daily.* 🍷 🦽
🍴 🎵 🍲 *AE, DC, MC, V.* 🍷🍷

The cobbled streets of the old fishing neighbourhood of Kumkapı are full of simple but popular *meyhanes*. Denizkızı is just one of these lively restaurants, serving good fish meals, sometimes to musical accompaniment. In warm weather tables are put outside.

Hünkar

Akdeniz Cad 21, Fatih. **Map** 1 C4.
📞 *(0212) 525 77 18.* ⏱ *11:30am–11pm daily.* 🍷 🎿 🦽 🍲 🍷🍷

For decades this family-run restaurant has been a haven of tasty Turkish food. Decorated with jars of colourful, pickled fruits and a small fountain, Hünkar offers typical Ottoman dishes, such as *hamsili pilav* (rice with a fish similar to anchovy), *kadınbudu köftesi* (meatballs), grilled meats, *böreks* and dolmas *(see p190)*. There is also an appetizing selection of sweets. Try the fig and apricot desserts.

Sedef

Fevzipaşa Cad 19, Fatih. **Map** 1 C3.
📞 *(0212) 532 82 33.* ⏱ *11am–midnight daily.* 🎿 🦽 🍷 🍲 🍷🍷

This bright and spacious restaurant specializes in meat dishes, such as lamb stew, kebabs, grills and hamburgers. The terrace with a fountain is perfect for outdoor dining. High chairs and small portions are provided for children. Alcoholic drinks are not served.

Develi

Gümüşyüzük Sok 7, Samatya.
📞 *(0212) 632 79 82.* ⏱ *noon–midnight daily.* 🎿 🍴 🍷 🍲 *AE, MC, V.* 🍷🍷

Develi devotes itself to the spicy meat specialities of southeastern Anatolia, such as kebabs with pistachios and the sharp-tasting loquat (*malta erik*, a yellow plum). *Keme kebabı* (with mushrooms) and *patlıcan kebabı* (with aubergine) are also good. For dessert try the *künefe* (syrup-coated pastry filled with sweet cheese).

Asitane

Kariye Hotel, Kariye Camii Sok 16, Edirnekapı. **Map** 1 B1. **(** (0212) 534 84 14. **◐** noon– 3pm, 7:30– 11pm daily. **🍴 ▮ ▾ ▾ ▤ 🎵 📶 🔩 🎗 🍽** AE, DC, M, V. **ⓣⓛⓣⓛ**

Housed inside the Kariye Hotel (see p183), Asitane offers Ottoman fare in a stylish setting. The menu consists of traditional dishes such as hünkar beğendi (meat with an aubergine sauce), sultan sarması (a fillet steak), and a selection of kebab and fish specialities. The kadırga pilavı (rice with almonds, pistachios and herbs) is excellent, as is the incir tatlısı dessert (figs with walnuts, cooked in syrup).

BEYOND TAKSİM

Bolkepçe

Muallim Naci Cad 41–9, Ortaköy. **Map** 9 F2. **(** (0212) 259 82 61. **◐** noon–2am daily. **▮ 🔩 ⓣ**

This small, intimate lokanta serves excellent Turkish home cooking. The hand-made curtains and rustic taste of the owner make it a warm and welcoming restaurant. The menu, which changes daily, includes soup of the day, cheese or meat börek (filled pastry), tas kebabı (meat stew), hünkar beğendi (meat with an aubergine sauce), mantı (ravioli) and ayran (a yoghurt drink, see p191).

The China

Lamartin Cad 17, Taksim. **Map** 7 E3. **(** (0212) 250 62 63. **◐** noon–3pm, 7–11pm Mon–Sat, 6–11pm Sun. **🍴 ▮ ▤ 🎗 🍽** AE, MC, V. **ⓣⓛⓣⓛ**

Opened in 1957, The China is still going strong despite all the other Chinese restaurants that have sprung up more recently. It has a light and unpretentious decor, albeit with the standard lanterns and fans found everywhere. İsa Wang, the friendly, multilingual owner, welcomes guests, while his mother is busy in the kitchen. The family grows its own beansprouts, makes its own soy sauce and imports the spices from China.

A la Turka

Hazine Sok 8, Ortaköy. **Map** 9 F3. **(** (0212) 258 79 24. **◐** noon–9pm daily. **▮ 🔩 🎵 🍽** MC, V. **ⓣⓛ**

Tucked away on a side street near the Ortaköy mosque, A la Turka is a modest but attractive restaurant. It serves simple, well-cooked classic Turkish dishes such as dolma (vegetables stuffed with meat), köfte (meatballs) and various types of filled pastries, such as börek, mantı and dürüm.

Hacıbey

Teşvikiye Cad 156/B, Teşvikiye. **Map** 8 A2. **(** (0212) 231 71 34. **◐** noon–10pm daily. **🔩 ▤ 🔩 🍽** AE, MC, V. **ⓣⓛ**

A bright and modern restaurant on two floors, Hacıbey caters to a chic crowd. Its speciality is an excellent Bursa kebab (served with butter, yoghurt and a tomato sauce, see p189). This is grilled over charcoal in the traditional manner, not under an electric grill as is now common. Try the red lentil soup and, for dessert, the kemalpaşa (a semolina and mastic sweet) from Bursa province.

Mezzaluna

Abdi İpekçi Cad 38/1, Nişantaşı. **Map** 8 A3. **(** (0212) 231 31 42. **◐** noon– 3pm, 7–11:30pm Mon–Fri; noon– 3:30pm, 7pm–midnight Sat & Sun. **▮ 🔩 ▤ 🔩 🍽** AE, MC, V. **ⓣⓛⓣⓛ**

Mezzaluna is part of an American chain, but it is not a cheap fast-food place. It is a young and trendy place and gets busy during lunch hours. The food is hearty Italian fare such as pizzas and pasta. Try cozze alla marinara – a mussel dish topped with tomato sauce. Fiery grappa is also served.

Rock House Café

Princess Hotel, Dereboyu Cad, Ortaköy. **Map** 9 F2. **(** (0212) 227 60 10. **◐** noon–3am daily. **▮ 🔩 ▤ 🎵 🍽** AE, DC, JCB, MC, V. **ⓣⓛⓣⓛ**

A successful imitation of the famous Hard Rock Café chain, this fashionable restaurant and bar is adorned with the gold records and guitars of famous rock stars. Rock House serves generous portions of hamburgers and ice cream, as well as Mexican, European and oriental dishes. During the day, the restaurant is popular with families with children. In the evening, the dance floor quickly fills up.

Park Şamdan

Mim Kemal Öke Cad 18, Nişantaşı. **Map** 7 F1. **(** (0212) 225 07 10. **◐** noon–3:30pm, 7:30pm–midnight Mon–Sat; 7:30pm–midnight Sun. **▮ ▤ 🎵 🍽**

A stylish restaurant which serves excellent food, the Park Şamdan is where Istanbul's high society comes to be seen. The cuisine is a combination of Turkish and international fare. Some of the gourmet European dishes include mutton soup, grilled cutlets, steak and chicken. Turkish specialities include ekmek kadayıfı (bread soaked in syrup with clotted cream).

Şark Sofrası

Swissôtel, Maçka. **Map** 8 A4. **(** (0212) 259 01 01. **◐** 7–11:30pm daily. **🍴 ▮ ▾ ▾ ▤** 🍽 AE, DC, JCB, MC, V. **ⓣⓛⓣⓛ**

Şark Sofrası, a wooden building in the garden of Swissôtel (see p184), is a top-class Turkish restaurant. The highly acclaimed specialities include kuzu incik (roast shin of lamb), balık buğulama (steamed fillet of fish with coriander and tomatoes), manca (fresh spinach in yoghurt) and sumptuous desserts.

Café du Levant

Hasköy Cad 27, Hasköy. **(** (0212) 250 89 38. **◐** noon–2:30pm, 7:30–10:30pm Tue–Sun. **🔩 ▾ ▤ 🍽** AE, DC, JCB, MC, V. **ⓣⓛⓣⓛⓣⓛ**

This stylish French bistro attracts gourmet diners and well-heeled Turkish families. Housed in the Rahmi Koç Museum (see p127), it is decorated with 19th-century hats, bags and posters.

Divan

Cumhuriyet Cad 2, Elmadağ. **Map** 7 F3. **(** (0212) 231 41 00. **◐** noon– 3pm, 7–11pm Mon–Sat. **▮ 🔩 ▤ 🎗 🍽** AE, DC, JCB, MC, V. **ⓣⓛⓣⓛⓣⓛ**

Opened in 1956, Divan serves elaborate dishes based on traditional Turkish cuisine. The restaurant has a tranquil ambience and the menu is extensive, ranging from simple olive-oil vegetable starters to extravagant meat specialities.

La Corne d'Or

Swissôtel, Maçka. **Map** 8 A4. **(** (0212) 259 01 01. **◐** 7–11:30pm Mon–Sat. **🍴 ▾ ▤ 🎵 🍽** AE, DC, JCB, MC, V. **ⓣⓛⓣⓛⓣⓛ**

La Corne d'Or (known as The Roof Garden in summer) is one of Istanbul's most authentic French restaurants, with stunning views over the city. The nouvelle cuisine dishes, prepared by a French chef, come in generous portions.

Miyako

Swissôtel, Maçka. **Map** 8 A4. **(** (0212) 259 01 01. **◐** noon– 3pm, 7–11:30pm Tue–Sun. **🍴 ▮ 🔩 ▾ ▮ 🎗 🍽** AE, DC, JCB, MC, V. **ⓣⓛⓣⓛ**

This restaurant, decorated in minimalist style, serves an assortment of sushis, teriyaki grills and deep-fried tempuras. The bright, well-ventilated dining area looks out on to a pretty miniature Japanese garden. This is one of the city's most expensive restaurants.

Spasso

Hyatt Regency Hotel, Taşkışla Cad, Taksim. **Map** 7 F3. **(** (0212) 225 70 00. ○ noon–3pm, 7–11pm Mon– Sat. 🅥 🛉 🍽 🖥 🍷 AE, DC, JCB, MC, V. ⓉⓁⓉⓁⓉⓁ

This fashionable Italian restaurant is decorated with black and white floor tiles, futuristic chairs and abstract paintings. From the bar guests can watch the preparation of dishes like saffron risotto, spinach tortellini and marinated salmon with mustard sauce.

LEVENT AND ETİLER

Şayan

Nispetiye Cad, Petrol Sitesi 8, Etiler. **(** (0212) 270 29 47. ○ noon–6am daily. 🅥 🛉 🍽 🖥 ⓉⓁⓉⓁ

Open round the clock, Şayan is a welcoming restaurant opposite the Akmerkez shopping mall. Its menu includes köfte (meatballs), mantı (ravioli), piyaz (beans with vinegar dressing) and excellent soups.

He-De

Nispetiye Cad 49, Etiler. **(** (0212) 263 67 74. ○ noon–midnight daily. 🛉 🍽 🖥 🍷 AE, MC, V. ⓉⓁⓉⓁⓉⓁ

He-De rose to stardom when Hillary Clinton ate here in 1995. It was, nevertheless, popular before then thanks to its excellent adana and urfa kebabs from southern Turkey, lahmacun (thin pizza, see p188) and various kebabs from the ocakbaşı grill bar.

THE ASIAN SIDE

Kanaat

Selmanıpak Cad 25, Üsküdar. **Map** 10 B2. **(** (0216) 333 37 91. ○ 10:30am–11:30pm daily. 🅥 🛉 🍽 ⓉⓁⓉⓁ

A busy lokanta serving traditional dishes from hünkar beğendi (meat with an aubergine sauce) to liver dolma (stuffed peppers or aubergines). The restaurant has been run by the same family since 1933, and its fasulye pilaki (a bean dish) is said to be the best in town.

Moda Park

Moda Cad 265, Moda. **(** (0216) 336 07 95. ○ noon–midnight daily. 🅥 🛉 🖥 🍷 ⓉⓁⓉⓁ

This large restaurant in the suburb of Moda, near Kadıköy, boasts beautiful views of the Sea of Marmara. It is still widely known by its former name, Koço. The

quality of its food, however, particularly its superb fish, never changes. The outdoor terrace is perfect for warm summer nights.

Huzur

Salacak İskele Cad 18, Üsküdar. **Map** 10 A3. **(** (0216) 333 31 57. ○ noon–2am daily. 🍽 🅥 ⓉⓁⓉⓁⓉⓁ

The view of Üsküdar and the good food make it worth the climb to this restaurant. Mezes are the main offering. Try the barbunya pilaki and fava purée (bean dishes with olive oil), and kabak tatlısı (stewed pumpkin with almonds).

THE BOSPHORUS

Bekriya

Birinci Cad 90, Arnavutköy, European side. **(** (0212) 257 04 69. ○ 7:30pm–12:30am Mon–Sat. ⓉⓁⓉⓁ

Decorated with rustic furniture and old photographs, Bekriya is a cosy meyhane with views over the Bosphorus. Balkan specialities are served including Macedonian, Bosnian and Serbian dishes.

Kebab's Ocakbaşı

Manolya Sok 2/1, Bebek, European side. **(** (0212) 257 71 41. ○ noon–11pm daily. 🛉 🍽 🖥 🍷 AE, DC, MC, V. ⓉⓁⓉⓁ

This spacious and airy restaurant has various southeastern meat dishes on the menu, as well as mezes. Its large ocakbaşı (grill bar) is in the dining area itself in the proper Turkish fashion.

Hıdiv Kasrı

Hıdiv Yolu 32, Çubuklu, Asian side. **(** (0216) 425 06 03. ○ 8:30–11am, noon– 10pm daily. 🍽 🅥 🛉 🖥 🍷 AE, DC, MC, V. ⓉⓁⓉⓁ

Perched high on a hill on the Asian shore, this former summer palace (see p142) stands in a beautiful park. Its large, formal restaurant serves traditional Turkish food, while the terrace on the ground floor is open for buffet lunches at weekends. Alcohol is not served; instead customers are encouraged to try sweet Ottoman sherbets.

Yedigül

İskele Meydanı 4, Anadolu Kavağı, Asian side. **(** (0216) 320 21 80. ○ noon–10pm. 🍽 🅥 🛉 🖥 🖥 AE, MC, V. ⓉⓁⓉⓁ

This is among the best of the many fish restaurants waiting for you as you disembark for lunch on a cruise up the Bosphorus.

Yedigül serves delicious fish and salad, köfte (meatballs) and deep fried mussels. If Yedigül is full, Yosun, also on the shore, is a reputable alternative choice.

Ali Baba

Kireçburnu Cad 20, Tarabya, European side. **(** (0212) 262 08 89. ○ noon–midnight daily. 🅥 🛉 🔥 🖥 🍷 🍽 MC, V. ⓉⓁⓉⓁ

This is a simple fish restaurant by the Bosphorus with a loyal clientele. Established in 1923, Ali Baba offers grilled and stewed fish of the day, memorable mezes and a delicious ayva tatlısı (quince dessert) served with clotted cream.

Façyo

Kireçburnu Cad 13, Tarabya, European side. **(** (0212) 262 00 24. ○ noon–midnight daily. 🍽 🅥 🛉 🔥 🍷 AE, DC, MC, V. ⓉⓁⓉⓁ

This unpretentious fish restaurant offers delicious seafood, which is complemented by a large variety of mezes. The levrek buğulama (steamed sea bass) and chocolate soufflé are especially good.

Hasır Beykoz

Beykoz Korusu, Beykoz, Asian side. **(** (0216) 322 29 01. ○ noon–11pm daily. 🍽 🛉 🔥 🍽 🖥 🎵 🍷 AE, DC, MC, V. ⓉⓁⓉⓁ

In a wooded area overlooking the Bosphorus, Hasır creates elaborate Ottoman fare, such as şiş kebab and chicken with soy sauce. But the keşkek kebabı (pounded wheat and meat), which is rarely on offer elsewhere, should not be missed.

Karaca Han

Yahya Kemal Cad 10, Rumeli Hisarı, European side. **(** (0212) 265 29 68. ○ noon–midnight daily. 🅥 🛉 🖥 🍷 AE, V. ⓉⓁⓉⓁ

This rustic restaurant serves fish and meze dishes in a lively, informal atmosphere. The terraces, which overlook the Bosphorus, are especially attractive on summer nights. Try kiremitte balık (fish cooked on an earthenware tile).

Pafuli

Kuruçeşme Cad 116, Kuruçeşme, European side. **(** (0212) 263 66 38. ○ noon–10:30pm. 🅥 🖥 🍷 MC, V. ⓉⓁⓉⓁ

This down-to-earth and lively restaurant specializes in hamsi, a Black Sea fish similar to an anchovy. An endless list of options has been devised using this inexpensive fish. It is served grilled, in bread, with pilav (rice) or as a börek. There is even a hamsi dessert.

Les Ambassadeurs

Cevdet Paşa Cad 113–15, Bebek,
European side. (*(0212) 263 30 02.*
◯ *noon–3pm, 7pm–midnight daily.*
V ▤ ♿ ⊞ AE, DC, MC, V.
TL TL TL TL

This restaurant has a superb setting
right at the edge of the Bosphorus.
The fine menu includes *lakerda*
(pickled tuna fish) and other
gourmet Turkish food, as well as
international dishes, including a
few Russian specialities. The
frozen vodka is very popular.

Deniz Park

Daire Sok 9, Yeniköy, European side.
(*(0212) 262 04 15.* ◯ *noon–*
midnight daily. V ♿ ♿ ⊞
TL TL TL TL

A firm favourite among the locals,
Deniz Park offers a good selection
of hot and cold mezes, including
shrimp stew and fried squid with
a walnut dip. For the main course
there is excellent fresh fish, accompanied by raki. The wooden terrace
affords fantastic sea views.

Yeni Güneş

Cevdet Paşa Cad 73, Bebek, European
side. (*(0212) 263 38 23.* ◯
noon–midnight daily. V ♿ ♿ ⊞
TL TL TL TL

Yeni Güneş is a simple, seafood
restaurant in an excellent location
at the water's edge. A variety of
high-quality mezes and fresh fish
dishes is prepared. The door is in
a narrow alleyway opposite the
taxi rank in Küçük Bebek Meydanı.

Ece Bar

Tramvay Cad 104, Kuruçeşme, European side. (*(0212) 265 96 00.* ◯
7pm–1am daily. ● *Jul–Aug.* V ♫
♿ AE, V, MC. TL TL TL TL TL

The owner of this restaurant uses
vegetables and herbs in simple
healthy cooking. One unusual meze
creation combines wild chicory
and nettles. Covered with a myriad
of small mirrors, the restaurant is
also known as "Aynalı Meyhane"
(the Mirrored Tavern). The terrace
has views over the Bosphorus.

Körfez

Körfez Cad 78, Kanlıca, Asian side.
(*(0216) 413 43 14.* ◯ *noon–3pm,*
7pm–midnight Tue–Sun. V ⊞ ♿
AE, MC, V. TL TL TL TL TL

This elegant waterside restaurant,
housed in a luxurious villa, has
candle-lit tables and a stunning
terrace. The house speciality of
sea bass is excellent, as are the
mezes. A private boat can be
reserved to carry guests over to
Rumeli Hisarı on the European side.

Pescatore

Kefeliköy Cad 29, Kireçburnu,
European side. (*(0212) 223 18 19.*
◯ *noon–midnight daily.* V ♿ ▤
⊞ ♿ ♿ AE, DC, MC, V.

Pescatore is a large restaurant
specializing in seafood. Fresh fish
is prepared in a wide variety of
ways. On the menu are fish balls,
octopus grill and seafood crêpes.
Pescatore's pride, however, is
tuzda balık: bream stuffed with
mushrooms, herbs and spices.

Süreyya

İstinye Cad 26, İstinye, European side.
(*(0212) 277 58 86.* ◯ *noon–*
2:30pm, 8pm–midnight, Mon–Sat.
▤ ♿ ♿ AE, DC, V. TL TL TL TL TL

Originally established by a White
Russian immigrant, this restaurant
is one of the top-notch culinary
landmarks of the Bosphorus, overlooking the bay of İstinye. The
staff still prepare some of the
recipes of its original chef, Süreyya
Usta. Caviar *blini*, chicken kiev,
beef stroganoff and lemon vodka
are always on the menu. Süreyya
also serves Turkish and other
international dishes.

EDİRNE

Lalezar

Karaağaç Yolu, Edirne. (*(0284)*
213 06 00. ◯ *11am–2am daily.*
⦿ ♿ ♿ ⊞ ♫ ♿ AE, MC, V.
TL

On the tree-lined bank of the
Meriç River, overlooking the
arched Meriç Bridge, Lalezar
serves mezes, kebabs and fish.
The restaurant interior can get
rather lively (and smoky), but a
waterside table in the garden is
pleasant on summer evenings. To
get here, take the Karaağaç dolmuş
heading south out of the city.

POLONEZKÖY

Leonardo

Köyiçi Sok 32, Polonezköy. (*(0216)*
432 30 82. ◯ *noon–10pm daily.* V
♿ ⊞ ♿ AE, MC, V. TL TL

Leonardo is a pretty restaurant
located in a restored country
house in a charming Polish village
(*see p158*). A wide variety of
Turkish and European fare is
served as a buffet meal at weekends and as an à la carte menu
during the week. The restaurant's
large garden makes it a perfect
spot to spend a day away from
the city and it is an ideal place to
go with children.

THE PRINCES' ISLANDS

Birtat

Gülistan Cad 10, Büyükada.
(*(0216) 382 68 41.* ◯ *11am–*
midnight daily. V ♿ ♿ ⊞ ♿ ♿
AE, DC, MC, V. TL TL

Birtat is a long-established restaurant
whose menu offers fresh grilled
fish and meat, and also tasty
mezes. Leave room for the *künefe*
dessert (syrup-coated pastry filled
with sweet soft cheese). The
restaurant's outdoor seating is in
the main street of Büyükada, near
the lively ferry pier.

İZNİK

Çamlık Moteli

Sahil Yolu, İznik. (*(0224) 757 16*
31. ◯ *8am–midnight daily.* ⦿ V
♿ ⊞ ♿ MC, V. TL TL

The lakeside restaurant of the
Çamlık Motel is an excellent place
to try the local specialities such as
yayın (catfish) or *inegöl köftesi*
(meatballs). This simple restaurant
has good views of the lake, İznik
Gölü, from the garden.

BURSA

Safran Hotel Restaurant

Safran Hotel, Arka Sok 4, Tophane.
(*(0224) 224 72 16.* ◯ *10am–*
midnight daily. V ♿ ▤ ♿
♿ AE, MC, V. TL TL

The rather shabby streets of the
Tophane district are an unlikely
location for this excellent restaurant within a comfortable hotel
(*see p185*). A wide selection of
mezes is offered, as well as
zeytinyağlılar (starters of vegetables
in olive oil), grilled meat and casseroles. For dessert the *kabak tatlısı*
(stewed pumpkin) is recommended.

Mercan

Hotel Kervansaray Termal, Çekirge
Meydanı. (*(0224) 233 93 00.*
◯ *8pm–midnight daily.* V ♿ ▤
⊞ ♫ ♿ AE, DC, MC, V.
TL TL

Dinner is served in the hotel's
elegant dining room or on the
rooftop terrace, from where there
are stunning views of the city and
surrounding countryside. The menu
includes international cuisine as
well as Turkish regional specialities. Try *kağıtta pastırma* (pastrami
cooked in paper) or *güveçte sultan*
mantısı ("sultan's ravioli" cooked
in an earthenware pot).

For key to symbols see p193

Light Meals and Snacks

Eating on the streets is very much a part of life in Istanbul. You cannot go far without coming across a café, street stall or pedlar selling snacks to appease the hunger of busy passers-by. Savoury snacks like kebabs, *lahmacun, pide* and *börek (see pp186–91)* are eaten at any time of day, as are sweets and puddings. On every street corner you will find a *büfe* (sandwich kiosk). If you want to sit down, try a traditional *kahve*, or one of the increasing number of European-style cafés in the more affluent and cosmopolitan parts of Istanbul. There are also dozens of American-style restaurants in the city, selling hamburgers, pizzas and other types of fast food.

STREET FOOD

A COMMON SIGHT on the streets of Istanbul is the seller of *simits* – chewy bread rings coated with sesame. The traditional *simit*-seller *(simitçi)* carries his fare on his head or on a wooden tray; better-off ones push a glass-fronted cart from which they also sell *poğaça* (flaky pastry filled with cheese or mince), *su böreği* (filled layered pastry), *açma* (a fluffy *simit* shaped like a doughnut) and *çatal* (sweeter, eye-shaped *simits* without sesame seeds). They are all best eaten fresh.

During the summer street vendors sell grilled or boiled corn on the cob *(mısır)*, generously sprinkled with salt. In winter they sell roast chestnuts.

Kağıt helvası, a sweet, is another summer snack. *Kağıt* means "paper", and the thin, crumbly layers of pastry filled with sugar melt in your mouth.

SANDWICH AND PASTRY SHOPS

D ELICIOUS SANDWICHES are on sale from small kiosks or *büfes,* usually near bus stops. They include inexpensive thin, toasted sandwiches *(tost)* and hot dogs *(sosisli sandviç)* with pickles and ketchup.

The snack bars of Ortaköy *(see p122)* specialize in pastries from southern Turkey like *göz-leme* and *dürüm*. Both consist of thin layers of bread, grilled on a hot sheet of iron and stuffed with meat, cheese and vegetables. *Dürüm* bread is cooked first, then stuffed and rolled, while *gözleme* is cooked with the ingredients inside, then folded over in a triangle.

FISH

F ISH SANDWICH SELLERS offer delicious grilled or fried fresh fish inside a half or a quarter loaf of bread. Their small boats line the jetties in Eminönü to meet the passing ferry passengers. *Midye tava* (fried mussels), dressed with ground hazelnuts, garlic and oil, are also served inside bread or on a stick.

Fish and mussel sandwiches are sold at the entrance to the Galatasaray Fish Market in Beyoğlu *(see p207)*. Here you can also buy *midye dolma,* mussels stuffed with pine nuts, rice and currants *(see p190)*. Mussels sold on street stalls may not be very fresh and you should never prize open a shell that has not opened during cooking.

KAHVEHANES

T HE TYPICAL Turkish café, *kahvehane* (or *kahve*), is a male-dominated local coffee shop. The original Ottoman name, *kıraathane,* means "a place to read", but such cafés are more a place where men play backgammon and cards, puff on a nargile (bubble pipe) and drink endless cups of coffee and tea. No alcoholic drinks or food are served.

In tourist areas like Beyazıt and Sultanahmet female foreigners will be welcome in *kahves* and, although they may be stared at, they will not be disturbed. **Çorlulu Ali Paşa Medresesi** *(see p96)* is a *kahve* popular with artists and students. Another traditional *kahve* is **Pierre Loti Café** in Eyüp *(see p120)*. Decorated

with memorabilia and antique wall tiles, it serves good apple tea. The publicity material claims it was the home of Pierre Loti *(see p42)*, but there is no evidence of this. **İsmail Ağa Café**, by the waterside in Kanlıca *(see p141)*, is famous for delicious yoghurt.

Next to the Bebek ferry jetty *(see p138)* and in the shadow of the mosque is **Bebek Kahvesi**. This café is a favourite with students and middle-class families who read their Sunday newspapers on the terrace while enjoying the breeze of the Bosphorus. Customers can buy *simit* and *poğaça* from street vendors. There are similar modest *kahves* beside the Bosphorus in Rumeli Hisarı *(see p140)*, all with wonderful sea views.

PATISSERIES AND PUDDING SHOPS

T HE BEST patisseries are in Beyoğlu, particularly in two hotels: the Divan *(see p184)* and Pera Palas *(see p104)*. **Divan** is known for its chocolates. **Patisserie de Pera** retains its charm with period decor, classical music and tasty biscuits. It has a good selection of English teas. **İnci Patisserie** is famous for its excellent profiteroles and baklava. Despite its run-down appearance, it is always busy.

Next door to the Atatürk Cultural Centre *(see p212)*, **Patisserie Gezi** sells handmade confectionery such as truffles and rich torte.

Pudding shops *(muhallebici)* sell traditional sweet milk puddings *(see p189)*. **Sütiş Muhallebicisi** is a long-established chain.

ICE CREAM SHOPS

I TINERANT ICE CREAM vendors are a common sight in residential districts in the summer. Turkish ice cream *(dondurma)* is thick and very sweet. It comes in milk chocolate and fruit varieties and is served in cones. One of the best places to eat ice cream is **Mado**, which has several outlets. Also try **Mini Dondurma** in Bebek.

EUROPEAN-STYLE CAFÉS

EUROPEAN-STYLE cafés serving light meals such as salads, croque monsieur, omelettes and crepes are now common in Istanbul. Sweets usually include cheesecake, chocolate brownies, tiramisu and ice cream in summer.

The best are around Taksim and İstiklal Caddesi in Beyoğlu (see pp102–3). The elegant, late 19th-century **Lebon** serves savoury dishes such as vol-au-vent, and sumptuous Viennese cakes. **Gramofon** is a cosy and relaxed café. Decorated with lace curtains and pictures of old Istanbul, it overlooks the square in Tünel.

Sultanahmet has a few chic, designer cafés. **Rumeli** was created by the interior architect who designed the Empress Zoe Hotel (see p180). It is decorated in stone and brick. Jazz, cabaret and classical music set the tone. **Sultan Pub** is a well-known café and restaurant with tables on the street in summer. The **Lale**

Pudding Shop, a hippie spot in the '70s, is now an inexpensive, self-service cafeteria restaurant serving casseroles and grilled chicken, as well as Turkish milk puddings.

Zanzibar, in the smart shopping district of Nişantaşı, is popular with a stylish young clientele. It serves dishes such as vegetable grill, Waldorf salad and toast provençale.

The area around Ortaköy is a haven of street food and light snacks. **Myott** is popular with a trendy set for its fruit muesli, fresh coffee and '60s furniture. In the early morning this tiny café fills with joggers.

On the shores of the upper Bosphorus, in Rumeli Hisarı, there is an exclusive English café called **Tea Room**. Decorated in a colonial style. Tea Room serves scones and a large variety of English teas.

Cafés are beginning to open on the Asian side as it begins to catch up with the booming trade on the European side. One of the most interesting is **Kadife Chalet** near Moda.

Housed in a 19th-century wooden building, it offers home-made cakes and dishes made with home-grown ingredients, and herbal teas.

BARS

DESPITE THE ISLAMIC edict against alcohol, there are plenty of bars in Istanbul. The majority of the city's fashionable cafés turn into bars in the evening, signalled by a change of music from soft tunes to loud pop. It is possible just to sit with a drink, but for those who wish to have food, many serve pasta, steaks, grills and salads at the bar. Even bars that are not cafés during the day will serve snacks. A few hotel bars, such as **City Lights** at the Ceylan Inter-Continental Hotel (see p183), offer more elaborate dishes. Other bars, like **Ziya** and **Zihni's**, have restaurant sections. Many bars feature live bands playing rock or jazz music. For further details see page 213.

DIRECTORY

KAHVEHANES

Bebek Kahvesi
Cevdetpaşa Cad 137,
Bebek.
[(0532) 261 98 69.

Çorlulu Ali Paşa Medresesi
Yeniçeriler Cad 36,
Çemberlitaş.
Map 2 C4 (4 B3).
[(0212) 528 37 85.

İsmail Ağa Café
Simavi Meydanı, Kanlıca.

Pierre Loti Café
Gümüşsuyu Balmumcu
Sok 5, Eyüp.
[(0212) 581 26 96.

PATISSERIES AND PUDDING SHOPS

Divan
Cumhuriyet Cad 2,
Elmadağ.
Map 7 F3.
[(0212) 231 41 00.

İnci Patisserie
İstiklal Cad 124, Beyoğlu.
Map 7 E4.
[(0212) 243 24 12.

Patisserie Gezi
İnönü Cad 5/1, Taksim.
Map 7 F4.
[(0212) 251 74 30

Patisserie de Pera
Pera Palas Hotel,
Meşrutiyet Cad 98–100,
Tepebaşı. **Map** 7 D5.
[(0212) 251 45 60.

Sütiş Muhallebicisi
Sıraselviler Cad 9/A, Taksim.
Map 7 E4.
[(0212) 252 92 04.

ICE CREAM SHOPS

Mado
Osmanzade Sok 26,
Ortaköy. **Map** 9 F3 .
[(0212) 227 38 76.

Mini Dondurma
Cevdetpaşa Cad 107,
Bebek..
[(0212) 257 10 70.

EUROPEAN-STYLE CAFÉS

Gramofon
Tünel Meydanı 3, Beyoğlu.
Map 7 D5.
[(0212) 293 07 86.

Kadife Chalet
Kadife Sok 29, Kadıköy.
[(0216) 347 85 96.

Lale Pudding Shop
Divanyolu Cad 6,
Sultanahmet.
Map 3 E4 (5 E4).
[(0212) 522 29 70.

Lebon
Richmond Hotel,
İstiklal Cad 445, Beyoğlu.
Map 7 D5.
[(0212) 252 54 60.

Myott
İskele Sok 14, Ortaköy.
Map 9 F3.
[(0212) 258 93 17.

Rumeli
Ticarethane Sok 8,
Sultanahmet.
Map 3 E4 (5 E4).
[(0212) 512 00 08.

Sultan Pub
Divanyolu Cad 2,
Sultanahmet.
Map 3 E4 (5 E4).
[(0212) 526 63 47.

Tea Room
Yahya Kemal Cad 36,
Rumeli Hisarı.
[(0212) 257 25 80.

Zanzibar
Teşvikiye Cad 60,
Teşvikiye. **Map** 8 A2.
[(0212) 233 80 46.

BARS

City Lights
Ceylan Inter-Continental
Hotel, Asker Ocağı Cad 1,
Taksim. **Map** 7 F3.
[(0212) 231 21 21.

Zihni's
Muallim Naci Cad 119,
Ortaköy. **Map** 9 F2.
[(0212) 258 11 54.

Ziya
Muallim Naci Cad 109,
Ortaköy. **Map** 9 F2.
[(0212) 261 60 05.

SHOPPING IN ISTANBUL

ISTANBUL'S SHOPS and markets, crowded and noisy at most times of the day and year, sell a colourful mixture of goods from all over the world. The city's most famous shopping centre is the Grand Bazaar and there are many other bazaars and markets to browse around (see pp206–7). Turkey is a centre of textile production, and Istanbul has a wealth of carpet and fashion shops. If you prefer to do all your

Contemporary glass vase

shopping under one roof, head for one of the city's modern shopping malls which offer a variety of international and Turkish brand goods. Wherever you shop, be wary of imitations of famous brand products – even if they appear to be of a high standard and the salesman maintains that they are authentic. Be prepared to bargain where required: it is an important part of a shopping trip.

Brightly decorated candle lanterns in the Grand Bazaar

OPENING HOURS

SHOPS ARE OPEN, in general, from 9am to 8pm Monday to Saturday; open-air markets from 8am onwards. Large shops and department stores open slightly later in the morning. The Grand Bazaar and Spice Bazaar open their gates at 8:30am and close at 7pm. Big shopping malls open from 10am to 10pm seven days a

week. Shops do not close for lunch, although a few small shops may close briefly at prayer times, especially for the midday prayers on Fridays. Most shops close for the religious holidays of Şeker Bayramı and Kurban Bayramı, but remain open on national holidays (see pp44–7).

HOW TO PAY

ALMOST ALL SHOPS that do business with tourists are more than willing to accept foreign currencies (especially US dollars), as well as Turkish lira. When buying expensive goods, paying in cash, especially a hard foreign currency, may get you a considerable discount. The shopkeeper will check the exchange rate in the day's newspaper.

Most large shops and those near tourist sights accept major credit cards, although they may charge a 5% commission. Visa, MasterCard and American Express are the most common. It is not usually possible to pay with

Euro or traveller's cheques, although carpet shops and some shops in the Grand Bazaar may accept them.

VAT EXEMPTION

VAT IS CHARGED on most items at a rate of 12–15% (8% for books). Foreign passport holders are entitled to a VAT refund on purchases made in Turkish lira from shops authorized for tax-free sales. These can be identified by stickers on their doors. To qualify for a refund, you must show your

Fezes for sale on a street stall

passport and obtain a special invoice (özel fatura) from the shop at the time of purchase. The invoice should then be submitted to the customs officer at the airport on your departure. After you have returned home, the shop will eventually refund the added tax, payable in your own country's currency. The procedure is time-consuming and not worth the effort for minor purchases. Shops may also offer a refund through a cash payment at the point and time of sale, or a bank cheque to be cashed in the customs area of the airport.

SIZES AND MEASURES

TURKEY USES continental European sizes for clothes and shoes. Food and drink are sold in metric measures. This book has a conversion chart on page 219.

Turkish delight and boiled sweets, sold by weight at market stalls

Antiques shop in Çukurcuma

BUYING ANTIQUES

Exporting rare and antique local artifacts, including carpets, is strictly forbidden and carries severe penalties. There is, however, no official definition of the age of an antique so an item that may be regarded as "antique" by the foreign visitor may not be classed as such in Turkey. In the case of antiques of European origin, permission must be obtained from the Directorate of Museums to take them out of the country. In spite of the restrictions, it is still worthwhile exploring Istanbul's antique shops (*see p204*). Reputable shopkeepers will advise you on whether you can export an item and help you with the necessary paperwork (which may take one or two days). **KÜSAV**, the Foundation for the Conservation and Promotion of Culture and Arts, is a source of expertise on the authenticity of antiques. KÜSAV also organizes auctions every other Sunday. Replicas of antique calligraphy, miniatures, ceramics, jewellery etc can be safely exported. Shops will provide a certificate to prove the item is a replica if needed.

SHOPPING MALLS AND DEPARTMENT STORES

Istanbul's modern shopping malls are popular with Turkish families and foreigners alike, for their entertainment as well as their shopping facilities. They have multi-screen cinemas, "food courts" selling fast food and chic cafés, as well as hundreds of shops.

Akmerkez in Etiler is an ultra-modern skyscraper where, besides branches of almost all the leading Turkish fashion companies, outlets for famous international names can be found. **Galleria**, next to the yacht marina in Ataköy, also offers a wide range of well-known clothes stores. The complex contains a branch of the French department store, Printemps, as well as an ice rink (*see p214*). **Carousel**, close to Galleria, in Bakırköy, is a smaller mall with branches of foreign shops, including Mothercare and British Home Stores.

International names alongside Turkish shops in Akmerkez

SEASONAL SALES

Clothes shops are the main places for seasonal sales (*indirim*), although department stores and a number of speciality shops also have them. They begin in June or July and continue to the end of September. The winter sales start as soon as New Year shopping is over in early January and continue until mid-April. There are no sales in bazaars – every day of the year offers bargains depending on your haggling skills.

HOW TO BARGAIN

In up-market shops in Istanbul, bargaining is rarely practised. However, you will probably do most of your shopping in the Grand Bazaar and the shops located in or around the old city (Sultanahmet and Beyazıt). In these places haggling is a necessity, otherwise you may be cheated. Elsewhere you can try making an offer but it may be refused.

Bazaar shopkeepers, characterized by their abrasive insistence, expect you to bargain. Always take your time and decide where to buy after visiting a few shops selling similar goods. The procedure is as follows:
• You will often be invited inside and offered a cup of tea. Feel free to accept, as this is the customary introduction to any kind of exchange and will not oblige you to buy.
• Do not feel pressurized if the shopkeeper turns the shop upside down to show you his stock – this is normal practice and most salesmen are proud of their goods.
• If you are seriously interested in any item, be brave enough to offer half the price you are asked.
• Take no notice if the shopkeeper looks offended and refuses, but raise the price slightly, aiming to pay a little more than half the original offer. If that price is really unacceptable to the owner he will stop bargaining over the item and turn your attention to other goods in the shop.

Haggling over the price of a rug

Where to Shop in Istanbul

Caviar in the Spice Bazaar

ISTANBUL IS HOME TO a vast range of shops and bazaars. Often shops selling particular items are clustered together, competing for custom. The Grand Bazaar *(see pp98–9)* is a centre for carpets and kilims, gold jewellery and leather jackets, as well as every type of handicraft and souvenir. Nişantaşı and İstiklal Caddesi on the European side, and Bağdat Caddesi on the Asian side, have a good range of clothes and shoes. The best choices for food are the Spice Bazaar *(see p88)* and the Galatasaray Fish Market *(see p207)*.

CARPETS AND KILIMS

ONE OF the best places to buy rugs in Istanbul is in the Grand Bazaar *(see pp98–9)*, where **Şişko Osman** has a good range of carpets, and **Galeri Şirvan** specializes in Anatolian tribal kilims. The **Cavalry Bazaar** *(see p71)* has many kilim shops, and **Hazal**, in Ortaköy, stocks a fine collection of kilims. **Sümerbank**, in Beyoğlu, has a modestly priced but extensive collection of handmade carpets.

FABRICS

AS WELL AS rugs, colourful fabrics in traditional designs from all over Turkey and Central Asia are widely sold. **Sivaslı Yazmacısı** sells village textiles, crocheted headscarves and embroidered cloths. **Muhlis Günbattı** *(see p98)* has rare Central Asian textiles,

Brightly coloured Central Asian *suzani* wall hangings

Uzbek and Turkmen *suzanis* (large hand-appliquéd cloths), silk ikats, and Ottoman kaftans, as well as carpets. The antiques dealer **Aslı Günşiray** sells both original Ottoman and reproduction embroidered cloths.

JEWELLERY

ISTANBUL'S substantial gold market centres on Kalpakçılar Bası Caddesi in the Grand Bazaar. Here gold jewellery is sold by weight, with a modest sum added for craftsmanship, which is generally of good quality. The daily price of gold is displayed in the shop windows. Other shops in the Grand Bazaar sell silver jewellery, and pieces inlaid with precious stones.

Icons for sale in the Grand Bazaar

Urart stocks collections of unique gold and silver jewellery inspired by the designs of ancient civilizations. **Antikart** specializes in restored antique silver jewellery made by Kurds and nomads in eastern Turkey.

LEATHER

TURKISH LEATHERWEAR, while not always of the best quality hides, is durable, of good craftsmanship and reasonably priced. The Grand Bazaar is full of shops selling leather goods. **B B Store**, for example, offers a good range of ready-to-wear and made-to-order garments.

Derishow is the top name in fashionable leatherwear, and **Desa** has a range of classic and fashionable designs.

ANTIQUES

THE MOST INTERESTING area in which to browse for antiques is Çukurcuma *(see p107)*, a slightly shabby but fashionable neighbourhood in the backstreets of Beyoğlu. Shops worth a visit are **Aslı Günşiray**, **Antikhane** and **Antikarnas** for their Turkish, Islamic and Western stock.

The antiquarian bookshops, such as **Librairie de Pera**, in and around Tünel *(see p102)* sell old postcards and prints.

HANDICRAFTS AND SOUVENIRS

ALL TYPES OF Turkish arts and crafts can be found in the Grand Bazaar. Ideal gifts and souvenirs include embroidered hats, waistcoats and slippers, mother-of-pearl inlaid jewellery boxes, meerschaum pipes in the shape of heads, prayer beads made from semi-precious stones, alabaster ornaments, blue-eye charms to guard against the evil eye, nargiles (bubble pipes) and reproductions of icons. At the **Istanbul Crafts Centre** *(see p76)* you can watch the traditional art of calligraphy being practised. **Rölyef** in Beyoğlu, the **Book Bazaar** *(see p94)*, **Artrium** and **Sofa** also sell antique and reproduction calligraphy, as well as *ebru* (marbled paintings) and reproductions of Ottoman miniature paintings.

POTTERY, METAL AND GLASSWARE

HUNDREDS OF SHOPS in the Grand Bazaar are stocked with traditional ceramics, including many pieces decorated with exquisite blue-and-white İznik designs *(see p161)*. Other types of pottery come from Kütahya – distinguished by its free style of decoration – and Çanakkale *(see p170)* – which uses more modern designs, often in yellows and greens. With its large and expertly selected stock of plates, bowls, Turkish coffee cups and vases, **May** is one of the best places in the Grand Bazaar. To purchase a modern piece of Kütahya ware, visit **Mudo Pera** which stocks a collection by Sıtkı Usta, a master of Kütahya pottery. Most museum shops also have a good range of pottery for sale, including reproduction pieces.

The Grand Bazaar and the Cavalry Bazaar *(see p207)* are centres of the copper and brass trade and offer a huge selection to the browsing visitor. For glassware, **Paşabahçe**, the largest glass manufacturer in Turkey, creates delicate *çeşmibülbül* vases (decorated with blue and gold stripes) and Beykoz-style ware (with gilded decoration).

FOOD, DRINK, HERBS AND SPICES

THE SPICE BAZAAR *(see p88)* is the place to buy nuts (especially pistachios) and dried fruits, herbs and spices, jams and the many types of herbal tea produced in Turkey. These include sage *(adaçayı)*, linden *(ıhlamur)* and camomile *(papatya)*. However, other foods can be bought here as well, including such luxuries as caviar. Another place with a wide variety of good quality herbs, jams, teas and spices is the Galatasaray Fish Market.

Several shops specialize in particular foods. **Şekerci Hacı Bekir** is renowned for its delectable Turkish delight and baklava. Also popular is **Bebek Badem Ezmesi**, on the Bosphorus, widely acclaimed for its pistachio and almond fondants. Over the course of more than a century in business, **Kurukahveci Mehmet Efendi** *(see p86)* has become the best known producer of Turkish coffee. The quintessential Turkish spirit, raki *(see p191)*, can be bought in any grocery.

Pickled fruits and vegetables, sold in markets and on street stalls

---

DIRECTORY

SHOPPING MALLS

Akmerkez
Nispetiye Cad, Etiler.
📞 *(0212) 282 01 70.*

Carousel
Halit Ziya Uşaklıgil Cad 1, Bakırköy.
📞 *(0212) 570 84 34.*

Galleria
Sahil Yolu, Ataköy.
📞 *(0212) 599 95 60.*

CARPETS AND KILIMS

Galeri Şirvan
Keseciler Cad 55–7, Grand Bazaar. **Map** 2 C4 (4 B3).
📞 *(0212) 520 62 24.*

Hazal
Mecidiyeköy Köprüsü Sok 27–9, Ortaköy. **Map** 9 F3.
📞 *(0212) 261 72 33.*

Şişko Osman
Halıcılar Cad 49, Grand Bazaar. **Map** 2 C4 (4 B3).
📞 *(0212) 526 17 08.*

Sümerbank
İstiklal Cad 302, Beyoğlu.
Map 7 D5.
📞 *(0212) 252 08 05.*

FABRICS

Muhlis Günbattı
Perdahçılar Sok 48, Grand Bazaar. **Map** 2 C4 (4 B3).
📞 *(0212) 511 65 62.*

Sivaslı Yazmacısı
Yağlıkçılar Sok 57, Grand Bazaar. **Map** 2 C4 (4 B3).
📞 *(0212) 526 77 48.*

JEWELLERY

Antikart
İstiklal Cad 207, Atlas Kuyumcular Çarşısı 32, Beyoğlu. **Map** 7 D4.
📞 *(0212) 252 44 82.*

Urart
Abdi İpekçi Cad 18/1, Nişantaşı. **Map** 7 F1.
📞 *(0212) 246 71 94.*

LEATHER

B B Store
Gani Çelebi Sok 46, Grand Bazaar. **Map** 2 C4 (4 B3).
📞 *(0212) 527 53 38.*

Derishow
Vali Konağı Cad 85, Nişantaşı. **Map** 7 F1.
📞 *(0212) 231 15 10.*

Desa
İstiklal Cad 140, Beyoğlu.
Map 7 D4.
📞 *(0212) 243 37 86.*

ANTIQUES

Antikarnas
Faik Paşa Yok 15, Çukurcuma. **Map** 7 E4.
📞 *(0212) 251 59 28.*

Antikhane
Faik Paşa Yok 41, Çukurcuma. **Map** 7 E4.
📞 *(0212) 251 95 87.*

Aslı Günşiray
Çukurcuma Cad 74, Çukurcuma. **Map** 7 E4.
📞 *(0212) 252 59 86.*

KÜSAV
Has Fırın Cad 305, Sinanpaşa İş Merkezi 3rd floor, Beşiktaş. **Map** 8 C3.
📞 *(0212) 227 34 85.*

Librairie de Pera
Galip Dede Cad 22, Beyoğlu. **Map** 7 D5.
📞 *(0212) 252 30 78.*

HANDICRAFTS AND SOUVENIRS

Artrium
9th floor, Swissôtel, Maçka. **Map** 8 A4.
📞 *(0212) 259 02 28.*

Rölyef
Emir Nevruz Sok 16, Beyoğlu. **Map** 7 D4.
📞 *(0212) 244 04 94.*

Sofa
Nuruosmaniye Cad 42, Cağaloğlu. **Map** 3 D4 (4 C3). 📞 *(0212) 527 41 42.*

POTTERY, METAL AND GLASSWARE

May
Koltuk Kazazlar Sok 10, Grand Bazaar.
Map 2 C4 (4 B3).
📞 *(0212) 526 68 23.*

Mudo Pera
İstiklal Cad 401, Beyoğlu.
Map 7 D5.
📞 *(0212) 251 86 82.*

Paşabahçe
İstiklal Cad 314, Beyoğlu.
Map 7 D5.
📞 *(0212) 244 05 44.*

FOOD

Bebek Badem Ezmesi
Cevdetpaşa Cad 238/1, Bebek.
📞 *(0212) 263 59 84.*

Kurukahveci Mehmet Efendi
Tahmis Cad 66, Eminönü.
Map 3 D2.
📞 *(0212) 511 42 62.*

Şekerci Hacı Bekir
Hamidiye Cad 83, Eminönü. **Map** 3 D3.
📞 *(0212) 522 06 66.*

Istanbul's Markets

İznik-style plate, Cavalry Bazaar

WHETHER YOU WANT to lose yourself in the aromas of exotic spices, rummage for old prints and miniatures among secondhand books, hunt for souvenirs or just shop for food, you will find a market or bazaar catering to your tastes somewhere in Istanbul. An obvious first stop is the Grand Bazaar, but several others are well worth visiting for their more specialized produce and their atmospheric settings. Every neighbourhood in Istanbul has its own open-air market on a specific day of the week. At these markets, crowded with budget-conscious housewives, you will find a huge variety of merchandise at the cheapest possible prices.

Spice Bazaar
The Spice Bazaar is an exotic trading house for dried herbs, spices and other foodstuffs (see p88).

Wednesday Street Market
One of Istanbul's colourful neighbourhood markets, the Wednesday market, is next to the Fatih Mosque (see p113) and sells everything from fresh produce and household goods to bulbs and seeds.

THE BAZAAR QUARTER

SULTANAHM

Book Bazaar
Next to the Grand Bazaar, the Book Bazaar (Sahaflar Çarşısı) offers a wealth of printed matter in various languages, from tourist guides to academic tomes and old magazines (see p94).

Grand Bazaar
The largest market in the world, the Grand Bazaar contains about 4,000 shops. In this roofed labyrinth of passages you can find every commodity associated with Turkey, from costly jewellery to basic foodstuffs. It has operated for hundreds of years (see pp98–9).

Beşiktaş Square Market
A splendid array of fruit, vegetables and fish is found in this interesting market near Dolmabahçe Palace (see pp128–9).

BEYOĞLU

BOSPHORUS

Ortaköy Flea Market
Every Sunday the main square of Ortaköy is filled with stalls selling souvenirs to suit every budget, from junk to fine jewellery and original Turkish handicrafts (see p122).

Galatasaray Fish Market
The best fish market in Istanbul runs along a historic alleyway. Constantly sprinkled with water to keep them cool, fresh fish from the Sea of Marmara and elsewhere lie waiting to be sold (see p103).

THE ASIAN SIDE

ERAGLIO POINT

Kadıköy Street Market
The main market on the Asian side of the city fills the streets around Mahmut Baba Sokağı. Clothes are sold on Tuesdays, and food on Fridays.

Cavalry Bazaar
Converted Ottoman stables are the setting for this bazaar below the Blue Mosque (see pp78–9). Carpets (see pp210–11) are the main items touted, but handicrafts and jewellery are also on sale (see p71).

| 0 metres | 500 |
| 0 yards | 500 |

What to Buy in Istanbul

Turkish slippers

W ITH ITS ENDLESS BAZAARS, markets, shops and stalls, Istanbul is a souvenir hunter's paradise. If you are seeking a bargain, jewellery and leather can be worth investing in. For something typically Turkish, there is a wide selection of ceramics and copperware based on the designs of traditional Ottoman handicrafts and arts. The city's antique shops (see p204) are also worth a visit. Istanbul is possibly most famous for its carpets and kilims (see pp210–11), but check the quality before you buy.

Copperware

Antique copperware can be very expensive. Newer items, however, are also available, at more affordable prices.

Copper goblets

Pipes

Classic nargiles (bubble pipes) are still used by older Turkish men. They make attractive ornaments even if you do not smoke.

Jewellery

Jewellery includes pendants made from gold, silver, semi-precious stones and other materials. A simple blue glass eye is said to ward off evil.

Blue glass-eye pendants

Antique copper water ewer

Ceramics

Ceramics form a major part of Turkey's artistic tradition. The style varies according to the area of origin. Blue and white pottery is in the İznik style (see p161); other areas of production include Kütahya and Çanakkale (see p170).

Colourful Kütahya ware

Green jugs from Çanakkale

Blue and white decorated plate

İznik-style tile

Miniatures

Istanbul has a history of miniature painting, examples of which can be seen in the city's museums, especially Topkapı Palace (see p57). These tiny works of art, often depicting the sultan at court, were once bound in books. Those for sale are copies of originals.

Miniature from the Grand Bazaar

Box inlaid with mother-of-pearl

Box with painted scenes on bone inlay

Handicrafts

Jewellery boxes crafted from wood or bone, alabaster figurines and other hand-made ornaments make unusual souvenirs.

Textiles

Hand-woven cloths, including ikat work (where the cotton is dyed as it is woven), fine embroidery and knits are just some of the range of textiles that can be bought.

Embroidered scarves, known as oyalı

Cotton ikat work

Glassware

This elegant jug is an example of the blue and white striped glass-ware, çeşmibülbül, made in the Paşabahçe works (see p147).

Çeşmibülbül jug

Local Delicacies

Delicious sweets (see p189) such as halva, Turkish delight and baklava are very popular. A huge range of fragrant spices, dried fruit and nuts are sold loose by weight in the city's bazaars.

Halva

Nuts in honey

Turkish delight

Mulberries

Sunflower and pumpkin seeds

Chickpeas

Dried red peppers and aubergines

Apricots

Almonds

Pistachio nuts

Turkish Carpets and Kilims

THE ANCIENT SKILL of weaving rugs has been handed down from generation to generation in Turkey. Rugs were originally made for warmth and decoration in the home, as dowry items for brides, or as donations to mosques. There are two main kinds of rug: carpets (*halı*), which are knotted, and kilims, which are flat-woven with vertical (warp) and horizontal (weft) threads. Many foreign rugs are sold in Istanbul but those of Turkish origin come in a particularly wide range of attractive colours. Most of the carpets and kilims offered for sale will be new or almost new; antique rugs are rarer and far more expensive.

A carpet may be machine-made or handmade. Fold the face of the rug back on itself: if you can see the base of the knots and the pile cannot be pulled out, it means that it is handmade.

Wool is the usual material for making a rug, although some carpets are made with silk.

Weaving a Carpet
Wool for rugs is washed, carded, spun and dyed before it is woven. Weaving is a cottage industry in Turkey; the women weave in winter leaving the summer months for farming duties.

CARPET
This reproduction of a 16th-century Uşak carpet is known as a Bellini double entrance prayer rug.

Indigo

Madder

Camomile

Dyes
Before chemical dyes were introduced in 1863, plant extracts were used: madder roots for red; indigo for blue; and camomile and other plants for yellow.

RUG-MAKING AREAS OF WESTERN TURKEY

The weaving industry in Turkey is concentrated into several areas of production, listed below. Rug designs are traditional to their tribal origins, resulting in a wide range of designs and enabling the skilled buyer to identify the area of origin.

ISTANBUL ① ANKARA ●
② ③ ④ ⑤ ⑥ ⑦ ⑫ ⑪ ⑩ ⑬ ⑧ ⑨

CARPETS
① Hereke
② Çanakkale
③ Ayvacık
④ Bergama
⑤ Yuntdağ
⑥ Balıkesir
⑦ Sındırgı
⑧ Milas
⑨ Antalya
⑩ Isparta

KILIMS
⑪ Denizli
⑫ Uşak

CARPETS AND KILIMS
⑬ Konya

The "prayer design" is inspired by a mihrab, the niche in a mosque that indicates the direction of Mecca *(see pp36–7)*.

The tree of life motif at the centre of the kilim is symbolic of immortality.

KILIM

Kilims are usually made using the slit weave technique by which a vertical slit marks a colour change.

The width of a rug is limited by the size of the loom. Most rugs are small because a large loom will not fit into a village house.

BUYING A RUG

Before you buy a rug, look at it by itself on the floor, to see that it lies straight – without waves or lumps. Check that the pattern is balanced, the borders are of the same dimensions, and the ends are roughly the same width. The colours should be clear and not bleeding into one another. Bargaining is essential *(see p203)*, as the first price given is likely to be at least 30% higher than the seller really expects.

Buying a good quality old rug at a reasonable price, however, is a job for an expert. The age of a rug is ascertained from its colour, the quality of the weaving and the design. Check the pile to make sure that the surface has not been painted and look for any repairs – they can easily be seen on the back of the rug. The restoration of an old carpet is acceptable but the repair should not be too visible. Make sure the rug has a small lead seal attached to it, proving that it may be exported, and ask the shop for a receipt.

Kilim pieces are used to make a variety of smaller craft objects, also for sale in carpet shops.

Burdock motif

Chest motif

Motifs

The recurring motifs in rugs – some of them seemingly abstract, others more figurative – often have a surprising origin. For instance, many are derived from marks that nomads and villagers used for branding animals.

Motif from wolf track, crab or scorpion

Modern motif of a human figure

ENTERTAINMENT IN ISTANBUL

ISTANBUL OFFERS A great variety of leisure pursuits, ranging from arts festivals, folk music and belly dancing to sports centres and nightclubs. The most important event in the cultural calendar is the series of festivals organized by the Istanbul Foundation for Culture and the Arts *(see pp44–6)*. The festivals take place between March and November, and have been drawing international performers and large audiences since 1973. Throughout the year, traditional Turkish music, opera, ballet, Western classical music and plays are performed

Belly dancer, Galata Tower

at the Atatürk Cultural Centre (AKM), the Cemal Reşit Rey Concert Hall (CRR) and other venues around the city. Beyoğlu is the main centre for entertainment of all kinds. This area has the highest concentration of cinemas in the city as well as several cultural centres, both Turkish and foreign. In the evening the bars and cafés here play live music. Ortaköy, on the European shore of the Bosphorus, is another popular venue where, on summer nights, dining, music and dancing continue into the small hours of the morning.

Copies of *The Guide*

ENTERTAINMENT GUIDES

ISTANBUL HAS A bi-monthly entertainment and listings magazine in English called *The Guide*. This publishes the programmes of the AKM and CRR, and information on other cultural events, as well as bars and nightclubs around the city. *The Guide* is sold at the larger, central newsagents and book shops. The English-language newspaper *Turkish Daily News*, available from newsstands, also has information on entertainment in Istanbul.

Lists of events taking place at individual theatres and cultural centres (including those attached to foreign consulates) can be obtained from tourist information offices *(see p221)*.

The Turkish Airlines in-flight magazine has details on major events in the city, and the daily Turkish newspaper *Hürriyet* has listings in Turkish.

BOOKING TICKETS

TICKETS FOR performances at the Atatürk Cultural Centre and Cemal Reşit Rey Concert Hall can be purchased one week in advance from their box offices. Both offer a 50 per cent discount for students and senior citizens, and a 20 per cent discount for groups of 30 people or more. The information desks inside the **Vakkorama** department store and **Galleria**, **Akmerkez** and **Capitol** shopping centres sell tickets for large pop and jazz concerts, and also for performances at the AKM and CRR. Payment is usually by cash.

LATE-NIGHT TRANSPORT

THE LAST late-night buses and dolmuşes leave at midnight from Taksim, which is close to many entertainment venues. Taxis run throughout the night. During the music festivals in June and July there is a special bus service which runs between show venues and central parts of Istanbul.

FESTIVALS

FIVE ARTS FESTIVALS, four annual and one biennial, are organized by the Istanbul Foundation for Culture and the Arts. The Film Festival runs from March to April every year, the Theatre Festival is in May and June, the Music and Dance Festival – the original and biggest festival – is in June

and July and the Jazz Festival is in July. The biennial Fine Arts Festival takes place in autumn. Tickets for all these festivals can be bought over the phone from the **Istanbul Festival Committee**, which also has programme details, and from the venues.

The Yapı Kredi Arts Festival, Akbank Jazz Festival and Efes Pilsen Blues Festival are also in the autumn *(see p46)*.

WESTERN CLASSICAL MUSIC AND DANCE

EVERY SEASON the Istanbul State Opera and Ballet companies, State Symphony Orchestra and State Theatre perform a wide repertoire of classical and modern works. The companies share the same venue: the purpose-built, 900-seat **Atatürk Cultural Centre** in Taksim. Early booking is essential for shows here. The **Cemal Reşit Rey Concert Hall** stages concerts of

Classical concert in the church of Haghia Eirene *(see p60)*

Folk dancing at Kervansaray, a long-established venue

Western classical music as well as hosting a wide variety of music and dance groups from all over the world. Concerts, operettas and ballets are also performed at smaller venues throughout the city.

Laser disc screenings of opera, ballet and classical music performances are held most days at 2pm and 6pm at the **Aksanat Cultural Centre**. It also sometimes stages live plays and music recitals.

ROCK MUSIC AND JAZZ

ISTANBUL HAS an increasing number of bars and clubs playing good live music. **Hayal Kahvesi** is a bar dedicated to jazz, rock and blues by groups from Turkey and abroad. It also has an outdoor summer branch next to the Bosphorus in Çubuklu. The **Q Club**, located in the grounds of the Çırağan Palace Hotel Kempinski (see p184), is an exclusive jazz bar which regularly invites well-known performers. Further up the Bosphorus, in Ortaköy, the **Rock House Café** (see p197) is an imitation of the famous Hard Rock Café. It has live bands on certain nights of the week.

In the city centre, **Kemancı** and **Roxy** feature live rock and heavy metal performers. In **Sappho** they play softer,

more sophisticated jazz and quality Turkish pop music. Other venues for Turkish pop are **Tribunal** and **Vivaldi**, while at **Beyoğlu Sanat Evi** they play Turkish pop with strong folk music influences.

NIGHTCLUBS

THE LUXURIOUS, summer-only **Club 29** is probably the most glamorous nightclub in Istanbul. It has a restaurant, swimming pool and torch-lit garden with glorious views of the Bosphorus. Every half-hour a boat ferries guests to and from İstinye on the European side. The bar becomes a disco after midnight. **Pasha**, also open in summer only, is the city's biggest nightspot, with a large dancefloor right beside the Bosphorus, as well as several bars and restaurants. **Majesty**, a chic bar and restaurant complex next to the Bosphorus, has a delightful outdoor balcony. Live bands play in the bar and there is dancing to Caribbean music. The restaurant features Turkish music and dance. The trendy club **DNA** plays House, Garage and Techno music on Wednesday, Friday and Saturday nights only.

Avoid the seedier-looking clubs in Beyoğlu, as these have been known to coerce clients into paying extortionate bills.

Musicians at the Jazz Festival

TRADITIONAL TURKISH MUSIC AND DANCE

TRADITIONAL Turkish music is regularly performed at the Cemal Reşit Rey Concert Hall. This includes Ottoman classical music, performed by an ensemble of singers and musicians, mystical Sufi music and folk music from various regions of Turkey. In summer, recitals of Turkish music are occasionally organized in the Basilica Cistern (see p76), which has wonderful acoustics. The Sultanahmet Tourist Office (see p221) has details.

Fasıl is a popular form of traditional music best enjoyed live in meyhanes such as **Ece**, **Kallavi** and **Hasır** (see p196). It is usually performed by gypsies on instruments which include the violin, kanun (zither), tambur and ut (both similar to the lute).

Belly dancing is performed mainly in nightclubs. Though often underrated, the sensuous movements of the female dancers are considered an art. Many clubs and restaurants stage belly dancing together with Turkish folk music and dance. Dinner is often included in the show. One of the best venues is the restaurant in the **Galata Tower** (see p105). Other venues featuring top performers are **Kervansaray**, **Orient House** and **Manzara**.

The Whirling Dervishes give a public performance of their extraordinary meditational dance at the Mevlevi Monastery (see p104) once a month.

The traditional ut, a lute-like instrument played in fasıl music

CINEMAS

THE LATEST foreign films are on general release in Istanbul at the same time as other European countries. They are screened in their original languages with Turkish sub-titles. Only a few cinemas show Turkish-made films.

The majority of the city's cinemas are on İstiklal Caddesi. Of these, **Alkazar** and **Beyoğlu** tend to show art-house films. There are also numerous cinemas in Kadıköy, on the Asian side, while all the main shopping centres have multi-screen cinemas.

The first screening of the day is half-price and many cinemas offer tickets at half-price all day on Wednesdays. Students with a valid card are entitled to a discount for all showings. Films tend to stop about halfway through for an interval.

THEATRE

PLAYS BY both Turkish and international playwrights are staged in Istanbul's theatres, but only in Turkish. One of the most popular companies is the Istanbul State Theatre, which is based at the **AKM**. The theatre season runs from September to June.

HEALTH CLUBS AND SPORTS CENTRES

THERE ARE a number of establishments with public sports facilities in and around Istanbul. All the main five-star hotels have good swimming pools and welcome non-residents for a daily fee. Health clubs such as the **Vakkorama Gym** and the **Alkent Hillside Club** can also be used by non-members for a daily fee.

At the edge of the Belgrade Forest, the **Kemer Country Riding and Golf Club** has stables and a 9-hole golf course. It also offers riding and golf lessons. The **Istanbul Golf Club** has an 18-hole course. **Enka Spor Tesisleri**, in Maslak, is a large sports complex with extensive facilities, including indoor and outdoor pools, and courts for tennis, basketball and volley-ball. For ice-skaters, there is a rink in the **Galleria** shopping centre *(see p203)* which is open to the public after 7pm. Skates are available for hire.

SPECTATOR SPORTS

FOOTBALL HAS a very large following in Turkey. The three Istanbul teams, **Beşiktaş**, **Fenerbahçe** and **Galatasaray**, all compete at international level and play in Istanbul most Sundays. Horse racing takes place at the **Veli Efendi** racecourse on Wednesdays and at weekends. In the summer months there are yacht regattas in the Sea of Marmara *(see p45)*. For an unusual spectator sport, head to Edirne at festival time, to see the grease wrestling *(see p154)*.

Galatasaray team logo

BEACHES

THE BEST PLACE to swim, water-ski and windsurf in Istanbul is the Princes' Islands *(see p159)*. Yörükali Plajı, on Büyükada, is a public beach, but it is safe to swim anywhere around the islands. It is no longer possible to swim in the sea closer to Istanbul, however, owing to heavy pollution.

There are large beaches at Kilyos *(see p158)* and Gümüş-dere on the Black Sea, about 30 minutes' drive from central Istanbul, and Şile *(see p158)*. The Black Sea can be rough at times, with big waves, but all the beaches have watch-towers, lifeguards and lifeboats for emergencies. The Marmara Islands *(see p169)*, are also popular for their beaches.

CHILDREN

LITTLE IN ISTANBUL has been designed with children in mind. Few neighbourhoods have decent playgrounds and there are not many large parks. Pavements are high, crowded and often bumpy, making it difficult to use a pushchair.

On a human level, however, children are welcome and will be made a fuss of almost everywhere they go. With a little thought you can find plenty of things for children to do. The State Opera and Ballet puts on children's musicals at the **AKM**, on Saturdays at 11am or 3pm.

Children are admitted free to the Archaeological Museum *(see pp62–5)*. It has a special children's section tracing the history of mankind, with a medieval castle and a Trojan horse to climb on.

There are big parks at Yıldız *(see pp124–5)* and Emirgan *(see p141)*. Another park near Emirgan, the **Park Orman**, is a family complex situated in woods, with picnic areas, a swimming pool and a theatre. On the Princes' Islands, where there are no cars, children can cycle safely, or take a tour in a horse-drawn carriage or on a donkey. **Tatilya**, 35 km (22 miles) from Istanbul, is a theme park with roller coasters and other rides, a small lake, a simulation cinema and shops, all under a huge glass roof.

Roller-coaster ride at Tatilya, a theme park near Istanbul

DIRECTORY

BOOKING TICKETS

Akmerkez
Nispetiye Cad, Etiler.
[(0212) 282 01 70.

Capitol
Tophanelioğlu Cad 1,
Altunizade. **Map** 10 C2.
[(0216) 391 18 34.

Galleria
Sahil Yolu, Ataköy.
[(0212) 559 54 44.

Vakkorama
Osmanlı Sok 13, Taksim.
Map 7 E4.
[(0212) 251 15 71.

ISTANBUL FESTIVAL COMMITTEE

[(0212) 293 31 33.
FAX (0212) 249 55 75.

WESTERN CLASSICAL MUSIC AND DANCE

Aksanat Cultural Centre
Akbank Building, İstiklal
Cad, Zambak Sok 5,
Taksim. **Map** 7 E4.
[(0212) 252 35 00.

Atatürk Cultural Centre (AKM)
Taksim Meydanı, Taksim.
Map 7 F3.
[(0212) 251 56 00.

Cemal Reşit Rey Concert Hall (CRR)
Darülbedayi Cad, Harbiye.
Map 7 F1.
[(0212) 231 51 03.

ROCK MUSIC AND JAZZ

Beyoğlu Sanat Evi
Abdullah Sok 22/1,
Beyoğlu. **Map** 7 E4.
[(0212) 252 61 96.

Hayal Kahvesi (Beyoğlu)
Büyükparmakkapı Sok 19,
Taksim. **Map** 7 E4.
[(0212) 243 68 23.

Hayal Kahvesi (Çubuklu)
Ağaçlı Mesire Yeri A Blok,
Burunbahçe, Çubuklu.
[(0216) 413 68 80.

Kemancı
Sıraselviler Cad 69, Taksim.
Map 7 E4.
[(0212) 245 30 48.

Q Club
Çırağan Palace Hotel
Kempinski, A Blok,
Beşiktaş. **Map** 9 D3.
[(0212) 236 24 89.

Rock House Café
Princess Hotel, Dereboyu
Cad, Ortaköy.
Map 9 F2.
[(0212) 227 60 10.

Roxy
Sıraselviler Cad, Arslan
Yatağı Sok 113, Taksim.
Map 7 E4.
[(0212) 249 48 39.

Sappho
İstiklal Cad, Bekar Sok 14,
Beyoğlu. **Map** 7 E4.
[(0212) 245 06 68.

Tribunal
Muammer Karaca
Çıkmazı 3, Beyoğlu.
Map 7 D5.
[(0212) 249 71 79.

Vivaldi
Büyükparmakkapı Sok 29,
Taksim. **Map** 7 E4.
[(0212) 293 25 99.

NIGHTCLUBS

Club 29
Paşabahçe Yolu 24,
Paşabahçe.
[(0216) 322 28 29.

DNA
Sıraselviler Cad 69/2,
Taksim. **Map** 7 E4.
[(0212) 293 67 99.

Majesty
Muallim Naci Cad,
Salhane Sok 10, Ortaköy.
Map 9 F3.
[(0212) 236 57 57.

Pasha
Muallim Naci Cad 142,
Ortaköy.
Map 9 F2.
[(0212) 259 70 61.

TRADITIONAL TURKISH MUSIC AND DANCE

Ece
Tramvay Cad 104,
Kuruçeşme.
[(0212) 265 96 00.

Galata Tower
Büyükhendek Cad,
Galata.
Map 3 D1.
[(0212) 245 11 60.

Hasır
Beykoz Korusu,
Beykoz.
[(0216) 322 29 01.

Kallavi
Kallavi Sok 20, Beyoğlu.
Map 7 D4.
[(0212) 251 10 10.

Kervansaray
Cumhuriyet Cad 30,
Elmadağ.
Map 7 F2.
[(0212) 247 16 30.

Manzara
Conrad Hotel, Yıldız Cad,
Beşiktaş.
Map 8 C3.
[(0212) 227 30 00.

Orient House
President Hotel, Tiyatro
Cad 27, Beyazıt.
Map 2 C4 (4 A4).
[(0212) 517 61 63.

CINEMAS

Alkazar
İstiklal Cad 179,
Beyoğlu.
Map 7 E4.
[(0212) 283 24 66.

Beyoğlu
İstiklal Cad 140,
Halep Pasajı, Beyoğlu.
Map 7 E4.
[(0212) 251 32 40.

HEALTH CLUBS AND SPORTS CENTRES

Alkent Hillside Club
Alkent Residential
Complex, Tepecik Yolu,
Etiler.
[(0212) 257 78 22.

Enka Spor Tesisleri
Sadi Gülçelik Spor Sitesi,
İstinye.
[(0212) 276 50 84.

Istanbul Golf Club
Büyükdere Cad,
Yeni Levent.
[(0212) 264 07 42.

Kemer Country Riding and Golf Club
Göktürk Beldesi,
Uzun Kemer Mevkii,
Eyüp.
[(0212) 239 79 13.

Vakkorama Gym
Osmanlı Sok 13,
Taksim.
Map 7 E4.
[(0212) 251 15 71.

SPECTATOR SPORTS

Beşiktaş FC
Spor Cad 92, Beşiktaş.
Map 8 A4.
[(0212) 227 87 80.

Fenerbahçe FC
Fenerbahçe Spor Kulübü,
Kızıltoprak, Kadıköy.
[(0216) 345 09 40.

Galatasaray FC
Galatasaray Spor Kulübü,
Hasnun Galip Sok 7,
Galatasaray.
Map 7 E4.
[(0212) 251 57 07.

Veli Efendi Hipodromu
Londra Asfaltı,
Bakırköy.
[(0212) 543 70 96.

CHILDREN

Park Orman
Fatih Çocuk Ormanı,
Maslak Cad,
Maslak.
[(0212) 223 07 36.

Tatilya
E5 Motorway,
Beylikdüzü.
[(0212) 872 55 30.

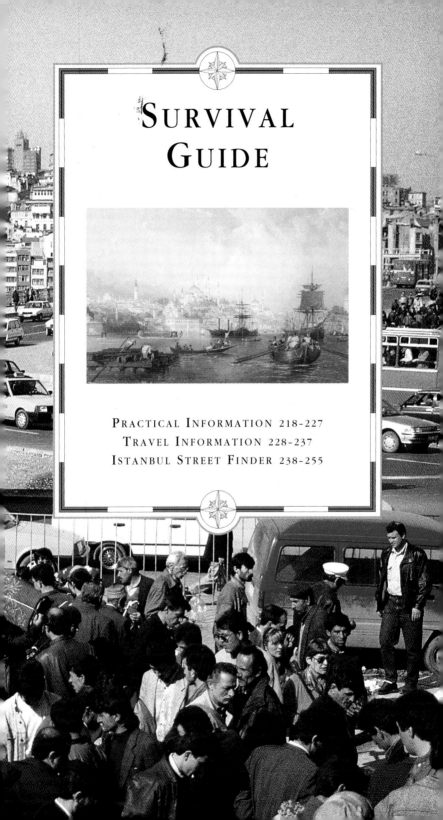

SURVIVAL GUIDE

PRACTICAL INFORMATION

IN RECENT YEARS Istanbul's infrastructure has greatly improved and it now has the transport, banking and medical facilities of any large modern city. However, it is still worth taking a few precautionary measures, especially if you intend exploring remoter suburbs of the city. A few bus tickets, a phone card, and at least one day's supply of hard currency or Turkish lira are a basic survival kit to carry at all times. Credit cards are still

Büyük Saray Mozaikleri Müzesi

Official sign to a tourist sight

not accepted everywhere, and it can be difficult to get cash outside bank opening hours away from the city centre. Certain aspects of Turkish culture may seem strange to the foreign visitor, especially if you have never travelled in a Muslim country. It is not considered rude to stare and foreigners are often objects of attention. In general, however, Turks are friendly and hospitable, and will appreciate any effort to show respect for their traditions.

VISAS

CITIZENS OF THE UK, Republic of Ireland and the USA require a visa. This is bought on arrival at the airport (or at land borders) and costs £10 or US$20, payable in cash only. It is valid for three months. Requirements vary for other EU countries. French, German and Greek nationals do not require visas, whereas Spanish passport holders must obtain a visa costing US$30–40 from a Turkish consulate in Spain. Canadians, Australians and New Zealanders can enter Turkey without a visa and stay for up to three months.

CUSTOMS

IMPORT LIMITS INCLUDE 200 cigarettes (400 if bought from a Turkish duty free shop), 200 g pipe tobacco (500 g if bought in Turkey), 75 cl alcohol, 1 kg chocolate, and 1.5 kg instant coffee. Details of cars and valuable electrical items will be entered in passports by customs officers to prevent their re-sale in Turkey.

There are strict rules on the export of antiquities (see p203). To export an antique carpet you must have the receipt, and the carpet should have a small lead seal attached to it (check when buying).

LANGUAGE

AS A RULE, Turks will make every effort to communicate with foreigners, even if they have to resort to sign language. In areas frequented

by tourists it is easy to find English speakers, although attempts to speak Turkish will be welcomed. Away from the main tourist circuit it can be harder to get your message across without some rudimentary grasp of the language. Useful vocabulary can be found in the phrase book on pages 271–2. Should you need one, there are several interpreting and translation agencies in Istanbul, including **Tercüme 80**.

SİGARA İÇİLMEZ

NO SMOKING

No smoking sign

ETIQUETTE

TURKS TEND TO dress smartly on all social occasions and for work. In cities, Turkish women usually cover their arms and legs in public, and increasing numbers include their heads. Men rarely wear shorts. Visitors are not expected to cover up in this way, but some Turks may be offended at exposed limbs in public

places. There are strict rules on dress in mosques (see p37).

Traditional rules of etiquette and hospitality are still an important aspect of Turkish society. Even though officials can often seem rude and the persistence of carpet salesmen can be annoying, always try to remain polite while firm. At all times show respect for Atatürk (see p29), whose picture you will see in offices, shops and public places.

Intimate physical contact with a person of the opposite sex in public is likely to cause offence: Turkish couples are rarely seen kissing, embracing or even holding hands.

Smoking is common in Turkey. Most public places, and even offices, tend to be very smoky. Smoking is permitted on most inter-city buses (see p236) but is forbidden on all local public transport and internal flights.

Fully veiled women, an increasingly common sight in Istanbul

◁ **The area between the New Mosque and Galata Bridge in Eminönü, a busy hub of trade and transport**

Newspaper stand where bus tickets and phonecards are also sold

TOILETS

PUBLIC TOILETS are found all over Istanbul. These can sometimes be very unpleasant: dirty squat toilets with no paper supplied and the floor awash with water. Entrances are marked *Bay* for men and *Bayan* for women. The attendant sitting outside, whom you pay on exit (a sign generally shows the charge), may supply toilet paper, but it is a good idea to carry tissues with you. Both toilet paper and tissues are available in groceries everywhere.

You may prefer to use the facilities in a good restaurant or hotel, which will have a European-style flush toilet. In most toilets, public or otherwise, there will be a bin beside the toilet. This is for used toilet paper, as the plumbing system cannot cope with it. Non-flushing toilets should be flushed using the jug provided in the cubicle.

BAY & BAYAN WC

Sign for a public toilet

TV, RADIO AND NEWSPAPERS

THE STATE-OWNED TRT (Türk Radyo ve Televizyon) has four television channels and three radio stations. Of these, TRT2 television has news bulletins in English, French and German at 7pm and 10pm. TRT3 radio (FM 88.2) broadcasts news in English, French and German at 9am, midday, 5pm, 7pm and 9pm.

Recent deregulation of the airwaves and the coming of satellite TV has meant a pro-liferation of private channels, from Turkey and abroad. Foreign channels which can be received include CNN, BBC Prime and MTV. Some hotels only receive Turkish satellite television. Check before booking in if you particularly want foreign channels.

There is also a wide variety of private radio stations, playing a range of western and Turkish pop, jazz and classical music. Voice FM (FM 90.6) broadcasts Voice of America programmes in Turkish, and news in English at 3pm. The BBC World Service can be received on short wave.

The only English language daily paper published in Turkey is the *Turkish Daily News* but day-old foreign newspapers can be obtained in tourist areas of the city, as can *Istanbul, The Guide (see p212)*. This has features on Istanbul and Turkish culture.

CONVERSION CHART

Imperial to Metric
1 inch = 2.54 centimetres
1 foot = 30 centimetres
1 mile = 1.6 kilometres
1 ounce = 28 grams
1 pound = 454 grams
1 pint = 0.6 litres
1 gallon = 4.6 litres

Metric to Imperial
1 centimetre = 0.4 inches
1 metre = 3 feet, 3 inches
1 kilometre = 0.6 miles
1 gram = 0.04 ounces
1 kilogram = 2.2 pounds
1 litre = 1.8 pints

ELECTRICITY

AS IN EUROPE, the electric current is 220V AC. Plugs have two round pins, and there are two diameters in use. The smaller one is more common. Adaptors should be bought prior to departure.

TIME

TURKEY IS TWO hours ahead of GMT. Between the end of March and the end of October it is three hours ahead.

Tips for Tourists

THE MAJOR MONUMENTS and museums of Istanbul are state-owned and charge a moderate entrance fee. Students and senior citizens are entitled to reduced or free entry to most sights, and should always carry proof of their status with them. In some museums there is a separate charge for a special section within the building, for example the Harem in Topkapı Palace (see pp58–9). Most sights are closed at least one day a week, usually Monday or Tuesday. Exhibits in museums are generally labelled in Turkish only, but some are labelled in English as well. If you intend to visit mosques (see pp36–7) remember that they close regularly for prayer, although people may be worshipping in them at any time of day.

Queuing for the Harem guided tour in Topkapı Palace (see pp58–9)

T.C.
TURIZM BAKANLIĞI
SULTANAHMET TURIZM DANIŞMA MÜDÜRLÜĞÜ
TOURISM INFORMATION

Sign for Sultanahmet tourist office

TOURIST INFORMATION

THE SIGN FOR a tourist information office is a white "i" on a light green background in a white box. The offices themselves are named in English and Turkish. They rarely have much printed information to give out, least of all public transport timetables, but the main office in Sultanahmet Square, in particular, will be able to answer questions on all aspects of your stay in Istanbul. The Directorate of Tourism in Beyoğlu does not give out information to casual passers-by, but if you book an appointment with them they will help with planning longer trips to places outside Istanbul and with mountaineering, walking and yachting expeditions. It is open on weekdays only.

Edirne, Bursa, İznik and Çanakkale all have tourist offices near the town centre. Most information offices are open from 9am to 5pm, Mon–Sat. Some stay open later in summer, while the one at the airport is open 24 hours every day of the year.

OPENING HOURS

MUSEUM OPENING times are generally 8:30 or 9am to 5:30 or 6pm, with a break for lunch in smaller establishments. Private businesses are open from 9am to 6pm, and government offices from 8am to 5pm. Shops open from 8:30 or 9am to 7 or 8pm (see p202). Most banks are open 8:30am to noon and 1:30 to 5pm, Monday to Friday, while exchange offices (döviz) are usually open until 8 or 9pm (see p224).

Public offices are closed on Saturdays and Sundays, and most shops on Sundays, although small grocers' are often open seven days a week.

Sign showing opening hours

GUIDED TOURS

SEVERAL TOUR operators run special-interest tours of Istanbul, as well as general guided tours of the city and further afield. **Plan Tours** has a variety of tours, including trips to Gallipoli, Troy and Bursa, Jewish heritage tours, and private yacht cruises along the Bosphorus (see pp144–9). **Gençtur**, which does "green" tours of Istanbul, offers discounts for young people. Companies running city tours

Entrance tickets for some of Istanbul's public monuments

include **Meptur** and **ITS Tourism**. For more companies offering trips to destinations outside Istanbul see page 237.

While sightseeing, you may be approached by people offering their services as tour guides. Some of these will be official guides licensed by the Greater Istanbul Municipality. Others may not be. Before you go anywhere with a guide, make it clear what you want to see and agree the fee. If you have little time, or do not wish to travel by public transport, it is often worth negotiating a private tour or visit to a sight with a taxi driver.

WOMEN TRAVELLERS

WOMEN TRAVELLING in Turkey may receive unwelcome attention from men, but are rarely in danger of physical attack. It is possible to avoid harassment by dressing respectably and looking purposeful when walking around. Avoid being out alone at night. Traditional cafés (see pp200–1) tend to be male preserves, but restaurants often have a section reserved for women (see p187).

VISITING MOSQUES

ALTHOUGH LARGE mosques are open all day, closing after last prayers in the evening, smaller ones open only five times daily, at prayer times *(namaz)*. At these mosques it may be difficult to gain entrance outside prayer times unless there is a care-taker around to open up for you. Non-Muslims should not enter any mosque during prayers. Instead, wait until most of the wor-shippers have left.

The times of prayer change throughout the year. They may be chalked up on a board outside the mosque, but they are always signalled by the call to prayer *(ezan)* from a loudspeaker fixed to the minaret of the mosque.

When visiting a mosque women and men should dress appropriately *(see p37)*. Some mosques can provide suitable attire at the door. Take your shoes off before entering and either leave them outside or carry them in with you. Make as little noise as possible inside and show consideration for anyone who is praying there.

Student with local women

Attendant on duty outside the Blue Mosque (see pp78–9)

STUDENTS

A FEDERATION OF International Youth Travel Organisation (FIYTO) Card will usually ensure free entry to sights, and an International Student Identity Card (ISIC) a 50% reduction. Reduced-price bus tickets are only available to those attending Turkish educational institutions, with a card to prove it. Non-Turkish students can get discounts on inter-city trains with an ISIC card. Officially, there are no discounts on coaches for non-Turkish students, but if you say you are a student when buying your ticket, you may be given a small reduction. Student accommodation is limited. In July and August you can get a bed in a student dormitory through Sultanahmet tourist information office. There are also a few youth hostels *(see p177)*, and plenty of cheap hotels and guest houses in the city centre *(see pp178–85)*.

DISABLED VISITORS

I STANBUL HAS FEW facilities for disabled people and the poor state of the streets can make it difficult to get around. Most mosques will not allow wheelchairs in, and very few museums have disabled access. Toilets with special facilities are also very rare. Conversely, museum staff and the public will go to great lengths to assist with entry to buildings, and there are some low-level public telephones and special-access buses *(see p231)*.

The **Turkish Tourist Office** in London publishes a guide to facilities for the disabled in Turkey. This contains specific details of hotels as well as general information. The **Turkish Association for the Disabled** (Türkiye Sakatlar Derneği), provides information and help for disabled people living in Istanbul, and can help tourists with specific queries.

PHOTOGRAPHY

M USEUMS OFTEN CHARGE for the use of a video camera, and sometimes even for cameras. Check whether or not a flash is allowed before paying. Flash is often forbidden in mosques, but discreet photography is usually allowed.

Avoid paying extortionate prices for film at tourist sights; you can buy film much cheaper in camera shops.

DIRECTORY

TOURIST INFORMATION OFFICES

Atatürk Airport
International Arrivals Hall.
((0212) 663 07 93.

Directorate of Tourism
Meşrutiyet Cad 57, Tepebaşı.
Map 7 D4. ((0212) 243 37 31.
FAX (0212) 252 43 46.

Hilton Hotel Arcade
Cumhuriyet Cad, Harbiye.
Map 7 F2. ((0212) 233 05 92.

Karaköy
International Maritime Passenger Terminal (Terminal 2). **Map** 3 E1.
((0212) 249 57 76.

Sultanahmet Square
Divanyolu Cad 3, Sultanahmet.
Map 3 E4 (5 E4).
((0212) 518 18 02.

Sirkeci Station
Sirkeci İstasyon Cad, Sirkeci.
Map 3 E3 (5 E1).
((0212) 511 58 88.

TOUR OPERATORS

Gençtur
Prof Kazım İsmail Gürkan Cad 14/4, Cağaloğlu. **Map** 3 D4.
(5 D3). ((0212) 520 52 74.

ITS Tourism
Kaya Aldoğan Sok 12/1, Zincirlikuyu. ((0212) 275 18 70.

Meptur
Büyükdere Cad 26/17, Mecidiyeköy.
((0212) 258 25 89.

Plan Tours
Cumhuriyet Cad 131/1, Harbiye.
Map 7 F3. ((0212) 230 22 72.

DISABLED VISITORS

Turkish Association for the Disabled
((0212) 521 49 12.

Turkish Tourist Office
170–73 Piccadilly,
London W1V 9DD.
((0171) 629 7771.
FAX (0171) 491 0773.

Personal Security and Health

Badge of the Turkish police

ISTANBUL IS AS SAFE AS other European cities, and visitors rarely encounter violence or theft. However, lone travellers should avoid certain suburbs of the city, especially those bordering the city walls and, as in any city, particular care should be taken at night. At all times be alert for pickpockets in crowded areas. In the event of any trouble, contact the Tourist Police.

There are public and private health clinics all over the city (some with English-speaking doctors) and a number of excellent private hospitals. For minor complaints, pharmacists will be able to provide advice.

POLICE

THERE ARE SEVERAL police forces in Turkey, distinguishable by their uniforms. The Security Police (*Emniyet Polisi*) is the main force in Istanbul. Its officers wear dark blue uniforms and caps, and pale blue shirts. The Tourist Police (*Turizm Polisi*) is a branch of the *Emniyet Polisi*. Most officers have some knowledge of one or two European languages. The Tourist Police station in Sultanahmet, opposite the Basilica Cistern (*see p76*), is open 24 hours a day, and has an English-Turkish translator available Monday to Friday, 8:30am to 5pm.

The Dolphin Police (*Yunus Polisi*) is a rapid-reaction branch of the *Emniyet Polisi*. Dolphin officers ride motor-

Dolphin Motorbike Police badge

bikes and wear black biking leathers with a red stripe.

The Traffic Police (*Trafik Polisi*) has the same blue uniform as the *Emniyet Polisi* but with white belt, hat and gloves. You will see these officers patrolling the streets in black and white cars equipped with loudspeakers. The Falcon Police (*Şahin Polisi*) is the motorbike branch of the *Trafik Polisi*. Their black leather uniform is similar to that of the Dolphin Police, but has a yellow stripe on the leathers instead of a red one.

The navy blue uniformed Market Police (*Zabıta*) is a municipal police force which patrols bazaars and other areas of commerce.

The Military Police (*Askeri İnzibat*), distinguished by an army uniform and white

helmet bearing the abbreviation "As İz", is responsible for the large numbers of military conscripts on city streets. The Gendarme (*Jandarma*), also a branch of the army, mainly polices rural areas and is unlikely to be found in the city.

PERSONAL PROPERTY

ON THE WHOLE, Turks are very honest people and will go to great lengths to return lost property. It is always worth returning to the last place the item was seen, or going to the Tourist Police. Pickpockets, however, are numerous and care should be taken in crowded areas. Property left on public transport can be reclaimed from the **Karaköy Gar** building.

HEALTH PRECAUTIONS

IT IS INADVISABLE to travel in Istanbul without medical insurance cover as EU reciprocal agreements do not cover Turkey. Your policy should allow for the cost of a flight home. No vaccinations are legally required before entering Turkey, but your doctor may advise inoculation against hepatitis A (spread through contaminated food and water), hepatitis B, tetanus and also typhoid.

Bottled spring water

Mosquitoes are more annoying than dangerous in Istanbul. Lorries run by the municipality spray the streets with repellent in the early evening, particularly in residential areas, but it is a good idea to bring some repellent lotion, spray or gel from your home country. ESEM Mat machines, electric vaporizers which release an effective repellent into the atmosphere, are available in Turkey. You can buy the machine and spare tablets in pharmacies, supermarkets and local groceries.

Many travellers to Turkey experience stomach upsets with diarrhoea and sometimes vomiting; this is often a result

Security policeman

Traffic policeman

Dolphin policeman

Turkish Security Police *(Emniyet Polisi)* patrol car

State ambulance in Istanbul

have ambulances, but the hospitals mentioned here either have their own service or have a contract with a private company. The **Night Ambulance** is a private service which will take you to any hospital you request, while a state ambulance will only take you to the nearest state hospital.

DIRECTORY

EMERGENCY NUMBERS

Ambulance
📞 *112.*

Night Ambulance
📞 *(0212) 247 07 81.*

Police
📞 *155.*

TOURIST POLICE

Yerebatan Cad 6, Sultanahmet.
Map 3 E4. 📞 *(0212) 527 45 03 or 528 53 69.*

LOST PROPERTY

Karaköy Gar
Rıhtım Cad, Karaköy. **Map** 3 E1.
📞 *(0212) 251 21 80.*

HOSPITALS

American Admiral Bristol Hospital
Güzelbahçe Sok 20, Nişantaşı.
Map 8 A2.
📞 *(0212) 231 40 50.*

Cerrahpaşa Hospital
Cerrahpaşa Cad, Cerrahpaşa.
Map 1 C5.
📞 *(0212) 588 48 00.*

European (Avrupa) Hospital
Mehmetçik Cad, Cahit Yalçın Sok 1, Mecidiyeköy. **Map** 8 A1.
📞 *(0212) 212 88 11.*

German Hospital
Sıraselviler Cad 119, Taksim.
Map 7 E4.
📞 *(0212) 293 21 50.*

International Hospital
İstanbul Cad 82, Yeşilyurt.
📞 *(0212) 663 30 00.*

---

of mild food poisoning. It is best to avoid drinking tap water altogether (bottled water is available everywhere), and some care should be taken when choosing restaurants and meals. Do not eat food that looks as if it could have been standing around, especially seafood. If you have a sensitive stomach avoid half-cooked meats (usually grilled), salads, and milk products other than yoghurt and *ayran (see p191).*

MEDICAL TREATMENT

Should you suffer from stomach troubles, remedies available from pharmacies include Lomotil, Ge-Oral (oral rehydration salts) and Buscopan. Drink lots of fluids – like bottled water, flat cola, weak black tea or soda water – and stick to a bland diet, eating only bread, yoghurt and rice until you recover. More serious bouts will require antibiotics.

The first port of call with a minor complaint should be a pharmacy *(eczane)*. Pharmacists are well-trained and many speak some English. If you need advice outside opening hours, look for a note in the window of a pharmacy giving the address of the local *nöbetçi eczane* (duty pharmacist).

There are excellent free public clinics *(poliklinik)* all over Istanbul, offering treatment for minor ailments. Private doctors often specialize in a particular branch of medicine, but there are general practitioners, called *tıbbi doktor*. Their clinics, located above shops in all the main shopping areas, are advertised by prominent signs outside.

Rabies poses a small threat in Turkey. If bitten or scratched by an animal, wash and cover the wound, and go straight to a hospital or health clinic.

Şişli Etfal Hastanesi

Sign for a state hospital in Şişli

HOSPITALS

State hospitals will take in non-Turkish nationals, but they are overcrowded, and treatment is not free. It is best to use private hospitals, or university teaching hospitals such as **Cerrahpaşa**. Foreign private hospitals, such as the **American Admiral Bristol**, **European**, **German** (which also has a dental clinic) and **International**, treat anyone, regardless of nationality. Not all foreign hospitals

Typical sign for a pharmacy in Istanbul

Banking and Currency

THERE IS NO LIMIT to the amount of foreign currency you can bring into Turkey. Most Turkish banks will change traveller's cheques and Eurocheques as well as cash. The best place to change cash, however, is at a *döviz*, or foreign exchange office. It is also possible to change hard currency in petrol stations, jewellers and any other business dealing with large amounts of money.

Payment by credit card is becoming more widely accepted, and cash dispensers are found outside an increasing number of banks. Rates of exchange are far better in Turkey than outside, so it is better to change a minimal amount of money before travelling. Inflation is high so only change a little money at a time – the rate may well go up the following day.

Cash dispenser with instructions in a range of languages

BANKS

MOST BANKS ARE open from 8:30am–midday and 1:30pm–5pm, Monday to Friday. However, the Garanti Bankası does not close for lunch and opens on Saturday mornings. There are branches in Sirkeci (Şehin Şah Pehlevi Caddesi), Sultanahmet (Divanyolu Caddesi) and Galatasaray (İstiklal Caddesi). The Vakıfbank at Esenler Coach Station is open daily 8:30am–11pm, and the Türkiye İş Bankası at the airport is open 24 hours.

There are many banks along Divanyolu Caddesi and İstiklal Caddesi. Nearly all banks have a foreign exchange desk, indicated by a sign in the window in several languages. Commission charges vary. Banks to look out for that offer good exchange rates and low or no commission are Akbank, Garanti Bankası, Yapı Kredi, Türkiye İş Bankası and Ziraat Bankası. A few foreign banks also have branches in Istanbul.

EXCHANGE OFFICES

FOREIGN EXCHANGE offices (*döviz*) are the best place to change foreign currency. They are efficient, open long hours (usually 8:30 or 9am to 8 or 9pm, Monday to Saturday) and give a better rate of exchange for cash than the banks. They do not charge commission on

cash. Daily exchange rates will be clearly displayed. *Döviz* offices are found all over the city. Those on Divanyolu Caddesi in Sultanahmet, however, give poor rates of exchange and should be avoided if possible. Instead use offices such as **Para Döviz** in the Grand Bazaar, **Ye-Ye Döviz** in Beyoğlu, and **Bamka Döviz** and **Çetin Döviz** in Taksim.

TRAVELLER'S CHEQUES AND CREDIT CARDS

TRAVELLER'S CHEQUES and Eurocheques should be cashed in banks or post offices. Many of the large banks, such as Garanti Bankası, do not charge commission on cheques. Post offices always charge commission but give a better rate of exchange. *Döviz* offices, shops and hotels rarely accept traveller's cheques.

To cash either Eurocheques or traveller's cheques you will need your passport, which will be photocopied with the cheque. You will also need a Eurocheque card for Eurocheques. You must then collect your money from the cashier. It is advisable to check the amount you receive against your receipt.

The major credit cards, such as VISA, American Express, MasterCard (Access) and Diners Club, are accepted in increasing numbers of hotels, petrol stations, shops and

Rates of exchange outside a *döviz*

restaurants. Credit cards and bank cards with PIN numbers can now also be used in the 24-hour cash dispensers of many banks, including Yapı Kredi Bankası, Garanti Bankası and Türkiye İş Bankası. They dispense Turkish lira.

Even if you have a credit card or traveller's cheques, it is a good idea to take some foreign currency with you into Turkey. Hard currency is in great demand and you will often be able to use sterling, US dollars or Deutschmarks to pay for larger items.

DIRECTORY
EXCHANGE OFFICES

Bamka Döviz
Cumhuriyet Cad 23, Taksim.
Map 7 E3. ((0212) 253 55 00.

Çetin Döviz
İstiklal Cad 39, Taksim.
Map 7 E4. ((0212) 252 64 28.

Para Döviz
Nuruosmaniye Sok 36, Kapalı Çarşı. **Map** 3 D4 (4 C3).
((0212) 513 38 52.

Ye-Ye Döviz
Turnacıbaşı Sok 229, Galatasaray.
Map 7 D4. ((0212) 252 73 58.

CREDIT CARD HOTLINES

American Express
((0212) 235 95 00 ext 205.

Diners Club, MasterCard and VISA
((0212) 211 59 60.

CURRENCY

THE CURRENCY of Turkey is the Turkish lira, abbreviated to TL. There are no smaller units. The lira has one of the lowest unit values in the world, with inflation sometimes reaching 2% per week. It may be useful to carry a small calculator as you will be dealing with millions of lira at a time. High denomination banknotes cannot always be changed in smaller shops, so try to carry a range of notes. Small change is so worthless that taxi drivers and shop assistants will often waive a few thousand lira in a transaction.

You can take up to US$5,000 worth of lira out of Turkey, but the rapid devaluation means that you will get a very poor rate if you exchange lira back for your own currency, so try to use up what you have left.

Banknotes

Turkish banknotes come in denominations ranging from 50,000TL to 5 millionTL. You may see red 20,000TL notes. These are no longer being printed, but are still officially legal tender, although you may have difficulty getting some shops to accept them. Be aware that the higher denomination notes are similar in colour to each other and can easily be confused.

50,000 lira

100,000 lira

250,000 lira

500,000 lira

1,000,000 lira

5,000,000 lira

Coins

The coins shown here (at their actual sizes) range in denomination from 500TL to 50,000TL. As with the banknotes, the head of Atatürk appears on one side of all coins. The 500TL and 1,000TL coins are of very little value.

500 lira

1,000 lira

2,500 lira

5,000 lira

10,000 lira

25,000 lira

50,000 lira

Telephone and Postal Services

PTT sign on a street letter box

POST OFFICES ARE identified by the letters PTT (Post, Telephone and Telecommunications) in black on a yellow sign. Most post offices are open for general business between 9am and 5pm, Monday to Saturday. If you just wish to buy stamps or post letters, stamp divisions in post offices are open from 8am to 8pm, and the telephone divisions are open every day until midnight. In the main tourist areas you can also buy stamps and post letters at PTT kiosks. Particularly useful is the kiosk in Sultanahmet Square.

The Turkish telephone network has been privatized and is now run by a company called Türk Telekom. Public telephones, which are mostly blue although you may see older yellow or orange ones, are found throughout the city. There is a variety of methods for paying for calls: with a *jeton* (token), a phonecard, by credit card or, at post offices, in cash for a metered call. Hotels generally add high surcharges to phone calls.

Small, independent kiosk selling phonecards and telephone tokens

CARD PHONES

CARD PHONES CAN now be found all over Istanbul. Phonecards *(telefon kartı)*, available at post offices and from street vendors and kiosks, come in units of 30, 60, 100, 120 and 180. Instructions on the phones are in English, French, German and Turkish.

Phonecards are the most economical method of making both international and local calls. Card phones are also considered more reliable than the older *jeton* phones. The disadvantages are that there are often long queues for them and you can be cut off with little warning, especially if you forget to press the "Card Change" button, labelled in English, when changing cards. Cheap rate is from 6pm to 8am on weekdays, and all day over weekends and holidays.

USING A CARD PHONE

1 Lift the handset and wait for the dialling tone.

2 Select instructions in the language of your choice.

3 Insert your card and wait for the remaining units to be shown on the screen.

4 Dial the number you require and wait to be connected.

5 To make another call press the follow-on button. If you have finished, replace the handset and the card will be ejected.

USING PUBLIC TELEPHONES

THE BEST PLACE to make a call from a public phone is at a post office. There is usually a row of phones, taking either phonecards or tokens, outside the office. Inside the office is an area reserved for *kontürlü* (controlled or metered) phones, for which you pay after making your call. Rates are slightly higher than for card or *jeton* phones, so there is not usually a queue. Groups of phone booths are also found in busy areas, such as public transport terminuses.

You can often find phones for making local calls in cafés, newsagents and grocers. Calls from such places are charged at slightly higher rates than those from post offices. You may need to buy special tokens at the counter, or you may be billed either a flat fee or by a meter after your call.

Phonecards depicting scenes of Turkey on the reverse side

REACHING THE RIGHT NUMBER

• Istanbul is divided into two area codes:
0212 (European side)
0216 (Asian side).
• To call a number in the same area, do not use the code. For another area, dial the code first.
• To call another city in Turkey, use the appropriate area code. For example, 0224 for Bursa.
• To call Turkey from abroad, dial 00 90 followed by the last three digits of the area code.
• To make an international call from Turkey, dial 00 followed by the code for the country eg:
Australia: 61.
Republic of Ireland: 353.
UK: 44.

OPERATOR SERVICES

Directory Enquiries
℟ 118.

Inter-City Operator
℟ 131.

International Operator
℟ 115.

Wake-Up Call Service
℟ 135.

Note: only international operators are guaranteed to speak English.

JETON PHONES

As THE QUEUES FOR *jeton* phones are usually shorter than those for card phones, it is worth carrying a few tokens as well as a phonecard. They can be bought in post offices, at newspaper kiosks and from vendors near groups of phone booths. Tokens come in two sizes, small *(küçük)* for local calls, and medium *(orta)*, for long-distance calls – however, it is better to use a card or metered phone for these. The slots on the phone for the tokens are usually labelled in English, but other

Medium and small telephone tokens

instructions appear in Turkish. To make a call, pick up the receiver and insert one *jeton*, or several if phoning abroad. When the red light goes out you will hear a tone. If you are making a local call dial the number, otherwise dial 0 for an inter-city call and 00 for an international call. When you hear the long-distance tone, dial the code and the number. If the red light comes on and pips sound during your call, insert more tokens.

CREDIT CARD PHONES

THERE ARE A FEW credit card phones in the central districts of Istanbul, at the airport and in some five-star hotels. They have comprehensive instructions in English on the front of the telephone.

Row of public telephone booths in Taksim Square

SENDING LETTERS

STAMPS ARE available only from post offices and PTT kiosks. These kiosks, found in tourist areas, also sell tokens and phonecards, and change travellers' cheques. Post offices are found throughout Istanbul. There are large branches, with a full range of postal services, at Sirkeci (Şehin Şah Pehlevi Caddesi), Taksim (Taksim

Square) and Beyoğlu (İstiklal Cad 192). These are marked on the Street Finder *(see pp238–48)*. Letters and postcards can be handed over the counter at post offices or posted in letter boxes, which are yellow and labelled PTT. Common signs indicating which box or slot to put your letter in are: Şehiriçi (local), Yurtiçi (domestic) and Yurtdışı (international).

POSTAL SERVICES

IT IS BEST TO USE air mail *(uçak ile)* when posting letters and parcels to another country as surface post is very slow. If you want to send a parcel by surface mail, use registered *(kayıtlı)* post. The contents of a package must be inspected at the post office, so take tape to seal your parcel at the counter.

International mail box

Folding boxes *(kutu)* for parcels are supplied free in larger post offices. You may be asked to show a receipt to prove you are not posting antiquities.
The express *Acele Posta Servisi* (APS) competes with private courier companies to provide a fast and efficient service. It costs more than air mail, but delivery is promised within three days.

POSTE RESTANTE

POSTE RESTANTE mail should be sent to the central post office in Sirkeci. Mail should be addressed with the recipient's name, then: poste restante, Büyük Postane, Büyük Postane Caddesi, Sirkeci, Istanbul, Turkey. A nominal tax is payable on collection.

Stamps in 10,000 and 50,000 lira denominations

TRAVEL INFORMATION

THE EASIEST WAY to get to Istanbul is to fly directly to the city's international airport, Atatürk Airport. There are regular, frequent flights, both scheduled and chartered, from most of the major European cities. There are also direct flights from the USA, but not from Canada, Australia or New Zealand. Package deals can be cheaper than the cost of a scheduled

Turkish Airlines (THY) aeroplane

flight and may include hotel accommodation. Coaches and trains run from many European countries to Istanbul, but any saving on the airfare may not be enough to make a much longer journey worthwhile. There are no direct ferry sailings from Europe, although cruises of the Aegean and Mediterranean usually include a one-day stopover for sightseeing in Istanbul.

Customs channels at the airport

ARRIVING BY AIR

TURKEY'S MAIN international airline, **Turkish Airlines** (THY), has direct flights to Istanbul from all major cities in Europe. Another Turkish airline, **Istanbul Airlines**, has scheduled flights from most countries in Europe. There are regular **British Airways** flights from London to Istanbul. It is always worth asking about discounted offers when buying a ticket for a scheduled flight. Various companies arrange chartered flights, at much cheaper prices, throughout the summer months. The flying time between London and Istanbul is roughly three and a half hours.

Turkish Airlines flies direct to Istanbul from New York and Chicago, and Delta Airlines flies direct from New York.

Passengers in the baggage hall of Atatürk Airport

ATATÜRK AIRPORT

ISTANBUL HAS ONE airport, Atatürk Airport (Atatürk Hava Limanı), with separate international (*dışhatları*) and domestic (*içhatları*) terminals. It is 25 km (16 miles) west of the city centre, in Yeşilköy.

Services provided in the international terminal include duty-free shops open 24 hours where, on arrival as well as departure, you can buy perfume, cigarettes, alcoholic drinks, sweets, personal stereos, watches and cosmetics. There are also gift shops, a café, a restaurant, a post office, 24-hour banking facilities, car hire outlets, a tourist information office and a hotel reservation desk.

Leave plenty of time (at least 2 hours) to check in for departures from Istanbul, particularly during the summer, as there are often long queues to get through security checks at the terminal building.

TRANSPORT FROM THE AIRPORT

TAXIS (*see p230*) are easy to find at the large rank just outside the arrivals hall of the international terminal. They are the most convenient means of reaching the city centre from the airport.

The airport bus is an efficient, cheaper way of getting to the city centre. Buses depart

approximately every half-hour between 6am and 11pm. The bus stop is marked '**Havaş**' (the name of the operating company) and is situated outside the main doors of the arrivals hall. The service into Istanbul makes one scheduled stop, on Mustafa Kemal Paşa Bulvarı in Aksaray, from where you can take a tram or taxi to Sultanahmet and Eminönü. It terminates in Taksim Square (*see p107*). If you want to get off somewhere else along the route, tell the driver before boarding.

Alternatively, there is a rail connection to the city centre from Yeşilköy, or you can take the Metro from Yenibosna as far as Zeytinburnu, and change on to the Tramway (*see pp232–3*). Both Yeşilköy and Yenibosna are some distance from the airport, however, and far less convenient than taking the bus.

Sign giving details of the Havaş airport buses

PACKAGE HOLIDAYS

A NUMBER OF travel companies organize package deals to Istanbul. These offer substantial savings on a stay in some of the city's top hotels, as well as the reassurance of having a company rep on hand to deal with any problems. Among the specialist companies in the UK which do package deals to Istanbul are **Anatolian Sky Holidays**, **President Holidays** and **Sovereign Cities**.

Sirkeci Station in Eminönü, where trains from Europe terminate

ARRIVING BY TRAIN

THE ORIENT EXPRESS *(see p66)* no longer runs as far as Istanbul and there has been a decline in train travel east through Europe since the break up of the former Yugoslavia. At present, the only direct route is from Thessaloniki, in Greece. The main overland route is from Munich via Salzburg, Vienna and Budapest, a journey lasting two and a half days. Passengers travelling from London can book the full trip through **British Rail International**.

Istanbul has two main-line stations: Sirkeci on the European side of the Bosphorus, and Haydarpaşa on the Asian side. Trains from Europe arrive at Sirkeci Station *(see p66)*. Trains from Anatolia and Asian cities terminate at Haydarpaşa Station *(see p133)*, from where you can get a ferry across to the European side.

Motorway sign showing Turkish and European road numbers

ARRIVING BY COACH

THE LEADING TURKISH coach companies **Ulusoy** and **Varan** operate direct services from several European cities to Istanbul. Ulusoy coaches run from Paris, Vienna, Munich, Milan and Athens. Varan runs from cities in Austria only, including Vienna and Salzburg.

Travelling by coach you will arrive at Esenler coach station *(otogar)*, 10 km (6 miles) northwest of Istanbul city centre. Esenler is also the main terminal for domestic connections *(see p236)*. Your coach company will probably take you into town in a courtesy minibus. If not, take the Metro *(see pp232–3)* from the station in the centre of the *otogar*, getting on at the platform marked Aksaray. The 83E and 91 buses also go to the city centre.

ARRIVING BY CAR

DRIVERS TAKING CARS into Turkey are asked to show registration documents and a valid driving licence at the port of entry. You will be given a certificate prepared by the Turkish customs authorities and this should be carried at all times, together with your driving licence and passport. You must have a Green Card (available from your insurance company) if arriving from Europe, and appropriate insurance if you wish to drive in the Asian part of Turkey. The car must also be equipped with a fire extinguisher, a first-aid kit and two warning triangles. Foreign drivers may find driving in Istanbul difficult and time-consuming as local traffic is either at a standstill in a traffic jam or travelling at dangerously fast speeds. There are public car parks, although it can be difficult to get a space. Your hotel may have its own parking facilities.

DIRECTORY

AIRLINES

British Airways
📞 *(0212) 234 13 00 (Istanbul).*
📞 *0345 222 111 (UK).*

Istanbul Airlines
📞 *(0212) 509 21 21 (Istanbul).*
📞 *(0181) 688 7555 (UK).*

Turkish Airlines (THY)
📞 *0212) 663 63 63 (Istanbul).*
📞 *(0171) 499 4499 (UK).*

AIRPORT

Atatürk Airport
📞 *(0212) 663 64 00.*

Havaş
📞 *(0212) 663 68 50.*

PACKAGE TOURS

Anatolian Sky Holidays
IMEX House, 52 Blucher Street, Birmingham, B1 1QU.
📞 *(0121) 633 4018.*

President Holidays
92 Park Lane, Croydon, CR0 1JF.
📞 *(0181) 688 7555.*

Sovereign Cities
First Choice House, Peel Cross Rd, Salford, Manchester, M5 2AN.
📞 *(0161) 742 2223.*

TRAIN TRAVEL

British Rail International
📞 *0990 848 848 (UK).*

INTERNATIONAL COACH SERVICES

Ulusoy
Esenler Coach Station.
📞 *(0212) 658 30 00.*

Varan
Esenler Coach Station.
📞 *(0212) 658 02 70.*

Coaches parked in front of their company offices at Esenler

GETTING AROUND ISTANBUL

IT IS POSSIBLE TO WALK between most major sights in Istanbul, and central areas are well served by an expanding system of metro and tram lines. Buses and dolmuşes provide city-wide transport, but take care to avoid travelling by road at rush hour times, when the main roads in and out of the city are congested with traffic.

Street sign at a junction in central Sultanahmet

As the public transport network grows, it becomes ever more confusing to work out the best means of transport

for any one journey, but the various forms of transport all link up so you can always get where you want to go somehow. See the map inside the back cover for more information.

Each type of transport has an individual ticket system, but there is also a travel pass, AKBİL *(see p233)*, which can be useful whatever the length of your stay. If time is short take a taxi. Istanbul's yellow cabs are relatively cheap, and their drivers can usually find a fairly traffic-free route.

ISTANBUL ON FOOT

THE DEVELOPMENT of semi-pedestrianized areas, such as İstiklal Caddesi and central Sultanahmet, has made it possible to walk with ease around some parts of Istanbul. This can be particularly pleasant in spring and autumn, when the weather is mild. It is also possible to walk around the city's quieter backwaters – like the area around the antiques shops of Çukur-cuma, near Galatasaray, or Eyüp *(see pp120–21)* – without encountering much traffic. For specialist tour companies offering walking tours around the city see page 221.

Sign for a pedestrian underpass

Wherever you walk, bear in mind that traffic only stops at pedestrian crossings controlled by lights, and always make use of pedestrian overpasses and underpasses on main roads.

Istanbul, like any city, has parts that should be avoided. If you are planning to walk in areas off the usual tourist track seek local advice, take extra care and try not to be walking in unfamiliar streets after dark.

TAXIS

TAXI CABS ARE ubiquitous in Istanbul, and fares are cheap in relation to other major European cities. Taxis operate day and night, and can be

hailed in the street or found at taxi ranks *(see pp238–48)*. Hotel and restaurant staff can always phone for a taxi.

Cabs are bright yellow, with the word "taksi" on a sign on the roof. They take up to four passengers. In all licensed taxis the fare is charged according to a meter. The daytime *(gündüz)* fare is applied between 6am and midnight; the night-time *(gece)* rate is 50% higher. If you cross the Bosphorus Bridge in either direction the bridge toll will be added to the fare at the end of your journey. The driver will not expect a sizeable tip unless he has helped you load luggage. The normal procedure for tipping is just to round up the fare to the nearest convenient figure.

Old-style dolmuş, still in use on some routes in the city

Most taxi drivers do not speak much English, if any. You may also find that some drivers are not familiar with routes to lesser-known sights, so it is a good idea to know which part of the city you want

to go to and to carry a map with you. It may also help to have the name and address of your destination written down.

DOLMUŞES

DOLMUŞES ARE a useful means of transport outside the city centre. These shared taxis with fixed routes are cheaper than regular taxis and more frequent than buses. In Turkish the word *dolmuş* means "full", and drivers usually wait until every seat is taken before setting off.

Four types of vehicle are used. The most distinctive are the large American cars made in the 1950s, which are yellow or black, and fitted with two rows of seats in the back. These are gradually being phased out and replaced with new, yellow diesel minibuses. There are also old-style mini-buses, often blue, known either as *minibüs* or dolmuş. Finally some yellow taxis operate as dolmuşes, and are only

Licensed Istanbul taxi cab with its registration number on the side

distinguishable from taxis by the sign with their destination in the front window. Dolmuşes run throughout the day until mid-evening, and later on busy routes, such as those starting from Taksim.

Points of origin and final destinations are displayed in the front windows of all dolmuşes, and passengers can get in and out anywhere en route. The fare depends on the length of your journey. State your destination, then hand your money to the driver or another passenger to pass forward. Any change will be returned. To stop the vehicle, simply say to the driver "*inecek* (pronounced eenejek) *var*" ("somebody wants to get out") and he will stop at the first opportunity.

Dolmuş ranks are marked by a blue sign with a black "D" on a white background. A main centre for dolmuşes is Taksim. Dolmuşes from here cross Bosphorus Bridge but, unlike taxis, do not charge passengers the bridge tariff.

GETTING AROUND BY BUS

L OCAL BUSES ARE either run by the municipality or rented out to private operators. The most common buses are **Belediye Otobüsü**, which are

owned and operated by the municipality. Tickets must be bought before boarding and you need one per journey, regardless of how far you are going. You can buy tickets at kiosks in bus stations, at newspaper stands near bus stops and (conveniently, but at a slightly higher price) from private vendors who set up small stalls near bus stops and telephone kiosks. On boarding, deposit your ticket in the metal box near the driver.

Recent deregulation of advertising has resulted in an array of brightly decorated buses, but the standard colours are red with an indigo stripe on the sides and front. A few Belediye buses run on natural gas. They are painted green and mostly run on the Asian side. There are also a few double-decker Belediye buses, on which all passengers are seated. They require two or three tickets depending on the journey. Some routes are served by special buses with wider doorways and lifts to facilitate wheelchair access. Useful routes with

An Özel Halk city bus, on which you pay a conductor after boarding

Full-fare and student tickets for Belediye buses

special access buses are the No. 12 from Kadıköy to Üsküdar, No. 25E from Eminönü to Sarıyer on the Bosphorus, and No. 28T from Beşiktaş to Topkapı (on the city walls; *see p114*) via Eminönü.

Some older Belediye buses are orange with a cream roof, but most of these are now

rented out to private operators. They are known as **Özel Halk Otobüsü** ("private buses of the people") and have this or "ÖHO" written on the side. On Özel Halk buses you do not buy a ticket in advance. A conductor will come round to collect your fare, which costs the same as a Belediye bus ticket. A few green double-decker buses are also leased to private operators.

On all buses, major destinations and bus numbers are shown on the front, and there is sometimes a fuller list of stops in the front kerbside window. Always get on through the front door. To stop the bus press the button above the rear or middle doors before reaching the required stop. There are big local bus stations in Taksim, Beşiktaş, Eminönü, Kadıköy and Üsküdar.

Most buses run between 6 or 7am and 9 or 10pm, although some run until midnight. There are no night buses.

Belediye bus advertising a brand of tomato purée

Getting Around by Metro, Tram and Train

T HE MODERN TRAM and metro systems are invaluable to both locals and visitors. Trams combine a congestion-free ride on popular routes with easy access and a comparatively comfortable journey, while the Metro provides an efficient means of linking the centre with the European suburbs and Esenler coach station. Greater Istanbul Municipality intends eventually to integrate the tram, metro and train systems into a more comprehensive network covering the whole city, with a tunnel under the Bosphorus linking the European and Asian sides.

Full-fare and student Tramway tickets, valid for one journey

THE MODERN TRAMWAY

T HE TRAMWAY (*Tramvay*) is a useful service on which you will probably travel more than once during the course of your stay. The line runs from

Eminönü, passing all the main sights in Sultanahmet, to Yusufpaşa, which is close to Aksaray – the first station on the Metro line. It then goes out past the city walls into the suburbs, ending at Zeytinburnu.

Trams travel on the right hand side of the street, so be sure to stand on the correct platform. To board a tram, buy a flat-fare ticket from the booth (*gişe*) near the platform, and put it into the receptacle at the top of the platform steps. Trams are frequent, running every 5 minutes between 5am and midnight, but get crowded during the rush hour.

Modern tram in Sultanahmet

THE METRO

I STANBUL'S METRO system has only recently come into operation, with much of it still under construction and still more at the planning stage.

The existing Metro runs from Aksaray out to Esenler coach station (Otogar). There it divides, with one line going on to the suburb of Esenler and the other continuing to Ataköy and Yenibosna. Running both above and below ground, the

Metro sign

TRAM AND METRO ROUTE MAP

Metro lines shown here as planned or under construction should be open by the year 2000. There are also plans to extend the metro line past Yenibosna to the airport.

KEY

— Metro

-- Metro planned or under construction

= Tünel

= Tramway

-- Tramway planned or under construction

= Old tram

Istanbul Metro is known locally by a variety of other names. These include Hızlı Tramvay (High Speed Tram), Hafif Metro (Light Metro) and LRT (Light Railway).

Trains run every 10–15 minutes seven days a week, starting at 5:40am and ending at 11:15pm. To board a train, buy a flat-fare ticket from the booth marked "Gişe" and feed it into the turnstile under the sign "Tek Geçiş". The final destination of each route is clearly indicated on the platform.

Turkish Railways sign on the side of a train

The Metro route will eventually extend across the Golden Horn to link the airport to the suburb of 4. Levent, with potential to go even further in the future. There are also plans to construct more overland Metro lines on the Asian side.

THE TÜNEL

INAUGURATED IN 1875, this French-built underground railway climbs steeply uphill for a distance of 500 m (550 yards) from Karaköy to Tünel Square in Beyoğlu, from where you can get the old tram up İstiklal Caddesi. The Karaköy station is set back from the main road just off the Galata Bridge (see p101). The best way to get to it is through the underpass at the end of the bridge. Look out for the exit marked "Tünel". To board it at either station you need to buy a token (jeton) from the booth and drop it into the turnstile at the entrance to the platform.

THE OLD TRAM

THE OLD TRAM (or Nostaljik Tramvay) covers a distance of just over 1 km (just under 1 mile) along İstiklal Caddesi from Tünel to Taksim Square. The trams are the original early 20th-century vehicles, taken out of service in 1966 but revived in 1989 for their historical value. The ticket collectors wear period costume. Tickets can be purchased from kiosks at either end of the line.

SUBURBAN TRAINS

SUBURBAN TRAINS (banliyö) run beside the Sea of Marmara between Sirkeci and Halkalı (on the European side), and Haydarpaşa and Gebze (on the Asian side). The service is slow, and stations are generally not close enough to tourist sights to be of much use to visitors. Exceptions are Yedikule (for Yedikule Museum, see p115), Ataköy (near Galleria shopping mall, see p203) and Yeşilköy (the airport station, see p228). On the Asian side, Bostancı is one of the ferry piers for the Princes' Islands.

A train ticket costs the same flat rate as a bus ticket, and should be retained for the whole journey. Suburban trains start daily at 6am and stop at 11:30pm. For further information on the rail network, see the map inside the back cover.

THE AKBİL TRAVEL PASS

THE AKBİL is a type of travel pass which can be used on almost all forms of public transport in Istanbul. Short for akıllı bilet, or "intelligent ticket", this metal token can be purchased from main bus

stations and other public transport ticket offices. It can be used on the Metro, the Tramway, the Tünel, ferries and sea buses, and most city buses.

When purchasing an AKBİL, you pay for a number of units in advance and also a deposit, which is refundable, for the token itself. More units can be added to the token at any time. The distinctive orange-coloured AKBİL machines are located at the entrances to stations and on buses. To use the AKBİL place the metal token in the socket on the front of the machine, near the display panel. The fare will then be deducted in units.

AKBİL passes

Old tram travelling along İstiklal Caddesi in Beyoğlu

Getting Around by Boat

PERHAPS THE MOST pleasant and relaxing means of getting around Istanbul is by the innumerable water-borne craft which ply the Bosphorus between the European and Asian sides. These range from small, privately operated motor boats to a fleet of high-speed catamarans. Travelling by boat, you will avoid the traffic jams

Token (jeton) for TDİ ferry

and tariffs of the Bosphorus road bridges. As well as being a relatively fast way to get around, a ride on a boat will also provide some great views of the city.

Passengers boarding a ferry

Old ferries at Karaköy

FERRIES

ACONSTANT TRAFFIC of ferries crosses the Bosphorus and the Golden Horn. Called *vapur*, they belong to the state-run TDİ (Turkish Maritime Lines).

The principal ferry terminus on the European side is at Eminönü *(see p87)*. Each of the six piers here has a boarding hall, with the destination written in large black letters on the outside. The three main piers are numbered. Pier 1 serves Üsküdar; pier 2 serves Kadıköy; and pier 3, labelled "Boğaz Hattı", is for all ferries travelling up the Bosphorus, including the special cruise. The other three piers are a short distance from Eminönü proper. On the west side of the Galata Bridge is the pier

for ferries up the Golden Horn (Haliç Hattı). To the east of pier 1, at Sirkeci, across the road from the station, is the departure point for car ferries to Harem. Further along from this, at Sarayburnu, is the final pier, labelled "Adalar", from which long-distance ferries depart. This is the pier for ferries to the Princes' Islands.

Another main terminus is Karaköy, opposite Eminönü, from which ferries run to Haydarpaşa and Kadıköy.

FERRY AND SEA BUS ROUTE MAP

There are numerous ferry and sea bus services departing daily from Eminönü and the other ports. In addition, a number of smaller, privately operated motor boats serve the same destinations as the state-run ferries.

EMİNÖNÜ PIERS
- ① Üsküdar
- ② Kadıköy
- ③ Bosphorus, Beşiktaş
- ④ Harem
- ⑤ Princes' Islands, Yalova, Marmara
- ⑥ Balat-Üsküdar

Galata Bridge

Sea bus

Beşiktaş / Anadolu Kavağı

KEY
— Ferry
— Sea bus
— Car ferry
— Motor boat

Balat
Fener
Kasımpaşa
BEYOĞLU
Kabataş
Üsküdar
Karaköy
Eminönü Piers
THE BAZAAR QUARTER
SERAGLIO POINT
Harem
Yenikapı
SULTANAHMET
Marmara *Princes' Islands*
Princes' Islands Yalova Marmara *Kadıköy*

The international dock, where cruise liners berth, is also here.

There are ferries from Eminönü to Kadıköy between 7:30am and 9pm, and from Eminönü to Üsküdar between 6am and 11:30pm, every 15 minutes (20 minutes at weekends). Other services are less frequent. If you want to explore independently using ferries, especially to hop between the villages along the Bosphorus, you will need to arm yourself with a timetable.

MOTOR BOATS

A NUMBER OF privately run craft cross the Bosphorus and Golden Horn at various points, and run up the Bosphorus. These routes are also served by TDİ ferries, but private motor boats are more frequent, though slightly more expensive. A conductor will come and collect your fare after the boat leaves the pier.

SEA BUSES

T HE MODERN, Swedish-built catamarans which are known as sea buses (deniz otobüsleri) are run by İDO, a municipal company. Their interiors resemble aircraft cabins, with long rows of comfortable, reclining seats, piped music and air-conditioning. Sea buses are considerably faster and more comfortable than ferries, but cost two or three times as much.

The most useful routes are Eminönü to Kadıköy (half-hourly from 7:40am to 7pm Monday to Friday, and 8:15am to 6:10pm at weekends); and Bakırköy to Bostancı (hourly between 8:15am and 10pm). In the summer, sea buses run

A sea bus catamaran, Istanbul's fastest form of water transport

Ferry for Kadıköy, docked at Eminönü's pier 2

from Kabataş and Bostancı to Büyükada on the Princes' Islands. For destinations outside Istanbul see pages 236–7.

THE BOSPHORUS TRIP

T URKISH MARITIME LINES runs daily excursions up the Bosphorus (see pp136–49). These are normal ferries on which light refreshments are served (at inflated prices) but no meals. They get crowded in the summer months, especially at weekends, so it is a good idea to arrive early to ensure a deck seat with a view. You should retain your ticket during the journey, as you must show it when boarding for the return trip. You can disembark at any pier along the way, boarding the next ferry that comes along with the same ticket; but if you make a second stop you will need to buy a new ticket. TDİ also offers a trip from Kadıköy in summer at weekends only.

There are alternatives to the official Bosphorus trip. The small private boats, which leave Eminönü just after the TDİ ferry sails in the summer months, only go halfway up the straits and do not stop on the way. If you decide to book a private cruise through a tour company, be sure to choose a reputable company, such as **Hatsail Tourism**.

Sea bus timetable

BUYING BOAT TICKETS

F OR FERRIES AND sea buses, you need to buy a flat-fare jeton from the booth (gişe) at the pier or from one of the unofficial street vendors who sit nearby and sell them at slightly higher prices. These jetons can be used for all local journeys. For ferries to the Princes' Islands or for the Bosphorus trip, you still need to buy a jeton which will cover the outward and return journeys, but it is more expensive than the normal TDİ fare.

To enter the pier put the jeton into the slot beside the turnstile, and then wait in the boarding hall for a boat.

A schedule of sailing times hangs in each pier and a copy of the timetable (tarife) can usually be bought at the ticket booth.

DIRECTORY

FERRY INFORMATION

[(0212) 244 42 33.

SEA BUSES

[(0216) 362 04 44.

PRIVATE CRUISES

Hatsail Tourism
[(0212) 258 99 83.

Travelling Beyond Istanbul

Courtesy minibus to and from the coach station

THE BEST WAY of getting from Istanbul to other towns and cities is by long-distance coach. A bewildering number of companies offer services to every conceivable destination in Turkey, with several companies serving any one intercity route. It is worth paying a bit extra to travel with a reputable company, to ensure a safe and comfortable journey.

The rail network is much more limited than the coach network. Trains go to only a limited number of cities in Turkey and the service is less efficient. Even express trains take longer than the same journey by coach. For destinations across the Sea of Marmara, ferries and sea buses are a relaxing means of transport.

INTERCITY COACHES

THE MAIN COACH station (*otogar*) for all domestic and international destinations is at Esenler, 10 km (6 miles) northwest of the city centre. It is served by the Metro. Facilities in the coach station include two banks, one of which is open until 11pm. There is another coach station in Harem, on the Asian side of Istanbul. Most coaches stopping here will be on their way to or from Esenler. Coach tickets can be bought from travel agents or coach company offices in the city centre, or direct from offices in the coach station. If you buy your coach ticket from a travel agency they will provide a service bus from their office to the coach station.

One of the many inter-city coaches from Esenler

At first sight Esenler coach station can seem daunting. The central courtyard is surrounded by over 150 ticket offices, their destinations displayed on signs. Company representatives walk around the station calling out destinations of coaches about to depart. If you cannot find the company or destination you want, there is an information office next to the Metro station, or you can ask any company representative, who will take you to the most suitable office. **Kamil Koç** (Bay 144), **Uludağ**

(Bay 99) and **Hakiki Koç** (Bay 7) have services to Bursa. The journey takes about four hours. Kamil Koç also goes to Çanakkale, taking six hours, and Gallipoli (about five hours). **Edirne Birlik** (Bay 109) has a service to Edirne, which takes three hours.

Smoking is generally permitted on coaches, but some companies now provide non-smoking (*sigarasız*) seats, so that at least the person next to you will not be smoking. A few companies have totally non-smoking services. Single passengers will usually be seated next to someone of the same sex. Couples can sit together. Mineral water, and sometimes other refreshments, are available on board free of charge. There will also be frequent rest and meal stops at service stations. On most coaches, the attendant will come round at regular intervals with a bottle of cologne which passengers are invited to use.

LONG-DISTANCE FERRIES

FERRIES AND SEA BUSES are a convenient means of travelling long distances from a city surrounded by water. TDİ ferries (*see p234*) are very good value, and cars are carried on many lines. Few concessions are made to comfort, however; seating is often rudimentary and the buffets are over priced and poorly equipped.

The trip to Bursa can be made by a combination of sea bus or ferry, and coach. The fastest route is to take one of four daily sea buses from Kabataş to Yalova, just an hour away. Ferries also sail from Sarayburnu, in Eminönü, to Yalova. The port of Mudanya is even closer to Bursa but boats are much less frequent. Sea buses go there from Yenikapı, ferries from Sarayburnu. Frequent buses meet incoming boats at Yalova and Mudanya.

In the summer, sea buses go from Yenikapı to Marmara. TDİ also has ferries to the Marmara Islands. Departing from Sarayburnu, they take 5 hours to reach Marmara and a further 45 minutes to reach Avşa.

Sea bus for Yalova about to depart from Kabataş on the Bosphorus

FLIGHTS TO BURSA

SÖNMEZ AIRLINES fly between Istanbul and Bursa twice daily, Monday to Friday at 9:30am and 6pm. The flight lasts one hour. Bursa airport is approximately 15 minutes' drive from the city centre.

TRAINS TO EDIRNE

THERE IS a daily train to Edirne from Sirkeci Station *(see p66)*. The journey takes six hours, twice the length of the coach journey. Advance reservations can be made at the stations in either city, or in certain travel agencies displaying the TCDD (Turkish State Railways) sign. Bursa is not on the rail network.

CAR HIRE

TURKEY'S comprehensive intercity coach network means that a car is not necessary for travelling to other cities. If you do wish to drive, car hire companies such as **Avis** and **Hertz** have offices in the airport, as well as in the city centre. You do not need an international driving licence; a normal licence from your own country will suffice.

All roads in Turkey, both in and out of the city, are made hazardous by reckless driving and extreme caution is recommended. Traffic drives on and gives way to the right, even on roundabouts. The Turkish Touring and Automobile Club

Car rental office in the arcade of the Hilton Hotel, Taksim

(Türkiye Turing ve Otomobil Kurumu, or **TTOK**, *see p175*), based in Istanbul, gives motorists advice on driving in Turkey, as well as offering assistance with breakdowns, accidents and insurance. It has reciprocal agreements with the British AA and RAC.

DAY TRIP TOURS

A NUMBER of companies offer day trips from Istanbul to the Princes' Islands, the Dardanelles, Bursa and villages on the Black Sea. Recommended tour operators are **She Tours**, **Türk Express** and **Plan Tours** *(see p221)*. **Arnica** specializes in trips to the countryside around Istanbul. Edirne is not usually included on tour company itineraries, although some will organize special tours there on request.

LOCAL TRANSPORT OUTSIDE ISTANBUL

THE MAIN means of public transport in both Bursa and Edirne is the dolmuş. These are either minibuses or saloon cars, with the destination displayed on signs on the roof. If you stay in the centre of either city and are moderately fit, you will find that all of the major sights are within easy walking distance.

In Bursa city centre, Heykel, at the eastern end of Atatürk Caddesi, is the main dolmuş terminus. From there you can get dolmuşes to most other parts of the city. There is also an efficient bus service.

Edirne is much smaller than Bursa, and the public transport system is not as comprehensive. To get from the coach station to the town centre, a distance of 2 km (1 mile), take a Merkez–Garaj minibus dolmuş, or a taxi.

There are no motor vehicles on the Princes' Islands. On Büyükada and Heybeliada there are phaeton carriages; otherwise you have to get around on foot or by bicycle.

Horse-drawn carriage (phaeton) on Büyükada

DIRECTORY	**Kamil Koç**	**AIRLINES**	**TTOK**
	İnönü Cad 35/B, Taksim.		I. Oto Sanayi Sitesi Yanı,
COACH STATIONS	**Map** 7 F4.	**Sönmez Airlines**	4. Levent, Seyrantepe.
	(*(0212) 252 72 23.*	Bursa Airport	(*(0212) 282 81 40.*
Esenler		(*(0224) 247 77 15.*	
(*(0212) 658 00 36.*	**Uludağ**	Atatürk Airport	**DAY TRIP TOURS**
	Esenler Coach Station.	(Istanbul)	
Harem	(*(0212) 658 06 00.*	(*(0212) 663 13 29.*	**Arnica**
Map 10 A5.			Mis Sok 6/5, İstiklal Cad,
(*(0216) 333 37 63.*	**FERRIES**	**CAR HIRE**	Beyoğlu. **Map** 7 E4.
			(*(0212) 245 15 93.*
COACH TRAVEL	**Sea Buses**	**Avis**	
	(*(0216) 362 04 44.*	Hilton Hotel, Cumhuriyet	**Türk Express**
Edirne Birlik		Cad, Harbiye. **Map** 7 F2.	Cumhuriyet Cad 47,
Esenler Coach Station.	**TDİ**	(*(0212) 246 52 56.*	Harbiye. **Map** 7 E3.
(*(0212) 658 19 07.*	Mudanya and Avşa:		(*(0212) 230 15 15.*
	(*(0212) 244 02 07.*	**Hertz**	
Hakiki Koç	Yalova and the Princes'	Küçük Bayır Sok 121,	**She Tours**
Esenler Coach Station.	Islands:	Dolapdere. **Map** 7 E2.	Cumhuriyet Cad 309/3,
(*(0212) 658 40 10.*	(*(0212) 249 16 95.*	(*(0212) 234 43 04.*	Harbiye. **Map** 7 F2.
			(*(0212) 233 36 70.*

STREET FINDER

THE MAP REFERENCES that are given throughout this guide refer to the maps on the following pages. Some small streets with references may not be named on the map. References are also given for hotels *(see pp174–85)*, restaurants *(see pp186–201)*, shops *(see pp202–11)* and entertainment venues *(see pp212–15)*. The map

Visitor to Istanbul consulting a map

below shows the area covered by the ten maps and the key lists the symbols used. The first figure of the reference tells you which map page to turn to; the letter and number indicate the grid reference. For an overview of Greater Istanbul see pages 108–9. The map on the inside back cover shows public transport routes.

KEY TO STREET FINDER

▢ Major sight	▣ Taxi rank
▢ Place of interest	▣ Tourist information
▢ Other building	▣ Hospital
▣ Ferry boarding point	▣ Police station
▣ Sea bus boarding point	▣ Turkish baths
▣ Railway station	▣ Mosque
Ⓜ Metro or Tünel station	▣ Synagogue
▣ Tram stop	▣ Church
▣ Cable car station	▣ Post office
▣ Main bus stop	▭ Railway line
Ⓓ Dolmuş terminus	▭ Tram line

▭ Motorway
▭ Pedestrian tunnel
▭ City walls

SCALE OF MAPS 1–3 & 6–10

0 metres	250
0 yards	250

SCALE OF MAPS 4 & 5

0 metres	200
0 yards	200

0 metres 750
0 yards 750